Buddhism
and Postmodernity

Buddhism and Postmodernity

Zen, Huayan, and the Possibility of Buddhist Postmodern Ethics

JIN Y. PARK

LEXINGTON BOOKS

A division of
ROWMAN & LITTLEFIELD PUBLISHERS, INC.
Lanham • Boulder • New York • Toronto • Plymouth, UK

LEXINGTON BOOKS

A division of Rowman & Littlefield Publishers, Inc.
A wholly owned subsidiary of The Rowman & Littlefield Publishing Group, Inc.
4501 Forbes Boulevard, Suite 200
Lanham, MD 20706

Estover Road
Plymouth PL6 7PY
United Kingdom

British Library Cataloguing in Publication Information Available

Library of Congress Cataloging-in-Publication Data

Park, Jin Y.,
  Buddhism and postmodernity : Zen, Huayan, and the Possibility of Buddhist
Postmodern ethics / Jin Y. Park.
      p. cm.
  Includes bibliographical references and index.
  ISBN-13: 978-0-7391-1823-8 (cloth : alk. paper)
  ISBN-10: 0-7391-1823-4 (cloth : alk. paper)
  1. Philosophy, Buddhist. 2. Postmodernism—Religious aspects—Buddhism. 3. Zen
Buddhism—Doctrines. 4. Huayan Buddhism—Doctrines. 5. Buddhist ethics. I. Title.
  B162.P37 2008
  294.3'3614997—dc22   2007048732

Printed in the United States of America

∞™ The paper used in this publication meets the minimum requirements of American
National Standard for Information Sciences—Permanence of Paper for Printed Library
Materials, ANSI/NISO Z39.48–1992.

To my father
Ki Won Park
(1928–2000)

Table of Contents

Abbreviations

C	Chinese pronunciation
HPC	*Han'guk Pulgyo chŏnsŏ* 韓國佛敎全書. Seoul: Tongguk taehakkyo ch'ulp'anbu. 1979.
J	Japanese pronunciation
K	Korean pronunciation
LPR	G. W. F. Hegel, *Lectures on the Philosophy of Religion*, 3 vols., edited by Peter C. Hodgson. Berkeley, CA: University of California Press, 1995.
Sk	Sanskrit
T	*Taishō shinshū daizōkyō* 大正新脩大藏經. Tokyo: Taishō issaikyō kankōkai, 1924–1932.
"WM?"	Martin Heidegger, "What is Metaphysics?"(1929) in *Martin Heidegger: Basic Writings*, edited by David Farrell Krell. San Francisco: Harper Collins Publishers, 1993, 89–110.

Acknowledgments

Thanks are due to the many people who have helped me in various ways at different stages of this book. I thank Sung Bae Park for his guidance in my study of Buddhism. A close reading of Buddhist texts with him became the basis of the discussions of Zen and Huayan Buddhism in this book. Park also brought to my attention the affinity between postmodern thought and the Huayan fourfold worldview. It took much longer than I expected to develop the connection between the two traditions into a philosophical paradigm as it appears in this book; however, the initial inspiration was always my encouragement when I became lost in the process of writing this book. I thank Hugh J. Silverman, to whom I owe my understanding of postmodern philosophy and deconstruction. His support and understanding of my comparative philosophy project throughout my graduate studies and afterwards has always been an invaluable asset that I have cherished in my academic career. I also thank Perry Meisel, who introduced me to postmodern thinkers.

I thank an anonymous reader for a very positive reading of the manuscript. I thank Robert Magliola, who read the manuscript and offered me invaluable advice. Being a pioneer thinker in the field of Buddhist–Western comparative philosophy, his scholarship and his support for my project convinced me the very "possibility" of this relatively new field. Gereon Kopf read the entire manuscript and spent an enormous number of hours on the phone with me, pointing out the gaps and fissures in my arguments. I thank him for his time, energy, and support for my project. I also thank him for bringing to my attention one of the methodological problems of comparative philosophy: that is, deciding how much of the basic concepts of each tradition—Buddhism and Continental philosophy—to spell out for readers who have not been exposed to either one of the traditions, without losing the interest of those who already have the basics of either tradition. Following his advice, I tried to provide as much background of basic conceptual frames of each tradition as possible without being redundant. Regardless of my own success or failure in handling of the problem in this book, the issue seems to remain one of questions comparative philosophers continue to discuss.

I thank Donald Lopez who read the first section, "Buddhism and Metaphysics," when it was in much poorer condition than it appears in this book. His comments were essential for a radical restructuring of the section, and as a result, the current section offers a more focused discussion of major issues relevant to the themes of the book. Steven Heine has always been generous in offering advice when I resort to him for guidance in my scholarship and academic career. I thank him for his guidance and support. Youru Wang also offered me valuable help in the preparation of this manuscript, for which I thank him.

I thank MacDuff Stewart and Patrick Dillon at Lexington Books for their help throughout the production process of this book. Tram Nguyen, Jeff Epstein, and Christopher Frascella helped me at the different stages in the preparation of this manuscript. I thank them for their time and effort.

CREDITS

A portion of Chapter Four, "Thinking and Violence: Zen Hermeneutics," appeared in *Universitas: Monthly review of Philosophy and Culture*, vol. 30, no. 3 (March 2003), 79–96, under the title "Zen Hermeneutics via Heideggerian and Derridean Detours." A portion of Chapter Nine, "Envisioning Zen Ethics through Huayan Phenomenology," appeared in *Journal of Buddhist Ethics*, vol. 13 (2006), 1–26, under the title "Wisdom, Compassion, and Zen Social Ethics: the Case of Chinul, Sŏngch'ŏl, and Minjung Buddhism in Korea."

Introduction

Buddhism and Postmodernity: Zen, Huayan, and the Possibility of Buddhist Postmodern Ethics is a response to some of the questions that have emerged in the process of Buddhism's encounter with modernity and the West. The questions are interwoven with different threads that constitute our philosophical, political, and cultural arena. By nature the questions are not specific to Buddhism but can be identified by generic issues that have haunted philosophical discourses. However, by the fact that the questions have appeared when two philosophical traditions collide in a historical moment, these questions become self-critical references for both Buddhist philosophy and for some of the Western philosophical traditions that are discussed in this book. The questions can be divided into three themes, each of which comprises one part of the book. The first is the question of the nature of Buddhist philosophy; the second is the meaning and function of violence in Zen Buddhism; and the third is how to envision ethics in the context of Zen and Huayan Buddhism along with postmodernism.

To some Buddhist scholars, the notion of Buddhist philosophy is problematic. These reservations about Buddhist philosophy have also appeared, if in a more unspoken manner, in the way Buddhism has been treated in American academic and philosophical circles. The reasons for the two groups' objection to understanding Buddhism as philosophy are not the same. Nonetheless, the phenomenon is one result of Buddhism's encounter with the Western categorical system. The very question of the existence or non-existence of Buddhist philosophy, then, is fraught with not only philosophical but political implications.

In the *Laṅkāvatāra Sūtra*, one of the Mahāyāna Buddhist texts, the Buddha repeatedly criticizes philosophers. "Philosophers," which is D. T. Suzuki's rendering in his English translation of this Sanskrit text, refers to Brahmins, the Buddha's philosophical opponents at the time. The major charge that the Buddha brings against the philosophy of the Brahmins is its substantialism. The Buddha contends that philosophers or Brahmins begin their practice of philosophy based on egoistic attachments, which results in the dualism of the self and others, and of the qualifying and the qualified.[1] The Buddha also criticizes philosophers for claiming that "there is a first cause from which continuation takes place."[2] Opposing this view of Brahmins, the Buddha contends that continuation takes place with no first cause of that continuation to be identified. That is so, from the Buddha's perspective, because the continuation is not an evolution of a certain independent and substantial essence but arises from the interaction of different elements involved in that action.

The nature of the Buddha's *philosophy,* demonstrated through his criticism of the Brahmins' philosophical orientation of substantialism and its metaphysical and dualistic tendency, is well inscribed in early Buddhist texts. For example, the Chinese Āgama collection, which contains dialogues of various lengths between the Buddha and his disciples, followers, and his contemporary inquirers, offers us the Buddha's philosophy as the "middle path." The Buddha considers the metaphysical substantialist philosophical orientation as either annihilationism or eternalism, and defines the middle path as a path which cuts off these two extremes. The middle path is frequently summarized by a passage, "because this happens, that happens; because that ceases, this ceases." One salient mode through which the Buddha demonstrates his position of the middle path is known as the "unanswered questions" or the Buddha's silence.

The Buddha refused to answer *certain* questions asked by his followers, and this silence of the Buddha has been subject to various interpretations. What is relevant in the context of our discussion is its philosophical implication. When the Buddha keeps silent on metaphysical questions, does the Buddha refuse philosophical discussion as irrelevant to his teaching? Or does he offer his own mode of philosophy as opposed to the one that he identified with the metaphysical and the substantial in his criticism of the philosophy of Brahmins? This raises a question regarding the position of metaphysics and philosophical discourse in the Buddha's teaching. One can further expand the scope of the question and ask: Is a philosophical discourse possible without in some way relying on a metaphysical foundation? (In this case, the "metaphysical foundation" should be understood liberally.) All of these issues have been grounds for some people's reservations in accepting Buddhism as a philosophical discourse. From the perspective of some Western Buddhist scholars, the basic position of the Buddha as represented by his silence to the questions on metaphysical issues is evidence that metaphysical discourse is not relevant to Buddhist teaching, and Buddhism duly belongs to the religious endeavor to save all human beings from suffering without resorting to any speculative mode. From a Western philosophical perspective, Buddhism's rejection of metaphysics and its lack of logical consistency becomes a ground for disqualifying the tradition as a philosophy. One of the questions that emerge in the course of parsing these issues in this book is that the term *philosophy* or the activities of philosophizing might need redefinition. This is not simply a philosophical issue but one that is related to a broader question of identity formation, categorization, and institutionalization.

The second theme of the book revolves around the meaning and function of violence in Zen Buddhist tradition. Zen Buddhism in the West has a relatively short history. In the United States, the official entry of Zen Buddhism is frequently dated to the 1893 Chicago World Parliament of Religions to which Japanese Zen master Shaku Sōen (1859–1919) was invited. More importantly to the development of Zen Buddhism in the United States, a young D. T. Suzuki accompanied Master Shaku Sōen to Chicago as his interpreter. Since then, with only about a hundred years of history, American Zen Buddhist scholarship has shifted in its evaluation of the school from one extreme to another. The first round of American scholarship characterizes Zen Buddhism as a non-dualistic doctrine, leading to the cultivation of a pure state of mind freed from the discriminatory function of the self's individualistic speculation influenced by language: Zen Buddhism in this regard is understood as creating harmony in an individual practitioner and in a society where its teachings are practiced. This understanding of Zen Buddhism, which has been frequently dubbed as Suzukean Zen, encountered a challenge in the late twentieth century. The new scholarship has fully geared its research to report how Zen Buddhism in reality is completely opposite to Suzukean Zen, and the expression is now a derogatory designation for a romanticized version of Zen Buddhism. The new understanding of Zen Buddhism criticizes the school for being rhetorical in its rendering of the Buddhist teaching, discriminating in its understanding of the world, and being violent in its social involvement, instead of being non-dual and harmony-oriented. The hostility to Zen Buddhism culminated when some scholars of Japanese Buddhism raised a strong voice against Japanese Zen Buddhism's involvement with Japanese imperialism and nationalism during World War II.

Steven Heine sums up these contrasting evaluations of Zen Buddhism with a neat paradigm of "Zen writes, Zen rites, Zen rights."[3] Through this rubric, Heine compares the faces of Zen Buddhism as they appear in the traditional Zen narrative and in Zen Buddhism's social and cultural manifestations. In the traditional Zen narrative, Heine tells us, Zen writes "ineffably," Zen rites promote non-duality, and Zen rights emphasize social harmony, whereas in the historical and cultural reality of Zen Buddhism, Zen writes with extensive use of language, Zen rites include various forms of rituals seeking for practical worldly benefits, and Zen rights have contributed to social discrimination.

Heine's research is based on Japanese Zen Buddhist tradition with references to Chinese predecessors. With some adjustment, one could expand this paradigm to other Zen Buddhist traditions. How, then, do we understand these contradictory elements within Zen Buddhism? John R. McRae's approach was to reconcile it through a symbolic reading, as he states in what he calls "McRae's Rules of Zen Studies," the first of which states: "It's not true, and therefore it's more important."[4] The implication is that by being aware of the gap in the record of Zen Buddhism, one can read the intended meaning.

Both Heine's and McRae's research are based on the cultural and historical approaches to Zen Buddhism. Looking into the philosophy of Zen Buddhism in an attempt to resolve the contradicting evaluations of the tradition, we can ask the question: what if Zen Buddhism's claim to ineffability is both real and rhetorical? What if Zen Buddhism's emphasis on non-duality contains the potential for both social harmony and discrimination? What if Zen Buddhism's focus on meditation is the gist of the school's identity and practice as has been claimed, and what if at the same time Zen Buddhism has always been amalgamated with more secular worldly rituals? The point to make is that no thought system is homogeneous. The desire to create the *one and only* coherent interpretation of a thought system is ubiquitous in philosophical tradition; however, satisfying that desire is possible only through suppression and exclusion. Its logic is rule by one authority, one truth, and one authentic interpretation. However, as Jean-François Lyotard states, "[o]ne side's legitimacy does not imply the other's lack of legitimacy,"[5] the meaning of which we discuss in the later part of this book.

Violence employed in Zen literature is one incidence through which the dual nature of Zen philosophy and logic can be examined. On the one hand, the physical violence in Zen narrative is a symbolic rendering of its emphasis on the cutting off of the dualistic and reified mode of thinking. Zen violence signifies the radical nature of the Zen Buddhist challenge to authority and at the same time the urgency with which Zen Buddhism presents the issue to the practitioner. On the other, when the message is articulated in language and enforced within an institution, be it a Zen monastery or a Buddhist community, the message and enforcement themselves become violence. Such violence could appear in several physical forms in culture and history. Jacques Derrida identifies three types of violence. Violence begins with articulation, when one makes distinctions through a linguistic system. The first layer of violence in the form of naming opens a door for the second layer of violence arising from the creation of and evaluation by an institutional system such as moral regulations and laws. Out of this second layer of violence, there emerges more empirical and physical violence, or "what is commonly called evil, war, indiscretion, rape."[6] To be noted in understanding Derrida's discussion of violence is that the original violence described here is not an optional element in life.

The fact that violence begins with our use of language, by making distinctions and naming, does not offer us the option not to use language. Zen Buddhism's emphasis on ineffability is an awareness of this original violence in any institution, including linguistic convention, habitualized mode of thinking, and social system. That the assertion for such awareness can itself become violence is the insight that has been frequently forgotten in our understanding of Zen Buddhist tradition.

The third theme of the book is related to the ethical domain of Zen Buddhism. The topic is a corollary of the first two questions. Soon after the entry of Buddhism into the American intellectual world, the question of ethics emerged. Criticisms and suggestions were made that if Buddhism wants to survive on Western soil, it must offer a clearer ethical blueprint. Among Buddhist schools, Zen Buddhism has been especially at odds with ethics both because of the radical nature of Zen's challenge to dualistic categorizations and because of Zen's antinomian tendency.

The problems of ethics that are raised against Buddhism, however, are not exclusively Buddhist issues but are shared by some recent philosophical developments in Western philosophy, especially in postmodernism and deconstruction. At the center of the distrust of Buddhism's capacity for ethics, as well as of postmodern philosophy, lie the Buddhist-postmodern claims for non-identity of identity, interconnectedness of opposite categories, and lack of transcendental foundation of an entity. This leads some to conclude that a philosophy of non-substantialism is anti-ethical in the sense that it cannot provide ethical agency because of its denial of distinctive subjectivity; it is incapable of offering clear ethical categories of right and wrong and good and bad because of its theory of relatedness; and it is impossible for such a philosophy to validate moral and ethical responsibility because it denies transcendental foundation.

As opposed to such a grim projection, an examination of Zen Buddhist literature and postmodern philosophy demands that the concept of ethics itself needs to be reconsidered. Normative forms of ethics, which are the result of metaphysical tradition, do not and cannot be the only form of ethics. The aporia and undecidability, which normative ethics could have considered as a dead end for ethical discourse, could offer a new ethical paradigm in the Buddhist-postmodern approach to ethics. I propose the "ethics of tension" as a new ethical paradigm that emerges from Buddhist and postmodern philosophy.

The discussion of the three themes of this book—that is, the nature of Buddhist philosophy, the meaning and function of violence in Zen Buddhism, and Buddhist-postmodern ethics in the form of the ethics of tension—are based on several sources in Buddhist tradition, but the most focused discussions appear in the hermeneutics of Zen and Huayan Buddhism, concentrating on Korean Zen master Pojo Chinul's (1158-1210) works with reference to Chinese Zen *gong'an* literature and Chinese Huayan Buddhist philosophy. Chinul's presentation of Zen Buddhism in the form of *huatou* meditation examines how Buddhist philosophy deals with the issues of subjectivity, of relation to the objective world, and of language and thinking. Chinul's Huayan Buddhism, which is discussed in this book in comparison with the Chinese patriarchs' rendering of Huayan Buddhist thoughts, offers a unique incidence in which Huayan Buddhist philosophy is utilized to overcome the limits of Zen Buddhism.

The three thematic questions of this book are presented through the paradigm which I identify as centripetality, centrifugality, and the tension between the two. Centripetality is the force moving toward a center whereas centrifugality is the force moving away from it. By its nature, the former centralizes and unifies, whereas the latter decentralizes and diffuses. Two points need to be made in advance for the discussion of centripetality and centrifugality. First, despite our habitualized value system, which is ready to evaluate unity and harmony as positive, and diffusion and disunity as negative, unity and disunity are value-neutral as such. Second, they never function separately, but are always already interfused. The tension as a state of the relationship between the two forces denotes recognition of the heterogeneous nature of centripetality and centrifugality and at the same time of their indissociableness. The tension in this case is not a provision for any type of final resolution; instead, the continued state of tension without ultimate resolution is to be understood as the nature of an entity.

These two types of forces have appeared in the history of philosophy in several different modes: the transcendental and the empirical, the noumenal and the phenomenal, the universal and the particular, the mind and the world, the subject and the object, the one and the many, the ontological and the ontic, and Truth and its dissemination. Buddhist tradition is not alien to this hermeneutic device, even though it has rarely been discussed in this way. The Buddha and sentient beings in Mahāyāna tradition, especially in Zen Buddhism, is one instance; the relationship between subitism and gradualism in Zen tradition is another; the normative linguistic and social convention and Zen *gong'an* language offers yet another set representing the centripetal and centrifugal forces and the relationship between wisdom and compassion also can very well be interpreted as the tension between the centralizing and decentralizing forces. That these two forms exist in a state of tension, mutually reinforcing, has not always been recognized; and when it is recognized, the tension is there only to be resolved, which becomes the *raison d'être* of the tension. What would it mean to understand the centripetal and centrifugal forces as in a relationship of tension with no final resolution on the horizon? First of all, it implies the openness of an entity, which also suggests the openness of a text and of a thought system. An openness of an entity is articulated in Buddhism with its no-self theory, dependent co-arising and emptiness; in the postmodern mode of thinking, the openness is described through the concepts of inter-subjectivity, *différance*, or an event. The openness by nature readjusts one's relationship with others as well as one's own identity. Hence, the openness of an entity cannot but be related to the political and the ethical.

Buddhism in general and Zen Buddhism in particular have demonstrated a keen awareness of the function of language in creating dualism in one's mode of thinking and thus language's inadequacy in articulating the non-substantial mode of truth that Buddhism supports. In analogous fashion, various philosophical discourses on language preceding the emergence of postmodern thought in Continental philosophy demonstrate the problem of truth and the role of language in the construction of truth. The awareness that truth is constructed, instead of being given, renders the discussion of language already as a political action. Postmodern discourse in this sense could be one of the most engaged philosophical discourses without explicitly naming itself a political philosophy.

Any consideration of the questions arising from Buddhism's encounter with the West—Western philosophy, Western culture, and Western scholarship—is charged with political implications that are reminiscent of the power relationship among the elements involved. As African-American thinker Charles Mills writes, "In a broad sense, virtually all African-American philosophy is 'political', insofar as the insistence on one's black humanity in a racist world is itself a political act."[7] The same can be said about thinking of the nature of Buddhist philosophy, its relation to dominant philosophical trends in American academia, and its ethical position. By bringing together "questions" on Buddhism with the philosophy of postmodernity, *Buddhism and Postmodernity* intends to move toward a new domain in our understanding both of Buddhism and of postmodernity.

Part I

CENTRIPETALITY:
BUDDHISM AND METAPHYSICS

Chapter One

The Silence of the Buddha

1. Buddhist Encounter with Modernity

The exact details of how Buddhism was first encountered in Europe are difficult to ascertain. Henri de Lubac notes in his *La rencontre du bouddhisme et de l'Occident*, "almost abruptly, for the Westerners, the great religion of the Orient finally 'emerged from the clouds'."[1] In the same context Lubac quotes Abbot Auguste Deschamps who states: "One has to admire with what speed, with its first contact with the spirit of investigation that characterizes our age, (Buddhism) has emerged from its profound obscurity and its long silence."[2] In the same vein, Stephen Batchelor's *Awakening of the West* describes the sudden emergence of Buddhism in the intellectual scene of Europe: "Until the 1840s the Buddha was vaguely conceived as a mythic god in the Indian pantheon. Then, almost overnight, he was revealed as an historical figure, comparable in an alarming number of respects to Jesus. In addition to the crisis of home-grown unbelief surging all around it, the Church now had to contend with the emergence of a fully fledged rival from Asia."[3]

Despite Deschamps' and Batchelor's strong characterizations, it is highly probable that the emergence of Buddhism in Europe was not such a dramatic event. As early as the sixteenth century, the Jesuits traveled to Asia and sent news about the Asian world back to Europe.[4] It is noteworthy, however, that the nineteenth century marks an increased interest in European scholarship regarding the Orient in general and Buddhism in particular. Roger-Pol Droit's *Le culte du néant, Les philosophes et le Bouddha* examines the development of the image of Buddhism in Europe during the nineteenth century, specifically focusing on the European understanding of Buddhism as "the cult of nothingness." Based on several important events, Droit divides the nineteenth century European understanding of Buddhism into three pe-

11

riods. "The Birth" begins in 1784 when Sir William Jones (1746–1794), an English philologist well-known for his claim for the common root of Indian and European languages, became president of the Royal Asiatic Society of Bengal, a group dedicated to the rational and systematic study of Asia. This period ends in 1831, Droit states, with the death of G.W.F. Hegel who said of Buddhism, "One should become nothing" in Buddhist religion. Hegel's statement is exemplary of the negative evaluations of Buddhism that predominated the nineteenth century European intellectuals. "The Threat" begins in 1832, according to Droit, when Eugène Burnouf (1801–1852), a prominent scholar among the first generation European Buddhologists, was elected to the Collège de France, marking the starting point of the scientific study of Buddhism in Europe. This second period ends in 1863 which marks the height of the controversy of the "cult of nothingness" in France, England, and Germany. The final period or "The Decline" comes to an end in 1893, which is the year of the Chicago Parliament of the World's Religions, an event which, for Droit, reflects the changed tone in the Western understanding of Buddhism. Droit concludes: "1893. The Parliament of Religion takes place in Chicago. The age of ecumenism, eclecticism, and occultism—in the background of literary pessimism—becomes a dream. Buddhism has ceased to be frightening."[5]

Even though Droit envisions 1893 as the end point of negative understanding of Buddhism in the West, it is questionable whether that has been the case. Throughout the twentieth century, Western understanding of Buddhism suffered from the ghost of Hegel's annihilation theory and the idea of Buddhism as "the cult of nothingness" ("*le culte du néant*") as the French thinker Victor Cousin (1792–1867) coined it. Nothingness as a characteristic expression for Buddhism, however, does not necessarily carry the nihilistic or negative connotation attributed by European thinkers in the nineteenth century. The issue is not whether Buddhism is actually a cult of nothingness, but how nothingness is understood in certain philosophical traditions. As we will discuss shortly, different modes of understanding nothingness are decisive factors in defining the nature of a certain philosophical tradition.

The first generation of German Buddhist scholars understood Buddhism as a religion full of negative, even "horrible and naïve" tenets.[6] To them, the negative aspects of Buddhism culminate in a negation or "annihilation" of being.[7] Burnouf translated nirvāṇa as "utter annihilation." Buddhism for him is a religion which seeks the "disappearance of individuality by way of absorption—into the Supreme Being or into the void (*śūnyatā*)." [8] Buddhist nirvāṇa for him meant "a fundamental change in the condition of the individual, which would, to all appearances, be utter annihilation."[9] Burnouf's identification of nirvāṇa with utter annihilation of the subject was further supported by his student, Max Müller (1823-1900), who wrote: "No person who reads with attention the metaphysical speculations of *Nirvāna* contained in the Buddhist canon can arrive at any conviction different from that expressed by Burnouf, *viz.* that *Nirvāna*, the highest aim, the *summum bonum* of Buddhism, is the absolute nothing."[10]

It is not accidental that Müller expresses his concern about Buddhism in the context of "metaphysical speculation." That is, Buddhism in the nineteenth century intellectual scene of continental Europe was inevitably understood through the lens of its philosophical tradition of modernist metaphysics. Andrew P. Tuck thus states in his *Comparative Philosophy and the Philosophy of Scholarship: On the Western Interpretation of Nāgārjuna*:

> The [European] Buddhologists' terminology of "annihilation," "extinction," and "nihilism" discloses an obsession with the metaphysical and a mistrust of any system that bypasses questions of ontology. Burnouf's principal concern was whether the individual is ultimately "absorbed" into a transcendental ground of existence or totally "extinguished" in *nirvāna*. And for all the scholars who followed him, the suspicion that the Buddhist *nirvāna* was in fact nothing—that there was no realm of reality behind the veil of appearance—made European acceptance of Buddhist philosophy impossible. Burnouf, Saint-Hilaire, and Müller saw nothing but annihilation of the individual, a denial of the reality of what Kantians were calling the "transcendental ego," what Hegelians were calling *Geist*.[11]

It remains debatable whether Buddhist philosophy "bypasses questions of ontology" and whether the Buddhist concept of reality is that there is no realm of reality behind the veil of appearance. However, as Tuck aptly points out, the problem of Buddhist annihilationism as conceptualized by European scholars lies not so much in the nature of Buddhism itself as in the metaphysical context in which Buddhism was evaluated. Tuck's statement together with that of Müller offers us a frame of reference through which Buddhism was understood during the initial phase of the tradition's encounter with the continental European intellectual world. One major component of the frame can be identified with Buddhism's relation to metaphysics. Its natural corollary includes the Buddhist view of self, its relation to transcendental reality, and the Buddhist conception of nothingness.

As noted in both Müller and Tuck, Buddhism's relation to metaphysics has played a significant role in the European evaluation of Buddhism, and it continues to be so in the Western understanding of the tradition. Buddhism has been frequently interpreted as a thought system that stands as a stark opposite to metaphysical tradition. Further expanding this idea, one finds the claim that Buddhism is anti-philosophical. The two theses—that is, the anti-metaphysical and anti-philosophical claims about Buddhism—are based on different aspects of Buddhism. The anti-metaphysics thesis focuses on the understanding that

Buddhist philosophy by nature negates transcendental foundation or foundationalism in general. The anti-philosophy thesis anchors its argument in a dualist approach to philosophy and religion; it claims that Buddhism's goal is to release practitioners from suffering and does not lie in abstract theoretical argument. Detailed discussions of each thesis shall appear as we move on in this book. The dualisms of metaphysics versus anti-metaphysics, philosophy versus religion, and theory versus practice are concepts that have deep roots in our philosophizing. However, a reconfiguration of the relationship between the binary poles in the above-mentioned dualisms leads us to a new vision in understanding the philosophical position of Buddhism and our way of philosophizing.

2. *Thinking as/and the Foundation of Being*

In considering Buddhism's relation to metaphysics as well as to the nineteenth century European evaluation of Buddhism, Descartes seems to be a good starting point. At the center of the Europeans' reluctance to admit Buddhist philosophy lies the legacy of the modern subject duly represented by the Cartesian Ego-Cogito.

Modernity in Europe began, among others, with the creation of the thinking subject, which had gradually replaced the power of God in various fields of human science. Works by René Descartes (1596–1650), especially his *Discourse on the Method* (1637) and *Meditations on First Philosophy* (1641), symbolically portray this transition, and the birth of the modern self in the form of Ego-Cogito. Through these works, Descartes set the orientation of the nature of philosophy, which will dominate continental metaphysics for the next three hundred years. The transition from God to the thinking subject (Ego-Cogito) as the foundation of knowledge, however, did not take place without the agonizing struggles of the critical mind which was keenly aware of the changing environments and which was also desperately searching for the grounds of existence and the certainty of human knowledge.

Descartes stands as a representative figure in this pursuit for a new direction in the relationship between men and God, on the one hand, and men and things, on the other. Objections from his contemporaries evidence the radical nature of his reasoning and the intensity of the struggle he had to go through in order to introduce the thinking subject as a major player in human understanding. In the *Discourse on the Method*, Descartes devotes his inquiry to a search for the fundamental law that guides the certainty of knowledge. The systematic doubts he carried out were based on his suspicion of the reliability of human knowledge. He asks whether the knowledge he had obtained through education was as reliable as he once used to think it was, and wonders whether he could reach perfection by working on knowledge imparted to him by others. The impossibility of finding the grounds to justify one view over another, and the realization that knowledge, and therefore judgment, is bound by ungrounded assumptions forced Descartes to put himself into an intellectual exile for nine years, during which time he "did nothing else but roam here and there in the world, trying to be rather a spectator than an actor in all the comedies that are played out there."[12] While keeping a neutral position and eliminating any ideas that might raise even minimal suspicion, Descartes had reached what he considers the unshakable ground of his being, and this ground was none other than his own thinking:

> I rejected as false all the reasoning that I had previously taken for demonstrations. . . . But immediately afterward, I took note that, while I wanted thus to think that everything was false, it necessarily had to be that I, who was thinking this, were something. And noticing that this truth—*I think, therefore I am*—was so firm and so assured that all the most extravagant suppositions of the skeptics were not capable of shaking it, I judged that I could accept it, without scruple, as the first principle of the philosophy that I was seeking. (Italics original.) [13]

Once the certainty of the thinking subject is self-confirmed, Descartes extends his inquiry to the issue of the immortality of the soul that exists apart from a corporeal body. And finally, the existence of God is to be confirmed as an inevitable foundation of his own existence and knowledge.

In the *Meditations on First Philosophy* written several years after the *Discourse on the Method*, Descartes reconfirms his own existence as well as that of God and the immortality of the soul. At the beginning of the *Meditations*, with the resolution that philosophy will not be sinned against twice, Descartes boldly declares that the existence of God and the immortality of the soul should be dealt with philosophically rather than theologically. With this declaration, the transition from the theocentric to the androcentric world that was already played out in the *Discourse on the Method* is rearticulated and reconfirmed. In *Meditations*, Descartes defines the certainty of his existence by the fact that he thinks. That he doubts his being at the very moment he does his thinking provides him the undoubted ground for his existence. Hence thinking itself becomes the nature of being for him. Descartes writes: "thought exists; it alone cannot be separated from me. I am: I exist–this is certain. . . . I am . . . precisely nothing but a thinking thing; that is, a mind, or intellect, or understanding, or reason–words of whose meanings I was previously ignorant. Yet I am a true thing and am truly existing; but what kind of thing? I have said it already: a thinking thing."[14]

The thinking itself in Cartesian reasoning not only represents the nature of one's existence but that of the soul as well: "I [am] a substance the whole essence or nature of which is only to think, and which, in order to be, does not have need of any place, and does not depend on any material thing. Thus this 'I' that is to say, the soul through which I am that which I am, is entirely distinct from the body, and is even easier to know than it, and, even if the latter were not at all, the soul would not cease to be all that which it is." [15] As Descartes finds the evidence of his existence within himself (he as a thinking being), so does he regard the existence of God: "the idea of God which is in us must have God himself as its cause."[16] This argument is a further elaboration of his view previously discussed in the *Discourse*: "that the things that we conceive very clearly and very distinctly are all true is assured only for the reasons that God is or exists, that he is a perfect being, and that all that which is in us comes from him. From whence it follows that our ideas or notions, being real things, and coming from God, in all that in which they are clear and distinct, cannot, in this, be anything but true."[17] The irony of Cartesian discourse is evident: Descartes derives God from the Cogito in order to confirm the certainty of Cogito itself. In his discourse, the role of God is reduced to the keeper of Ego-Cogito. Descartes' contemporary, Blaise Pascal, is credited to have said: "I cannot forgive Descartes: in his whole philosophy he would like to do without God; but he could not help allowing him a flick of the fingers to set the world in motion; after that he had no more use for God." [18]

A review of the Cartesian thinking subject offers us possible sources we can look to for the understanding of the nineteenth century European evaluation of Buddhism. The research of Buddhism in Europe became possible under the assumption that Buddhism (that is, a non-Christian religious tradition) was an object of an objective and scientific study. However, the sociopolitical imbalance of power between the East and the West—concretized by the reality of colonialism—and a different set of philosophical assumptions and traditions hindered European understanding of Buddhism. From the perspective of modernist metaphysics, the goal of Buddhism was none other than "annihilation" of being, the Cartesian Ego-Cogito. Such an anti-metaphysical system that denies the foundation of existence could not but create horror.

However, we need to discern what a thought system would actually entail when it is labeled as anti-metaphysical. Does anti-metaphysical denote that the thought system "bypasses the issue of ontology" as Tuck claimed? If an anti-metaphysical system refuses to deal with the issues that are commonly categorized as "metaphysical," what are the concerns of that system? Does that simply disqualify the system as a philosophy or does an anti-metaphysical thought system offer its own way of dealing with the issues that constitute the core of metaphysical discourse? These questions about metaphysical and anti-metaphysical systems are poignant not only in the Buddhist encounter with the Western world and Western philosophical system but also in philosophy's encounter with postmodern thought. In order to further explore the issue, let us examine the Buddhist concept of self and its positions on metaphysical discourse.

3. Buddhism and the Contingency of Self

One of the classic texts in the Buddhist tradition that deals with the Buddha's view on metaphysical discourse is a dialogue between the Buddha and Māluṅkyāputta. Māluṅkyāputta is especially well-known for the ten questions on metaphysical issues he posed to the Buddha, which Buddhist tradition has identified as the "undeclared" thesis (Pāli: *avyākata*; Sk. *avyākṛta*). According to the dialogue, when the venerable Māluṅkyāputta was meditating, a reasoning mind arose in him, raising the following questions:

> The following views were set aside, ignored, and not fully explained by the World Honored One. That is, (1) whether the world is eternal or (2) the world is not eternal; (3) whether the world has an end or (4) the world does not have an end; (5) whether life (the soul) is the same as the body, or (6) life (the soul) is one thing, the body another; (7) whether the Tathāgata dies, or (8) the Tathāgata does not die; or (9) the Tathāgata both dies and does not die, or (10) the Tathāgata neither dies nor does not die. I do not like [that these issues have not been explained], I would not put up with that, nor let it go."[19] (Numbers added.)

With this doubt, Māluṅkyāputta went to see the Buddha and asked him these questions. Prior to asking, he had decided that if the Buddha failed to produce satisfactory answers to his questions, he would disavow the Buddha's training and go back to secular life. In our discussion of Descartes, we mentioned that through his doubts, Descartes discovered three aspects of his existence: the "I" as the "thinking thing," the existence of soul, and God as the ground for both. This trinity of subjectivity, rationalism, and God as the transcendental foundation of both provided Descartes with the security of human existence as well as the certainty of knowledge. Māluṅkyāputta could have been a Descartes in Buddha's time. Like Descartes, Māluṅkyāputta wanted to have a clear knowledge about the nature of his existence in this world, afterlife, and their foundation. However, the Buddha flatly rejected his Cartesian inquiries on the nature of the universe, the afterlife, and the soul as irrelevant to Buddhist discourse. The Buddha responded to Māluṅkyāputta that the reality of life remains the same regardless of one's position on the issues he raised. The Buddha asks Māluṅkyāputta: "Māluṅkyāputta, are you following me because I told you that the world is eternal?" Māluṅkyāputta said no. Then, the Buddha explained the situation with a well-known story. If someone was shot with a poisoned arrow, the first thing the person should do is to get rid of the arrow and save his life. If the person insisted that he needed to know, before he removed the arrow, who shot the arrow, what the arrow was made of, and why the person shot him, he would risk his life. Those questions do not help him to save his life. By the same token, the questions as to the eternity of the world, the relationship between body and the mind, or to the immortality of the Tathāgata do not help people solve the issue of life and death. Whatever the answers to the above questions might be, the Buddha contends, one is born into this world, gets through the sufferings of life, gets old and eventually dies. The Buddha thus tells Māluṅkyāputta: "Those who believe that the world is eternal also go through birth, aging, sickness, grief and sadness, worries, agony, and create in that way a bunch of suffering. Similarly, those who believe that the world is not eternal go through birth, aging, sickness, grief and sadness, worries, agony and create in that way a bunch of suffering."[20]

One conventional interpretation of this dialogue holds that Buddhism takes metaphysical discourse to be unnecessary because the goal of Buddhism is to save practitioners from suffering which cannot be alleviated through theorization or logical (or illogical) arguments.[21] A more nuanced interpretation of this dialogue can be gained by examining John Hick's views of "unanswered questions" and "unanswerable questions" in religious tradition. For Hick, "unanswered questions" are "legitimate questions to which there are presumably true answers, but to which we do not in fact know the answers," whereas "unanswerable questions" are "about realities transcending the systems of categories available in our human thought and language."[22] Hick categorizes the first six of Māluṅkyāputta's questions as unanswered questions. He contends that the Buddha intentionally withheld the answers to these questions since they are irrelevant to the teachings of the Buddha. The goal of the Buddha's teaching, according to Hick, prioritizes soteriological edification and to know the answer to these questions would not serve that goal. The simile of the poisoned arrow and subsequent advice by the Buddha to Māluṅkyāputta appear to support Hick's argument. As for the questions (7) through (10), in which Māluṅkyāputta asks about the status of the Tathāgata after death, Hick explains them as both "unanswered" and "unanswerable." According to Hick, these are questions regarding a state which is too deep and profound for common people to understand. Based on his ideas of "unanswered" and "unanswerable" questions, Hick tentatively concludes that the Buddha's insight is based on a "need-to-know" basis and for the Buddha "what we need to know is soteriological rather than metaphysical."[23] Hick's argument is persuasive and fits nicely with conventional wisdom in Buddhist studies.[24] However, it is debatable whether soteriological and metaphysical concerns can be so clearly distinguishable in a religious tradition such as Buddhism. Can a religious tradition be maintained by simply dismissing metaphysical issues and emphasizing the primacy of a soteriological goal?

The Buddha's silence to Māluṅkyāputta's questions could represent the Buddhist mistrust of metaphysical discourse per se. Or it could be another way of addressing the issues that are conventionally considered metaphysical. It is true that in the above mentioned dialogue the Buddha refused to discuss

Mālunkyāputta's inquiry on the soul, the universe, the relation between soul and body, the afterlife and the meaning of death. However, in other dialogues in early Buddhist texts, the Buddha implicitly and explicitly addresses these topics. The Buddha's concept of self, or, rather, his theory of no-self, explains the relationship between self (or soul) and body; this, in turn, shed light on the meaning of life, death, and afterlife. Without directly answering Mālunkyāputta's questions, the Buddha was indeed answering them. The point is not whether or not the Buddha answered these questions, but how the Buddha addresses the issue and how Buddhist tradition has directed our interest, curiosity, and desire to learn about these issues.

Let us go back to the ten questions and examine how these questions and the Buddha's handling of them represent the Buddha's way of addressing metaphysical issues as well as Buddhism's soteriological goal. Mālunkyāputta's questions can be categorized into four metaphysical issues: "the first two pairs of propositions refer to the duration and the extent of the world, the third, to the nature of the soul, and the last four, to the state of the dead saint."[25] These questions were posed from two distinct philosophical positions: the eternalist position and the annihilationist (or materialist) position. The former contends that existence continues after the destruction of the tangible, material reality of the body and the world, whereas the latter asserts that existence is terminated together with the extinction of material reality. In his tenfold inquiry to the Buddha, Mālunkyāputta asks the Buddha whether he is a materialist (annihilationist) or eternalist. By maintaining silence to Mālunkyāputta's questions, the Buddha declares that he is neither. Not only can the Buddha's position not be categorized as either materialist or eternalist, but the very impossibility of complying with the dualistic model constitutes the core of his philosophical frame. Several sections in the Chinese Āgama, in which the Buddha openly maintains the position of "non-declaration," demonstrate this stance. One example comes from a dialogue entitled "Sūtra of Having Self" in which one of the Buddha's followers has a doubt about the meaning of no-self and asks the Buddha as follows:

"Dear World-Honored One, how would you say? Does 'I' exist?" the Buddha remained silent to this question. Vatsa asked the same question three times and the Buddha kept silence each time. Disappointed by the Buddha's silence, Vatsa thought that the Buddha was not capable to answer his questions and was about to leave the Buddha. Ananda, who was watching the incident, tells the Buddha. "World Honored One, Vatsa asked you three times. Why did you avoid answering his questions? Your silence could raise a suspicious idea in him and make him think that you were unable to answer his question." The Buddha replies to Ananda: "If I said 'I' exists, that will only deepen the wrong view Vatsa already has in his mind; if I said 'I' does not exist, that means that there was 'I' and now 'I' does not exist, which will deepen the suspicion in Vatsa's mind. If I say, 'I' originally existed, that will be the view of permanence; if I say, 'I' is annihilated, that will be the view of annihilation. Tathāgata stays away from both extremes and teaches the dharma of the middle. That is, because this exists, that exists. Because this happens, that happens."[26]

In this dialogue, the Buddha refuses the views of both eternalists and annihilationists regarding the existence of self and explains it according to the Buddhist theory of "dependent co-arising." Hence the Buddha states: "because this exists, that exists." Existence, from the Buddha's perspective, occurs dependently, and not through a maintenance or extinction of a certain independent quality of an entity. The Buddha's dialogue with Ananda in the above passage indicates that his silence is his way of communicating the impossibility of choosing between the eternalist and annihilationist positions.

A close connection between the Buddha's silence and his philosophical paradigm is also articulated in his dialogue with Kāśyapa. In the dialogue, Kāśyapa asks to the Buddha whether the suffering, with which the Buddha characterizes the life of unenlightened beings, is of one's own making or created by causes other than oneself.

Kāśyapa asks the Buddha: "What would you say, venerable one? Is suffering of one's own making?" The Buddha tells Kāśyapa: "As to the question of whether suffering is of one's own making, the Buddha keeps silence." Kāśyapa asks again: "What would you say, then, venerable one? Is suffering caused by others?" The Buddha tells Kāśyapa: "As to the question of whether suffering is caused by others, the Buddha also keeps silence." Kāśyapa asks once again: "What would you say, venerable one? Is suffering caused both by oneself and others?" The Buddha says to Kāśyapa: "As to the question of whether suffering is caused both by oneself and others, the Buddha also keeps silence." Kāśyapa asks again: "Is suffering caused neither by oneself, nor by others, and thus by nothing?" The Buddha responds again: "As to whether suffering is caused neither by oneself, nor by others, and thus by nothing, the Buddha keeps silence." Kāśyapa asks once again. " . . . when I asked whether suffering is of one's own making, you answered that that cannot be answered; when I asked whether suffering is caused by others, or both by oneself and others, or neither by oneself nor by others, thus has no cause, you answered that that cannot be answered. Then, is it the case that suffering does not exist?" The Buddha says to Kāśyapa, "Suffering does not not exist; suffering does exist."

Kāśyapa tells the Buddha, "I'm glad to hear that. You said that suffering does exist; please teach me about that, so that I can learn about suffering and see into it." The Buddha tells Kāśyapa, "If feeling [of suffering] is one's own feeling, I would obviously say that suffering is caused by self; if the feeling is others', and thus others are the ones who receive the feeling, I would obviously say that suffering is caused by others. If feeling is one's and others' feeling, and thus suffering is caused by the self and others, I keep silence. If suffering is caused neither by self nor by others, and thus without cause comes into being, I also keep silence. Tathāgata leaves two extremes and thus teaches the middle path. Because of this, that happens; because this arises, that arises"[27]

I cited the episode in its entirety in order to demonstrate the pattern of argument the Buddha employs in the section where the "undeclared" issues are discussed. In all three dialogues, the Buddha responds by maintaining silence as to certain questions. In the dialogue with Mālunkyāputta, the Buddha emphasizes the soteriological irrelevancy of the questions; with Vatsa, the Buddha identifies the problem of Vatsa's questions as eternalist-annihilationist dualism, which the Buddha claims to go against his own position of interdependency of existence. In the dialogue with Kāśyapa, the Buddha further clarifies his position. He admits that his silence on the cause of suffering does not negate the existence of suffering. Suffering "does exist." The Buddha is yet to explain how he would confirm the existence of suffering if he keeps silent as to the cause of suffering. However, at least one thing is clear: the Buddha is not merely refusing to discuss the issues that are brought up to him by his students because the issues are not related to the soteriological goal. Instead, through his declaration of "undeclarability," the Buddha reveals that the mode of question itself needs to be reconsidered.

As Steven Collins explains, the questions asked by Mālunkyāputta, Vatsa, and Kāśyapa are, from the Buddha's perspective, linguistically ill-formed.[28] The questions the Buddha refuses to answer are unanswerable not because the questions deal with the reality that transcends our experience and linguistic expression as described by Hick, but because the questions themselves are flawed and based on untenable presuppositions. The undeclared thesis of the Buddha is the incident of logical and linguistic impasse that occurs when interlocutors do not share basic assumptions of their dialogue. The gap between the inquisitors deprives one side of linguistic, logical, and philosophical tools to respond, which results in the silence of one side.[29] One frequently cited popular version of this example goes: "Have you stopped beating your wife?" The question is unanswerable if the interlocutor considers himself as free from the charge of beating his wife. Neither positive nor negative answer will enable the dialoguer to make the point that the question is itself irrelevant to his situation.

The Buddha's silence in the undeclared thesis offers a salient point about Buddhism's relation to metaphysical discourse. In all the three dialogues between the Buddha and his followers we examined here, the Buddha's silence is followed by the Buddha's exposition of his own mode of thinking. While refusing to answer the questions in the manner the questions were posed, the Buddha proposes his position by explicating the idea of the middle path, which is not subject to either/or logic. Hick's explanation of the Buddha's dismissal of metaphysical issues as unnecessary information based on his "need-to-know" teaching system stems from his belief that the Buddha's priority was always soteriological. Furthermore, this raises the assumption that metaphysical issues are by nature unrelated to a soteriological goal. Our examination of the Buddha's silence in the undeclared cases suggests the contrary. As opposed to the claim that the Buddha took an anti-philosophical stance through his silence, one can argue that the Buddha employed his silence to actively get involved with his own philosophical argument and, by so doing, he was demonstrating his own logical system.[30]

When the Buddha refused to give a direct answer to Māluṅkyāputta, he explains the reason for his dismissal of Māluṅkyāputta's questions as follows: "As to whether the world is eternal or not, I have not explained it at all. Why is it so? Because it does not comply with the meaning of things, nor the Truth, nor the fundamentals of pure living. It does not lead one to attain wisdom, nor awakening, nor nirvāṇa. That is why I have not explained it at all."[31] In this passage, the Buddha offers six categories that constitute the value system of his discourse: meaning of things, achievement of truth, exercise of the fundamentals of pure living, achievement of wisdom, achievement of awakening, and achievement of nirvāṇa. Each category reflects what one could take as technically Buddhist concepts, but it is not too difficult to convert them into more generic philosophical terms. The first two categories, translated as "the meaning of things" and "the Truth," have to do with the philosophical search for the meaning of things and ultimate truth; the next two categories, "the fundamentals of pure living" and the attainment of "wisdom," are related to the subject's relationship to the first two categories. In other words, the fundamentals of pure living imply an ethical and virtuous life as well as religious practice. The attainment of wisdom—wisdom being a special type of knowledge from the Buddhist perspective—is the subject's capacity to get through the reality of things, and the final two categories suggest the result that will follow when the philosophical investigation of the first four categories is performed properly. When the subject comes to have a correct understanding of the objects and of truth, and, when such understanding complies with one's ethical behaviors and internalized knowledge of things, the subject will eventually become one with things and truth, which leads one to liberation.

Based on this analysis, we can say that the Buddha does not suggest that he keeps silent to the questions raised by Māluṅkyāputta because they are irrelevant to the goal of his teaching. Instead, the Buddha clarifies that they do not "comply with" the reality of things, of truth and, thus, one's ethical and religious life in the way the Buddha sees the world. The problem the Buddha finds with Māluṅkyāputta's questions are not so much the questions themselves but the way questions are posed and the way those issues are framed. Having explained the six categories of his own value system, the Buddha informed Māluṅkyāputta: "What is it that has been explained by me? I have explained: suffering, accumulation of suffering, cessation of suffering, and the path leading to the cessation of suffering. These are what I have explained."[32] These four aspects of the Buddha's teaching, known as the Four Noble Truths, is the way the Buddha explains the structure of and one's relation to the world. An elucidation of the relationship between the Four Noble Truths and the six categories of value system the Buddha offered to Māluṅkyāputta will further clarify the Buddha's philosophical position.

In this context, one can interpret the simile of the poisoned arrow that appeared in the Buddha's dialogue with Māluṅkyāputta as part of the Buddha's philosophical endeavor. The conventional interpretation of the simile claims that the Buddha in this episode flatly rejects philosophical curiosity as a waste of time. However, as Yi Chungp'yo, a Korean scholar of early Buddhism, argues,

One cannot say that the person is merely exercising her/his curiosity when s/he refused to remove the poisoned arrow [before s/he learns about the nature of the arrow itself]. The person must have thought that the source of her/his suffering lies in the poisoned arrow, and s/he makes the arrow itself an issue because s/he thought that by learning about the arrow, s/he can remove the source of her/his suffering. It is true that the cause of suffering is not 'the existence' of the poisoned arrow, but the 'reality' of being shot by the poisoned arrow. Hence, the Buddha advises that one should remove the poisoned arrow, without being concerned about the existence of the arrow itself, and through this the Buddha tells us what is the correct way of doing philosophy if one wishes to be relieved from the reality of suffering; but the Buddha does not negate philosophy itself.[33]

If a distinction is made between philosophy and religion, this argument leads us to the conclusion that the Four Noble Truths demonstrate the Buddha's philosophical paradigm as much as his religious goal. Another dialogue in the Chinese Āgama further clarifies the issue:

Kaccāyana asked the Buddha: "World Honored One, what is the Right View that you teach? How is it the Right View and how do you explain it?"
    The Buddha responded to Kaccāyana: "One's worldview relies on either one of the following two: existence and non-existence [or being and non-being]. People become attached to what they encounter. Getting attached to what they encounter, some people rely on existence in their understanding of the world, and others on non-existence. If one does not get attached, even when the mind is constrained by phenomena, the mind will not be attached to them, and thus will neither stagnate nor calculate. [In that situation] one takes the arising of suffering as arising of suffering and its cessation as cessation, without being suspicious or being confused. Without relying on others, one knows. This is called

the Right View. This is the Right View the Tathāgata has explained. Why is it so? If one has a clear view about the appearing of things in the world, there is no thing that does not exist; and if one has a clear view about the disappearance of things in the world, there is no thing that exists. This is called cutting off two extremes and explaining the middle path. That is to say, because this exists, that exists; because this arises, that arises.[34]

This dialogue with Kaccāyana clearly elaborates the philosophical implication of the Buddha's silence. In the dialogues with Māluṅkyāputta, Vatsa, and Kāśyapa, the Buddha tells his inquisitors that he would keep silent on the issues brought up by them. The Buddha in all three dialogues tells his inquisitor that his teaching is based on the dependent nature of things: "because this exists, that exists." In the Kaccāyana dialogue, the nature of this dependency of beings develops into a most fundamental issue in philosophical discourse: that is, the question of being (existence) and non-being (or non-existence). The Buddha claims that philosophical discourses as well as views in the world come to emerge when things are viewed from a substantialist perspective, which creates a dualism of being and non-being. Refusing to answer the questions when the questions were posed based on the substantialist perspective, the Buddha offers his position as the middle path. As opposed to the substantialism of metaphysics, we can identify the Buddha's philosophical paradigm as a *non-substantialist* perspective. The point to note here is that, even though being and non-being, or existence and non-existence, take the form of a dichotomy in common-sense logic, in the Buddha's system, they belong to the same category in the sense that both being and non-being anchor themselves in the idea of the substantial existence of an entity either through affirmation or negation.

The Buddha teaches that when one realizes the dependent nature of existence, one attains Right View and then, "without relying on others, one knows [the reality of the encountered phenomenon]." The Buddha's claim in this passage raises a question: if one knows the Right View, who is the subject of this act of knowing? If the Buddha rejects the subject who exists as a separate entity, how does he identify the subject who knows the reality of phenomena? In another dialogue in the Āgamas, the Buddha illuminates the issue as he explains what is known as the Twelve Chains of Dependency. The Buddha's inquisitor asks:

"Dear World Honored One, who is it that exists?"
   The Buddha responded: "I did not say that someone exists. If I had said that someone existed, you are right in asking 'who is it that exists?' You should ask, 'Depending on what does existence come into being?' Then, I would answer: "Dependent upon attachment, existence comes into being, which becomes the cause of the future contact. This is called existence."[35]

The nature of the question asked here is similar to the instances in which the Buddha allegedly remained silent. The Buddha in this dialogue takes the active position of correcting his inquisitor. As Steven Collins states that the ten undeclared questions are linguistically ill-formulated, the Buddha is pointing out that the form of question already forecloses the possible answer. In an analysis similar to that of Steven Collins, Henry Cruise states: "The point of the analogy would seem to be that . . . what is assumed by the very framing of the question . . . is unacceptable. So much so that to deny the question is not enough; one must deny the assumption in the question, and one does this by rejecting the question as not legitimate."[36]

The Buddha's sensitivity to the forms of interrogation is not mere formality, or an addendum to his philosophy, but is his philosophy itself. As it will become clear, in philosophical investigation, "how" the enunciated is articulated is as important as "what" is enunciated. A shift of concern from "what" to "how" in a philosophical articulation also demonstrates a change in philosophical paradigm. When the "what-ness" of an entity occupies the main concern of a philosophical discourse that philosophical system takes the form of substantialism, and the system's discourse develops according to identity-principle. As a discourse underscores the problem of "what-ness" based logic and addresses the issue of "how," as the Buddha does in his undeclared thesis, that philosophy takes the position of non-substantialism. The "how" in this case does not indicate an applicative dimension of "what": "how" itself constitutes the non-whatness of the what, or the non-identity of identity. When the discourse of "how" encounters the logic of "what" that dominates the linguistic convention of the time, the former has to reconfigure the logic and language it employs. The Buddha's silence functions as a provisional logic and language that demonstrates the gap between the philosophical paradigm of substantialism and that of non-substantialism.

The non-substantial position of the Buddha frequently puts him in a linguistic conundrum as demonstrated in the cases of the undeclared thesis. The annihilation theory used by nineteenth century European intellectuals to characterize Buddhism is what the Buddha rejected as an inappropriate measure to discuss his position. The act of annihilation by nature requires an object to be annihilated. Based on this logical premise, the Europeans accused Buddhism of being nihilistic. And nihilism is disparaged as pessimistic because it is based on a tendency or an intention to destroy and deny that which has been assumed to exist, be it existence of an entity, a moral value, a social structure, or the meaning of life. Nihilism is also understood as negative based on the assumption that the nihilist destruction, negation, and denial of that which exists are usually not accompanied by an alternative to replace that which will have been removed. The result is anarchism in a society, decadence in moral and ethical position, or radical skepticism in philosophy.

When the European thinkers and European Buddhist scholars identified Buddhism with the annihilation theory, or "the cult of nothingness," a pessimistic tone was inevitable because the idea of no-self cannot but be interpreted as the removal of the existing self. The Buddha's position as revealed through our examination of the dialogues in the Chinese Āgama demonstrates that the Buddha's theory of no-self has little to do with "removing" or "annihilating" self. The concept of "removing" or "annihilating" is an ill-formulated argument because the Buddha's claim of no-self denotes the non-substantial nature of self, not the annihilation of it. Self exists only as a contingent reality, not as a permanent and independent essence.

As we compare Buddhist understanding of self and metaphysical issues with those in Continental modern metaphysics, we note that what is at stake is the attitude as much as the contents of a discourse. What I mean by "attitude" is a basic assumption maintained by the agent in carrying out a philosophical inquiry. What makes Descartes the author of the Cartesian thinking is not so much the clarity and authenticity of his logic, but his desire and determination to create an unshakable ground of his existence at all cost. Mālunkyāputta shares with Descartes this desire to find answers to his questions. Thus the attitude with which Descartes and Mālunkyāputta pose these questions prefigures their answers. Metaphysical discourse is derived from the determination of a human subject who wishes to put the world in an orderly manner and keep it within the scope which can be manipulated by human will. The gap between reality and the human desire to measure reality is what the Buddha calls "suffering."

Was the Buddha completely free from such a desire? In theory, the Buddha should be, since enlightenment is a state in which a being is liberated from desire. Desire by nature presupposes a division between the desiring subject and the desired object. The subject-object division is a basic structure for desire to take place. The division is connected through "intentionality," the direction of the subject toward the desired object. Similar to Brentano's concept of intentionality in phenomenology, Buddhist intentionality, the core element in the creation of karma, characterizes the subject-object relationship in the unenlightened state. Enlightenment as described in the Chinese Āgama is characterized by the disappearance of this division. When the Buddha pointed out to his inquisitor that the question should have been posed as "dependent on what does existence come into being?" instead of "who is it that exists?" the Buddha was claiming that assuming an individual identity based on the division between the subject and object is not a correct way of understanding reality. The subject is already other in the Buddha's philosophical paradigm, because the subject's existence is dependent upon the elements of non-subject, which nullifies the concept of the subject itself. When the subject is identified as other, intentionality cannot take place. There is neither direction nor space that the subject's desire can move through and toward.

The Buddha considered any attempt to understand a being in terms of "what" as an ill-formed question. In all the dialogues we have examined, the Buddha advises his inquisitors that one can ask "how" but not "what." Despite the English expression "dependent origination," the Buddha's philosophy does not tell us the origin of things; it only tells us things are "dependently originating." This method of the Buddha seems to relieve him from the burden of identifying the Transcendental Signifier, or the Unmoved Mover, for which Descartes had to resort to the conception of God. However, was the Buddha really free from such a burden? Without foundation, how does the Buddha legitimize his theory of dependent origination? On what grounds does his philosophy claim its truth over what he calls the "heretical views" of substantialist visions? The Buddha's explanation of being and the world is purely epistemological. He uses the method of *epoché*-ing—to borrow the phenomenological expression—regardig the issue of the ontological foundation of being.[37] Where then does the Buddha's epistemological statement anchor itself?

Dialogues in the Chinese Āgama indicate that the Buddha did not completely negate the possibility of the transcendental legitimacy of his theory. When asked by a monk whether the theory of dependent origination was created by the Buddha or others, the Buddha responded: "The law of dependent origination was made neither by me nor by anyone else. Regardless of the appearance of the Tathāgata [the Buddha] into this world, the *dharmadhātu* [or the realm of reality] exists permanently. The Tathāgata came to realize this law, attain equal and right enlightenment, and explain it for the benefit of the people."[38] The passage suggests a complex situation Buddhism situates itself with regard to metaphysics. If the Buddha claimed that either he or anyone else had created the law of dependent origination, this leads to positing the original cause of the world. This is self-destructive, because providing the originator of the law of dependent origination contradicts the very nature of the Buddha's law that things are dependently arising. To identify the origin or the originator requires isolating an entity from its dependent nature and confirming the independent nature of its existence. On the other hand, by negating any originator, and affirming it as the way things are, the Buddha concedes the responsibility of legitimizing the law to the natural world. By naturalizing the law of dependency and thus relieving himself from the burden of contradicting his own theory, the Buddha creates his own metaphysics. In this sense, Yi Chungp'yo claims that the philosophical position of the Buddha does not destroy metaphysics, but criticizes false metaphysics. Yi states:

. . . metaphysics always contains the instance of transcendentality. In other words, it deals with trans-experiential reality. The Buddha's awareness that the *dharmadhātu* exists permanently is not something that he obtained through experience. This is so because since our experience is finite, one cannot experience the permanence of the *dharmadhātu*. Therefore, if the Buddha attained the realization of the law of dependent origination and revealed it to sentient beings, one cannot but say that the law of dependent origination is another form of metaphysics. The logic then goes that the goal of the undeclared thesis did not lie in destroying metaphysics; instead, its goal should be understood as critique of the problem of existing metaphysics.[39]

In the context of Yi's argument, we can ask following questions: If European modernist metaphysics is characterized by the universalization of a regional value constructed through the reification of a specific human faculty whose legitimacy is derived through God—as we discussed it through the case of the Cartesian Ego-Cogito—, in what sense, does the Buddha's naturalization of dependent origination, which leads to the Buddhist theory of no-self, distinguish itself from metaphysics? Is metaphysics possible only in a substantialist mode of thinking such as European Continental modernist philosophy, or is a non-substantialist metaphysics possible, for which the Buddha's discourses in the Āgama could be a candidate? The reasoning we are evoking here is not about naming. We are not simply asking whether a certain philosophical system is qualified to be identified as metaphysical. Instead, the question is whether a thought system, be it philosophy or religion, is possible without to some degree relying on a certain type of metaphysical foundation. In the end, our discussion is not just about either metaphysics or a-metaphysics, but about our habitual mode of thinking that generates a clear border between the two: metaphysics and a-metaphysics.

In one of the classic pieces of scholarship on the undeclared thesis of the Buddha, T. R. V. Murti interprets the undeclared thesis as the moment when the dialectic was born. Identifying the three major interpretations of the silence of the Buddha as "the practical, the agnostic, and the negative," Murti claims that they are "specimens of an incorrect reading of Buddhism."[40] The practical interpretation claims that the Buddha did not answer Māluṅkyāputta's questions because the Buddha considered them to be of no help to the practitioner in overcoming suffering. The agnostic position understands the Buddha's silence as an indication that the issues brought up by Māluṅkyāputta could not be answered because the nature of the issues is related to the realm beyond the experiential. The negative interpretation considers that by silence the Buddha suggested that the self is not and nirvāṇa is annihilation. Murti contends that the Buddha's silence cannot be agnostic because agnosticism "is an attitude of doubt and despair, but Buddha's answer is decisive."[41] Nor can the Buddha's silence be understood as nihilistic, Murti argues, because the Buddha explicitly denies annihilationism together with eternalism as wrong views. Against these interpretations of the unanswered questions of the Buddha, Murti states:

> Criticism is the very essence of Buddha's teaching. He was aware of the anti-nomical character of reason. His refusal to answer questions about the beginning and extent of the world or of the unconditioned existence of the soul (jīva) and the Perfect being (tathāgata) was the direct outcome of the awareness of the conflict in Reason. It is at the same time an attempt to transcend the duality of reason. Dialectic was born. . . . Dialectic, . . . is the consciousness of the total and interminable conflict in Reason and the consequent attempt to resolve the conflict by rising to a higher standpoint.[42]

Murti contends that the dialectic in the unanswered thesis is only suggested and the suggestion becomes systematized in Mādhyamika thought. To Murti, the dialectic itself is the philosophy of the Buddha, and that was the case throughout the evolution of Buddhism from the Buddha in early Buddhism to Buddhist philosophy in Mādhyamika thought. Murti contends that early Buddhism's rejection of eternalism, annihilationism, and the theory of permanent self does not imply that the Buddha rejected metaphysics; the Buddha was critical of the dogmatism of a philosophical system, of which speculative metaphysics of the Buddha's time was guilty. Transcending the dogma of speculative metaphysics through the dialectical consciousness of thesis and anti-thesis was the Buddha's way of revealing the indescribable nature of the absolute, the ultimate reality, without being trapped by Reason's tendency toward theorization. In this sense, the Buddha, for Murti, is not only a philosopher, but a prime metaphysician who demonstrated the inexpressibility of the absolute without being caught in the conflict of Reason.

Contrary to Murti, David J. Kalupahana contends that Buddhism in its original form is exclusively based on empirical and anti-metaphysical philosophy. Developments in Buddhism after the death of the Buddha, Kalupahana argues, turned the tradition into metaphysics and elevated the Buddha to the position of a transcendental being. Kalupahana states:

> It is rather unfortunate that the 'saintliness' (buddhatta, Sk. buddhatva or ara-hatta, Sk. arhatva) that is attained as a result of an understanding of the 'con-stitution of things' (dhammadhātu) and the consequent elimination of craving (rāga, taṇhā, and so on) and grasping (upādāna) did not satisfy the ordinary man. What he needed was an awe-inspiring breath-taking, transcendental father-figure, or a being, even though invisible, through whom he could hope to save himself. . . . The Buddha rejected any ultimate principle like the individual 'self' (ātman) or the Universal Reality (loka = Upaniṣadic Brahman). His rejection

was based on the fact that any such Ultimate Reality, which was recognized as nonsensuous, indescribable, and transcendental, is also *metaphysical*. Metaphysics, as the Buddha saw, was a field where common sense may run riot and where there is no standard measure (*na pamāṇam atthi*) to determine whether there is any reality or not.[43] (italics original)

In this sense, Kalupahana understands the Buddha's silence to Māluṅkyāputta's questions as well as other incidents of the unanswered questions in the Pāli Nikāya and the Chinese Āgama to be demonstrations of the Buddha's rejection of metaphysical discourse. In making this claim, Kalupahana is careful to suggest that there exists a difference between early Buddhist and modernist philosophical conceptions of "the metaphysical." That is, "early Buddhism regarded questions pertaining to the origin and extent of the universe, the nature of the 'soul' or 'self' and the state of the saint after death as being metaphysical. . . . But problems such as causal uniformity and survival of the human personality, which are considered metaphysical in modern philosophy, were not looked upon as such in early Buddhism."[44] Kalupahana challenges the claim that identifies Buddhism as a religion but not a philosophy and contends that the Buddha himself did not reject philosophy per se; rather the discourse of the Buddha was nothing but philosophical, but the Buddha's philosophy was based on empirically obtained knowledge. For Kalupahana, the religious aspect was an off-shot of later developments of Buddhism that developed after the death of the Buddha. The religious aspect went hand in hand with the emergence of Buddhist metaphysics which, Kalupahana claims, the Buddha, in his teachings, rejected as heretical.

We began our discussion with an attempt to juxtapose and thus reveal the dichotomous position between the Cartesian thinking subject and Buddhist no-self, the former as an example of a metaphysical, substantialist mode of thinking in European Continental modernist philosophy and the latter as an a-metaphysical, non-substantialist mode of thinking in "Eastern" philosophy. Our discussion demonstrated the differences between these philosophical paradigms; however, it also led us to the point at which the borderline between the two begins to be blurred. Once we come to realize the vulnerability of the border between metaphysics and a-metaphysics, we will also realize that its implications run deep in our philosophizing.

Chapter Two

Hegel and Buddhism

Buddhism's encounter with Continental modern metaphysics reaches a culmination in Hegel's interpretation of Buddhism. An examination of Hegel's reading of Buddhism offers us with a concrete incidence in which the non-substantialist position of Buddhist philosophy is re-written through the lenses of metaphysics.

Hegel gave four lectures on the philosophy of religion during the last ten years of his life. Those lectures were given in 1821, 1824, 1827, and 1831 at the University of Berlin and were posthumously published as Lectures on the Philosophy of Religion. In four lectures, Hegel makes radical changes in his interpretation of different religions. In *Phenomenology of Spirit* (1807) Hegel categorizes religion into three types: natural, aesthetic, and revealed religions.[1] The three types of religion become modified into two levels in his lectures on the philosophy of religion: the determinate religion and the consummate religion. The natural and aesthetic religions in the previous categories become determinate religions, whereas revealed religion is now called consummate religion.

In Hegel's lectures on the philosophy of religion, discussions of Buddhism do not appear until the 1824 lectures. The 1821 lectures do not have a separate section on "immediate religion" (*die unmittelbare Religion*), with which Hegel will later categorize Buddhism. In the 1821 lectures, Hegel's account of "immediate religion" is mostly devoted to explaining how immediate natural objects were identified with the concept of God at the early stage of the development of religious consciousness. Hegel categorizes it as a pre-religious stage. As examples of this stage, Hegel mentions the concept of Heaven in Chinese religions and Brahman in Indian religions, about which he offers only a sketch without detailed discussion. Buddhist religion is not mentioned. In the subsequent three lectures given in 1824, 1827, and 1831,

Buddhism is introduced and understood through different traits. The 1824 lectures categorize Buddhism as an example of the "Being-within-Self" (*In-sichsein*) under the rubric of the "Religion of Magic" (*Religion der Zauberei*). In the 1827 lectures, Buddhism is no longer treated as a religion of magic; it is understood as the religion of the "Being-within-Self" in the category of "Religions of Substantiality" (*Religionen der Substanzialität*). In the 1831 lectures, Buddhism is identified as the religion of "Being-within-Self" in the category of the "Internal Rupture of Consciousness" (*die Entzweiung des Bewußtseins in sich*; literally, the division of consciousness itself). In these three lectures on religion, not only does Hegel's understanding of Buddhism change, but the themes Hegel discusses through Buddhism also change. In the 1824 lectures, Hegel pays special attention to the Buddhist theory of transmigration; in 1827, Hegel's focus changes to the concept of Nothing (*Nichts*) in Buddhism; and the 1831 lectures define Buddhism as a religion of annihilation (*Vernichtung*). Moving forward, we will look at the details of Hegel's understanding of Buddhism in his lectures of 1824, 1827, and 1831 and try to identify the inner structure of the transformation that took place in his understanding of Buddhism.

1. The Absolute Spirit and Transmigration: The 1824 Lectures

In the Hegelian system, religion is defined as "the unity of the finite and infinite, of concept and reality."[2] The finite refers to "the immediate and subjective self-consciousness" (i.e., a human being) whereas the infinite represents objective universality, in Hegel's words, "the general power of the spirit over the contingent, the sensuously external" (*LRP II*, 304). Explaining the phenomenon of religion as a unity of these two elements, Hegel describes the development of religion through the process of the finite's awareness of the infinite existing within itself and the finite's movements towards an eventual union with the infinite. The key in this movement is the finite's determination, its consciousness of the existence of the infinite, divinity, or the absolute, within itself, which facilitates the sublation of the finite into the infinite. Theoretically speaking, the relationship between the finite and the infinite is reciprocal. Hegel states: "Even as the content, God, determines itself, so on the other side the subjective human spirit that has this knowledge determines itself too. The principle by which God is defined for human beings is also the principle for how humanity defines itself inwardly, or for humanity in its own spirit" (*LRP II*, 515). The degree of determination, or the distance between the finite and the infinite, determines the level of a religion in the entire spectrum of Hegel's projection as to the evolution of world religions.

The religion of "Being-within-Self," with which Hegel describes Buddhism, is the stage in which the finite (human beings) for the first time comes to the determination that it is free. This stage virtually marks the beginning of religion because "here in this being-within-self the place of divinity in general emerges for the first time" (*LPR II*, 305). However, the finite's recognition of the infinite within itself, at this stage, is yet to be complete. That is because the finite, which is particular, empirical, and thus subject to contingency, distinguishes itself from the infinite rather than sublates itself into pure freedom, which is the infinite. Since the finite is yet to fully realize its self-identity with the absolute, it needs time to evolve to the final stage, which is to Hegel the meaning of Buddhist transmigration.

In Hegel's view, the doctrine of transmigration attests to the necessity of temporal movement in the process of facilitating the final reconciliation between the finite and the infinite. The self-completion of the Spirit and the finite's capacity to speculate about the essence that survives physical death is, for Hegel, the very meaning of transmigration. Such an understanding of the Spirit and the finite's relation to this Spirit, Hegel argues, is a proof that man is a thinking being:

> Those who have made the transition to the theoretical know that there is a being that is at rest within itself, something truly essential; having arrived at this intuition, they know themselves as thinking beings, they know themselves too to be *theoretical* beings—*fixed, enduring, substantive; and what is termed immortality of the soul (in the broadest sense) is what now for the first time emerges [in Buddhism]. As thinking beings they have consciousness of their eternity, of their unaltering, unchanging inner being, which is thought, the consciousness of thought.* (*LPR* II 309, emphasis mine.)

For Hegel, thinking capacity is a precondition for the possibility of transmigration. The subject that goes through rebirth is defined as "unchanging inner being," which is further identified with "thought," and the "consciousness of thought." The line of argument employed here is unmistakably Cartesian. Like Descartes, who finds reason, or the thinking being, to be the foundation of existence, Hegel identifies the unchanging inner being that he thought he found in Buddhism as thought and consciousness of thought.

Hegel's discussion of transmigration can be summarized with the following four aspects: First, transmigration theory confirms the existence of an eternal soul, of unchangeable reality, and of divinity; Second, not only does the "being-within-self" endorse the existence of the unchanging reality beyond the realm of the finite, it demonstrates the fact that the infinite exists in relation with, not in separation from, us, the finite. That is, divinity, the infinite, is not something existing outside us, but within us; Third, the transmigration theory confirms that the evolution of religion is the dialectic movements of the Spirit. The movement is linear and teleological both for the Spirit and for an individual soul as its microcosmic version. Fourth, transmigration offers another occasion to confirm that man is a thinking being, and this thinking being (the being-within-self) is equated with thought itself. Underlying the above four features in Hegel's understanding of Buddhism is the idea that there *exists* something permanent. (1) The *presence* of thought; (2) the *existence* of the Spirit; (3) the immortality of the soul; as well as (4) the linear movement from the finite (the incomplete) to the infinite (the complete): all guarantee the benefit of rebirth as a period for self-training.

A real religion for Hegel is a state in which the finite is sublated to the infinite, and the Buddhist theory of transmigration for him fell short of having evolved into the state of a real religion. Hegel contends that in Buddhism, immediate nature, such as a human being, has been confused with and respected as the representation of the infinite. This confusion about and misunderstanding of the relationship between the finite and the infinite demonstrates, from Hegel's view, that Buddhism is yet to attain the status of a religion. Hegel argues that the elevation of the finite to the infinite in Buddhism is possible only through the pseudo-religious action, which is magic. This is why Buddhism in Hegel's 1824 lectures is categorized as a religion of magic. Hegel writes: "The transmigration of souls is based on the image of the being-within-self of spirit, which is raised up above change; and associated with it is magic" (*LPR* II, 314). Hegel contends that because the finite is yet to realize the identity between the Spirit and the finite, the Spirit "make[s] a halt at this stage" (*LPR* II, 307). This is the reason why, for Hegel, practitioners of Buddhism fall to idolatry instead of sublating themselves to the absolute. Hegel writes:

> This is the source and origin of the innumerable masses of idols and images that are worshiped wherever the veneration of Fo holds sway. Four-footed beasts, birds, insects, and reptiles, in a word the lowliest forms of animal life, have temples and are venerated because God in his reincarnations can dwell in individuals of all kinds, and each animal body can be inhabited by the human soul. (*LPR* II, 311-2)

Hegel claims that the incomplete awareness of the nature of the being-within-self, and of its relation to the finite, led the followers of Buddhism to distort the meaning of the transmigration, resulting in Buddhism's failing to overcome its bond with magic and superstition:

> Here magic again enters on the scene, the mediation of the human priests who belong to the higher realm of the supersensible and yet at the same time have power over the configurations that humans assume; in this way the aspect of power and magic comes to be associated once more with this theoretical image. Adherents of the Fo religions are in this respect extremely superstitious. They represent to themselves that our human shape passes over into every possible shape, that of a cat, a snake, a mule. (*LPR* II, 313)

In Hegel's interpretation, the Buddhist theory of transmigration has two sides. On the one hand, it proves the existence of the eternal soul, and of human beings' awareness of it, in the earliest stage of the historical development of religion. On the other hand, it still enslaves human beings with magical and superstitious ideas. In Hegel, transmigration as "thought" and the finite as a "thinking being" are celebrated whereas the transmigration of bodies into different shapes is condemned.

Magic and superstition need to be overcome for any pre-religions to develop into a real religion. Therefore, Buddhism could not attain the status of a full-fledged religion in Hegel's paradigm of the evolution of religions. Nevertheless, Hegel in his 1824 lectures values Buddhism in the sense that it provided evidence for the historical reality of one of the stages in his philosophy of religions. In Buddhist transmigration, Hegel sees that the "purely theoretical moment" of the being-within-self is expressed and "[h]as come to intuition . . . among this people" (*LPR* II 313). Hegel concludes his 1824 lectures on Buddhism with a statement which confirms that Buddhism as a religion of "being-within-self" represents "the general basis of any idea of divinity" and in Buddhism "for the first time we have a genuine foundation for religion" (*LPR* II, 316).

2. Buddhism, Nothingness, and Pantheism: The 1827 Lectures

Hegel's discussion of Buddhism in his 1827 lectures is a development from his 1824 lectures but with changed focus, which is clearly reflected in the repositioning of Buddhism in his system of religions. In the 1827 lectures, Buddhism is still within the group of Nature Religions, but is no longer categorized under the rubric of the "Religion of Magic." This time Hegel positions Buddhism, still as a religion of "being-within-self," at the second stage of Nature Religion under the rubric "Religion of Substantiality." The Buddhist theory of transmigration and its relation to magical and superstitious aspects, the main topics of the 1824 lectures, are no longer Hegel's main concern.[3] Instead, the 1827 lectures are focused on the identity of the being-within-self. In particular, Hegel pays close attention to the meaning of nothing in Buddhism.

By 1824, Hegel had already noted the importance of the concept of nothing in Buddhism. He contended that, in Buddhism, the Being as the infinite existed in the finite as the "being-within-self," and this Being was identified with nothing. Hegel wrote: "The principle of the Fo religion is that 'nothing' is the principle, the beginning and the end of everything existing. Our first ancestors came from nothing and to nothing they have returned . . . . However varied people and things may be, there is thus only one principle from which they stem, in which they are, through which they subsist, completely unqualified, simple and pure"(*LPR* II, 312). With this statement, Hegel proposed nothing as the ontological foundation of Buddhism.

Earlier we noted that the first generation European Buddhist scholars understood nothing in Buddhism only in a negative light and identified this nothing with the negation of being and self. Compared to this simple understanding of nothing as a lack of being, Hegel's exposition of Buddhist nothing is rather complex. In the 1824 lectures, Hegel explained Buddhist nothing as "not nothing in the sense of not being, but it is what is purely identical with itself, undetermined, a substantive being; it is thus completely pure, wholly simple and undifferentiated, eternally at rest; it has neither virtue nor power nor intelligence; it lacks these determinate distinctions, being quite free of determination" (*LPR* II, 312).

Nothing in this sense was self-identity; it was a state of pre-individualization. For Hegel, Buddhist salvation was a return to the pre-individualized state of nothing, the realization of which was achieved by removing all the transitory elements accrued as a result of individuation. Hegel understood the Buddhist practice in this context as follows:

> As for the relationship of human beings to this principle [of nothing], the rule is that in order to be happy they must endeavor, by dint of continuous speculation, continuous meditation and continuous self-conquest, to resemble this principle, to resolve or wish for nothing, to do nothing, have no passions, no inclinations or activities. With the attainment of this state of perfect impartiality or absence of concern, there is no longer any question of virtue and vice, reward and punishment, atonement, immortality of the soul, worship, and so on. All this has passed away, and human sanctity consists in finding union, in this silence, with God. In this cessation of all bodily movement or animation, all movement of the soul, therein consists happiness, and once human beings have reached this level of perfection, there is no longer any change, their souls have no further wanderings to fear, for they become completely identical with the God Fo. (*LPR* II 312-3)

For Hegel, the finite in the religious evolution goes through transmigration so as to be united with the Absolute Spirit. This Absolute Spirit, or the infinite, was identified by Hegel as substance. In the above passage, Hegel identifies the ultimate state of being in Buddhism with nothing. Hegel also mentions that nothing in Buddhism is not nothing in the sense that it does not exist but is something that is purely self-identical. How then is the nothing which means "to do nothing, have no passions, no inclinations or activities" related to the nothing which is the self-identity of being? The two meanings of the Buddhist nothing in Hegel—nothing as absence of being (or actions) and nothing as self-identity of being—become clearer in his discussion of pantheism.

Pantheism is a prominent theme in his 1827 lectures on Buddhism. And his discussion of pantheism is much related to his understanding of Buddhist nothing. In the 1827 lectures, Hegel describes Buddhist nothing as follows:

> [I]n the religion of Fo, the ultimate or highest [reality] is . . . nothing or not-being. They say that everything emerges from nothing and everything returns into nothing. This is the absolute foundation, the indeterminate, the negated being of everything particular, so that all particular existences or actualities are only forms, and only the nothing has genuine independence, while in contrast all other actuality has none; it counts only as something accidental, an indifferent form. For a human being, this state of negation is the highest state: one must immerse oneself in this nothing, in the eternal tranquility of the nothing generally, in the substantial in which all determinations cease, where there is no virtue or intelligence, where all movement annuls itself. . . . Human holiness consists in uniting oneself . . . with nothingness, and so with God, with the absolute. A human being who has reached this holiness, this highest level, is indistinguishable from God, is eternally identical with God; and thus all change ceases. (*LPR* II, 565-6)[4]

Hegel in this passage offers an elevated explanation of the role and meaning of nothing in Buddhism. He claims that nothing (non-being) does not mean non-existence; rather, it implies fullness of being. It is a state in which determinate elements of the finite are nullified and thus transformed into the indeterminate of the infinite. Nothing in this sense is "the indeterminate" and "the substantial in which all determinations cease" which is "the absolute" and God. When we say that God is nothing, Hegel argues, we do not mean that God does not exist. Instead, we mean that "God is infinite" and "God is the essence." God is nothing, because God is nothing determinate; He is the indeterminate. God is nothing because, after the removal of all that is determinate, all that is left is nothing. Hence, from the perspective of the finite, we say that God is "emptiness" (*das Leere, LPR* II, 568).[5] God who exists after the removal of all the features of the finite and the determinate is the God of the infinite, God as the One, which, in Hegel's view, is the real meaning of Buddhist nothing.

In this context, Hegel connects his concept of Buddhist nothing with what he considers as the authentic form of pantheism. Hegel argues that when we discuss the relationship between God and the finite in the context of pantheism, two different interpretations are possible. The first is the idea that "the All is God." In this case God is the One who encompasses everything. The second interpretation of pantheism is a claim that "everything is God" (*LPR* II, 573).[6] In this case, God exists in each individual finite entity. Hegel contends that this second understanding is a wrong interpretation of pantheism. The real pantheism, Hegel argues, is to understand God as "the one and absolute substance" (*LPR* II, 575).[7] This is also what is referred to by Buddhist "being-within-self," which, to Hegel, indicates absolute substance and absolute spirituality.

Hegel sees Buddhism as an Oriental form of authentic pantheism. Through the existence of "being-within-self," the absolute spirit becomes real in the actual world. Buddhist nothing in this sense refers to the omnipresence of God as in the case of Spinoza's philosophy of substantiality. This is also why Hegel identifies Buddhism in his 1827 lectures as the religion of substantiality.

However, Buddhism, Hegel claims, confuses the omnipresence of absolute spirituality with the existence of spirituality in individual, concrete things. Buddhism for Hegel thus remains as immediate spirituality. Hegel writes: "at the level of nature religion . . . this spirituality [absolute spirituality] is not yet spirituality as such, it is not yet a spirituality that is thought or universal; instead it is sensible and immediate spirituality. Here it is a human being as a sensible, external, immediate spirituality: a [particular] human being" (*LPR* II, 575).

If the Buddhist understanding of the Absolute Spirit remains at the level of "sensible and immediate" spirituality and fails to reach the spirituality "that is thought or universal," is it not the case that Buddhism should be defined as a false pantheism—in Hegel's definition—instead of the real one? In the 1824 lectures, Hegel understood Buddhism as the former, which he employed as a reason for Buddhism's failure to evolve into a real religion. His evaluation of Buddhism in the 1827 lectures appears to be more positive than the 1824 lectures, but he still categorizes Buddhism as a nature religion. The reason for that categorization is that Buddhism is yet to realize the universal spirituality in its entirety. Similar to his 1824 lectures, in the 1827 lectures, Hegel appears to be satisfied with the observation that Buddhism manifests an early stage of the union between the finite and the infinite and the finite's recognition of the existence of the Spirit. He closes the 1827 lectures on Buddhism with this statement: "We are still at the standpoint of the substantiality that is indeed necessarily bound up with subjectivity, with spirituality; but here what is spiritual is still in immediate, sensible existence, and this subjectivity is still in an immediate subjectivity" (*LPR* II, 579).

Roger-Pol Droit claims in his *Le culte du néant: Les philosophes et le bouddha* (The Cult of Nothingness: the Philosophers and the Buddha) that unlike Jesuit missionaries and Orientalists who, since the seventeenth century, evaluated Buddhism as a nihilist and destructive religion, Hegel provided a new interpretation of Buddhist nothing by understanding it as God, as the Absolute Spirit.[8] A separate claim made by Yi Dong-hee, a Korean scholar of Hegel, in his "Hegel ŭi Pulgyo ihae" (Hegel's Understanding of Buddhism) also asserts that Buddhism in Hegel's *Lectures on the Philosophy of Religion* played an important role for Hegel to defend his own philosophy. Yi's claim is based on his understanding that Hegel employed Buddhism to explain the true meaning of pantheism when his philosophy was criticized as pantheism by the followers of Schleiermacher (1768-1834).[9]

In order to fully evaluate these claims, we need to consider the inner conflicts that exist in Hegel's treatment of Buddhist nothing. The conflicts can be summarized into the following two points. First, Hegel's interpretation of Buddhist nothing reveals the same double edged-ness as we encountered in his interpretation of the theory of transmigration in the 1824 lectures. Hegel has a positive take on Buddhist nothing as a theory: nothing is pure abstraction of pure spirit and thus nothing is understood as absolute being. Hegel also emphasizes that the finite's awareness of nothing marks the very beginning of religious consciousness. However, when the nothing is actualized in a person—as in the case of the Buddha or a lama—Hegel degrades the phenomenon as evidence of Buddhism's under-developed state as a religion.

Secondly, the nature of nothing in Hegel's discussion needs clarification. In the 1827 lectures, nothing, on the one hand, implies the infinite. This is how he identified nothing with God. In this case, nothing is absolute being. However, absolute being, or the infinite is not and cannot be the collection of the finites. On the other hand, Hegel also explains that one becomes nothing by eliminating the features belonging to the finite. When he claims that in Buddhism the finite desires to become nothing by getting rid of its finite elements, this interpretation raises a question about the relationship between the finite and the infinite: can the accumulation of the finite make the infinite? By the same token, can we create absolute being by removing the elements of the finite being? Nothing as absolute being accords with what Hegel defines as true pantheism, whereas nothing created by removing the features of the finite is another version of what he defines as a false pantheism. Hegel employs Buddhism in his 1827 lectures as a true form of pantheism, and by so doing, he actually contradicts his own definition of true pantheism.

For Hegel, Buddhism is a failed synthesis: the finite takes up the status of the infinite by erasing the features of the former. This is usurpation. As the finite *ad infinitum* cannot arrive at the infinite, the emptying out of finite elements cannot secure for a finite being the position of the infinite. This is what Hegel calls a bad infinite. In the 1831 lectures we will see how the contradictions involved in Hegel's treatment of the Buddhist nothing in the 1827 lectures become the foundation of Hegel's evaluation of Buddhism as a religion of annihilation.

3. Religion of Annihilation: The 1831 Lectures

In the 1831 lectures, Hegel once again re-organizes his system of the philosophy of religion. Peter Hodgson, the editor of Hegel's *Lectures on the Philoso-*

phy of Religion, claims that the position of Asian religions had been improved in the new system (*LPR* II, p.72).[10] However, upon closer examination, one cannot but doubt whether that is the case.

In the lectures of 1824 and 1827, Hegel interpreted Buddhism as a stage in which the immediate nature, which is human being, began to realize within itself the existence of the absolute spirit. In the 1824 lectures, Hegel identified Buddhism as the religion of magic, focusing his discussion on the theory of transmigration. In the 1827 lectures, Buddhism was identified as the religion of substantiality, and pantheism was at the center of his discussion. The 1831 lectures develop around the theme of the religious consciousness revealed in Buddhism. Buddhism now is categorized under the rubric of "The Internal Rupture of Religious Consciousness," and is no longer classified as the Natural Religion. In this stage, the finite realizes inside itself the relationship with the infinite and this realization creates a rupture. Under this category of the internal rupture of religious consciousness, Hegel includes Chinese religion, Hinduism, Buddhism, and Lamaism.

In the section that discusses Buddhism and Lamaism, Hodgson adds a subtitle, "the religion of annihilation." In this context, we realize that the expression annihilation, which rarely appeared in the previous lectures, appears frequently in the 1831 lectures. We also encounter Hegel's statement: "the acme [of Buddhism] is to be united with Buddha, and this *annihilation* is termed nirvana" (*LPR* II, 736). Annihilation, together with nothing, was an expression frequently associated with Buddhism in the first-generation European Buddhist scholars' evaluation of the tradition. How did Hegel make a transition from his 1824 and 1827 lectures to the annihilation in the 1831 lectures? What happens to the religious consciousness when annihilation takes place in Buddhism? And what made Hegel give up his previous endorsement of Buddhist nothing as representing absolute being, and interpret it this time as annihilating power? In his introduction to the English edition of the *Lectures on the Philosophy of Religion*, Hodgson asks why Hegel identified Buddhist nirvāṇa with annihilation in his 1831 lectures when he had expressed more positive views on Buddhism in his previous two lectures.

A close reading of the 1831 lectures reveals that Hegel no longer maintains the ambivalent position he previously held with regard to the theory of transmigration and Buddhist concept of nothing. In the 1824 lectures, transmigration to Hegel had a positive meaning in that it facilitates the voyage the finite needs to go through in order for the eventual unification with the absolute spirit to take place. When the transmigration was actualized in the shapes of human body, Hegel condemned it as superstition. In the 1827 lectures, Hegel portrayed Buddhist nothing as an authentic form of pantheism which reveals omnipresence of the absolute being; when this nothing is realized in a real entity such as the Buddha or Lamas, Hegel took it as an evidence of Buddhism's status as an under-developed religion. In 1831, Hegel points out the superstitious nature of the idea of transmigration without mentioning the positive function he assigned to it in the earlier lectures. Also, in discussing the Buddhist concept of nothing, he reconfirms the meaning of nothing in Buddhism as the beginning and end of the religion, and that Buddhist practitioners try to overcome the status of the finite by removing the features of the finite, thereby becoming one with nothing. However, he does not mention the positive evaluation of nothing as a manifestation of the authentic form of pantheism. Seen from this perspective, one can say that Droit's claim that Hegel evaluated Buddhist nothing positively and Yi's claim that Hegel had a positive view of Asian religions might not be entirely wrong but reveal only a limited view of Hegel's treatment of Buddhism. Hegel does not clarify in his lectures why he gave up in the 1831 lectures the positive values he had assigned to the theory of transmigration and the concept of nothing in his previous lectures. However, Hegel's positive interpretations of Buddhist transmigration and Buddhist nothing were already charged with internal contradictions, which could be one reason, if not the only reason, for Hegel's modification of his evaluation of Buddhism in the 1831 lectures. Based on our analysis of Hegel's three lectures on Buddhism, we can construct the following interpretation to explain Hegel's movement from Buddhist nothing as the infinite to Buddhist nothing as annihilation.

Religion to Hegel is "the union of the finite and the infinite, concrete and absolute." At stake in this definition is the relationship between the finite and the infinite. They are no longer fitted into the two poles of binary opposites, but postulated as participants engaged in a temporary conflict, which will eventually be reconciled. In Hegelian dialectics, the irreconcilable other in pre-Hegelian thinking finds its place within the non-other, as dualism opens itself to a shared space in which opposites unite in the dialectical movements. In this process of reconciliation between the finite and the infinite, Hegel takes the essence of the finite to its limit. He declares that "fully developed, the finite is an 'other', namely, the infinite; the finite is simply this, to be the infinite," and thus, the finite "does not have its being in itself but in an 'other', and this 'other' is the infinite" (*LPR* II, 257). "The other" in this case is no longer outside; the other is in "me."

Despite the mutual inter-dependence of the finite and the infinite, in Hegel's system the finite is there only to be sublated, and, by sublating itself to the infinite, and by becoming the infinite, the finite finds its *raison d'être*. The other side of the subject is, from the beginning, encompassed within the negation of the subject, only to be sublated in the final stage of absolute subjectivity. In the Hegelian system, the finite remains as it is, instead of being *lifted up*. Jacques Derrida thus contends that the negative moment in Hegel is simply contradiction, the cancelling of what is there to be cancelled in its turn by the negation of the negation, which (re-) establishes identity: contradiction or difference is there in Hegel only "to lift it up . . . into the self-presence of an onto-theological or onto-teleological synthesis."[11] The negative moment is there only when it is already within the synthesis; when it is not a part of the system, it will be cancelled out. In Hegel, the finite remains in its finite state, despite the happening of sublation. The frozen finite, which cannot be lifted up despite being lifted up, creates a hierarchy in each stage of Hegel's philosophy. Hierarchy is an ordering of fixed identity, a closedness of being.

If the dialectic in Hegel assigns the synthesis a position higher than those being synthesized, the dialectical movements travel from the lowest and emptiest constituents of the dialectic toward the highest and fully embodied existence. In Hegel's terms, in the lowest lies pure being, which is empty and, thus, which is nothing, and at the highest level exists the all encompassing absolute spirit. The irony at this point is that both the lowest and the highest can be identified with nothing in Hegel's reading of Buddhism. Nothing as non-existence marks the lowest point in the structure of his dialectic, whereas nothing which is self-identity, and with which God is identified, is located in the highest position. In Hegel's interpretation of Buddhism, Buddhist nothing was first understood as the latter, when Hegel identified Buddhism as an Asian version of pantheism in his 1827 lectures. In his 1831 lectures, Buddhist nothing is treated as the former, that is, nothing as a being without content.

In the lectures of 1824 and 1827, Hegel understood nothing as the essence which is the one substance and which is pure self-identity. Nothing in this case exists as a figurative device, not as an ontological entity. In other words, nothing is a linguistic device to clarify the nature of the Absolute Being. It is a negative theology to express God as the infinite, the absolute. However, in Hegel, this rhetorical meaning of nothing is not the only function of nothing. Another nothing in Hegel still exists as being, that is, nothing as a lack of being, which is another form of being. The nothing as a rhetorical device, the nothing as a negative expression of the absolute, cannot annihilate because there is nothing to be annihilated. When he declares that Buddhist nothing is annihilation, Hegel declares the hierarchical relationship between being and nothing, and admits that nothing as *something* cannot be on the same level with being. A hierarchical understanding of nothing and Being is not an alien theme in metaphysical tradition as we shall see in the next chapter. The hierarchical relationship established between being and nothing in this manner expands itself into the socio-cultural realm in Hegel's exposition of Buddhism.

4. Buddhism and Ethnography in Hegel

It is not clear which Buddhist texts, publications by contemporaries, or other sources on Buddhism were available to Hegel when he modified his interpretation of Buddhism. By all appearances, his claims suffer from insufficient materials on Buddhism. Throughout his lectures on the philosophy of religion, Hegel's discussion of Buddhism and other Oriental religions suffers significantly from inaccurate information. It does not seem that Hegel was aware of the difference between Hinduism and Buddhism, to say nothing of the differences among the different Buddhist schools; he misunderstood Buddhism as being older than Hinduism. Both in the 1824 and 1827 lectures, Hegel placed Buddhism and Lamaism before Hinduism. Hodgson defends Hegel by claiming that the general understanding in Hegel's time was to place the life of the Buddha around 1,000 BC (*LRP II* , 308, n. 193). However, Hegel stated in reference to the birth of Gautama Siddhartha: "Gautama is supposed to have lived some forty years before Christ"(*LPR II,* 308). Hegel also mistook a Hindu figure for the Buddha. Hegel's description of the image of Buddha with "feet and arms intertwined so that a toe extends into the mouth . . ." (*LPR* II, 564), which to him represented Buddhism's tendency of "the withdrawal into self," and "absorption in oneself," is not actually a representation of the Buddha but of a Hindu figure. In his footnote, Hodgson speculates that Hegel was probably referring to "fig. 2 in plate xxi of the volume of illustrations accompanying Friedrich Creuzer's *Symbolik und Mythologie der alten Völker* (Leipzig and Darmstadt, 1819)," in which Creuzer identifies the figure as Brahmā Narāyama, a Hindu figure from the cosmology of the Code of Manu. What does such erroneous information amount to in our understanding of Hegel's Buddhism? The parameter of our discussion in this case is not limited to pointing out wrong or missing information about Buddhism in Hegel's philosophy. Instead, our investigation is about how information is processed, digested, and eventually domesticated in a discourse.

What this examination reveals then is a process through which a discourse creates its identity in the manner which Jacques Derrida calls "centrism." The identity-creation is followed by a power-play exercised by the discourses at the center over the marginalized discourses. When an identity is based on a substantial reality, a hierarchical logic becomes its corollary. A hierarchical world-view further expands itself into other categories in life, including ethnicity and gender. Once we realize the relationship between religio-philosophical discourses and their sub-categories in the cultural arena, we enter a new domain in understanding the nature of truth-claims in various fields in the humanities, including philosophy. The synergic relationship between a certain mode of thinking in philosophy and its socio-cultural manifestations might at first appear tenuous or even dismissible. In fact, this relationship has been frequently dismissed in our philosophical investigation. However, once its thread receives our attention, we come to realize that not only is the relationship between philosophy and its manifestations in cultural realms visible, but each member of the relationship mutually enforcing and consolidating the other's position. This phenomenon seems quite relevant to Hegel's understanding of Buddhism.

In his 1824 lectures, after his discussion of transmigration, Hegel criticizes what he considered to be the superstitious nature of those who practice Buddhism. In the 1827 lectures as well, immediately after he defines Buddhism as a religion of nothing with its final goal of abandoning all that is transitory and human, Hegel applies this trait of the religion to describe the character of the people who practice the religion: "Hence the character of the people who adhere to this religion is one of tranquility, gentleness, and obedience, a character that stands above the wildness of desire and is the cessation of desire" (*LPR II,* 564). The feminine qualities Hegel applied to the practitioners of Buddhism accord with his characterization of Asia in his *Philosophy of History*, where he portrays the feminized East in his discussion of Buddhism. Hegel states:

> These Lamas lead a thoroughly isolated life and have a feminine rather than masculine training. Early torn from the arms of his parents the Lama is generally a well-formed and beautiful child. He is brought up amid perfect quiet and solitude, in a kind of prison: he is well catered for, and remains without exercise or childish play, so that it is not surprising that a feminine susceptible tendency prevails in this character. [12]

The "feminine susceptible tendency" which Hegel characterizes as isolation and quietude implies the "lack" of positive qualities possessed by masculinity. The hierarchical relationship between being and nothing at this point takes the form of the hierarchical relationship of masculine and feminine qualities, which are also applied to the characterizations of the West and the East. Femininity understood as the absence of positive nature of masculinity finds its philosophical ground in the concept of nothing, which is here assessed as inferior to being. Thus, it follows that people whose religious ideal is anchored in nothing are inferior to those whose religious ideal lies in the ultimate Being. The line of pseudo logical inference continues that as their understanding of the infinite is limited, so are Easterners (or Buddhist practitioners) limited in their capacities for life:

> The Orientals have not attained the knowledge that Spirit—Man as such—is free; and because they do not know this, they are not free. They only know that one is free . . . That one is therefore only a Despot; not a free man. The consciousness of Freedom first arose among the Greeks, and therefore they were

free; but they and the Romans likewise, knew only that some are free—not man as such . . . The German nations, that man, as man, is free: that it is the freedom of Spirit which constitutes its essence.[13]

Like people, Gods are also classified according to Hegel's hierarchical understanding of the world and being. Hegel declares: "an inferior god or a nature god has inferior, natural and unfree human beings as its correlates; the pure concept of God or the spiritual God has as its correlate spirit that is free and spiritual, that actually knows God" (*LPR* II , 515).

Hegel depicts religions practiced in the East as the most primitive of religions. History for Hegel moves towards its completion, and its beginning is a thing of the past:

The History of the World travels from East to West, for Europe is absolutely the end of History, Asia the beginning. The History of the World has an East . . . for although the Earth forms a sphere, History performs no circle around it, but has on the contrary a determinate East, viz., Asia. Here rises the outward physical Sun, and in the West it sinks down: here consentaneously rises the Sun of self-consciousness, which diffuses nobler brilliance.[14]

Hegel probably is not the only philosopher who projects a feminized, castrated, and despotic East. In Hegel, however, we find an instance in which a philosophical discourse becomes expanded into the social and cultural realms and thus proffers theoretical foundations for what we now identify as discrimination. Discrimination in this case is multi-layered; it includes geographical, ethnic, gender, and religious systems. At the bottom of this hierarchical postulation of different dimensions of life one finds the hierarchical relationship between being and nothing. Being as the ultimate substance and essence is postulated as superior to nothing that is understood as a lack and absence of the traits of Being. We can identify this as "metaphysical discrimination" or "philosophical discrimination." In this scheme, by default, Being is privileged over nothing, masculinity over femininity, Europeans over non-Europeans, and the West over the East. A complete categorical discrimination reveals a package of Eurocentric, phallocentric, and ethnocentric metaphysical thinking.

Hegel's Buddhism succinctly demonstrates the philosophical paradigm that explains the nineteenth century European evaluation of Buddhism. Needless to say, understanding Buddhism as a cult of nothingness leaves much to desire to be an accurate description of the tradition. However, the limits of the nineteenth century European evaluations of Buddhism, including that of Hegel, do not merely lie in that aspect. They did not consider the possibility that their understanding of nothing itself might need a redefinition, and this fact constitutes the very limits and closedness of their approach to Buddhism.

Before Buddhism makes it an issue, a self-critical realization of this possibility has occurred within the Continental philosophy as it made a transition from a modern to a postmodern mode of thinking.

Chapter Three

The Logic of Nothing
and A-Metaphysics

1. Heidegger and Nothing

In our philosophical imagination, "nothing" inhabits a unique position. This is so because "nothing" by definition is not *some thing* that can be identified in language or through our speculation. Since we have no proper language to identify nothing, our deliberation on nothing tends to hover near the periphery of being. This idea of understanding nothing as the opposite, and thus a negation, of being has been one most convenient mode of reflecting upon nothing. However, it has also been a prime cause of pulling nothing away from its own nature. Since Buddhism's initial encounter with the West in the nineteenth century, nothing has been at the center of the European evaluation of Buddhism. As we noted, in both the European intellectuals' response to Buddhism and Hegel's analysis of the tradition, nothing provides a theoretical ground for their negative understanding of this Asian religio-philosophical system. "Nothing" also occupies an important position in our efforts to articulate the relationship between the metaphysical and the a-metaphysical in a philosophy because nothing is a locus in which these two modes of thinking collide. It is a venue in which the differences between Buddhist and European modernist metaphysical frames become visible. The nature of difficulty involved in our investigation of nothing also connects it to the silence of the Buddha we discussed in chapter one. In this context, Heidegger's short essay "What is Metaphysics?" offers an instance to examine the complexity involved in our investigation of nothing.

At the beginning of the essay, Heidegger points out that human science has been exclusively focused on the investigation of beings. That which is not being—that is, nothing—has been treated as irrelevant to the study of being. Questioning the efficacy of this centuries-old neglect of the investigation of the nothing, Heidegger contends that the study of beings inevitably leads us to question that which is not being, and by finding answers to the question of that which is not being, the meaning of being can be illuminated. Heidegger asks: what is this nothing which does not exist? Heidegger identifies two major sources that are responsible for the concept of the nothing in the West. The first is the classical metaphysics, which claims that "from nothing, nothing comes to be." [1] In this understanding, the nothing is non-being, the "unformed matter which is powerless to form itself into 'being' and cannot therefore present an appearance." The second concept of the nothing emerges along with the introduction of Christianity, through which the nothing comes to designate the "counterpart to being proper, the *summum ens.*"

Heidegger argues that Western thought has been forgetful of the contradiction involved in this binary postulation of being and nothing. Heidegger states: "if God creates out of nothing precisely He must be able to relate Himself to the nothing. But if God is God he cannot know the nothing, assuming that the 'Absolute' excludes all nothingness" ("WM?" 107–108). The problem of this line of argument, Heidegger contends, is not just the contradiction itself but the fact that the metaphysical tradition has been blind to this contradiction. Instead of addressing the logical conflict involved in the relationship between God (Being) and the nothing as articulated in the above, philosophy has imposed an unchanging value on Being and subjugated the nothing to it.

Challenging this tradition, Heidegger asserts that a question of nothing is not just one question among many questions, but "the first of all questions," and "the fundamental question of metaphysics," the range of which "finds its limit only in nothing, in that which simply is not and never was." Heidegger further observes: "Everything that is not nothing is covered by this question, and ultimately even nothing itself; not because it is *something,* since after all we speak of it, but because it *is* nothing"[2] (emphasis original). By marking a distinction between *something* and *is*-ness of nothing, Heidegger wishes to locate his discourse on nothing in the realm of fundamental ontology. By doing so, he also makes the question on nothing the primary issue in metaphysics. The task Heidegger takes on himself with this project is a challenging one because to place a discourse of nothing within the realm of ontology and consider it as a primary issue in metaphysics cannot but raise the fundamental question of the very definition of ontology and metaphysics. Heidegger thus asks:

What is nothing? Our very first approach to this question has something unusual about it. In our asking we posit the nothing in advance as something that "is" ["ist"] such and such; we posit it as a being. But that is exactly what it is distinguished from. Interrogating the nothing—asking what and how it, the nothing, is—turns what is interrogated into its opposite. The question deprives itself of its own object. Accordingly, every answer to this question is also impossible from the start. For it necessarily assumes the form: the nothing "is" this or that. With regard to the nothing question and answer alike are inherently absurd. ("WM?," 96–97)

In this short passage, Heidegger identifies what he considers to be the basic problem the metaphysical tradition has to deal with in the understanding of the nothing: that is, whether it is possible to discuss the nothing in the existing structure of metaphysics, which has been basically a study of beings. Metaphysics, Heidegger contends, has treated the nothing without considering this basic problem involved in the investigation of the nothing. Since metaphysics has been a study of beings, regardless of the real nature of the nothing, the nothing has been understood in the shadow of beings, as that which exists on the other side of beings. Heidegger asserts that any investigation of nothing requires a new mode of philosophizing that is different from the mode one applies to the investigation of beings. Furthermore, this new philosophical mode demands a fundamental reconsideration of one's approach to metaphysics. In this sense, Heidegger understands the issue of the nothing not just as one among many inquiries in metaphysical discourse but that which holds the core of metaphysics itself.

Once we recognize the impact of the imbalanced position of Being and nothing in our philosophical investigation, our discussion of the nothing turns into another incidence of an "undeclared" thesis. Despite the conventional practice in which questions regarding the nothing have been answered with "nothing is this and nothing is that," the question of "what is the nothing?" is itself a linguistically ill-formulated question. The question is asked with the presupposition that the nothing exists (that is, "is") and the nothing has an identity (the "what-ness") of its own, which, as Heidegger tries to expound in the passage above, contradicts the very nature of nothing. Heidegger's discussion on nothing raises a series of questions regarding the relationship between the investigation of the nothing and metaphysics, which we can roughly summarize with the following three points:

The first is a question of the nature of metaphysical inquiry: what is metaphysics? Heidegger points out that if metaphysics (according to the Greek etymology) is an inquiry about "beyond" ("meta") "beings" ("physics"), it is only natural and more appropriate to consider that such an investigation requires us to go beyond individual beings toward the foundation of beings. The foundation of beings is possible through the encounter with the Being of beings, which, Heidegger contends, can be revealed through the meditation on nothing. The paradox of this claim that the Being can be revealed only through nothing is the salient part of Heidegger's deliberation on the nothing.

The second question has to do with the issue of how to "do" metaphysics. Traditionally, Aristotelian logic has been considered the general foundation of logical thinking, and logic has been understood as the basic rule for metaphysics. However, a discussion of nothing reveals to us the impossibility of maintaining the rules of identity, contradiction, and the excluded middle. If the nothing, by definition, denotes that which does not exist, that which does not exist cannot follow the rule of identity, and, by the same token, cannot violate the rule of contradiction. Understanding the nothing under the constraints of the rules of identity, contradiction, and the excluded middle, is not possible, unless one is already under the assumption that the nothing is a part of being and thus subjugates the nothing to being. For Heidegger, the fact that logic has been the foundation of metaphysical thinking demonstrates that metaphysics has limited the scope of its investigation only to beings.

This leads us to the third and most fundamental question: is philosophy possible when logic is violated and nothing is privileged over being? This is a question the consequence of which will bear a radical impact on our philosophizing, if the investigation is executed properly. Heidegger thus asks:

> [A]re we allowed to tamper with the rule of "logic"? Is not intellect the taskmaster in this question of the nothing? Only with its help can we at all define the nothing and pose it as a problem—which, it is true, only devours itself. For the nothing is the negation of the totality of beings; it is nonbeing pure and simple. But with that we bring the nothing under the higher determination of the negative, viewing it as the negated. However, according to the reigning and never-challenged doctrine of "logic," negation is a specific act of the intellect. How then can we in our question of the nothing, indeed in the question of its questionability, wish to brush the intellect aside? Are we altogether sure about what we are presupposing in this matter? Do not the "Not," negatedness, and thereby negation too represent the higher determination under which the nothing falls as a particular kind of negated matter? Is the nothing given only because the "not," i.e., negation, is given? Or is it the other way around? Are negation and the "Not" given only because the nothing is given? That has not been decided; it has not even been raised expressly as a question. We assert that the nothing is more original than the "not" and negation. ("WM?," 97)

By accepting the limits of logic and allowing nothing identity beyond the simple negation of being, Heidegger opens up a new dimension not only in our discussion of the nothing but in our philosophical imagination.

In his discussion of the influence of the *Daode jing* on Heidegger's philosophy, Reinhard May states that Heidegger's thinking on the nothing "ultimately distinguishes itself from everything else that has been thought and said in Western philosophy about the topic of Nothing."[3] This rather dramatic statement on Heidegger's understanding of the nothing earns much validity not only from Heidegger's own statements as cited earlier but also as we review different receptions of Heidegger's discussion of the nothing. Responses to Heidegger's "What is Metaphysics?" over the past seventy years confirm the radical nature of Heidegger's thought on the nothing and at the same time the complexity that is involved in the discussion of the nothing that Heidegger addresses in his philosophy. Immediately after the publication of the essay, Heidegger's discussion of the nothing was criticized as being irrational and "ambiguous" in its use of the nothing, and as having violated logic through the strange use of the term "nothing." Even in the 1970s, Heidegger's discussion of the nothing was treated as an odd irregularity in philosophical discourse, as we read: "There is no doubt, . . .—by all ordinary criteria—he [Heidegger] misuses 'nothing' and goes against logic."[4] When Heidegger's discussion of the nothing receives a positive evaluation, it is understood as a kind of mysticism. Michael Zimmerman thus claims that "the mystical origins of Heidegger's idea of nothingness" are a result of the influence of mystics such as Meister Eckhart.[5]

A seemingly more positive evaluation also appeared, and in that interpretation, the nothing in Heidegger was understood not as a candidate for philosophical irrationalism which violated the logic of philosophy but as a confirmation of fundamental ontology in which the nothing is identified with the being-ness of entities. That is, Heidegger's nothing was read as a confirmation of the ontico-ontological difference.[6] Interpretations of Heidegger's treatment of the nothing, then, have made a full circle: it was first understood as the stark opposite of traditional metaphysical thinking, then as mystical openness of being, and finally as a confirmation of the metaphysical foundation of entities in the form of ontico-ontological difference. The conflicting readings themselves reflect the position of Heidegger in the evolution of Western understanding of the nothing. In "What is Metaphysics?" Heidegger distances himself from the previous metaphysical discourse on the nothing, but is still a part of the legacy that he wishes to overcome. The second part of this statement needs further elaboration. In order to do so, we need to go back to the three questions we raised as major points of the discussion in "What is Metaphysics?" That is, the relationship between nothing and the nature of metaphysical inquiry, the nothing's relation to logic, and the Heideggerian nothing and the possibility of philosophy.

Why indeed is the investigation of nothing a legitimate path to do metaphysics? For Heidegger, nothing reminds us of the Being of beings. Dasein's awareness of the Being is possible only when Dasein holds itself out to the nothing, without which Dasein remains as a finite being. The nothing in this sense provides a possibility of the ontological interrogation of a being:

Only because the nothing is manifest in the ground of Dasein can the total strangeness of beings overwhelm us. Only when the strangeness of beings oppresses us does it arouse and evoke wonder. Only on the ground of wonder—the revelation of the nothing—does the "why?" loom before us. Only because the "why" is possible as such can we in a definite way inquire into grounds, and ground them. Only because we can inquire and ground is the destiny of our existence placed in the hands of the researcher. ("WM?" 109)

The nothing to Heidegger is revealed in anxiety (*Angst*), when we have an uncanny feeling. This experience of being ill-at-ease with our being and our world makes us retreat. This "repelling from itself" or "expelling into" is the function of the nothing, which Heidegger calls the nihilation of the nothing:

this wholly repelling gesture toward beings that are in retreat as a whole, which is the action of the nothing that oppresses Dasein in anxiety, is the essence of the nothing: nihilation. It is neither an annihilation of beings nor does it spring from negation. Nihilation will not submit to calculation in terms of annihilation and negation. The nothing itself nihilates. ("WM?" 103)

Both annihilation and negation presuppose the existence of being as an object to be annihilated or negated. When Hegel and European Buddhologists understood Buddhism as a religion of annihilation, the deliberation inevitably presupposed existence of being or self. The nothing in this case was lack, deprivation, and absence of being. With the above statement, Heidegger distances himself from the two common understandings of the nothing: the nothing as the annihilation of being, and the nothing as negation. The nothing is neither of them, Heidegger contends, because the awareness of the nothing, or nihilation of the nothing, is the moment when an entity faces its existential reality through an encounter with the totality of its being. Heidegger thus states:

We 'hover' in anxiety. More precisely, anxiety leaves us hanging because it induces the slipping away of beings as a whole. This implies that we ourselves . . . in the midst of beings slip away from ourselves. At bottom, therefore it is not as though 'you' or 'I' feel ill at ease; rather it is this way for some 'one'. In this altogether unsettling experience of this hovering where there is nothing to hold onto, pure Dasein is all that is still there. ("WM?" 101)

A being's awareness of the nothing makes possible the being's being with itself. With the realization of the nihilation of the nothing, "pure Dasein,"—a being which encounters, face to face, the anxiety of the human condition of being "thrown into the world,"— emerges. The realization of the nihilation of the nothing creates moments in which Dasein turns away from beings of everyday life to nihilative activities of the nothing. Only with this realization, Heidegger contends, do beings obtain "selfhood" and "freedom," and thus overcome nihilism.

The nothing for Heidegger is no longer an incomplete form of a being; it is the unnameable source of a being, which allows the awareness of the ground of the being's existence. The nothing "functions" as a source for Dasein's awareness of the Being, but as it is, it does not have identity. This is a tactic, one might say, that Heidegger employs in order to avoid the trap of turning the nothing into a being. The intertwining of a being and the nothing in their mutual revelation is a movement which distinguishes Heidegger from his predecessors in the discourse of nothing.

In its function as a revelator of the Being to Dasein, Heidegger's nothing also reveals the remnant of the onto-theological aspect of Heidegger's thoughts. In Heidegger we encounter a certain "returning of the Being" through a detour of the nothing, which makes his discussion of the nothing ambivalent. In Hegel's discussion of Buddhism, the nothing is understood through the logic of being, whereas in Heidegger, the nothing is both the ground for a being's encounter with the Being of beings and at the same time the source of its dread and anxiety. The *raison d'être* of nothing, for Heidegger, becomes the revelation of beings in its entirety: "The essence of the originally nihilating nothing lies in this, that it brings Dasein for the first time before beings as such" ("WM?" 103). Heidegger further contemplates: "Holding itself out into the nothing, Dasein is in each case already beyond beings as a whole. This being beyond beings we call 'transcendence'. If in the ground of its essence Dasein were not transcending, which now means, if it were not in advance holding itself out into the nothing, then it could never be related to beings nor even to itself . . . Without the original revelation of the nothing, no selfhood and no freedom" ("WM?" 103). In this existentialist approach to nothing, the transcendental is reinstated and the Being of beings reconfirmed as Dasein exerts its capacity to face the impossibility of its own existence. In Heidegger, "Being as a theoretical problem is not dissolved in his thinking, it is generated and regenerated primordially, presumably by the Being-process itself."[7] Jacques Derrida's criticism that Heidegger's philosophy remains in the realm of onto-theology, despite his attempt to stay away from metaphysics, does not seem completely groundless.[8]

At least two major contentions have been repeated in the Western reluctance and eventual refusal to "grant" Asian thought a membership in "philosophy." The first is the claim that Asian thought is not philosophy but religion. The second is the assertion that Asian thought does not have a logical structure and thus cannot be considered philosophy. Heidegger's awareness that discourse on the nothing inevitably violates this universal logic of philosophy and that such a violation does not negate the possibility of either philosophy or metaphysics bridges different modes of philosophizing in the East and the West.[9] A rather visible aspect of this bridge can be found in the

"Postscript to 'What is metaphysics?'" which Heidegger added in the 1943 edition of "What is Metaphysics?"

In this "Postscript" Heidegger states that his meditation on the nothing has created much misunderstanding. He summarizes the "mistaken views about the lecture" in the following three points. That is, people criticize that:

> 1. The lecture makes "Nothing" the sole subject of metaphysics. But since Nothing is simply the negatory (das Nichtige), this kind of thinking leads to the idea that everything is nothing, so that it is not worthwhile either to live or to die. A "Philosophy of Nothing" is the last word in "Nihilism."
> 2. The lecture raises an isolated and, what is more, a morbid mood, namely dread, to the status of the one key-mood. But since dread is the psychic state of nervous people and cowards, this kind of thinking devalues the stout-hearted attitude of the courageous. A "philosophy of Dread" paralyses the will to act.
> 3. The lecture declares itself against "logic." But since reason contains the criteria for all calculation and classification, this kind of thinking delivers all judgements regarding the truth up to a chance mood. A "Philosophy of Pure Feeling" imperils "exact" thinking and the certainty of action.[10]

Heidegger's summary of his critics' position on the nothing resembles the nineteenth century European intellectuals' evaluation of Buddhism. Like Heidegger's critics, the first generation European Buddhist scholars found Buddhist no-self, impermanence, and the nothing manifestations of Buddhist nihilism. In the same context, Hegel employed Buddhist nothing and no-self theory to identify Buddhism as a solipsistic religion with enervating femininity. As a result, he placed Buddhism at the primitive stage in his philosophy of the evolution of world religions.

As Heidegger states, logic is "only *one* exposition of the nature of thinking" (emphasis original).[11] To follow the rules of logic might be the most "exact" thinking; however, the most exact thinking does not guarantee "the strictest thinking." Moreover, the discussion of the nothing makes us "face up to the decision concerning the legitimacy of the rule of 'logic' in metaphysics" ("WM?" 108), and eventually, "the idea of 'logic' itself disintegrates in the turbulence of a more original questioning" ("WM?" 105), which, for Heidegger, is the question of the meaning of the nothing.

Why is the nothing so important to Heidegger and our philosophical investigation? For Heidegger, the nothing is not one isolated theme in our philosophizing, but that which is closely related to the structure of one's mode of thinking. The structure is in general characterized as dualistic and hierarchical. A dualistic thought system understands a being as a closed entity, whereas a new understanding of nothing introduces the openness of beings. Heidegger thus states, "For human existence the nothing makes possible the openness of beings as such. The nothing does not merely serve as the counter-concept of beings; rather it originally belongs to their essential unfolding as such" ("WM?" 104). He further contends, through the nothing, "we liberate ourselves from those idols everyone has and to which they are wont to go cringing" ("WM" 110). In these passages Heidegger postulates a being as "unfolding" itself and such an unfolding liberates a being from the constraints created by the identity principle that views an entity as an independent essence. The underlying implication seems very much Buddhist, despite the distance of the two philosophies on the surface.[12] In the following section, we will look into the liberating aspect of nothing by examining the function of nothing in a Buddhist text.

2. Buddhism, Nothing, and Emptiness

Nothing is neither an ontological nor an epistemological category, nor can it be concretized as any philosophical scheme. A discourse on nothing is justified only when understood as a figurative device. Such caution is required in order to avoid subjugating nothing to beings. Only by constantly problematizing existing identity, and thus violating the identity principle, nothing functions as nothing. Nothing in this case cannot be the "lack" or "privation" of being; instead, it opens up the limits that a being retains within itself in an attempt to maintain its identity as an entity.

Since no affirmative language can represent the nothing, the language for the nothing takes the form of contextual language as opposed to the substantial or representational mode. The forms of the contextual language are diverse. Most notable is the figurative language of literature as opposed to the substantialist language of metaphysics. The figurative language is characterized by its dependency on the context and thus constantly violates the rules of semantics in which linguistic expression is subject to a fixed meaning system. Contrary to the figurative language, in the substantialist language, or the language of metaphysics, linguistic expression is understood as a re-presentation of the essence and identity of an entity. To express the nothing without sacrificing it to the language of being is to use language in such a way that absence becomes tactical but not real. Since the nothing belongs to neither existence nor non-existence, both affirmation and negation with regard to the nothing are only tactical. The same can be said about the silence of the Buddha. The Buddha's silence does not indicate that the Buddha dismisses the issues raised by his interlocutor or that he withholds an answer to the posed question. His silence was another way of articulating the middle path, the manifestation of which was foreclosed because of the different presuppositions between the logic of the Buddha and that of the language his interlocutor brought into the dialogue. The logic of nothing can be explained in a similar manner. Our linguistic and philosophical paradigms are dominated by the logic of being.

Since the nature of nothing does not follow the same logic, a discussion of nothing suffers from ineffability. That the ineffability of nothing has its own philosophical function as much as the eloquence of being is what has been frequently forgotten in our philosophical investigation.

In the *Nirvāna Sūtra*, one of the Mahāyāna Buddhist texts, the Buddha discusses the middle path by using the relationship between being and nothing (or non-being). The *Sūtra* states: "The Buddha nature neither exists nor does not exist/ both exists and does not exist/... being and nothing combined/This is what is called the middle path."[13] The middle path here is characterized by its non-static position. It is both being and nothing and at the same time neither being nor nothing. In this passage not only the identity of nothing, but that of being as well, becomes problematic from the perspective of conventional logic. If a being is both and neither of being and nothing, negation, which traditionally falls into the realm of nothing, cannot take place, since one cannot negate without identifying that which is being negated. From the logic of this *Sūtra*, a discourse on being cannot but be that on nothing and vice versa. Nothing is understood as the opposite of being in the above passage, but the binary postulation of being and nothing in this *Sūtra* does not comply with the hierarchical values frequently associated with these terms.

The nothing as the opposite of being in the *Sūtra* is distinguished from the middle path which is defined as a mutual revelation of being and the nothing. In this context, one can make a distinction between two different understandings of nothing: the nothing (non-being) as absence of being, which is the nothing the *Nirvāna Sūtra* employs here, and the nothing as openness of being, which Heidegger eventually comes to denote by the expression in his "What is Metaphysics?" One can distinguish these two understandings of nothing as the relative nothing and absolute nothing, following Se Geun Jeong, a Korean scholar of Asian philosophy, in his speculation about nothing. Jeong writes: "I do not know nothing, because it does not exist. However I speak of the nothing. Is this wrong? The absence of that which does not exist means the presence of all things. The non-existence of that which exists means a mere absence. How about then the absence of all that which does not exist? Is this existence or non-existence?"[14] In these questions, Jeong articulates the delicate relationship not only between being and non-being (or nothing) but between non-being (or nothing) and Non-being (or Nothing), which we just identified as the relative and absolute nothing respectively. The former understands nothing as the opposite of being, whereas the latter locates nothing beyond the category of either being or non-being. Jeong's questions evoke the specific nature involved in our meditation on the nothing. That is, is "the absence of all that which does not exist" existence or non-existence? The question is unanswerable, because that which does not exist cannot be absent as much as it cannot be present; it is neither existence nor non-existence. To discuss nothing in the context of either existence or non-existence is itself an ill-formulated argument. Jeong further pursues his meditation on nothing as he states:

> What is absolute Nothing? It does not have its other. The absolute negation here is not the same as relative negation. Since it does not have its other, negation is not possible either. Is the absolute negation the same as absolute affirmation? No. The absolute negation, which must take place in the world of the absolute, cannot come down to the affirmation which is in the world of the relative, nor does the negation of negation become affirmation [in the world of the absolute]. The moment the absolute Nothing encounters beings, it falls into the position of the relative nothing. The relative nothing as a mere image or illusion of being occupies only a degraded position. Nothing, then, should not be articulated through positive expressions. Nothing will remain forever in the world of negation. However, even though Nothing remains in the negation, it cannot be negated.[15]

How does one speak of nothing which cannot be articulated in positive expressions and which should remain in the world of negation without being negated? Since nothing cannot be articulated in positive expression and should remain in the world of negation without being negated, it can only be expressed in figurative language which defies the essentialist view of language. In this sense, the absolute Nothing is openness of and from being, rather than a lack of it. It opens the fixed identity of a being and thus frees being from its boundary. Such an understanding of nothing demands constant efforts to open up the boundary of nothing itself because the moment we domesticate nothing, it already loses its "identity" as nothing. Such an effort involves a problematization of language's capacity to represent reality, because nothing does not represent anything.

Jeong's view of the absolute Nothing shares its characteristics with what Buddhist philosophy denotes by the expression "emptiness" (Sk. *śūnyatā*). In its English translation, "emptiness" is more often than not used interchangeably with nothing. This practice of identifying emptiness with nothing in the English language, without noting a distinction between the relative and absolute nothing, has offered one cause of misunderstanding the Buddhist concept of emptiness. The Buddhist conception of emptiness and its relation to the relative and absolute nothing is well articulated in a group of literature known as the *Prajñāpāramitā Sūtras* (Scriptures of the Perfection of Wisdom). The *Heart Sūtra*, which is the shortest version in this group of literature, succinctly demonstrates how a text in the non-substantialist tradition—to which we assign the Buddha's silence and our deliberation of nothing—manifests itself through substantialist mediums such as language and the physical reality of an entity.

The discourse on the emptiness in the *Heart Sūtra* begins by identifying emptiness with a being. The Buddha tells Śāriputra: "Śāriputra, form does not differ from emptiness, / emptiness, form; / that which is form is emptiness, / that which is emptiness, form."[16] To say that form is emptiness is to negate form. How and what does the Buddha negate when he declares form as emptiness? The basic structure of the *Heart Sūtra* is a step-by-step negation of all the classifications and impersonal categories that previously served as the main thematic structures in the Buddhist tradition. At the outset of the *Sūtra*, the Five Aggregates, which the Buddha employed to explain the theory of no-self, are negated. The Buddha states, "In emptiness, there is neither form, nor sensation, nor perception, nor mental formation, nor consciousness." The negation of the Five Aggregates is followed by the negation of what is known as the Eighteen Elements. Through the paradigm of the Eighteen Elements, early Buddhism explains the entire range of the subject-object interactions. The Eighteen Elements consist of the six sense faculties, which are eyes, ears, nose, tongue, body, and mind; their six objects, which are form, sound, smell, taste, touch, and ideas; and the six corresponding functions. When eyes encounter a form, seeing takes place; when ears meet sound, hearing takes place; with nose and smell, olfactory activities become possible; the combination of tongue and taste, palatal; and that of body and touch, sensation; and finally, the combination of ideas and mind brings about thinking and reasoning.

In the *Sūtra*, the Buddha negates all of the six sense faculties, their six objects, and their corresponding functions as we read, "no ear, nor eyes, nor nose, nor tongue, nor body, or mind; no color, no sound, no smell, no taste, no touch, no objects of mind / no realm of eyes, and up until we come to no realm of consciousness." In this manner, not only does the Buddha negate all the entities, but he also negates all the epistemological function of the subject. After the Buddha negates both ontological and epistemological structures of his philosophy, he further negates the Twelve Chains of Dependent Co-arising. The Twelve Chains of Dependent Co-arising is one of the paradigms through which the Buddha expounds the theory of conditioned causality in early Buddhism. The Buddha negates the idea as he states, "There is no ignorance, nor the realm of consciousness." And finally, he negates the Four Noble Truths, the very contents of his enlightenment: "No suffering, no arising of suffering, no cessation of suffering, nor the path leading to the cessation of suffering."

Negating the Four Noble Truths is equivalent to negating the Buddha's enlightenment itself. Hence, immediately after the *Sūtra* denies the existence of the Four Noble Truths, it declares, "No wisdom, also no attainment." Negation at this point reaches its apex: not only are the ontological and epistemological aspects of the subject negated, but the basic structure of the Buddha's worldview is denied through the negation of his enlightenment itself.

The moment of this negation, however, marks an ironic turning point. After the *Sūtra* negates all the elements that can be negated, it turns to affirmation: "Since there is nothing to obtain,/ bodhisattvas, relying on the perfection of wisdom, obtain the ultimate nirvāṇa. / The Buddhas from the three worlds, relying on the perfection of wisdom, / attain the unsurpassed, right, and perfect enlightenment." The *Sūtra* ends with the encouragement that everybody should practice the perfection of wisdom and obtain enlightenment as bodhisattvas and Buddhas have done. If bodhisattvas and Buddhas have obtained enlightenment with the help of wisdom and, thus, are relieved from suffering, there *is* wisdom, there *is* suffering to be removed, and there *is* the enlightenment and nirvāṇa to obtain. In the first half of the *Sūtra*, the Buddha negates all the categories of existence and enlightenment. In the second half, he affirms their existence. This seeming contradiction constitutes the Buddhist logic in the *Heart Sūtra*.

The seemingly contradictory logic of the *Heart Sūtra* begins to make sense when we look into the nature of the relationship between being and non-being, or between form and emptiness, in this text. In the first half of the *Sūtra*, the narrative of negation dominates. The Five Aggregates, the Eighteen Elements, the Twelve Chains of Dependent Co-arising, the Four Noble Truths, wisdom, and the attainment of enlightenment are all negated. However, to negate these features is not to remove them from the realm of being and relocate them in the realm of the nothing. When the *Sūtra* negates them, it does not by default indicate the "lack" or "privation" of these elements. Negation, in this case, is a figurative device to indicate the limits of existing concepts and their linguistic expressions. When form is equated with emptiness, the expected effect is not the disappearance of, nor replacement of, either one by the other; instead their boundaries become blurred, as their identity is re-conceptualized through the inter-subsumption of parties involved in the discourse.

When the Buddha negates all the components of his teaching in the first half of the *Sūtra*, there was a condition that the Buddha set for this sweeping negation. Just before he denies the existence of the Five Aggregates, the Eighteen Elements, the Twelve Chains of Dependent Co-arising, and the Four Noble Truths, the Buddha mentions that they do not exist, "when one sees them from the perspective of emptiness." The identity principle of an individual entity holds only a tentative significance, if seen from the perspective of emptiness. Like Heidegger's nothing, which facilitates the experience of existential totality for Dasein, reality understood from the position of emptiness in the *Heart Sūtra* opens the limitations of individual concepts and entities whose existence on the phenomenal and linguistic levels is possible through the identity principle. Once one realizes the inner structure of entities and concepts, the phenomenal and linguistic boundaries become blurred, but the blurring of boundaries does not negate them on the phenomenal level. Seen from the perspective of emptiness, individual identities lose their validity; from the phenomenal perspective, they remain as individual. This idea of simultaneously affirming and negating boundaries between entities is an important point in Zen Buddhist and Huayan Buddhist discourse as we shall see later.

The form is now to be understood with its relation to emptiness. Negation is a strategic device, and in that sense, has a function similar to the silence of the Buddha. The negation of beings (or affirmation) is counterbalanced by the negation of nothing (negativity). With this double negation, the *Heart Sūtra* prevents a hypostatization of either being or nothing in a way similar to the Buddha's undeclared thesis in which he refutes both eternalism (being) and annihilationism (non-being) and declares the middle path. In a similar vein, in the *Heart Sūtra*, a declaration, "that which is form is emptiness," is immediately followed by its reverse, "that which is emptiness is form." The absence in this sense is only functional but not ontological. Absence is functional because presence itself is functional.

To understand being and nothing without subjecting them to a hierarchical relationship makes it possible to be aware of the reverse-hierarchy, that is, the privileging of nothing over being. The history of Buddhism has been sensitive to this issue. The seventh-century Korean Buddhist monk Wŏnch'ŭk (613-696) interprets the identity between form and emptiness declared in the *Heart Sūtra* in the context of the mutual cancellation of hierarchical relationship between being and nothing. In his comments on the passage regarding wisdom, meditation, and emptiness, Wŏnch'ŭk writes, citing Badhuprabha:

> Badhuprabha comments: "A thousand years ago, the teaching of the Buddha was consistent; now that a thousand years have passed, debates on being and the nothing have emerged. [. . .] In order to help sentient beings to enter the world of the Buddha, the school of being and the school of the nothing were established. Both follow the teachings of the Buddha. Bodhisattva Bhāviveka [490-570 ca.] relied on emptiness and removed being, and that was to warn against the attachment to [or privileging] being. Bodhisattva Dharmapāla [530-561] relied on being and removed emptiness, and that was to warn against the attachment to [or privileging] emptiness. Emptiness does not contradict being, thus it is possible to construct the principle of emptiness ["form is emptiness"]. Being [lit. no-nothing] does not contradict emptiness, thus, it is possible to construct the discourse of being ["emptiness is form"]. Put together, the two levels of truth of "both emptiness and being" are constructed. Adding to "both emptiness and being" and "neither emptiness nor being," the middle path is explained. This is the core of the Buddha's teaching."[17]

The double negation and double affirmation employed in the *Nirvāna Sūtra* is repeated in Wŏnch'ŭk's explanation. Being and the nothing are both affirmed and negated, because the relationship between negation and affirmation as well as that of being and non-being are non-dual. Not only is the philosophical discrimination of privileging being over nothing fended off, but the possibility of a reverse discrimination of privileging the nothing over being is prevented.

3. Philosophical Discrimination and Philosophical Imagination

Philosophical discrimination is a salient indicator of our desire for centripetal power. The centripetal mode of thinking, which privileges unity and order, accompanies substantialism as its corollary or foundation. The Buddha's silence is a silence-action toward, not a dismissal of, the questions when those questions are posed in an effort to create and consolidate a centripetal power. The Buddha's silence, however, is not a mere negation of a certain centripetal force to be replaced with another form of centripetality. The middle path, with which the Buddha responded to his inquisitors, serves to relativize the centripetal force. Its generic format, "when this arises, that arises; when this ceases, that ceases," deprives it of its independent identity, and reminds his inquisitors of the contextuality of existence. The contextuality of an entity as well as the constituents of that entity is presented through the paradoxical language in the *Heart Sūtra* with its strategy of alternating affirmation and negation. When affirmation and negation are understood from the perspective of a substantialist mode of thinking, they are in a dichotomous relationship; the identity of the one cannot overlap with that of the other. From the perspective of a non-substantialist mode of thinking, affirmation and negation are mutually indebted: affirmation by nature already encompasses negation in its concept and vice versa.

Let us for a moment unfold our philosophical imagination in which the boundaries that have been so dear to our philosophical investigation become blurred. As the borders between affirmation and negation, reason and imagination, philosophy and literature, logos and mythos, and truth and fiction become blurred, the centripetal force placing them in respective positions becomes loose as well. The Cartesian revolution opened a new path in the relationship between philosophy and religion. Hegel, like Descartes before him, redefined the border between philosophy and religion by incorporating the religions in his philosophical system. In Descartes' *Discourse on the Method* and *Meditations on First Philosophy,* reason begins a journey to claim itself as the sole legitimizing authority in discourses on humanities. The God of Abraham would be replaced with the God of philosophers.[18] The journey reaches the apex when Hegel introduces the concept of philosophy of religion in which religion is sublated into philosophy.[19] It might sound ironic; however, in the process of reason's journey in Descartes' and Hegel's philosophy, reason frequently speaks figurative language instead of philosophical language, if one can make a clear distinction between the two. Can figurative language speak truth? Does figurative language speak through reason? Can literature tell the same truth that philosophy claims to tell us? Is metaphysics possible when philosophy speaks a figurative language? Has metaphysics (and philosophy) ever spoken other than figuratively? Can we ask whether philosophy is a fiction?

Metaphysics has claimed the truth of philosophical language and has been critical about the figurative nature of literary discourse. The poet was the one who should be expelled from the republic ruled by the philosopher. At the threshold that foretells the "closure" of metaphysics and the impossibility of remaining "on the fringes of Hegelian discourse," Philippe Lacoue-Labarthe asks, "What if, after all, philosophy were nothing but literature?"[20] What would it mean to think of philosophy as literature?

In a reading of Descartes, Dalia Judovitz demonstrates how the birth of modern subjectivity in Cartesian texts was carried out not through philosophical language but literary devices. Judovitz contends that in Descartes' text, especially in his *Meditations*, the creation of subjectivity is mediated by a special representation, that of the evil genius, which makes the text "a representation of fiction par excellence."[21] Judovitz further claims that the Cartesian reason is possible only by employing fictional devices and that this is an "index of a metaphysical crisis": the fiction of madness and hyperbolic doubt fosters "the Cartesian illusion of a philosophical system that can define itself autonomously."[22]

Once we begin to see the metaphysical tradition as embedded within the literary tradition, we begin to note a certain pattern in the function of the literary trope in the construction of philosophical discourse. The relationship between imagination and reason in Kant provides another such occasion. Paul de Man, thus, notes in his discussion of the fate of imagination in Kant's *Third Critique*, "What could it possibly mean, in analytical terms, that the imagination sacrifices itself, like Antigone or Iphigenia—for one can only imagine this shrewd and admirable imagination as the feminine heroine of a tragedy—for the sake of reason?"[23] De Man answers his own question with a claim that "instead of being an argument, [Kant's *Critique*] is a story, a dramatized scene of the mind in action" in which "the faculties of reason and of imagination are personified, or anthropomorphized."[24]

Hegel's texts are no exception in the employment of literary figures for philosophical arguments. In Hegel's grand narrative on the journey of the Spirit, one finds a *Bildungsroman* in which Hegel describes how the Spirit wages its journey to be a grown "man":

These stages [of Spirit in process] can be compared to the stages of human life. The child is still in the first, immediate unity of will and nature (both its own nature and that which surrounds it). The second stage [is] youth, this individuality, this becoming-for-self, this spirituality blossoming into life, still setting no particular purpose for itself but questioning, searching this way and that, paying heed to everything that comes its way, taking heart from it. The third stage, maturity, is that of work for a particular purpose, to which adults subject themselves, to which they devote their strength. Hovering above maturity, finally, the fourth stage is old age, the age of thought, having the universal before itself as infinite purpose, recognizing this purpose—the age that has turned back from particular forms of activity and work to the universal purpose. (*LPR* II, 237-8)

The same literary trope can be found among the advocates of the Hegelian system. Defending Hegel against the Derridean deconstruction of dialectics, Rowan Williams writes, "It is of course true that Hegel believes there to be only one story to tell of the life of the mind . . . Absolute spirit is characterizable as ultimate self-presence, but... it is at least debatable whether, in the Hegelian system, it could actually make any sense to claim that Absolute Spirit was realizable as the term of any specific historical process."[25] With this doubt, Williams reaches a conclusion similar to de Man's, namely, "all that is *said* about this *telos* has a necessarily *quasi-fictional character*: it has the negative force of insisting that we don't take for granted *any* level of dualism between self and world, the perceived and the real, the concept and the 'brute fact', and so on."[26] The distance between mythos and logos does not seem as far apart as philosophy has claimed. In this context, one might even claim that philosophical discourse has been using literary trope and by doing so, it has generated its own legitimacy: fable has been the foundation of the self-legitimation of logos.

What would it mean to think of fiction, instead of philosophy? Lacoue-Labarthe states, "*Muthos* and *logos* are the same thing, but neither is more true (or false, deceptive, fictional, etc.) than the other; they are neither true nor false; both are the *same* fable."[27] That is because, Lacoue-Labarthe contends, "the 'becoming-*logos*' of the world in the metaphysics that is accomplished in Hegelian logic is nothing other than its 'becoming-*muthos*'."[28] To think of philosophy as literature without allowing the traditional dichotomy between literature and philosophy, or fiction and truth, is to think about the world without the outside. To cite Lacoue-Labarthe again, "To think fiction is not to oppose appearance and reality, since appearance is nothing other than the product of reality. To think fiction is precisely to think without recourse to this opposition, *outside* this opposition."[29] In our philosophical discourse, the suppression of mythos for the privileging of logos could offer us one barometer to reflect the nature of the presuppositions we employed in our philosophizing. This mode of philosophizing could be more visible in a certain philosophical tradition than others; when this mode comes to take the position of exclusivism, resorting to strictly dichotomous views on the usual binary opposites, including logos and mythos, reason and emotion, truth and fiction, and being and nothing, we come to note that the power to hold the center becomes strongest. The power entertains our desire to keep things in order, give entities their unified identity, and enable society to concretize normative value systems and codes of behaviors.

The Cartesian Ego-cogito could be one of the strongest manifestations of the power of such a desire, which we identified earlier as centripetality, the force concentrating toward center, maximizing its power to hold things together. As forces gather together in the creation of its power, frequently forgotten is the fact that the centripetality goes along with the centrifugality. This is true in nature, and so is in human society, in an individual's life, and in a philosophical discourse. Centrifugality is the power distracting the centralizing forces; it allows individual constituents of a group their own separate identity, diversity, and room for nonconformity. The nonconformity could take place as an intentional action of an agent, when the agent realizes that certain norms of society, ideology, culture, or politics do not serve the interest of the agent. The agent's action to ameliorate the existing structure follows. Nonconformity of the agent in this case is facilitated by the external forces, and the agent is reacting to the outside stimuli by challenging the unfavorable environments. Nonconformity, however, also arises through the internal logic of an entity because of heterogeneity existing within an entity. In this case, nonconformity takes place as an internal rupture that constantly influences the subject's existence and function as a unified agent of action.

One might ask whether the internal and external constituents of nonconformity can be so decisively separated. Our discussion of Buddhism and metaphysics has already revealed the nebulous nature of this division. On a surface level, the silence of the Buddha is externally incurred since the Buddha is challenging the dominant discourse of the time, that is, eternalism of the Brahmanical tradition and annihilationism of the heretics. When the Buddha eventually identifies the meaning of his silence as the middle path, his logic gets close to the centrifugal dispersive power over the centripetal desire to hold the center. However, when the Buddha declares this middle path as the universal law of the world, we ask whether the middle path, centrifugal in its content, marks another metaphysical turn resorting to the centripetal forces. In the case of the Buddha in the Āgamas, the coexistence of centripetality and centrifugality is still debatable. In the next section, we shall examine how centrifugality is articulated in Zen Buddhist literature and at the same time how centripetality is employed to secure self-legitimation in the same tradition.

Part Two

CENTRIFUGALITY:
LANGUAGE AND VIOLENCE

Chapter Four

Language and Thinking: Subjectivity and Zen Huatou Meditation

1. Acting Out Silence

The philosophical imagination we experimented with at the end of the last chapter is not far from the imagination exercised in Zen Buddhist literature. The mixture of what is traditionally considered "literary trope" with philosophical ideas and religious doctrine has made the Zen tradition subject to various types of misunderstanding and created a perception of Zen Buddhism as a strange, illogical, and mystical tradition. At the center of this image of Zen as "impenetrable" lies language.

As we discussed in length, the Buddha's silence in the "undeclared thesis" of early Buddhism is not the indication of literal silence, but a demonstration of the inadequacy of the language employed by his interlocutor. Zen Buddhism is the Buddhist school which most effectively and rigorously employs the complex meaning of the Buddha's use of silence; moreover, it turns this silence into "language." Because the silence is at the core of the school's teaching, and at the same time the Zen school has never remained silent, the paradox of asserting silence by not remaining silent has complicated the hermeneutic endeavors of scholars of Zen Buddhism. To understand the relation between silence and language in Zen Buddhism is one key to unraveling Zen literature in this context. Let us, then, begin our discussion of Zen Buddhism with a meditation on silence.

What does "silence" denote in our communication? Despite the relatively simple and unsophisticated dictionary definition of the word, which usually identifies the expression as "absence of sound and noise" and thus "absence of mention," the range of hermeneutical possibilities that this expression affords is exceedingly rich. The absence of mention can be an expression of extreme happiness or of despair, of indifference or of resistance, of authority or of subservience. One can keep silence but also be silenced. In Buddhist tradition, one also practices silent meditation. In other words, being silent never means being silent. In addition, one does not merely keep silence. One is noted, recorded, or said to keep silence. Silence, then, like any other linguistic expression, is a communal language. One can feel happy all by oneself, but one does not keep silence by oneself. Silence by nature is one's response to outside stimuli: it is the subject's evaluation of the object, the nature of which ranges from one's opinion on various daily events to linguistic, philosophical, cultural, and political agenda. In this encounter between the subject and the object presented to the subject's evaluation, silence as the subject's response to the object contains meanings that often include opposite ideas.

Despite the wide range of hermeneutic possibilities with which silence is impregnated, there exists a commonly shared aspect of different interpretations of silence; that is, silence as a speech act is characterized by a certain gap between the subject and the object or between the subject and the outside world. The lack or delay of an immediate verbal response is a suggestion that what is presented to the subject does not properly fit into the thought system that the subject maintains at the moment the object is presented. The period of the subject's adjustment to the challenge of the current situation is expressed through the momentary lack of sound or comment, which is silence. Silence, in this sense, is a speech act of asymmetry that takes place at the moment of the subject's encounter with the object.

Even before the appearance of Zen Buddhism, the use of silence has been one dominant speech act in Buddhist literature. A frequently cited passage from the *Laṅkāvatāra Sūtra* claims that the Buddha said nothing in his forty-nine years of teaching: "It is said by the Blessed One that from the night of the Enlightenment till the night of the Parinirvana, the Tathagata in the meantime has not uttered even a word, nor will he ever utter; for not speaking is the Buddha's speaking."[1] This expression, which caused both eighteenth century European historians and twentieth century Buddhist scholars much hermeneutical embarrassment, is a superb rhetorical employment of the multi-layered meaning of silence.[2] Bernard Faure, thus, asks:

> The "originality" of Chan may be that there is no originary teaching, since the Buddha allegedly "never spoke a word during his forty-nine years of predication." But was there even an "originary" or "pure" experience? What we seem to find are "traces" in the Derridean sense of signs pointing to an origin that was never more than virtual. Paradoxically, the very insight that there is nothing to obtain comes to play the role of an original insight, and thus constantly risks becoming hypostasized, even and particularly when signified by the (meaningfull) silence of the Buddha or of Vimalakīrti."[3]

As noted by Faure, the silence of Vimalakīrti is another incidence in which a lay practitioner Vimalakīrti acts out the Buddhist philosophy of non-duality by keeping silence. In a section entitled "Entering the Gate of Non-duality" in the *Vimalakīrti Sūtra*, participating members of a conversation are asked to describe non-duality. After each member expresses his vision of non-duality, the same question is put to Vimalakīrti:

> Then Manjushri said to Vimalakirti, 'Each of us has given an explanation. Now, sir, it is your turn to speak. How does the bodhisattva enter the gate of nondualism?'
>
> At that time Vimalakirti remained silent and did not speak a word.
>
> Manjushri sighed and said, "Excellent, excellent! Not a word, not a syllable—this truly is to enter the gate of nondualism!"[4]

The Buddhist silence—beginning with the silence of the Buddha in his undeclared thesis, then, in the non-utterance claim in the *Laṅkāvatāra Sūtra* to the silence of Vimalakīrti—takes a new turn in the East Asian Zen Buddhist tradition. Zen Buddhism did the best job of "acting out" the silence of the Buddha and thus "speaking out" silence and, at the same time, explicitly denying the use of language. Ironic as it might sound, "speaking out silence" and "denial of language" belong to the same philosophical endeavor. When one approaches Zen literature without considering the dual nature of Zen language, the Zen Buddhist attitude toward language turns out to be a source of various conflicting contentions regarding the role of language in Zen Buddhism. This situation has been very visible in Zen Buddhist scholarship for the past several decades.

Major questions addressed in scholarly investigation of Zen literature have been focused on the relationship between language and thinking. That is: Is language a tool to communicate our thought or is it part of our thinking? Is thinking possible without language? If so, can we assume a pure state free from linguistic constraints? Zen Buddhist scholars have attempted to locate Zen literature within the scope of answers to these questions. Based on the evaluation of the relationship of language and thinking, we can categorize recent Zen Buddhist scholarship in the West into two opposing views: linguistic and non-linguistic approaches.

According to the linguistic approach, Zen Buddhism asserts a flat rejection of the linguistic system. From that perspective, Zen sees distortion as inevitable in our use of words and theorization, and sees enlightenment as an experience of human reality that takes place beyond the realm of linguistic communication. This vision of linguistically pure Zen Buddhism explains the school as searching for a "pure experience" of the "primordially given" original nature of human beings, when the practitioner frees herself or himself from the linguistically constructed reality of the world. In this approach to Zen

Buddhist language, Zen Buddhism is understood as an effort to reach the realm where language "halts," as Roland Barthes writes: "All of Zen . . . appears as an enormous praxis destined to halt language . . . perhaps what Zen calls satori . . . is no more than a panic suspension of language, the blank which erases in us the reign of the Codes, the breach of that internal recitation which constitutes our person."[5] When this idea of Zen rejection of language is pushed to the extreme, Zen is blamed for its "monopoly of inarticulation." As Koestler states: "Painters paint, dancers dance, musicians make music, instead of explaining that they are practicing no-thought in their no-mind. Inarticulateness is not a monopoly of Zen, but it is the only school which made a monopoly out of it."[6] Whether Zen can be charged with a monopoly of inarticulation is very much a debatable issue. It is further questionable whether Zen inarticulation, if such a phenomenon does exist, has been drawn from a rationale similar to the painters', dancers', or musicians' use of communicative methods other than language. Is language completely missing in their expressions? Is what we call language limited to verbal expressions or to linguistic signs?

The idea that Zen Buddhist enlightenment reflects an aspiration for a linguistically pure realm in human experience encounters opposition when postmodern and post-structuralist theories of language come into play. When Zen enlightenment is viewed as a non-linguistic pure state, language is understood mainly through its representational function. Language represents truth, but as such it is not a constituent factor in the construction of truth. Understanding of language as a medium, or a carrier, of truth not only prevents language from participating in the message of truth itself, but makes it a liability for one's understanding of truth. In the space between the truth and its receiver stands language. This being the space in which the distortion of the original message of the truth takes place, the only way to overcome this unwanted play of the intermediary power, one could argue, is to completely remove this stage.

The idea that language or linguistic communication not only participates in one's experience of truth but is its indispensable element introduces a linguistic approach to Zen language. In this context, mainly two interpretations have been suggested: the first is to understand Zen language as a rhetorical discourse and the second is to interpret it as a specific language game. Mark Lawrence McPhail's discussion of Zen language in connection with post-modern narrative takes the first stance. According to McPhail, Zen language is to be understood with its "rhetorical aspect," rhetoric here indicating its positioning on the other side of argumentative and critical language based on the identity principle of dualistic thinking. Reading the tradition of encounter-dialogue in Zen Buddhism from a rhetorical perspective, McPhail evaluates Zen as a "radically emancipatory understanding of language and life."[7] McPhail thus claims that language in Zen tradition is fully operating in Zen discourse, instead of something that needs to be removed for the experience of Zen enlightenment.

Dale S. Wright pushes the idea of the rhetorical function of Zen language further and claims that Zen tradition, rather than denying the use of language, has developed its own language game, which Wright calls a "monastic language game." Wright brings our attention to the fact that language is not an optional element in one's life nor is the pre-linguistic state, if such exists at all, accessible to human beings. In this context, Wright proposes the "monastic language game" as an alternative to "a fundamental component of Western-language interpretations of Zen experience—the idea that Zen enlightenment is an undistorted 'pure experience' of 'things as they are' beyond the shaping power of language."[8] Challenging the purely non-linguistic approach to Zen language, Wright contends that "awakening would consist, among other things, in an awakening to rather than from language . . . . Zen monastic training would be understood to require a fundamental reorientation of one's sense of language."[9] Wright's interpretation not only secures an essential role for language in Zen enlightenment, but also creates a special position for it: "Language is taken to be the power to form that commonality and to shape and sustain the monks' shared concern for the possibility of 'awakening'."[10]

Bernard Faure also finds the combination of Zen language and power (in this case, the emphasis is on social rather than monastic power) to be an attractive alternative to the naïve argument for alinguistic pure experience in Zen Buddhism. Faure states: "The question [in Zen discourse] is never that of language in abstracto, but always that of legitimate language and of the power from which it derives and to which it gives access."[11]

In the examples I have provided so far, one finds a spectrum that ranges from a complete denial of language to a full acceptance of it. The linguistic and nonlinguistic approaches deal with Zen language at different stages in Zen practice. The non-linguistic approach is mainly concerned about the role of language in the state of enlightenment, whereas the linguistic approach focuses on the role of language in the process of attaining enlightenment. This distinction, however, should not pose a serious obstacle to our line of argument because, if language in the ultimate stage of Zen practice is to be forgotten, language in the process of reaching that goal cannot have any major role either. Also, if language is understood as essential in Zen practice and as a pre-condition for it, the goal reached through that practice cannot be free from linguistic power. Our focus does not lie in the distinction between the two approaches but in the fact that these seemingly contradictory understandings regarding the role of language in Zen Buddhism are not, as they seem, mutually exclusive; rather, they coexist like two sides of a coin in various Zen discourses. At the same time, note that the two different approaches to Zen language reflect the change of the position of language in Western philosophical discourse, as it evolves from a modern to postmodern mode of thinking. A brief examination of the role of language in modernist and postmodernist philosophies will suffice to demonstrate this point.

In the traditional formula of 'I speak', the speaking subject is believed to posit meaning through the medium of a linguistic system. Language, in this understanding, is a means of bridging the gap between the thinking/speaking subject and the things articulated by that subject. Not only is the gap between thinking and speaking left unaddressed; the subject here predicates objects both through linguistic structure and the mode of thinking. Posited in this manner as an object, like any other object of thought, language cannot possibly play any role other than that of a communicative tool.

At the birth of the modern self, Descartes did not consider the role of language in thinking; thus his dictum, *Cogito ergo sum*, confirms the certainty of one's existence via the thinking subject. A full reversal of the situation takes place in postmodern and post-structuralist understanding of language. An example can be found in the Lacanian modification of the Cartesian dictum. Echoing the Freudian formulation, *Wo es war, soll Ich werden* (Where it was, there shall I become),[12] Lacan writes: *Cogito ergo sum, ubi cogito ibi sum* (I think, therefore I am; where I think, there I am).[13] To put it another way, our existence is predicated by our thinking, which in turn is located where we are doing the thinking, and we do the thinking in language. To Lacan, then, the Cartesian thinking subject is none other than language, as his famous phrase goes: "The unconscious is structured like a language."[14]

In the Cartesian thinking, the subject posits meaning, and language is meaning's servant, whereas in the Lacanian model, meaning (thinking and the thinking subject) is governed by language, which Lacan calls the symbolic order. Reciprocity between the two worlds—the subject *vis-à-vis* the object, thinking (meaning) *vis-à-vis* language, and the self *vis-à-vis* the other—is closed. The occupier of the center has changed from the Cartesian to the Lacanisn model, but the structure of subordination has not. In the Cartesian world, one would say: 'I speak language', whereas in the Lacanian world, it could be modified into: 'I am spoken'. The shifting position of language from Descartes to Lacan inevitably affects the position of the human subject in the process of signification. In the Cartesian model, the subject is an active agent of the meaning-giving action, whereas in the Lacanian model, the subject disappears into the margin as we note in other postmodern and post-structuralist philosophy. The nonlinguistic and linguistic models of Zen language in their own ways reflect this change in the view of language from the modernist to postmodernist perspectives. In the case of Zen language, however, the two models do not stand in linear relationship but they co-exist. This has been a cause of confusion for the readers of Zen Buddhism in understanding the role of language in the Zen Buddhist tradition.

Confusion about the Zen Buddhism attitude toward language and contradictory interpretations of it are not exclusively a modern phenomenon but one that scholars repeatedly encounter in traditional Zen Buddhist literature. Consider the conventional definition of Zen Buddhism, attributed to Bodhidharma, which has been cherished as a declaration of the goal and identity of Zen Buddhism. Zen is: "A special transmission outside the scripture,/Not dependent on words and letters,/ Directly pointing at the human mind,/Seeing into one's nature and becoming a Buddha." [15] These passages have been used, too frequently and too easily, as a proof of the Zen school's rejection of a linguistic system. The history of Zen Buddhism provides ample examples of such expressions supporting the negative evaluation of language in Zen tradition. However, at least two issues are frequently forgotten when one accepts this negative tone of Zen rhetoric toward language. The first is the fact that the rejection of linguistic system in Zen literature more often than not accompanies a complete acceptance of the system. The second is the question of why language is considered unreliable in Zen tradition. We will come back to the second issue shortly and here will take up the first issue.

Consider the following statement by Bodhidharma on language: "The ultimate truth is beyond words. Doctrines [Theories or teachings] are only words. They are not the Way. The Way is originally wordless. Linguistic expressions are illusions. They are no different from things that appear in your dreams at night." [16] In this typical Zen statement on language, the non-linguistic approach finds a solid ground for its argument. The truth is beyond linguistic expression, for language is as unreliable as things in one's dreams. However, Bodhidharma is also recorded as having stated, "There is no language that is not Buddhist teachings . . . . The original nature of language is liberation. Language cannot cause attachment. Attachment originally cannot be caused by language" (translation modified). [17]

This seeming contradiction within Zen tradition as to the function of language appears in a more complicated and sophisticated form in the *Diamond Sūtra*, one of the major texts in Zen Buddhism. The narrative in the *Diamond Sūtra* is characterized by its use of paradox. The *Heart Sūtra*, the shortest version among the *Prajñāpāramitā* texts, which we discussed earlier, also incorporates the logic of simultaneous use of negation and affirmation in order to disturb the hypostatizing nature of linguistic expression. In the *Diamond Sūtra*, the paradoxical play of negation and affirmation is further enforced. The following passages from the *Diamond Sūtra* offer us a good example to explore the logic employed in this text.

(1) What is called Buddhist *dharma* refers to what is not Buddhist *dharma*.[18]

(2) I will lead all the sentient beings to *nirvāṇa*; though I said "I will lead all the sentient beings to *nirvāṇa*," there actually are no sentient beings.[19]

(3) Tathāgata means that all *dharmas* are as such. Some people might say that the Tathāgata has obtained unsurpassed, right, and equal enlightenment; however, Subhūti, there is no such *dharma* as unsurpassed, right, and equal enlightenment. In the unsurpassed, right, and equal enlightenment that the Tathāgata obtained, there is nothing real nor unreal, and that is why the Tathāgata says that all the *dharmas* are Buddhist *dharmas*, and again, Subhūti, what is called all the *dharmas* are not "all the *dharmas*"; their names are "all the *dharmas*."[20]

(4) Do not assume that there is *dharma* to be explained by the Tathāgata. Do not think like that. . . To talk about *dharma* (*dharma*-talk) means that there is nothing to talk about, that is why it is called *dharma*-talk.[21]

These quotations provide evidence of how the simultaneous usage of affirmation and negation, which I have described as a characteristic feature of the Zen attitude toward language, develop into Zen logic in a text like the *Diamond Sūtra*. As Bodhidharma teaches language as illusion and at the same time liberation, the *Sūtra* in the first passage identifies *dharma* with no-*dharma*. In the second passage, the existence of sentient beings is affirmed and immediately negated. The third passage begins by negating the belief that the Tathāgata has attained enlightenment. This negation is immediately revoked by the admission that he did attain enlightenment. The final passage again identifies *dharma* with no-*dharma*.

The discourse obviously violates the logic of language, not to speak of the logic of logic. If "a" is identified with "not-a," language cannot function; or language might still function in such a state but it loses its meaning; or language will function only if the user of the language learns it in a way that is different from linguistic convention. This might suggest that Zen training, as the linguistic approach claims, includes the capacity to decode the logic of the seeming illogic of Zen discourse as exemplified in the *Diamond Sūtra*. This in turn justifies the claim that mastery of a specific use of a language game is essential to Zen enlightenment and to the power of Zen masters in Zen monasteries. Such a conclusion brings us back to the beginning of our query into Zen language. The rejection of language in Zen discourse supports the non-linguistic approach whereas the counterbalancing statement that accepts the linguistic system and the logic of illogic in a Zen text like the *Diamond Sūtra* also provides a justification for the linguistic approach. As a way to resolve this dilemma of accepting both linguistic and non-linguistic approaches, and to map out the synergy of the two approaches in a Zen text, let us examine how language is explained in the *Platform Sūtra* by the Sixth Patriarch Huineng.

In the text, Huineng explains one's relation to language by employing thirty-six parallels. Huineng writes:

[Things] arise and cease, and thus leave two extremes. When explaining any *dharma*, do not stay away from the nature and characteristics [of things]. If someone asks you about *dharma*, use language so that the two extremes are completely explored [and exhausted]. All explanation should be given using parallels to show that things originate from each other, and eventually the two extremes [dualism] will be exhausted [explored to their end], and find no place to set themselves up.[22]

The thirty-six sets of parallels Huineng postulates are examples of individual entities which convention views as opposites. To name things is to give them an individual identity through opposition and contrast, and this process constitutes a major function of language. By claiming the independence of each being and giving it a separate identity, language functions against the idea of dependent co-arising. This world of provisional appearances, however, eventually reveals itself as only half of the truth, for when a name is used, it brings with it the other side of itself, that is, invisible aspects within the visible reality, which is the rupture of the other within the self. As Huineng states, "Darkness is not darkness by itself; because there is light there is darkness. Darkness is not darkness by itself; with light darkness changes, and with darkness light is revealed. Each mutually causes the other."[23]

The name, darkness, is understood by virtue of its relation to its other, that is, light. A problem arises *only when* one represses the invisible other within the name, and the name, darkness, claims an independent identity, refusing to admit its relation to light. Zen both confirms and rejects the linguistic function of naming by employing language to reveal the interrelatedness of each pair of oppositions. Huineng thus warns:

When you speak, outwardly, while remaining within form, free yourself from form; and inwardly, while remaining within emptiness, free yourself from emptiness. If you cling to emptiness, you will only be increasing your ignorance. If you cling to form, you will slander *dharma* with your false views. Without hesitation, you will say that one should not use written words. Once you say one should not use written words, then people should not speak, because speech itself is written words.[24]

With this citation, it is not difficult to see the echo of the Buddha's claim for the middle path as demonstrated in his undeclared thesis. The use of the similar pattern in the *Heart Sūtra* and the *Diamond Sūtra* has been pointed out, which we identified as acting out silence by refuting language. Linguistic expression, as Huineng states, must contain within itself the other side which articulation cannot bring forth because language functions based on its capacity to make distinctions. If light and darkness are understood as identical, language cannot function; not only that, if they are identical, why does one need two different linguistic expressions? On the other hand, the concept of light cannot stand by itself but exists dependently with darkness. This identity of difference and difference of identity becomes a core synergic relationship in Zen understanding of language. Despite the seemingly paradoxical nature of this definition of language in Zen, this is only another way of saying that language is an arbitrary sign system. Buddhist terminology for this arbitrariness would be emptiness. Language itself is a good example of emptiness. Being an arbitrary sign system, no signifier in a linguistic system can claim anything about the nature of the signified. Language functions on a tentative agreement between the signifier and the signified. That this agreement is tentative, however, is frequently forgotten: in the naming process, the signifier is identified with the essence of the signified, and this essence is further reified, paving the way to create a fixed Truth, which in turn assumes a central role in one's understanding of the world and of being.

A mistaken approach to language, with regard to the relationship between language and one's mode of thinking, is well articulated in the *Platform Sūtra* through an episode about a monk named Fada. After seven years' study of the *Lotus Sūtra*, Fada was still unable to realize the true meaning of the *Sūtra*. Reasoning that his failure was caused by the problem of the *Lotus Sūtra*, not by his capacity to decipher the text, Fada asks Huineng to resolve his doubts about the validity of the text. Huineng responds:

> If you practice with the mind, you turn the *Lotus*; if you do not practice with the mind, you are turned by the *Lotus*. If your mind is correct, you will turn the *Lotus*; if your mind is incorrect, you will be turned by the *Lotus*. If you open [your] Buddha-view, you turn the *Lotus*; if you open the sentient-being's view, you are turned by the same *Lotus*. Practicing by relying on *dharma*, you will turn the *Lotus*. Fada, upon hearing one word, you will be greatly awakened.[25]

What Huineng tries to teach to Fada is still meaningful in our time in understanding the role and function of language in Zen Buddhism. Language, like any entity in the world, is first of all a "form," and is in itself neither positive nor negative. As one's own tangible existence as a form is empty and at the same time is subject to the logic of dependent co-arising, so is language. If one rejects language because of its function of naming which provides a tentative identity for each entity named, then one should also reject one's own physical existence in favor of emptiness, against which the Buddhist discourse strenuously warns. The problem of language that Zen Buddhism takes pains to teach has less to do with the function of language as such than one's inability to read the identity of difference between form and emptiness.

2. From the Hermeneutical to the Existential

The co-existence of negation and affirmation of language, and thus of speaking out silence and negating language, reaches its peak in Zen Buddhist encounter-dialogue technique. In this context Korean Zen master Pojo Chinul's (1158–1210) posthumous work, *Kanhwa kyŏrŭi ron* (Treatise on Resolving Doubts about Huatou Meditation 1215; Henceforth *Treatise on Huatou Meditation*) offers us an instance to examine how the Buddha's silence, and the paradox of the *Prajñāpāramitā* literature, goes though yet another transformation in the Zen Buddhist tradition. Unlike most encounter dialogue literature which contains just a collection of dialogues between Zen masters and their disciples, in this work, Chinul deliberates on the meaning of encounter dialogue technique in the form of *huatou* meditation and offers his theory of Zen Buddhism as well as of encounter dialogue.

Before we move on, we need to clarify two different layers of Zen language. We will call the first layer the hermeneutical, and the second, the existential. By the hermeneutical, I refer to linguistic renderings of Buddhist doctrines. When we mention the alternative use of affirmation and negation in the *Heart Sūtra* and the *Diamond Sūtra* as well as in the Bodhidharma's teaching, the text is mainly addressing the problem of language on the hermeneutical level. The hermeneutical dimension in Zen language underscores the gap between the basic function of language, which is based on individual identity, and the reality Buddhism envisions through its theory of the middle path, which is relational. Huineng advised his students to use language so that binary opposites come together and shed light on each other and that the boundary marking the limits of an entity becomes invaded and redefined by others. In this deliberation of the relationship between language and identity, Huineng was illuminating the hermeneutical dimension of Zen language.

The existential dimension deals with language's relation to the subject. The existential dimension of Zen language concerns how linguistic rendering of Buddhist doctrine can be actualized in the existential reality of the subject. Deliberation of the existential dimension also includes the commonly held binary opposites of theory *vis-à-vis* practice, or theory *vis-à-vis* experience. The Fada episode in the *Platform Sūtra* belongs to this category. Huineng's advice to Fada, however, distinctly deviates from the conventional way of explaining the relationship between theory and practice.

When the theory and practice become an issue of a discourse, a common assumption is that these two exist on separate levels, and the relationship is established through a linear movement from the former to the latter. Huineng, however, suggests that Fada's understanding of his own nature changes his understanding of the contents of the text, not the other way around. Here we are approaching one of controversial issues in Zen Buddhism: the subitist and gradualist paradigms of enlightenment. We will not get into the discussion of the issue now,[26] but it should at least be mentioned that hermeneutic subitism is shared by both the subitist position of the Southern school of Zen Buddhism and the gradualist position of the Northern School of Zen Buddhism as their philosophical ground of Zen Buddhism itself. In this sense, hermeneutic subitism needs to be distinguished from existential subitism and existential gradualism. The basic Zen Buddhist tenet holds that the mind of the sentient being is the Buddha. Since Zen Buddhism defines enlightenment as the realization of one's own mind, enlightenment is sudden, immediate, and unmediated. Whether this journey from "me" to "my mind" will take place suddenly or gradually in physical clock time is a different issue. It is necessary to make a distinction between these two levels of subitism because the problem of language in both hermeneutical and existential dimensions has much to do with the subitist claim of the Zen hermeneutics of enlightenment.

The Zen hermeneutics of enlightenment poses a set of questions that deserve our consideration. First, if the realization of one's own mind constitutes the content of enlightenment, how does this internal and subjective movement of Zen enlightenment make a connection with the outside world? Secondly, if the mind is the Buddha, what is the function of the Buddhist scriptures and Buddhist doctrine itself? Fada himself did not ask this question to Huineng, when the latter explained how a text (*The Lotus Sūtra* in this case) would be turned around by the subject, which will take place only "after," not before, the subject realized the nature of her/his mind. Buddhist scripture by nature means teachings by the Buddha. If the subject needs to get to a stage of awakening in order to understand the meaning of scriptures, which were written to awaken the subject, we encounter a circular logic. It is not difficult to see that the myth of Huineng, who was illiterate at the time of appointment to patriarchship and remained so throughout his life, was designed to downplay the role of a text in Zen practice. However, the relative underplay of Buddhist scriptures in various Zen literature should not be read literally. The underplay should be understood within the context in which the story is built. On the other hand, it is also true that by overly emphasizing the subject's function in the process of one's realization of the ultimate reality and at the same time foregrounding the subject's independence from textual authority, the *Platform Sūtra* places itself in a position of being subject to a mysticism of its own creation.[27]

In his *Treatise on Huatou Meditation*, Chinul maps out the synergy involved in the multilayered relationship between language and meaning, the hermeneutical and the existential, and textual authority and Zen introspection.[28] In his exposition of these issues in the *Treatise on Huatou Meditation*, Chinul constantly compares Zen Buddhism with other Buddhist schools, especially the doctrinal teaching of Huayan Buddhism.

According to the Huayan theory of the fourfold realm of reality, the ultimate goal of enlightenment is the realization of the unobstructed interpenetration of phenomena (C. *shishi wuai*). The phenomenal world consists of diverse particularities. Each element, in its individuality, seems to exist independently, sometimes coming into conflict with others. Based on the basic tenet of dependent co-arising, which claims the interconnectedness of all beings, Huayan Buddhism posits the ultimate stage of enlightenment as the realization that the variety of existence in the phenomenal world is originally interrelated and, if understood from the perspective of the ultimate reality, devoid of conflict. Contrary to this, Zen Buddhism claims that the mind is Buddha.

From the Huayan Buddhist perspective, Zen Buddhism falls short of the Huayan teaching in its emphasis on the identity between the mind of the sentient being and that of the Buddha. Huayan Buddhism claims that when one practices Zen meditation, one tries to achieve enlightenment only in the realm of the noumenal by retreating into the realm of one's mind, which Huayan Buddhism interprets as a self-closure within Zen training. Huayanists consider the Huayan Buddhist teaching more comprehensive than that of Zen Buddhism because, whereas the Zen school teaches that "the mind is Buddha," thus limiting itself to the realm of the subject, the Huayan school emphasizes "the contemplation of the unimpeded interpenetration of all phenomena," encompassing diverse existence in the phenomenal world. This is exactly what a Huayan lecturer tried to teach Chinul, as described in the "Preface" to *Hwaŏmnon chŏryo* (Excerpts from the Exposition of the *Huayan jing*, 1207), which contains a biographical portrayal of one of three incidents of Chinul's awakening experiences.[29]

Chinul begins the "Preface" by entertaining his contemplation about how Huayan Buddhism's teaching of awakening would be different from that of the Zen school. Chinul writes: "In the autumn of the Year of the Snake of Great Stability (1185), I began a retreat on Mountain Haga, always keeping deep in my heart the Zen school's teaching that the mind is the Buddha, and thought to myself: 'if one does not meet this teaching, even though one practices for multiple kalpas, one will not be able to reach the realm of the sage'."[30] Even though Chinul was convinced of the authenticity of Zen teaching, he seems still unsure of the differences between Huayan and Zen approaches to awakening and eventually his query leads him to consult the issue with a Huayan lecturer, who advises Chinul: "If you contemplate only your own mind and do not contemplate the unimpeded interfusion of all phenomena, you will lose the fruit of the perfect virtue of the Buddha's enlightenment." Chinul is not convinced by this remark, thus he thinks to himself: "if one uses the mind to contemplate the phenomena, since the phenomena must have obstacles [among themselves] one will have to pursue worries in one's mind and there will be no end of it. If one is only to clear up one's mind and clarify its wisdom, then one hair and the world will become interfused, and this cannot possibly be something that happens outside of one's mind" *(HPC* 4.767).

On a surface level, Chinul poses his question as if it is a mere curiosity about the differences between Huayan and Zen Buddhism. However, Chinul's doubt is neither a passing curiosity nor about Huayan Buddhism, but is about the validity of the basic position of the Zen Buddhist claim that the mind is the Buddha. Otherwise, there would be no reason for Chinul, who just ascertained that the Zen teaching of the mind qua the Buddha is the only way to enter into the realm of the ultimate reality, to spend the next three years leafing through Buddhist scriptures, as he records in this "Preface." Further, if Chinul was fully convinced about the validity and efficiency of the mind being the source of one's awakening, and if he literally believed that brightening one's own mind is the only way to reach the realm of the ultimate reality, he did not need to scrutinize Buddhist scriptures.[31] Whatever caused Chinul's doubt in its deep level,—be it Zen teaching, Huayan theory, or the relationship between the two,—Chinul spent the next three years examining Buddhist scriptures, searching for the evidence of the validity of Zen teaching. After three years' perusal of Buddhist texts, Chinul arrives at the conclusion, which he describes as follows:

> What the World Honored One said with his mouth constitutes the teachings of the scholastic schools. What the patriarchs transmitted with their minds is Zen. What the Buddha said and what the patriarchs transmitted can certainly not be contradictory. Why do [students of both scholastic and Zen schools] not explore what is at the core [of these teachings], but instead, complacent only in their own training, vainly involve themselves with debates and waste their time? (*HPC* 4.767 c)

A certain disparity seems to exist between the issue over which Chinul agonized earlier and the conclusion he has arrived at here. Chinul's meditation on Huayan and Zen Buddhism began with his inquiry into the relationship between the subjective world emphasized by Zen as the locus for awakening and the objective world which Huayan Buddhism presents as a goal to be mastered in one's path to enlightenment. This can also be identified as a seeming gap between the world of noumenon in Zen Buddhism and the world of phenomena in Huayan Buddhism. The conclusion of Chinul's speculation as described above was to confirm the fundamental identity between the authority of the Buddha and of patriarchs. How did the subject-object polarization raised by Zen versus Huayan Buddhism lead Chinul to a conclusion of the intrinsic identity between the Buddha's teaching in the scholastic school (linguistic rendering) and the Zen patriarchs' emphasis of the mind-training (non-linguistic claim of Zen Buddhism)? In order to fill the gap, let us reconstruct the thought process that Chinul went through to reach his conclusion.

When Chinul consulted with the Huayan lecturer, he was concerned about how the introversive movement in Zen practice can be related to the external world. Zen Buddhist teaching for Chinul is characterized by the phrase "The mind is the Buddha" (K. *chŭksim chŭkpul*). If one's mind is the Buddha, and thus realization of the mind amounts to achieving awakening, how does this subjective action and realization not fall into solipsism but embrace the objective world? If the mind in Zen Buddhism is the source of enlightenment, how does Zen introversive exploration come to the understanding of the world without creating its own subjective idealism? Or is Zen meditation of the mind a form of subjective idealism? The Huayan master with whom Chinul consulted must have thought it was. Chinul himself seems to confirm the possibility of the solipsistic nature of Zen practice when he questions the validity of the Zen Buddhist emphasis of the mind over the Huayan teaching of contemplating phenomena.

Supposing one is able to realize the nature of one's mind so that one can experience the awakening to the interfusion of the subject and object, how, then, does one come out of this subjective world and prove its objective validity? If one is able to overcome the subjective confinement of this process of attaining awakening through the contemplation of the mind, why should any object in the outside world not play the same role as the mind does? One might consider that one's mind has a function which objects in the outside world do not have, because, after all, the mind is the locus through which we construct our views of the world. If this commonly held dualism between the mind and non-mind objects, and further of the subject and object, is relevant to Chinul's deliberation on the relationship between the Zen claim of the mind being the Buddha and the Huayan position on the unobstructed interpenetration of all things, two issues need clarification: first, how does this dualism fit in with the basic Buddhist tenet of dependent co-arising and emptiness?; secondly, how does the subjectively obtained insight into the ultimate reality earn its authenticity and legitimacy in this case? Ironically, Chinul finds answers to these questions in Huayan Buddhist doctrine.

One unique aspect of Chinul's Buddhist thought lies in the employment of Huayan Buddhism as a philosophical underpinning of Zen Buddhist doctrine. In this context, Robert E. Buswell evaluates Chinul's exposition of Huayan Buddhism in *Wŏndon sŏngbul ron* (The Treatise on the Complete and Sudden Attainment of Buddhahood) as the most important contribution of Chinul to East Asian Buddhism. Buswell writes: "By demonstrating the Hwaŏm [Huayan] thought can be used for the philosophical underpinnings of the Sŏn [Zen] approach, this work [*Wŏndon sŏngbul ron*] can, without exaggeration, be considered Chinul's most important contribution to East Asian Buddhist philosophy"[32] In a similar spirit, a Korean scholar subtitled his translation of Chinul's *Treatise on Huatou Meditation* as "The Dialectic of Huayan and

Kanhua Zen," underscoring the importance of Zen-Huayan connection in Chinul's Zen philosophy.[33] The amalgamation of Huayan philosophy of the doctrinal school and Zen Buddhism of meditation in Chinul also became a source of criticism by contemporary Korean Buddhists against Chinul's Zen Buddhism.[34] However, a close examination of Chinul's use of textual authority offered by Huayan Buddhism as a legitimation of the Zen claim of the mind qua the Buddha clarifies several issues essential to Zen Buddhism, about which many Zen texts offer only ambiguous explanations.

Chinul describes his journey from the time of his conversation with the Huayan master until his arrival at the above cited conclusion as follows:

> Having returned to the mountain [after the encounter with the Huayan lecturer], I sat down and examined scriptures, searching for the Buddha's words which would comply with the school of the mind. Three winters and summers had passed by, when I came to read in the chapter of "Appearance of the Tathāgata" of the *Huayan jing* a metaphor stating "A single mote contains a thousand volumes of scriptures." The passage is later explained with, "The wisdom of the Tathāgata is like that. It is equipped in the bodies of the sentient beings; however, the common and foolish people do not know it, nor do they realize it." I placed the scripture on my head [with joy] and was not aware of tears coming out. (*HPC* 4.767 c)

Chinul had initially rejected the Huayan lecturer's advice that the mind-training of Zen Buddhism would lead one to solipsism. Chinul also considered that the contemplation of the phenomenal world would cause unceasing obstacle to the practitioners. However, the above passage indicates that Chinul admitted the validity of the Huayan teaching of the unobstructed interpenetration of phenomena. We can construct Chinul's reasoning at the moment of his awakening described above as follows.

First, if even a single mote can contain a thousand volumes of Buddhist scriptures, the symbolic meaning of this metaphor suggests that all the entities in the world have equal ontological values. In this case, the superiority of the mind as an object for contemplation is rejected and the mind versus non-mind dualism is therefore resolved.

Second, if a single mote and the mind of the practitioner have the same ontological value, then, looking into one's mind cannot create a solipsistic introversive approach to the ultimate reality; instead, the realization of the nature of the mind should be equal to the realization of the reality of any entities in the world; the potential danger of the subject-object dualism is removed.

Third, the metaphor of one mote containing a thousand volumes of scriptures also resolves the tension between the linguistic rendering of the scholastic school and the Zen emphasis of the mind-training in rejection of textual authority. The linguistic versus non-linguistic dualism is resolved.

Fourth, if a single mote and the mind of the subject are ontologically equal and, at the same time, they are all reflections of the wisdom of the Buddha, the investigation of the mind earns its own validity and authenticity as the realization of the Buddha's teaching. All the Buddhist scriptures themselves should be the endorsers for Zen meditation of the mind. The problem of the authenticity and legitimacy of the Zen school is settled.[35]

By resolving these problems in the manner we have discussed thus far, Chinul inevitably encounters a new problem. By admitting the Huayan doctrine as a philosophical underpinning of Zen Buddhism, Chinul actually came to refute the very identity of Zen Buddhism. That is, with the confirmation of the above four points, the superiority of the mind-meditation over the phenomenal world was rejected; the emphasis of the non-linguistic dimension of Zen Buddhism was denied; and at the same time, the claim of a non-textual based teaching was negated as well. If this is the case, what is the point of having Zen Buddhism as an independent school separated from Huayan Buddhism? What is the difference between the doctrinal school of Huayan Buddhism and the meditational school of Zen?

Chinul's *Treatise on Huatou Meditation* addresses this exact issue. In the text, Chinul poses five questions asked by a fictional inquisitor, who demands answers from Chinul on why Zen Buddhism claims to be an independent school when its teaching is all spelled out in Huayan school's doctrines. From the perspective of Huayan Buddhism, there is no reason for the Zen school to reclaim its superiority when Huayan teaching offers the most complete teaching of the Buddha. In response to the claim, in the *Treatise* Chinul has the imaginary inquisitor make the following five challenges regarding the legitimacy of the Zen school's *huatou* meditation. The inquisitor asks:

1. "Huayan Buddhist teaching has already clearly expressed that there is nothing to take or reject in the unimpeded dependent co-arising of the realm of reality (*dharmadhātu*).[36] How then does the Zen school define the 'ten diseases' as that which should be rejected and insist on *huatou* meditation?" (*HPC* 4.732 a)

2. "It has been mentioned that the nature of an entity is characterized by complete interpenetration with other entities and that the doctrine of dependent co-arising postulates that there should be no conflict among entities. If that is the case, supposing one has established one's own mode of thinking, how could it bring about obstacles?" (*HPC* 4.733 b)

3. "The *Prajñāpāramitā Sūtra* [Scripture of the Perfection of Wisdom] states, 'there is neither wisdom nor attainment,' and the Sudden school teaches, 'if one thought does not arise, that is called the achievement of the Buddha nature'. Is what you said not the same as these teachings, in terms of the idea that one should free oneself from linguistic expressions and eliminate speculation?" (*HPC* 4.733 b)

4. "The Sudden school is also critical of verbal teachings and encourages the practitioner to leave words and speculation, eliminate form, and get free from the mind. The same is the case with the *huatou* of the Zen school: it aims for the destruction of bad knowledge and bad understanding, and, by dismantling attachments, reveals the essence of the school. Both schools share the same method of initiating students. How then do you say that in the Sudden school one accomplishes the Buddha nature only on the theoretical level and has yet to realize the non-obstruction of the realm of reality, whereas the explosive power of the shortcut approach of Zen Buddhism enables one to experience in person the One Mind of the realm of reality and naturally embodies the virtue of non-obstruction? Since both practices are based on freeing the practitioner from the constraints of language and speculation, how can it be that one is biased, the other, perfect?" (*HPC* 4.733 c-734 a)

5. "[Based on your argument, one should say] those who attain enlightenment in the Zen school belong to the same category as followers of the Complete school, though not with those of the Sudden school, in that they realize the unimpeded interpenetration of the realm of reality. Why is, then, the Zen school so persistent in identifying itself as an esoteric teaching separated from the Complete school of Huayan Buddhism?" (*HPC* 4.736 b)

The entirety of the five questions are cited here in order to demonstrate the rigorousness with which Chinul pursues the topic of the relationship between Huayan and Zen Buddhism as well as his agonizing efforts to clarify the identity and differences between the two. A number of issues need clarification in order to fully digest these questions. However, at least one thing should be clear: the entire treatise is about the identity of Zen Buddhism. In answering these questions, Chinul does not claim that in its teaching Zen is any different from the teachings of many other Buddhist schools that appeared in the evolution of Buddhism. Chinul admits that Zen Buddhism does not offer any doctrinal renovations. Chinul repeatedly convinces his inquisitor that the idea of cutting off language (non-linguistic claim) does not exclusively belong to the Zen school. Nor is the nature of the achieved goal through Zen practice different from that described by Huayan Buddhism. Chinul's ready admission of the identity between Huayan teaching and Zen Buddhism leads Chinul's inquisitor to ask at the end: if there is no difference between the two, why should Zennists be so insistent that they follow a special teaching through the training of the mind?

Our earlier definition of the hermeneutical and the existential can be of help in answering this question. To Chinul, Zen teaching, especially Zen *huatou* meditation, is first of all a movement from the hermeneutical to the existential dimensions in Buddhist teaching. This transition from the hermeneutical to the existential is closely related to the way language functions in Zen discourse and its influence on one's thought system. Chinul's own classification of Buddhist schools offered in this *Treatise* meaningfully demonstrates this aspect of Chinul's Zen Buddhism. Compared to the five layered taxonomy of Buddhist schools proposed by Fazang, the alleged third patriarch of Huayan Buddhism,[37] Chinul's classification is much simpler. It contains only two layers, namely, the scholastic schools and the Zen schools. The former category is composed of the non-Huayan scholastic schools and Huayan Buddhism; the latter is composed of Huayan Zen and Huatou Zen. This demonstrates how much Chinul felt close to Huayan Buddhism, even while he was advocating the efficiency of Zen *huatou* meditation. The measure to distinguish among the four groups, that is, non-Huayan scholastic teachings, Huayan Buddhism, Huayan Zen, and Huatou Zen, is the proportion of the hermeneutical and the existential in these teachings. We can locate the Non-Huayan scholastic teachings on the far end of the hermeneutical side and Huatou Zen on the far end of the existential side; in between these two extremes we find Huayan Buddhism and Huayan Zen.

Chinul's responses to the five questions posed in the *Treatise* are repetitive but increasingly emphatic assertions regarding the identity and difference between Zen Buddhism and other Buddhist schools culminating in the final section where he endorses the necessity of practicing *huatou* meditation. Chinul tries to quell the doubts of his inquisitor by confirming the intrinsic identity between Zen Buddhism and Huayan teaching on the hermeneutical level. Gradually, Chinul leads the challenger to the realm of difference between the two schools in the existential dimension.

In the first question, the inquisitor asks the validity of the Zen school's criticism of what are known as the Ten Zen Diseases. The Ten Zen Diseases are ten incorrect ways of practicing *huatou* meditation, which Chinul created based on the twelfth century Chinese Zen Master Dahui Zonggao (1089-1163)'s discussion on *huatou* meditation.[38] Chinul enumerates the Ten Zen Diseases one by one in the later section of the *Treatise on Huatou Meditation.*[39] What is at stake with the Ten Diseases, however, is not so much its content as the very act of making distinctions. If there were to be right and wrong ways of practicing *huatou* or of anything, this in itself indicates a conflict with the Huayan teaching of the unobstructed interpenetration of all things. To the inquisitor in the *Treatise*, who represents the Huayan Buddhist position, the idea of counting something wrong, and thus making distinctions between right and wrong, is problematic. One might wonder, if Huayanists (and Zennists as well) consider the distinction between right and wrong so problematic, what would be the position of ethics in Huayan philosophy. We will take up this issue in the later sections of this book.

Chinul agrees with his inquisitor that in terms of "meaning, theory, and analysis," the Ten Zen Diseases are also subject to the conditioned causality and thus cannot be either right or wrong as they are. He, thus, concurs with his inquisitor in denying the validity of identifying the Ten Diseases, and writes: "If one is ready to make a distinction and choose between the destroyer and the destroyed, between what should be taken and rejected, that is an obvious indication that one is still under the sway of the trace of words, which disturbs one's mind. How then could that be called the right way of confronting a *huatou*, whose only function is to be a guide?" (*HPC* 4.733 a). However, Chinul also emphasizes that as much as the Ten Diseases do not have intrinsic essence of their own, it is also true that there are some modes of approaches that the subject needs to avoid in order to realize the ultimate reality. The Ten Diseases do not exist as an objective reality but all the same they do in the mind of the subject. The Zen discursive pattern of coexistence of the negation and affirmation is employed again by Chinul to explain the relationship between the objective world of the ultimate reality as postulated by Huayan Buddhism and the existential reality of the subject that Zen addresses.

Chinul does not consider the scholastic rendering of the ultimate reality deficient as it is. In fact, he defends the validity of the linguistic rendering of the ultimate reality offered by the Huayan school and confirms that the Ten Zen Diseases are only provisional. However, Chinul is also clear about his position that the hermeneutically rendered reality of the objective world is not always reflected in the existential reality of the subject. From the reality of the hermeneutical dimension "All kinds of obstacles are themselves the ultimate enlightenment" (*HPC* 4.732 c) [40] because obstacles themselves do not have self-nature and are subject to the conditioned causality. However, as much as this ultimate reality is true, it is also true that the existential dimension does not always follow it. What are the causes of the gap between the hermeneutical and the existential in the subject's world? Chinul states: "The theories [describing the ultimate state of Huayan Buddhism], though most complete and marvelous, are [expressions of] what one heard, understood, thought, and calculated based on one's consciousness and feelings" (*HPC* 4.733a). Chinul in this context cites Dahui to warn about the structural problem in one's thinking process: "the influence of established thought being so strong, the mind in search of enlightenment itself becomes a barrier and thus the correct knowledge of one's mind has rarely obtained a chance to manifest itself. However, this barrier does not come from outside nor is it something that should be regarded as an exception" (*HPC* 4.732c). Chinul further states: "The very basis of the so-called Ten Diseases is in fact one's desire to get enlightened" (*HWP* 4.732 c). The problematics of the situation at this point become internalized and subjectivized. Subjectivity, which is at the core of modernist thinkers, is also a major theme in Chinul's Zen Buddhist philosophy. After all, it is the subject's desire that creates a gap between the ultimate reality and the reality of the subject.

The problem of subjectivity appears as an important issue in Chinul's response to the second question. By subjectivity I mean the subject's capacity to perceive, understand the outside world, process thoughts, and respond to external outside stimuli. On the hermeneutical level, the traditional opposition between the subject and object cannot have much meaning in the context of Zen Buddhism. However, the division between the two still exists in Zen Buddhism on the existential level. For Chinul, Zen Buddhism addresses, among other issues, the problem of subjectivity.

In the first question, Chinul juxtaposes Zen with Huayan, equating them in terms of its vision of the ultimate reality and at the same time distinguishing them in terms of how to approach it. In the second question, Chinul's inquisitor still holds onto the identity between Huayan and Zen and demands that Chinul provide a further explanation. Chinul responds:

> Do you not understand? *The Complete Enlightenment Sūtra* states: "If someone has managed to completely eliminate worries, his realm of reality has been purified. But the idea that one has acquired purity of the realm of reality will create a barrier, which shows that one has not yet obtained the freedom of complete enlightenment."[41] If even realizing the purity of the realm of reality become an impediment because of acquired knowledge, what more can we say about students in our time who try to configure by means of their feelings and six consciousnesses the conditioned arising that is totally free from all obstacles? How could they earn a true view born of liberation? (*HPC* 4.733 b)

The subject's capacity to create selfhood by means of "feelings and six consciousnesses," the accumulation of which modern philosophy frequently identifies as 'subjectivity,' is the very ground that distorts the knowledge obtained by the subject from Chinul's Zen Buddhist perspective. The feelings and six consciousnesses (K. *sikjŏng*), which Chinul repeatedly identifies in the *Treatise* as the cause of the problem for the practitioner, are also the very condition for understanding the ultimate reality proposed by the Buddha. Chinul's discussion of subjectivity, then, has two sides, and the investigation of one's mind is critical in this sense. The mind is allegedly the locus in which the gap between the existential reality of the subject and the hermeneutical reality represented in linguistic rendering takes place. But the irony of this approach is that it is also only through the mind that this distortion can be 'corrected.' The movement is circular, but this seemingly circular logic is to be differentiated from tautology in the sense that this circle is like the "hermeneutic circle,"—to borrow the term from the twentieth century Continental philosophy—in which the emergence of meaning becomes possible.

Both Chinul's Zen Buddhism and the hermeneutics of the twentieth century Continental philosophy attempt to address the problem of subjectivity without creating another subjectivity by envisioning shared space that belongs neither to the subject nor to the object. Complexity arising out of identifying subjectivity as a determining feature of Chinul's view of Zen Buddhism is similar in nature to those in various Buddhist situations. That is, the point is not that subjectivity is wrong, but subjectivity is not possible without being the subject's illusion. As Chinul states, "Seen from the perspective of the ultimate sense, deluded thought itself is empty, since it lacks self-nature. It is then not possible to remove it. All the dharmas are themselves originally true nature, and it is not possible to cut off or destroy the marvelous functioning of dependent co-arising" (*HPC* 4.734 b).

By identifying Chinul's Zen Buddhism as philosophy addressing the problem of subjectivity, we challenge one of major criticisms against Zen Buddhism: that is, Zen subjectivism. Even though Zen Buddhism emphasizes the importance of the mind, it does not subscribe subjectivism; instead, for Chinul, Zen problematizes subjectivity and Zen practice demands constant deconstruction of subjectivism. In this context, Zen Buddhism is keen to the function of language in the subject's mode of thinking. As Chinul emphasizes, to mark the limits of language and thought is not a Zen specific feature but is visible in other non-Zen Buddhist schools. Chinul addresses this issue in his response to the third question, in which the inquisitor challenges Chinul about the major difference between the Sudden school and Zen *huatou* meditation, Chinul states:

> . . . the idea of leaving language behind and eliminating speculation is found in all five teachings. Each teaching has something to say about being free from linguistic constraints in order to teach the practitioner to overcome linguistic description and grasp the seminal message. . . . Inside the gate of enlightenment [i.e., at the final stage of enlightenment] they all free themselves from linguistic expressions as well as established frames of thought. If language and speculation are not to be overcome, how can we say that one has experienced enlightenment? (*HPC*, 4.733c)

By the same token, both the Sudden school and Huayan Buddhism teach that the nature of the principle leaves language and abandons forms. Thus the Sudden school also teaches, "If even one thought does not arise, that is called the achievement of Buddhahood" (*HPC* 4.733 c). The Huayan school as well teaches, Chinul explains, that "The fruition of enlightenment leaves thought behind and is transmitted by mind" (*HPC* 4.733 c). The point to Chinul, however, is that all these teachings "discuss from the perspective of those who have already entered into realization" (*HPC* 4.733 c). This is another way of saying that in all of these approaches, the teachings are discussed from the hermeneutical level without a consideration of the existential reality of the subject. This is also why Chinul characterized the awakening in the Sudden school as the realization of "the inexperienced *dharmakāya* Buddha" (K. *sobŏpsin*) (*HPC* 4.733 c).[42]

For Chinul, all five schools that appear in Fazang's taxonomy explain the "theory" of the process of awakening. The movement from scholastic schools to Zen can then be identified as that from doctrine to soteriology and also from theory to practice. Even though these characterizations cannot be wrong, they also cannot be sufficient, because, if Zen is an expression for the primacy of soteriology over doctrine and practice over theory, does this imply that other Buddhist schools are not concerned about ultimate realization and practice? One cannot make such a radical gesture, without a specific intention in mind and without risking over-generalization. Earlier we identified this movement as that from the hermeneutical to the existential which is similar to the previous two paradigms in the sense that the hermeneutical dimension is close to the doctrinal and theoretical level whereas the existential dimension is close to the soteriological and practicing level.

If we follow Chinul's logic in the *Treatise*, we come to a rather interesting conclusion. First, the Zen school does not offer any doctrinal renovation of Buddhism; hence one can even say that the main concern of Zen Buddhism is not Buddhist doctrine itself, since Buddhist doctrines are all already spelled out by existing Buddhist schools, especially by Huayan Buddhism. At the same time, the Buddhist teaching which Zen represents is not and cannot be different from the teachings expounded by these other schools. Second, the problem Zen tries to address concerns how this linguistic rendering of the real is related to the existential reality of the subject. This justifies Zen emphasis on the mind which is the cause of potential distortion of the hermeneutical efforts of the subject in understanding the linguistic dimension of Buddhism as it appears in Buddhist scriptures. As cited earlier, Chinul confirmed that written texts are "what the World Honored One said with his mouth" and, if this is the case, there is no way, at least for Chinul, that Zen Buddhism can be a negation of language or scriptures. Instead, Zen addresses and further foregrounds the subject's relation to language and language's function in the subject's understanding of reality.

Chinul considers that language in Buddhist teachings other than *huatou* meditation is understood as a tool to impart the hermeneutical aspect of the Buddha's teaching. The *huatou* employs language not to communicate meaning but to facilitate an environment in which the subject makes a transition from the hermeneutical to the existential. That is, *huatou* is neither a healer of disease (K. *p'abyŏng*) nor a presentation of truth (K. *chŏnje*). Chinul writes: "The moment one tends toward the slightest idea that the *huatou* must be the presentation of the ultimate truth or that it enables one to treat one's defects, one is already under the power of the limitations set by linguistic expression" (*HPC* 4.733 b). The *huatou* is like a catalyst: as it is, it is not pertinent to what is happening to the subject; it simply facilitates the process of enlightenment without itself being involved or changed by the transformation. The transforming function of the *huatou* is also for Chinul the *raison d'être* of Zen Buddhism. This being the case, in his responses to questions four and five, Chinul extensively discusses the nature and function of the encounter-dialogue (or *gong'an*) and *huatou* meditation, focusing on the inner alchemy operating between the subject and language.

3. *Huatou Language and Zen Awakening*

In discussing the synergy between the subject and language in *huatou* meditation, Chinul proposes three paradigms as the key to understanding this operation. The first is the distinction between the "live word" (K. *hwalgu*; C. *huoju*) and the "dead word" (K. *sagu*; C. *shiju*), second, between the "direct involvement with word" (K. *ch'amgu*; C. *canju*) and the "direct involvement with meaning" (K. *ch'amŭi*; C. *canyi*); and third, the Three Mysterious Gates (K. *samhyŏnmun*; C. *sanxuanmen*).

Chinul emphasizes the importance of the first distinction by citing Dahui: "If one obtains enlightenment by a direct confrontation with the live word, one will not ever forget it; if one works with the dead word, one will not even be able to save oneself [not to speak of being unable to provide help for others to become awakened]" (*HPC* 4.737a).[43] Later in the *Treatise*, Chinul also states: "Practitioners in our time, in their attempt to resolve doubts, work vainly on the former [the direct involvement with meaning] and have yet to practice the latter [the direct involvement with word]" (*HPC* 4.737a). The Three Mysterious Gates is believed to have first been proposed by Chinese Zen master Linji (?-867). The Three Mysterious Gates contain the threefold mystery: Mystery in the Essence (K. *ch'ejunghyŏn*; C. *tizhongxuan*), Mystery in Words (K. *kujunghyŏn*; C. *juzhongxuan*), and Mystery in the Mystery (K. *hyŏnjunghyŏn*; C. *xuanzhongxuan*). The context in the *Treatise* indicates that Chinul urges practitioners to practice the live word, not the dead word, and to get involved with word, not with meaning so that one can embody the Mystery in the Mystery. What is not clear is exactly "what" these categories—the live word over the dead word, the direct involvement with word over with meaning, and the Mystery in the Mystery—denote, and "why" the first category in the first two groups and the Mystery in the Mystery is preferable to the rest in one's practice of Zen Buddhism.

Frustrations the readers of the *Treatise* have to deal with in their attempts to understand these three groups are related to the perennial Zen problem: Chinul never clearly defines exactly what each set represents. The only places in which one gets a glimpse of the possible meaning of these terminologies turn out to be less than satisfactory in helping us to understand them. Consider the following passage. Chinul states: "The Zen practitioner with unbounded capacity, in practicing the *huatou* and learning its clandestine meaning, does not fall into the ten diseases of speculative understanding; . . . Shaking the foundation all of a sudden, the realm of reality will emerge in lucidity, as unimpeded virtue becomes clear by itself" (*HPC* 4.733 c). Or, "One by one, free yourself from them [the ten diseases] and further free yourself from even the idea of whether or not you've freed yourself, or whether or not you are under the influence of the ten diseases. All of a sudden the flavorless and groundless *huatou* will explode as if shaking the earth, then the realm of reality of the One Mind will illuminate itself" (*HPC* 4.735 a).

Despite the frustration arising out of the difficulty in systematically interpreting Chinul's three paradigms, one should resist a temptation to transform the frustration into its opposite and makes a claim for Zen romanticism, Zen mannerism, or Zen naturalism. We will not go into detailed discussion of the tendencies I have identified here as Zen romanticism, Zen mannerism, and Zen naturalism. To give them a rather rough definition, Zen romanticism is a tendency to explain away the hermeneutic difficulty involved in Zen literature with a claim that Zen does not rely on language, so by getting rid of language—hence no clear definition of terms employed in Zen literature—one will *naturally* understand the teaching of Zen Buddhism. Zen naturalism takes a similar path by further emphasizing that Zen considers theorization as an artificial creation by humans; by removing theorization, one will *naturally* reach the teaching of Zen Buddhism. Zen mannerism combines the above two, and would consider even such attempts themselves to contradict the gist of Zen teaching which Zen mannerism claims to be "let-it-happen" or "just-do-it."

Consolidation of the three tendencies creates what John R. McRae dubbes as the "Zen of Anything," a Zen genre which he explains as "the inevitable side-effect of D. T. Suzuki's missionary success" in Western Buddhism.[44] This Zen of Anything contends that "Zen is simply an attitude of undistracted concentration that can be applied to any human endeavor,"[45] and thus by getting rid of whatever is considered to be an obstacle to achieve one's goal—most of the time the victims in such a sweepstake are language, thinking, and theorization—one will find a way to accomplish the goal in an authentic way.

Instead of entertaining such an idea, we should consider the possibility that the reluctance or impossibility of offering a definite description of the live word or the involvement with word can be read as a message of its own. This applies as much to Chinul's *Treatise* as it does to many other Zen Buddhist literature. The radically open invitation to interpretation in Zen literature cannot be an attempt to negate language or theory. Like the Buddha's undeclared thesis, which resists classification and representation of the existing logic, Chinul's live word and the involvement with the word is another occasion of speaking out silence, carrying the philosophical spirit of acting out the limits of the existing mode of thinking. The Buddha's undeclared thesis was one of such incidents, as was the alternate use of negation and affirmation in the *Prajñāpāramitā* literature and to some degree Heidegger's discussion of the nothing.

Let us then try to unpack the meaning of the three paradigms Chinul employs in his exposition of *huatou* meditation. We will begin with the Three Mysterious Gates since, compared to the other two paradigms, the threefold mystery is relatively well-described in the text. Chinul presents the Three Mysterious Gates as a step-by-step measure, the higher stage ameliorating the problems in the lower stages. Whether this actually involves the gradualism in a physical clock time or whether Chinul employed them as hermeneutically gradual is still debatable.

In the first stage, which is named the Mystery in the Essence, one realizes the ultimate reality on the level of noumenon. This stage is more or less equivalent to the unobstructed interpenetration of phenomena in Huayan Buddhism. In the second stage of the Mystery in Words, the first stage of the Mystery in the Essence becomes a target of criticism, primarily because the realization in the first stage is considered to have been attained only on a theoretical level. This is also relevant with Chinul's argument as to the sameness and differences between Huayan and Zen schools. The unobstructed interpenetration of phenomena, which Huayan Buddhism projects as the ultimate reality, is itself "mystery" (K. *hyŏn*; C. *xuan*) in the sense that the vision violates the common sense logic. However, since the mystery here is presented through theorization, Chinul considers that this theorization is inevitably subject to subjectivity in the process of the subject's assessment of the vision, which undermines the subject's understanding of the content of the mystery. Hence, the second stage of the Mystery in Words. For the examples of this second stage, Chinul uses well-known *huatous*, or "critical phrases," including "A dog does not have the Buddha nature," "A dried shit stick," or "Three pounds of flax." With these *huatous*, the subject faces a situation in which the common sense logic goes bankrupt and language is used against itself. In the process of this experience, the subject becomes deprived of the room to entertain its own subjective interpretation. We will come back to the issue of why the critical phrases of *huatou* facilitate such an experience in the subject. Chinul maintains that the subject's overcoming of subjectivity in the second stage of the Mystery in Words is not sufficient for the final enlightenment, and his reason for this is noteworthy. In the second stage, the very idea of one's being free from the fetters of subjectivity will in turn become an obstacle and constrain one's freedom. The subject, thus, must go through one more step, the Mystery in the Mystery, in which s/he shakes off the very idea that s/he has dismantled all the limitations imposed on her/himself.

Each of the three stages is a step that the subject needs to overcome in order to move on to the next stage. The threefold mystery, however, could have four, five, six, or any number of stages in the sense that each new stage points out the limits of the previous stage. That is not because the previous stage contains a default as it is, but because in the process of the subject's digestion of the message, the subject subjectifies the message. The subject creates a gap between the original message and the one s/he internalized. In that manner, the process generates constraints on the subject. The process of delimiting the existing mode of thinking itself, then, should be one major activity of this paradigm of the threefold mystery.

To further clarify what we have discussed so far, let us incorporate the other two paradigms into the discussion of the Three Mysterious Gates. By putting them together, we can create three mixed groups: the first group includes the dead word and the Mystery in the Essence pair; the second group, the involvement with meaning and the Mystery in Words pair; and the third group includes the live word, involvement with word, and the Mystery in the Mystery. Below are examples Chinul employed to explain each group, which I identify by number:

> (1) If one thought does not arise, that is called the Buddha. (*HPC* 4.734 b)
> (2) "The oak tree in the garden."[46]
> (3) Master Shuiliao asked Mazu, while they were out gathering rattan: "What does it mean that Patriarch Bodhidharma came from the west?"
> "Come close, I'll let you know," Mazu replied.
> As soon as Shuiliao approached him, Mazu kicked him in the chest, knocking him to the ground. Shuiliao picked himself up without being aware of it, and burst into a big laugh, clapping his hands.
> "What did you learn that makes you laugh like that?" Mazu asked.
> "A hundred thousand teachings on dharma, countless mysterious meanings, all are understood to the core at the tip of one hair," Shuiliao said. Mazu suddenly didn't care about him. (*HPC* 4.735 b)

The first quotation provides a theoretical rendering of Buddhist doctrine, especially of the unimpeded interpenetration of Huayan Buddhism. Compared to the first quotation, the second passage, which is one of the well-known *gong'ans,* uses terse language and opaque logic. The entire dialogue goes as follows: "A monk asked Zhaozhou: 'What is the meaning of the First Patriarch's coming from the West?' 'The oak tree in the garden', Zhaozhou replied." The student in the third passage asks: "What does it mean that Patriarch Bodhidharma came from the West?" This time the answer Shuiliao received from Mazu was neither a logical explanation nor a mysterious response. He was kicked by Shuiliao and the story presents it as a moment of enlightenment. Gestures like shouting, silencing, and striking are given as examples of the Mystery in the Mystery.

Having presented the Mazu episode, Chinul observes: "How is it possible that Shuiliao understands a hundred thousand teachings on *dharma* and countless mysterious meanings to the core by being kicked by Mazu? The episode clearly expresses that, for those with the ability to encompass the Zen approach, entering into awakening has nothing to do with the Sudden school's method, which insists on cutting off language to create the state of leaving thought behind" (*HPC* 4.735 b).[47] The implication is that "at the final stage of enlightenment one does not need many words," not that one should not use language at all (*HPC* 4.735 c).

In respect to the function of language, in the transformation from the first to the third stage of non-linguistic gesture, two aspects are noteworthy. The first is a movement from a theoretical rendering (a neutral expression) to performance (which is wholly context bound). The second is a movement from prosaic expression to poetization. As the narrative style changes from prosaic philosophical discourse to poetization pregnant with literary imagination, the relationship between the subject and language also changes. In theoretical renderings such as "one phrase is so clear that it encompasses all the phenomena in the world" (*HPC* 4.733 a), the gap between the subject and object as well as between the reader and linguistic expression is clear. Applying the idea to religious practice, we find that theoretical renderings provide the goal (or the enlightened state) at which the practitioner is aiming to arrive. The goal, however, is described without concern for the practitioner's existential reality. Nor does the phrase provide any means for the practitioner to achieve this goal. This is why Chinul emphasizes several times in his *Treatise* that Buddhist teachings other than *huatou* meditation express the goal to be achieved and describe it from the perspective of those who have already attained enlightenment.

Chinul criticizes passages like "In this endless world, between me and others, there is no gap even as infinitesimal as the thinness of a hair" (*HPC* 4.733 a) as an example of the dead word because "they create in the practitioner's mind barriers derived from understanding" (*HPC* 4.733 a). In opposition to the dead word, Chinul makes this observation about the live word:

> Considered in terms of the short-cut approach [of *huatou* meditation], when one experiences in person the esoteric transmission, the experience takes place at the point when one frees oneself from the influence of linguistic expressions and interpretations as well as from what s/he has heard and been thinking. If even such a great theory as the unimpeded dependent co-arising of the realm of reality risks the danger of becoming an obstacle due to the limitations of one's interpretation, unless one was born with a great capacity equipped with great wisdom, how could one clearly understand it and make it his/her own?" (*HPC* 4.733 b).

Once again we encounter the issue of subjectivity. From the perspective of Chinul's Zen Buddhism, the subject's desire and capability to create a harmonized and understandable interpretation of the world around the subject and of others creates, ironically, a gap between the subject and the outside world. Incomplete knowledge of the object in the subject's mental picture of the world and subsequent distortions regarding the nature of the object are the inevitable consequences of the subject-object dualistic paradigm. The subject is "not" the object, and thus cannot have the perfect knowledge of the object. The seeming harmony that the subject believes to have achieved in the process of the subject's acquaintance with the reality of the object is reconciliation at best, and the reconciliation was attained from the position of the subject. At worst, it is violence that the subject exercises on the object in order to place the object within the perimeter of the subject's thought system so that the outside world stops being a threat to the subject by remaining in the realm of the unknown.

When Zen Buddhism constantly criticizes language and theorization, it is because they are the very tools for the subject to carry out this process of domesticating the outside world and tailoring it according to the mode of thinking most familiar to the subject. What we call self-knowledge goes through the same process of the subject's taming of the object. In this case the subject would put her/himself in the position of the object, which makes the entire process an oxymoron. The Ten Zen Diseases, with which Chinul opened his *Treatise*, can be understood as ten philosophical items that the subject employs in the process of the subject's efforts to realign outside reality with the subject's established mode of thinking. When Chinul states that the practitioner's desire to obtain enlightenment is the cause of the Ten Zen Diseases, Chinul's logic reflects our discussion.

The *huatou* meditation, especially the live word and the direct involvement with word are tools to readjust the subject-object relationship so that it acts out the Buddha's silence, or the middle path, or the non-substantial identity. The nature of non-substantial identity is such that it demands a radical change in the subject-object relationship. We will at this point describe the new subject-object relationship Chinul tries to facilitate through the three paradigms as emerging in the art of interrogation.

4. Huatou Meditation and the Art of Interrogation

Zen encounter dialogue, or *gong'an* practice, is characterized by a gap between the question asked by students and the answer given by Zen masters. Students pose a query about the nature of Buddhism or of Zen practice, and Zen masters respond to the query with undecipherable answers, which usually leaves students in a state of bewilderment. Readers in our time might understand this situation in such a way that they might wonder why ancient Zen masters were so unwilling to share their knowledge with their students. However, we should understand this reluctance of Zen masters in the context of the silence of the Buddha. Consider Zhaozhou's *wu huatou*, one of the most well known *gong'an* cases. A student asked whether a dog has the Buddha-nature, and Zhaozhou is recorded to have answered with "wu" (literally no, or nothing). If we take the answer literally, there are only a limited number of interpretations that can be drawn from this answer: (1) No, the dog does not have the Buddha nature; (2) no, I do not know; (3) no, it is none of your concern. The practitioner eventually arrives at a dead-end, the point where possible answers are exhausted. Wither does this exhaustibility and exhaustion of the answer lead the questioner?

When a question is answered, the question ceases to be a question and turns into a statement. When a question "What is 'A'?" is posed, "A" is in an open state. The moment this "A" is answered, "A" is no longer "A," but *the* "A," as defined by the subject. To ask "what is . . . ?" is to ask about the essence of that which is being asked about. The question demands definition, distinction, and naming. By asking about what is asked and expecting a logical answer, the person who asks the question tries to determine the identity of the object of questioning. This determination, or meaning-giving act, of the subject, by its own nature, limits what is determined and thus leaves some parts out. This process of self-delimiting of linguistic practice does not limit itself to our use of language but creates a boundary of one's mode of thinking. By creating a gap between questions and answers, and thus producing a state in which no definite answer resolves the tension between the question, the answer, and the questioning subject's desire to control the relationship between the two, *huatou* practice challenges the existing mode of thinking of the questioning subject. Until the questioning mode inquiring "what is it?" is challenged and broken down, until the subjugation of the other by the questioning subject through the subjectified vision of others is itself put into question, until what is asked about exposes itself, instead of being defined by the questioning subject, the discrepancy between the question and the answer in *huatou* remains wide open.

As the range of possible answers to a given question becomes exhausted, the separation between the subject who asks the questions and answers which are conventionally controlled by the speaking subject begins to be blurred. Zen Buddhist scholar Heinrich Dumoulin suggests that, in order to solve the seeming riddle involved in *gong'an* meditation, the practitioner should "become one with the *koan* [*gong'an*]," so that s/he "will so completely appropriate it that it no longer stands as a separate object."[48] To identify the *gong'an* with oneself is to change the direction of questioning activity. The subject's inquiry in this case no longer heads toward the external object but becomes internalized, and the nature of the inquiry changes from the investigation of the identity of the object in question to the existential reality of the questioner. This transformation of a linguistic question into an ontological one in the process of *huatou* meditation can be explained through the art of interrogation. The transition from the hermeneutical to the existential, from linguistic to ontological, and from Huayan to Huatou, which can also be identified in Chinul as that from the dead word to the live word and from the involvement with meaning to involvement with word, takes place through the act of questioning. Huatou meditation, in this sense, is sometimes translated as "questioning meditation."[49]

Through his silence, the Buddha demonstrated his disapproval of the presuppositions based on which his interlocutors posed their questions. The *gong'an* encounter dialogue functions through a similar synergy. Responses from Zen masters are considered non-sensical because they fail to comply with the presuppositions within whose boundary questioners formulated their inquiries. Both the silence of the Buddha and *gong'an* encounter dialogues function at the borderline of communicative presuppositions. In both cases, the rigid borderline that encapsules the identity of participating elements becomes loosened, as each side of the border retreats and advances at the same time through intermingling of different identities, and a communal space emerges through inter-subsumption of participating identities. This space is the locus in which interrogation takes place. The image reflects the hermeneutical circle, in which meaning looms through the interactive functioning of the constituents of the hermeneutic circle.

What does an act of interrogation entail? The interrogative mode in our linguistic practice does not mean a mere syntactic change from the declarative mode. When a mode of narrative changes from the declarative to the interrogative, the speaking subject's relation to the addressed object changes as well. When a question "What time is it?" arises in the mind of the questioner, it opens up a space which connects the subject with the object of the inquiry. In our daily conversation, the created space is quickly closed out with the responding statement: "It is eight thirty." However, this is not necessarily an indication that there are specific questions that raise a philosophical inquiry as opposed to a question exclusively limiting itself to a matter-of-fact of life. The division between philosophy and non-philosophy does not lie in the object being investigated but in the mode of investigation. Such a seemingly simple question as, "What time is it?", also opens up a space between a being and the world and installs the questioner in the milieu of others, thus initiating its relationship with them. This is because when a question arises in the mind of the questioner, the questioner is already opening herself/himself to the world outside her/his existence. With the question, "What time is it?" the questioner exposes herself/ himself to the temporal provisions of her/his existence. During the brief moment between the time when the question is posed and an answer is given, the subject floats in the realm of uncertainty and its identity lingers on the border between the subject and the objective world. In daily routines, the opening created through questioning is immediately closed up as the subject attains an answer that fits in with the logic of the subject. In case of *gong'an* meditation, since the answer fails to be part of the subject's existing logic, the gap created by the question (or Zen Master's answers) becomes widened, until there emerges a radical readjustment between the subject and the object. There are, then, at least two kinds of questions: the question as a temporary absence of signification and the question as an exposure of one's relationship with others.

French philosopher Maurice Merleau-Ponty explains the art of interrogation as a chiasmic movement. When one interrogates things, between the interrogator and the interrogated there arises a relationship similar to the two lines in the Greek letter "chi" ("X"). The interrogator in this relationship cannot have any privilege over the interrogated. Nor is the interrogated an "empty thing" waiting to be filled by the desire, intention, and meaning provided by the interrogator. Instead, their relationship is totally mutual; there is a "crisscrossing" or "intertwining" of the two. Merleau-Ponty elaborates this concept in terms of the chiasm of visibility. According to Merleau-Ponty, the conventional understanding that "my eyes" see "things" explains only half of the phenomena of visibility. When one sees things, one inscribes one's vision among the visible and this inscription is already a reaction to the visible. The seer then not only sees the visible, but at the same time is being seen by the visible. The reciprocal activity between the seer and the seen, and the dual function of the subject and the object, preclude the substantialist attempt to define the relationship as one over the other. Hence Merleau-Ponty writes: "the seer and the visible reciprocate one another and we no longer know which sees and which is seen."[50] This chiasmic visibility represents the synergy through which philosophical interrogation functions. Philosophical interrogation cannot be the kind of question that passively waits to be filled in by ready-made answers. When a question is raised, between the questioner and the question itself there emerges a relationship similar to the seer and the visible in visibility. The dissonance and disturbance within the questioner designates a gap between the two and leads him to the "openness upon the world" (*ouverture au monde*).

In this context, Merleau-Ponty offers a view of language that is comparable to Chinul's paradigm of the live and the dead words. According to Merleau-Ponty, when philosophy turns the doubts and anxiety of the interrogative into the certitude and security of the declarative, it also deprives language of its relation with the world. As signification is sedimented and institutionalized through the advocate of the essence within and without, the language employed becomes suffocated. Merleau-Ponty calls this "sedimented language" (*le langage parlé*). The sedimented language effaces itself in order to yield its meaning.[51] As opposed to the death or near-death of language in "sedimented language," "speech" (*le langage parlant*) for Merleau-Ponty is language "which creates itself in its expressive acts, which sweeps me on from the signs toward meaning."[52]

Sedimented language consists of "the stock of accepted relations between signs and familiar signification."[53] Like the kind of philosophy which confines the being and the world within the realm of the known through the institutionalization of thought process, sedimented language limits one's experience to ready-made expressions. The dream of sedimented language is the dream of the objective science of language. Unlike sedimented language, speaking language (or speech) creates a secret meaning out of already existing signs and signification. "Speaking language" does so by listening to the voice of "silence" or "indirect language." The silence of the Buddha did not remain in the realm of silence. As much as his silence was an indirect communication of his position regarding the presuppositions of his inquisitors, the Buddha eventually came to turn his silence into an explicit message through his doctrine of the middle path. Merleau-Ponty's "speaking language" is the mode that takes place when the rebellious silence encompassing and appropriating the silenced voice turns into articulation. The indirect language, Merleau-Ponty contends, connects language to "the mute things it interpellates and those it sends before itself and which make up the world of things said."[54] This is a process in which the subjective and objective worlds come to subsume each other.

Like Merleau-Ponty's sedimented language, Chinul's dead word subjugates itself to a sign-system. As opposed to the dead word, the live word becomes the mediator between the practitioner and his original state of the mind. Like Merleau-Ponty's speech (or speaking language), the live word realizes the philosopher's attempt to communicate the muteness of beings, the silence of original nature, which is articulated through the silence of the Buddha and that of Vimalakīrti.

By employing two levels of language, both Merleau-Ponty and Chinul attempt to resolve the difficulty of initiating a transition from a substantialist to a non-substantialist vision of being and the world. This transition is based on the philosophical underpinning that an entity is not a self-sustaining unit with identifiable essence or substance, but a being which is always already in communication with others. From the Zen Buddhist perspective, this mutual subscription of the self and others is the original nature of a being. When the subject fails to see this mutuality, the inevitable result is a promotion of subjectivity, which brings about the reification of a provisional perspective of the subject. Chinul specifically explains this point by citing a passage from the *Awakening of Faith* (*Dasheng qixin lun*):

Though all *dharmas* are spoken of, there is neither speaking subject nor spoken object; also, though all *dharmas* are thought of, there is neither thinking subject nor thought object. If one comes to understand this, that is called, "to understand the principle" (K. *susun*). If one enables to make oneself free from thought in one's thinking, that is called "to enter into enlightenment." (*HPC* 4.734a-b)[55]

Having cited this passage, Chinul comments that a verbal statement as this is aimed for those who have already freed themselves and thus are in the state of freedom. The purpose of *huatou* meditation is to get the practitioner into this state. Chinul's *Treatise*, hence, clarifies how the radical change in the subject's relation to the object will facilitate the way to freedom by elaborating on the three paradigms relevant to the practice of *huatou* meditation.

Chapter Five

Thinking and Violence:
Zen Hermeneutics

Two themes seem to appear repeatedly in Zen Buddhist discourse: language and violence. The former is overly explicit throughout the history of Zen Buddhism and has played a significant role in the construction of Zen identity, whereas the latter seems hidden and has failed to attract the attention of Zen scholarship despite the fact that the narrative of violence dominates the literature of Zen Buddhism. No-killing (and hence non-violence) is the first precept for both lay and ordained Buddhist practitioners. It is also one of the commonly shared features across different Buddhist schools. How then does the Zen discourse of violence fit into the context of Buddhism? Is this violence rhetorical, symbolic, or empirical?

Here are some well-known examples from the Zen Buddhist tradition. Legend has it that Bodhidharma, the alleged founder of Zen Buddhism, once dozed off during his meditation. He was so upset that he cut off his eyelids so that it would not happen again. The portraits of Bodhidharma describe him with big eyes without eyelids. In the conventional interpretation, the physical violence in this episode has been symbolically translated, and thus, the story serves as a model for the rigorous meditation practice of the alleged founder of the school. A similar case occurs in the story of Huike, the retroactively appointed Second Patriarch of Zen school. In an effort to demonstrate his resolution to receive the teachings from Bodhidharma, the future Second Patriarch of Zen Buddhism cut off his left arm and presented it to Bodhidharma. The *Transmission of the Lamp* (*Chuandeng lu*) records the incident as follows:

> The Master said, "The supreme, unequalled, spiritual Way of the Buddhas is accessible only after vast eons of striving to overcome the impossible and to bear the unbearable. How could a man of small virtue, little wisdom, slight interest, and slow mind attain the True Vehicle? Striving for it would be vain effort."

After listening to this exhortation from the master, Shen Kuang [later re-named Huike by Bodhidharma] took a sharp knife and cut off his own left arm, placing it in front of the Master.

Realizing that he was a good vessel for the Dharma, the Master said, "All Buddhas in search of the Way have begun by ignoring their bodies for the sake of the Dharma. Now you have cut off your arm in front of me. You may have the right disposition."[1]

Bodhidharma's complementary statement on Huike's determination for dharma training in the story explicitly symbolizes and dilutes the intensity of the physical violence involved in this episode. An episode from the *Platform Sūtra of the Sixth Patriarch* (*Liuzi tanjing*) also reports another instance of violence. Immediately after Huineng was appointed as the Sixth Patriarch, the Fifth Patriarch Hongren advises him to run away under cover of darkness, worried that the monastic community might not accept the authenticity of the newly appointed patriarch and harm him. Violence in this case is not yet committed but impending. Another story details one of the most exciting versions of violence in Zen literature: the well-known *gong'an* encounter dialogue titled "Nanquan Cuts the Cat in Two." In this episode, Zen Master Nanquan kills a cat in front of a group of monks. We will examine this story in detail shortly. An equally sophisticated rhetoric of violence is found in the well-known passage by Zen Master Linji (?–866), who was recorded to have advised his students:

Followers of the Way, if you want to get the kind of understanding that accords with the Dharma, never be misled by others. Whether you're facing inward or facing outward, whatever you meet up with, just kill it! If you meet a Buddha, kill the Buddha. If you meet a patriarch, kill the patriarch. If you meet an arhat, kill the arhat. If you meet your parents, kill your parents. If you meet your kinfolk, kill your kinfolk. Then, for the first time you will gain emancipation, will not be entangled with things, will pass freely anywhere you wish to go."[2]

In an attempt to mitigate the shock caused by the violence involved in this passage, the English translator Burton Watson added a footnote to this passage: "All this talk of killing is of course intended merely to warn students not to be led astray by external goals or considerations, though the violence of Lin-chi's language has often shocked readers."[3] A somewhat moderate version of violence is also found in another *gong'an* encounter dialogue, in which a Zen master cuts off a finger of a boy apprentice, through which the boy allegedly attains enlightenment. Case number three, "Judi Raises a Finger" in *The Gateless Gate* (*Wumen guan*) records the story as follows:

Whenever Master Judi was questioned, he would just raise a finger. Later a servant boy would also raise a finger when outsiders asked him what the master taught.

When Judi heard of this, he cut off the boy's finger with a knife. The boy ran out screaming in pain, but Judi called him back. When the boy turned his head, Judi raised a finger. Suddenly the boy attained enlightenment.

When Judi was about to die, he said to a group, "I attained my teacher Tianlong's one-finger Zen, and have used it all my life without exhausting it." So saying, he passed away.[4]

Here we have an odd collection of images of Zen masters in classical Zen Buddhist texts: a picture of the founder of the school who cut off his eyelids upset by his own physical reality; the second patriarch of the school voluntarily slicing off his arm in an attempt to get recognition from his teacher; another patriarch running away from impending violence from the monastic community; a Zen master exhorting his students to kill the founder and teachers of Zen Buddhism; another Zen master murdering a cat, and yet another Zen master chopping off a poor apprentice's finger: the episodes of violence continue in Zen literature.

Recent Buddhist scholarship in the West brings our attention to yet another type of violence. Japanese Zen Buddhism's support for nationalism and imperialism during the first half of the twentieth century and its employment of Zen doctrine to exhort the military action during the Second World War raise the question as to the ethos of Zen Buddhism. This scholarship challenges the conventional interpretation of Zen enlightenment, Zen discourse, and its history, and asks whether ethics is conceivable in the context of Zen Buddhism. This research adds to the complexity in our consideration of the meaning and function of violence in Zen literature.

Religion and violence is not a theme that is found exclusively in Zen Buddhist tradition, nor did the problem of violence in Zen Buddhist tradition begin with Japanese Zen Buddhism's involvement with military operations during the Second World War. Violence and voluntary suffering constitute elements that are found at the heart of most of religious traditions as one notes in sacrificial rituals involving the killing of animals, ascetic practice mortifying one's body, and martyrdom, not to mention wars waged in the name of religion. In Buddhist tradition as well, a connection between violence and religion has been on the horizon, even though it has not always attracted due attention from Buddhist scholars.

Some popular assumptions about the identity of Zen Buddhism make the pairing of Zen and violence an odd couple on several different levels. First of all, Buddhism has been known as a religion of non-violence, its first precept being no-killing. Secondly, Zen Buddhism's radical challenge to the status quo and any forms of authority in its search for freedom has generated a tendency to make it a default character of Zen Buddhism that Zen is against violence. Thirdly, Zen emphasis on meditation gives the tradition an image that Zen is about peace and harmony and devoid of the conflicts that characterize the life-world.

With these preliminary deliberations on Zen Buddhism and violence, one might want to dismiss the possibility that the Zen narrative of violence is in any way related to empirical violence. Some questions, however, still beg to be answered in this context. Supposing that the violence in Zen literature is only symbolic, how is this violence related to the Zen mode of thinking? Was it necessary for the Zen tradition to consistently resort to the rhetoric of violence?[5] How is the physical violence displayed in Zen literature interpreted in the context of the Buddha's rejection of ascetic self-mortification in preference of the middle path? Are there any suggestions that the symbolic violence can develop into a social and political one? If Zen Buddhism's involvement with violence on the institutional level, as claimed by some contemporary scholars of Japanese Buddhism, is not related to the traditional vision of Zen Buddhism, where do we find the source of the emergence of such violence? These questions suggest that a certain endeavor to untie the multi-layered meaning structure involved in Zen violence will be required in order to better understand Zen language and the Zen mode of thinking. To answer the questions posed here, let us first analyze the symbolic function of Zen violence by taking the *gong'an* "Nanquan Cuts the Cat in Two" as a sample case.

1. The One and the Truth

The fourteenth episode in *The Gateless Gate* is entitled "Nanquan Cuts the Cat in Two." The story also appears in *The Blue Cliff Record* (*Biyan lu*) as two cases, numbers sixty-three and sixty-four. Zen master Nanquan (748-834) was the teacher of Zhaozhou, a well-known figure in the Zen *gong'an* tradition. Let us read the entire episode as told in *The Gateless Gate* and continue our discussion.

> Nanquan saw monks of the Eastern and Western halls quarreling over a cat. He held up the cat and said, "If you can give an answer, you will save the cat. If not, I will kill it." No one could answer, and Nanquan cut the cat in two.
>
> That evening when Zhaozhou returned from an outing, Nanquan told him of the incident, Zhaozhou took off his sandal(s), placed it (them) on his head, and walked out. "If you had been there, you could have saved the cat," Nanquan remarked.[6]

To the first time reader of this *gong'an*, the episode could be stunning. No-killing is the first Buddhist precept, and this episode depicts a Zen master killing a cat in a Buddhist monastery in front of a group of monks. The extreme and unrealistic situation seems to confirm that the story should be read symbolically. What were the monks arguing about concerning the cat? The story does not provide that information. But the point came when the Zen master Nanquan felt that it was inevitable for him to intervene in this argument. He grabbed the cat, held it up, and said to the monks that if anybody could say a smart word (or the truth), he would save the cat; otherwise, the cat would be dead. The monks were stunned. The life of the unfortunate cat depended on their words. Nobody dared to say anything. Without hesitation, Nanquan cut the cat in two. In the version from *The Blue Cliff Record*, case number sixty-three ends here, demonstrating that this portion can also serve as an independent *gong'an*. However, as the verse in *The Blue Cliff Record* suggests, Zhaozhou's reaction gives a final twist to the *gong'an*. When Zhaozhou returned from the outing that evening, Nanquan told him what had happened during his absence. Zhaozhou's response to the story was as extraordinary as his behaviors in other *gong'an* episodes: he took off his sandal/sandals made of grass, put it/them on his head and walked away, and his teacher confirms that the gesture is a "correct" answer which would have saved the cat.

As with any other *gong'ans*, the reader of Nanquan's cat and Zhaozhou's sandal(s) remains perplexed. The killing of a cat was stunning, while Zhaozhou's gesture was comic, and Nanquan's reaction to Zhaozhou mysterious. Still confused, we recap the entire story, and most likely, our thoughts stop to muse about the one word Nanquan demanded of the monks. What could be the one word that Nanquan demanded of the monks? If the monks did not know the answer, Zhaozhou must have known it, for that was what Nanquan indicated. But how could Zhaozhou possibly have saved the cat by carrying his sandal(s) on his head? At this point, we lose track of any clue that might have guided us further in our investigation of the word, the answer, the truth, which must be the very teaching of this *gong'an*. Confused and feeling helpless, we naively fall for the well-known Zen cliché allegedly given by Bodhidharma. That is, Zen does not rely on words or language; it directly points to the mind to see the self nature and realize the Buddhahood; and thus any attempt to logically interpret Zen *gong'an* is a way to commit a cardinal sin.

This option of falling for what Thomas Cleary calls the "irrationalist fallacy" has been overplayed during the course of the history of Zen Buddhism. The idea that one should not try to find a logical explanation about a *gong'an* encounter dialogue, and thus should not try to find a "correct" answer to *gong'ans*, has been used as a panacea for the difficulties one faces in understanding Zen Buddhism. This tendency in Zen Buddhism claims that the mystery of the Zen *gong'an*, the weirdness of Zen masters' deportment, and their uncanny expressions, are not subject to our hermeneutic endeavors and should be accepted as they are without an interpretative medium because they are the signs of the enlightened mind. Surely, Zen masters' verbal expressions and bodily gestures must flow from their enlightened nature. However, practitioners who encounter them are still in the realm of the unenlightened world and need to decipher those signs in order to learn from Zen masters' teachings.[7] In that sense, hermeneutics is inevitably a part of Zen practice and

Zen philosophy. However, hermeneutics in this context cannot be simply a search for "the" meaning of the Zen masters' deportment; it is a discourse that actively involves itself in the problematization of a certain mode of thinking. The hermeneutics of Zen Buddhism, then, bears a strong resemblance to the trend in recent Continental philosophy. Hermeneutics as a science of meaning production did not begin with a recent philosophical school in Continental philosophy but has a long history in the Talmudic tradition and Biblical exegesis.[8] However, a distinction can be made between the recent hermeneutical school and traditional hermeneutics in the sense that the latter's goal lies in finding the authentic meaning of religious texts whereas the former focuses on the process of meaning production. Furthermore, hermeneutics in recent Continental philosophy can be understood within a broader stream of contemporary philosophical trends, in which the metaphysical tradition, especially with regard to its clear dualism of subject-object and the optimization of the rationalized subject's construction of the world and being, has been problematized.[9] Zen *gong'an* encounter dialogues in this context provide a challenging environment for hermeneutics in Buddhism.

Zen hermeneutics, especially in the context of *gong'an* meditation, is inevitably connected with the Zen use of language. In discussing the function of language in Zen *gong'an*, Wŏnch'ŏl Yun and Inhae Kang identify it as subversive, liberating, spontaneous, and performative.[10] They further state that Zen language can be understood in the context of Wittgensteinean language-game theory. That is, the Zen *gong'an* produces meaning only when it is understood as a religious language-game specific to Zen Buddhism,[11] which Yun and Kang characterize as anti-metaphysical and anti-intellectual. Yun and Kang quote a *gong'an* also related to Zhaozhou as an example of the anti-metaphysical nature of Zen *gong'an* language:

> A monk asks Zhaozhou: "Ten thousand things return to one. To where does this one thing return?"
> Zhaozhou replies: "When I stayed in Qinzhou, I made clothes, which weighed seven pounds."[12]

One cannot miss the similarity involved in the above *gong'an* and "Nanquan Cuts the Cat in Two." Earlier we asked what the one word that Nanquan demanded of the monks might be. We also wondered how Zhaozhou's quixotic behavior of putting his sandal(s) on his head could be a "correct" answer to Nanquan's question. What is the relationship between the question on the One ultimate reality, or the one word, and Zhaozhou's reactions in these two *gong'ans*? Yun and Kang interpret the above *gong'an* as follows: "To the metaphysical question asking for the One as the ultimate reality, Zhaozhou responds with the totally anti-metaphysical language of everyday communication, causing an embarrassment to the questioner. Since the world exists only as dynamics of relationship (*pratītiyasamutpāda*) but not as a part of the ultimate reality which contains self-identity, a metaphysical question which presupposes the existence of the One needs to be deconstructed through an anti-intellectual answer."[13] In a similar manner, when asked by his master for the one ultimate word to save the cat, Zhaozhou responds with a gesture which is beyond the normality of language, thus problematizing the issue of identifying the essence or the ultimate truth.

If truth cannot be revealed by identifying and articulating the One ultimate reality, how is truth, even in an anti-metaphysical sense, to be understood? If truth does not lie in the one word, how does the truth occur? When truth is believed to be expressed in one word, the one word—be it logos, essence, or Truth—is the locus of the truth one is looking for. However, Zhaozhou's clothes, which weighed seven pounds, or the sandal(s) that Zhaozhou put on his head itself/themselves, is/are not truth per se. How is the truth, which cannot be identified either linguistically or non-linguistically, encountered at all by practitioners of Zen Buddhism or philosophers in search of truth? This seems the point at which Zen Buddhist performative language meets the hermeneutics of Continental philosophy in its efforts to explain the anti-metaphysical nature of the hermeneutic meaning production. The hermeneutics I have in mind at this point is Heideggerian ontological hermeneutics.

2. Truth and Subjectivity

One of the concepts that Heidegger emphasized in the later years of his career with regard to our understanding of truth is the idea of *aletheia* as the emergence of truth, as opposed to the understanding of truth as *veritas*. The understanding of truth as *veritas* locates the essence of truth in the conformity of mind with object. This "agreement or conformity of knowledge with fact" has long been understood as the reality of truth.[14] However, Heidegger contends that the concept of truth as conformity between knowledge and fact solicits a question that has been blindly disregarded: that is, how does one obtain the facts which will lead one to truth? If the constituent of truth lies in the agreement of knowledge with fact, how does one acquire knowledge that is required to reach a truth? In order to earn knowledge, relevant facts should be understood. But before truth is revealed, how is fact passed to the subject who will eventually go through the process of conformity with his/her knowledge and the fact? The vision is tautological: in order to reach truth, we need knowledge; in order to acquire knowledge, we need fact; in order to understand fact, we need knowledge; both knowledge and fact need to be truthful for a thought system to be valid, but at this point we have yet to acquire either knowledge, fact, or truth. The problem we are encountering here is similar to the one involved with one's attempt to overcome existential anxiety in a capitalist society. In order to get over the anxiety arising from the uncertainty of the world, one needs to exert one's power to control others so that one can create security—the security based on one's illusion of domesticated reality. However, the project should continue ad infinitum, because the subject's ownership of the outside world always falls short of the mastery of the outside world in its entirety. As long as the gap remains between the subject and the outside world, so does anxiety. By the same token, if the truth means conformity between fact and knowledge, as far as the fact remains as the reality outside of the thinking subject, and thus as an object to be understood by the subject, the gap between the fact and thinking subject remains open. Heidegger thus asks: "the fact must show itself to be fact if knowledge and the proposition that forms and expresses knowledge are to be able to conform to the fact; otherwise the fact cannot become binding on the proposition. How can fact show itself if it cannot itself stand forth out of concealedness, if it does not itself stand in the unconcealed?"[15]

In order to overcome the tautological circling among the three factors—fact, knowledge, and truth—, truth as *veritas* understands truth as being grounded on certainty and correctness. The beginning point of the searching for truth here is that there already should exist something that is grounded, the validity of which we do not ask. Truth as *veritas* has led philosophers to understand Being as something that is already grounded, when the ground itself is questionable. This unquestioned grounding of existence and truth has been the foundation of metaphysical thinking, be it the logos, the Idea, the Spirit, or the Cartesian Ego Cogito. This is the world of the One word in which Nanquan's students were trapped. This is the One word that Zhaozhou's questioner wanted to hear from Zen master Zhaozhou.

Heidegger considered the task of thinking "at the end of philosophy" as something similar to what Nanquan and Zhaozhou might have wanted to teach to their students who were eager to find the One word. Heidegger claims that the epoch in which philosophy finds security by grounding itself without foundation has come to an end. That such a metaphysical mode of philosophy has come to an end does not suggest that the task of thinking, which is the propeller of philosophy, has also reached an end. At this turning point of philosophy's understanding of its own function, Heidegger brings our attention to a new dimension of truth, which he defines as the taking place of truth, that is, *aletheia*. As opposed to truth as *veritas*, in which the truth is acquired as a result of the conformity or correspondence between knowledge and fact, truth as *aletheia*,—a Greek term, literally meaning "disclosedness"—envisions truth as something that is uncovered, that which reveals itself. Heidegger further visualizes this taking-place of truth in the image of "the opening": "The quiet heart of the opening is the place of stillness from which alone the possibility of the belonging together of Being and thinking, that is, presence and perceiving, can arise at all."[16]

Philosophy, Heidegger contends, has been obsessed with the assumption that what is present is grounded and always present. This is an inevitable corollary of maintaining truth as the conformity between the knowledge and fact. Since grounding is a required element for truth, the conformity or identity of the Being and beings, thinking and truth, has been the foundation and justification of philosophers' search for truth. However, once we begin to question the ground of grounding the Being, essence, and the ultimate truth, we realize that the task of thinking is not to identify truth. Instead, its role is to remain on the horizon of a continuing quest for truth. This quiet opening is the space in which the individual's quest for truth is taking place. The taking place, or happening, of "belonging together of the Being and thinking" does not confirm the nature, or essence, of the Being or thinking; instead it only opens up the possibility in which philosophy can work on its own search for truth. Like Zen *gong'an* encounter dialogue, which introduces this interrogative mode of thinking through the gap between the question (e.g. "To where does the one thing return?") and the answer ("I made clothes, which weighted seven pounds."), Heideggerian hermeneutics places the questioner at the junction of the individual's quest for meaning and truth.

Nanquan demanded one word of the monks in the hall. When the one word is understood as the unchanging prescriptive truth, as the monks did, one will fail to respond to Nanquan's demand: according to their presumption of prescriptive truth, who would be capable of expressing the ultimate truth in one word? However, when truth is understood in a Heideggerian way, as un-concealed-ness, which emerges in the hermeneutical circle—the very space in which truth shall emerge—, the seeker of the truth becomes a part of the emergence of truth itself; the ultimate truth is no longer a complete form, or a coherent whole, standing out there as an object for the subject to grasp. Nor does the seeker of truth, in this case, stand as an observer of the truth, but s/he is a participant of the taking place of truth. Heidegger thus identifies the relationship between the Being and thinking, or philosophy and truth, in terms of "belonging togetherness" but not in terms of "possession" or "ownership." This belonging togetherness of truth and being, the Being and thinking, and the Being and beings, has the color of the chiasmic movements of visibility in the Merleau-Pontean world. The subject and object belong together in the mutual revelation with no final point of destination fixed.

Only when truth is understood as an unchanging essence can one dream of "possessing" the truth. Understanding truth in terms of ownership contains limits within its own structure and thus ironically reveals the impossibility of owning truth. If truth is something that can be owned, the owner of truth does not own the truth because the truth is the object of the subject who owns it. The owner owns truth, but is not part of truth, and therefore is excluded from truth. Since one owns truth, one can employ it to exert its power over non-owners of truth. But in an ultimate sense, both owners and non-owners of truth are in the same state in that they are outside of truth. By replacing the idea of truth as *veritas* or the conformity between knowledge and fact with the truth as *aletheia* or disclosure, Heidegger invites the subject to the realm of truth that is to take place according to the changing contexts of reality. Once one gives up the idea of owning the truth, thereby stopping the objectification of truth, which is another way of putting limits on truth, then the first way to approach truth becomes an opening up of one's subjectivity, which the monks at the Nanquan's monastery failed to realize.

The idea of hermeneutics as a philosophy in which the interpreter shares the horizon of truth with the object of his/her interpretation is also expressed in the understanding of hermeneutics as a philosophy that combines theory and praxis. Why did Nanquan's monks fail to react to their master's demand, even when they knew that their reaction was the only way to save the cat and help their master avoid committing the violation of the first precept of Buddhism and keep themselves from being accomplices in their master's committing violence and the violation? The extreme situation symbolically demonstrates how far away the monks were from learning the teaching they were seeking. As one scholar suggests, it is not the cat but the monks and we, the readers of the *gong'an*, who die when Nanquan murders the cat as we fail to get the meaning of the *gong'an*.[17] The impasse of the monks is the symptom of their attachment to the truth, and, at the same time, their alienation from truth. To the mind of those monks, the one ultimate truth exists as an object to be obtained, an object which is a forlorn and untouchable reality, of which we are admirers and worshippers, but not participants.

Paying special attention to the participatory elements in hermeneutical discourse, Hosŏng Kim identifies the shared realm of Buddhist philosophy and hermeneutics as self-philosophy (K. *cha'gi ch'ŏrhak*), in which philosophical thinking and reading of a text contribute to an individual's looking into one's own reality.[18] Kim calls this belonging together of an individual and the text, "the horizon of praxis" (K. *silch'ŏn chip'yŏng*). In self-philosophy, an individual acts out her/his hermeneutical capacity in understanding and applying philosophical discourse to one's life. As Kim writes: "the pragmatic reading in which we [readers] actively interpret texts based on the context of our reality cannot help but introduce new self-philosophy all the time. . . . That is because all interpreters work on different horizons of praxis."[19] Unlike the traditional approach to a text, in which "the" meaning of a text is fixed in the sense that a text delivers the intention of the author, hermeneutics as self-philosophy brings our attention to the fact that meaning of a text arises only when the reader of the text brings her/his experience into the reality of the world presented by the text. In this sense, meaning production is always already an inter-textual endeavor.

In self-philosophy, interpreters, thinkers, and readers actively involve themselves in the context of life where truth is being constantly encountered, instead of being discovered as a ready-made fact. Nanquan's monks failed to embody self-philosophy when they stood in the meditation hall as spectators of the cat's fate, waiting to recover a ready-made truth. They refused to see truth as part of their existence because truth to them should be the finality which is correct and complete. If hermeneutics is a science concerning the production of meaning, and the process of meaning production does not confine this procedure to a discovery of pre-existing and prescribed meaning within a text or a situation, a hermeneutical endeavor will have to open itself up to the "belonging togetherness" of truth and the seeker of the truth.

The Heideggerian hermeneutical circle in this context provides a paradigm that we can apply to the hermeneutics of Zen Buddhist *gong'an* (con)texts. A *gong'an* dialogue functions as *gong'an* only when it situates itself within its own context. When we separate sentences and expressions in a *gong'an* from their context, each sentence takes on a different meaning, as any linguistic expression does. The fact that Zhaozhou's clothes weighed seven pounds or that he placed his sandal(s) on his head is uncanny within the context of the *gong'an* in which it occurs; however, its uncanniness would be lost if expressed in a different situation. Like in the hermeneutical circle, the situation should be put into the opening in which the tripartite participants of the situation—that is, the *gong'an* episode, the being who asks the meaning of the *gong'an*, and truth—work together for the happening of truth of which all of them are part.

3. Subjectivity Unbound and the Rhetoric of Violence

Why did Nanquan's monks fail to react to their master's demand? We explained that the failure was caused by their objectification of truth. But what are the actual ramifications of this idea that truth should be understood in terms of "belonging togetherness" instead of ownership? This question leads us to a double-binding or the two-fold existence that is found both in hermeneutics and Buddhist philosophy.

Heidegger once traced the etymological origin of "hermeneutics" to the Greek god Hermes. "Hermes is the divine messenger. He brings the message of destiny."[20] Hermes brings the message from Zeus to mortals. Hermeneutics for Heidegger brings out the message Hermes brought from the god, the message which "bring[s] out the Being of being." As Richard Palmer tells us, the importance of Hermes as the god of hermeneutics does not lie in the fact that he delivers the message from divinity, but in that

Hermes crosses different ontological thresholds—the thresholds between Zeus and humans and between the underworld and mortals. Hence, "liminality or marginality is his very essence."[21] The awareness of liminality or marginality in one's relation to the Being marks Heidegger's de-metaphysical understanding of the Being and truth, which Heidegger defines as the task of fundamental ontology. Heidegger states that the emergence of the Being of beings in hermeneutics is no longer metaphysical, but it is "such that Being itself will shine out, Being itself . . . the presence of present beings, the two-fold of the two in virtue of their simple oneness. This is what makes its claim on man, calling him to its essential being."[22] The Being and a being are not identical, neither are they completely separate. Dasein locates itself in the ontico-ontological difference, asking the meaning of its existence. Like Hermes, Dasein is a being which is fully aware of its own liminality as the basis of its existential ground. A being in Buddhism is also explained in its two-fold nature as explicated in the theory of the two-levels of truth by Nāgārjuna:

> The Buddha's teaching of the Dharma/ is based on two truths:/ A truth of worldly convention/ And an ultimate truth// Those who do not understand/ The distinction drawn between these two truths/ Do not understand/ The Buddha's profound truth// Without a foundation in the conventional truth/ The significance of the ultimate cannot be taught./ Without understanding the significance of the ultimate,/ Liberation is not achieved.[23]

As Nāgārjuna expounds, the existential reality of a being from the Buddhist perspective is like a hinge which locates itself between the ultimate and conventional truths. A being on its phenomenal level is an individual who has a separate physical body and life. However, in its ultimate existential condition, a being cannot exist independently because it is always already a combination of different factors orchestrated together through multi-level causation. The double-séance of human existence or the non-duality of individual entity in the provisional level and non-substantial reality in the ultimate level cannot be realized until the individual, who is the Zen practitioner in Zen Buddhism, the reader of *gong'an* in Zen hermeneutics, and Dasein in Heidegger's ontology, realizes the fundamental link between the two. The two levels of truth are explained in the *Heart Sūtra* through the identity and difference between form and emptiness. In Chinul, the idea appears as a relationship between the hermeneutical and the existential. The two levels of truth are a philosophical interpretation of what we characterized as a Buddhist narrative pattern of the simultaneous use of affirmation and negation.

Nanquan's monks failed to see the oneness of this twofold vision. Asked by their master for the one word of ultimate reality, the monks had to fumble to objectify the ultimate level, the Being in Heidegger's terminology, into a substantial entity existing beyond their own existence. As long as the ultimate reality is understood as separate from one's reality, it cannot escape the process of substantialization, which eventually will postulate the existence of the transcendental foundation. The transition from Nanquan's one word to Zhaozhou's sandals in the *gong'an* episode warns us of the pitfall that exists in playing with the one word when the idea of ultimate reality is not fully dispersed and disseminated. This is exactly the point Derrida asserts in his reading of Heidegger. To Derrida, "Heideggerian thought reinstates rather than destroys the instance of the logos and of the truth of being as 'primum signatum'."[24] To Derrida, metaphysical thinking is already embedded in our linguistic structure. As far as one makes recourse to the Being, or essence, as the ground of being and its truth, one is already within the frame of metaphysics. By the same token, if the *gong'an* "Nanquan Cuts the Cat in Two" ends with Nanquan's killing of the cat, the *gong'an* could be interpreted as another occasion of reinstating the reality of the one word. Hence, Zen Master Dōgen (1200-1253) commented: "If I had been Nan-ch'üan [Nanquan], I would have said: 'Even if you can speak, I will cut the cat, and even if you cannot speak, I will still cut it'."[25]

What is intriguing in the reading of Zhaozhou and Derrida is the comic relief in their reaction to the metaphysical, and even tragic, development of a search for truth in Heidegger and among Nanquan's monks. Derrida's writings, especially his early works, have the taste of Zen *gong'an*. The playfulness of Derrida's works, like the seeming nonsense and absurdity of *gong'an* episodes, brings us a comic relief which does not aim for innocent laughter. As Heidegger once said—ironic as it may sound to cite the passage in criticism of Heidegger himself—this is a comic relief which is "a playful thinking that is more compelling than the rigor of science."[26] Seriousness of philosophy, as Derrida notes in his comments on Hegel, begins with philosophy's declaration of its separation from myth and its entering into the investigation of logos. [27] Once the status of logos is put into question, and the boundary between mythos and logos becomes blurred, the logic of philosophy reveals its own chasm. Our discussion of logos and mythos in earlier chapter has much relevance here.[28]

The comic play of Derridean deconstruction shines clearly in his essay "Restitutions." The essay revolves around a correspondence between Meyer Schapiro and Martin Heidegger. The issue of the correspondence is the ownership of the shoes in Van Gogh's painting: that is, to whom do the pair of shoes in Van Gogh's painting belong? What interests Derrida about this debate on the ownership of the shoes is the idea of pairing up the shoes. There are obviously two shoes in the painting, which we are ready to identify as a pair of shoes, most likely out of habit. But as Derrida claims, there is no reason that two single shoes put together should make a pair. From the beginning of "Restitutions," Derrida plays with and plays around the idea of pairing the shoes, and asks: what makes Heidegger and Schapiro so sure that the shoes in Van Gogh's painting are a "pair" of shoes? There is no indication in Van Gogh's painting that the shoes are a "pair of shoes." However, Heidegger pairs them up without a suspicion and assumes that they belong to a peasant woman who would walk to the fields from early in the morning till late into night.[29] One might wonder what is the significance of a pair or a non-pair of shoes in Van Gogh's painting to Derrida. Let us look into some details of the debate between Heidegger and Schapiro on Van Gogh's shoes, and then hopefully we will be able to see how Derrida's reading of their debate approximates the message of Zhaozhou's sandal(s) on his head.

A work of art to Heidegger is a locus in which "truth is put into the work"[30]; it is the disclosure of the particular being in its being, and the happening of truth.[31] Placing the origin of a work of art in the hermeneutic circle of art, a work of art, and artist, Heidegger meditates:

> What happens here? What is at work in the work? Van Gogh's painting is the disclosure of what the equipment, the pair of peasant shoes, *is* in truth. This entity emerges into the unconcealedness of its being. The Greeks called the unconcealedness of beings *aletheia* . . . If there occurs in the work a disclosure of a particular being, a disclosing what and how it is, then there is here an occurring, a happening of truth at work.[32]

This is the instant in which Heidegger describes how truth reveals itself through the hermeneutical paradigm of letting it happen as opposed to the metaphysical imposition of truth. However, Meyer Schapiro, an art historian, had a different idea. In an essay "The Still Life as a Personal Object: A Note on Heidegger and Van Gogh," Schapiro confronts Heidegger's view on Van Gogh's shoes. Schapiro claims that the pair of shoes in Van Gogh's painting does not belong to a peasant woman as Heidegger would like to believe, but to the artist himself who was, at the time he created the painting, a city dweller. Schapiro criticizes Heidegger for the imaginary projection of his own personal life onto Van Gogh's shoes and argues that Heidegger contradicted his own claim about the beingness of the work of art by imposing his own subjective interpretation. The issue of this debate might sound odd for some readers. The point here however is not whether one would side with Heidegger or Schapiro, but that both Heidegger and Schapiro are determined to reveal *the* truth without relying on metaphysical underpinning. Schapiro's criticism of Heidegger is based on the fact that Heidegger projected his own subjectivity in his interpretation of the painting, and by so doing, violated his own presupposition of the emergence of truth in the work of art.

Using this debate between Heidegger and Schapiro as one motive for his essay on truth in/and painting, Derrida brings our attention to the conditions

Heidegger and Schapiro established in order to bring forward their versions of "truth" in Van Gogh's painting. Heidegger had no doubt that the shoes in Van Gogh's painting are "a pair of shoes." Nor does Schapiro have any doubt that the shoes make a pair when he opposed Heidegger's claim that they belong to a peasant woman. There is no indication in the title or in the painting itself that the shoes make a pair, and both Heidegger and Schapiro claim that they are a pair of shoes belonging either to a peasant woman or to Van Gogh himself. Pairing up the shoes, Derrida contends, reflects the desire to set up the subject. Without being appropriated as a pair, the shoes lose their utility function and thus their identity. Unpaired shoes will be abandoned without an owner, and without an owner, to whom the truth of the painting should return, there cannot be subjectivity. If subjectivity is the condition of the truth, such a truth cannot but be subjective. Both Heidegger and Schapiro can claim the truth in Van Gogh's painting only after they tied up the shoes, rendering them, restituting them, and returning them to a peasant woman or to the painter. The ghost of Ego-Cogito hangs around in Heidegger's "Origin of the Work of Art," despite his criticism of subjectivity in metaphysical thinking and his claim for the truth as *aletheia*. Thus the voices in Derrida's essay ask:

> - what makes him so sure that they are a pair of shoes? What is a pair?
> - I don't know yet. In any case, Heidegger has no doubt about it; it's a pair-of-peasant-shoes (*ein Paar Bauernschuhe*). And *ça revient*, this indissociable whole, this paired thing, from the fields and to the peasant, man or even woman. Thus Heidegger does not answer one question, he is sure of the thing before any other question. So it seems.[33]

Here again we are reminded of the one word that Nanquan's monks failed to produce. Both Heidegger and Schapiro had to pair up the shoes because without the subject who owns the shoes, the truth of the painting cannot be revealed. Only after setting up the ownership of the truth, the truth of the painting can be established. By the same token, only after the owning of the truth is confirmed, would the monks have been able to say the word, the truth. Until the truth is set up, and its ownership is clarified, the monks would remain silent. The impasse of the monks and the consequent death of the cat contain an ethical message stronger than any ethical codes. Violence is not committed by Nanquan alone who killed the cat in a literal sense; instead, the monks who failed to respond to Nanquan and we, who thus failed to realize the meaning of Nanquan's question, became accomplices. Violence is not committed only by our active involvement with physically violent actions. The inchoate origin of violence lies in our non-action and failure to see the world as it is. Violence, then, begins with our thinking. The *physical* violence of killing a cat, be it actual or symbolic, was caused by the monks' inability to *think*.

Despite the bleak atmosphere of Nanquan's monastery, Zen Buddhism rarely subscribes to a tragic vision. Instead, the *gong'an* eventually ends with a comic gesture of Zhaozhou. As Derrida's shoes are charged with a deconstructive scheme, Zhaozhou's sandal(s) provide(s) its (their) own deconstructive turn in the episode. What is the truth involved in this sandal/sandals which the Zen master had worn all day during his outing and put on his head as an expression of the truth his teacher asked of the other monks in the monastery? Heidegger and Schapiro tied up the shoes into a pair, returned them to their owner, and ended up creating subjectivity as a ground for their truth claim. Zhaozhou untied his sandal, detached it from its owner, and put it on his head, a most inappropriate place for a sandal to be. The sandal is totally detached from both its owner who is Zhaozhou (the subject) and from the most familiar environment which is his foot (its utility function and thus its identity). Detachment of the sandal(s) dissolves the ownership, thus dissolves the subjectivity. Without subjectivity, truth cannot be returned to the owner. Without the subject, there is no truth that can be summarized in one word.

Does this suggest that truth does not exist? Like Zhaozhou's sandals, which are completely detached from their utility function, and Derrida's shoes, which are untied from their paired-ness, truth is untied from its subject and has become a part of the world that has neither subject nor object. As truth is untied from the subject, the gestures of Zhaozhou and Derrida disseminate language and linguistic meaning production instead of assembling them into a coherent interpretation. Both the Zen *gong'an* "Nanquan Cuts the Cat in Two" and Derrida's reading of Heidegger remind us how strong our affinity with the centripetal force is. The desire to hold a center, and thus create a coherent world view, demonstrates its power through devices which range from philosophical themes like subjectivity to our daily linguistic expression like "a pair of shoes." It is not just philosophers who dream of the world which makes sense to humans. Dissemination of that dream in the life-world becomes a constituent power of institutional violence in human society.

The radical nature of the rhetoric of violence in Zen literature indicates the seriousness of the symptom in the way Zen Buddhism assesses it. Zen Buddhist *gong'an* dialogues suggest that attaining the truth requires a constant deconstruction of the human tendency to construct a coherent reality and meaning structure. Generating a provisionally coherent meaning system is an inevitable stage of everyday life. A cup needs to be understood and named as a cup in order for us to communicate and for it to function as an entity in daily life. However, Zen Buddhist *gong'an* also emphasizes that a cup is not just a cup in its ultimate reality. The simultaneous emphasis on the provisional and ultimate levels of truth is a recurring theme in *gong'an* dialogues.

The indivisibility of these two levels is demonstrated in the *gong'an* like "Judi Raises a Finger" in which Zen Master Judi chops off a finger of the apprentice. As the apprentice boy "repeats" his master's action of raising one finger, the master punishes him by cutting off his finger. But the master in turn teaches the suffering boy through the same action of raising one finger. The irony of the difference of identity and identity of difference is at work again. The truth does not lie in the action of raising one finger, but it does not exist outside of this action, either. Raising one finger does not represent truth, but at a given moment and given context, it could function as the representation of truth as any other action or a statement at other moments in other contexts. Raising a finger, even though repeated every day by the boy's master, is not the same raising of a finger. Each time the finger is raised, the sameness of the phenomenal action is encroached by different contexts. As Merleau-Ponty states, "I cannot think of identically the same thing for more than an instant. . . . Thought does not bore through time. It follows in the wake of previous thoughts, without even exercising the power (which it assumes) of retracing that wake . . . ."[34] The encroachment of thoughts of the past, of the present, and even of the future leaves one's encounter with one's own thought as anachronic. And there was no original thought, other than as a potential, whose original form can never be retrievable.

An empirical action, like raising a finger, cannot be different from the mobility and heterogeneity of one's thought process. The sameness on the phenomenal appearance is a provisional understanding of its non-sameness with the previous and future action of raising a finger. The non-duality of the provisional and ultimate truths so oddly expressed in "Judi Raises a Finger" often appears in a more placid tone in other *gong'an* dialogues. One example is a well-known *gong'an*, "Wash Your Bowl." Case number seven of *The Gateless Gate* records the *gong'an* as follows:

A monk asked Zhaozhou, "I have just joined the community, and I request the teacher's instruction."
Zhaozhou inquired, "Have you had your breakfast gruel yet?"
The monk said, "I have had my gruel."
Zhaozhou said, "Then go wash your bowl."
The monk had an insight.[35]

Another example of a *gong'an* episode in this category is case number nineteen, "The Ordinary Mind is the Way," which is also recorded in *The Gateless Gate*:

Zhaozhou asked Nanquan, "What is the Way?" "Ordinary mind is the Way," Nanquan replied. "Can it be approached deliberately?" Zhaozhou asked. "If you try to aim for it, you thereby turn away from it," responded Zhaozhou. "How can I know the Way unless I try for it?" persisted Zhaozhou. Nanquan said, "The

Way is not a matter of knowing or not knowing. Knowing is delusion; not knowing is confusion. When you have really reached the true Way beyond doubt, you
will find it as vast and boundless as outer space. How can it be talked about on
the level of right and wrong?" With these words, Zhaozhou came to a sudden
realization.[36] (Translation modified.)

In reading these two cases, one feels a tension emerging. In Zhaozhou's
"Wash Your Bowl," the ultimate reality is described as the same as any daily
activities. This leads to the question of how to make distinctions between
knowing and not-knowing the ultimate truth as we read in Nanquan's "The
Ordinary Mind is the Way." The Zen narrative pattern of the simultaneous
use of affirmation and negation is again at work in the *gong'an* literature
that attempts to confirm the identity of truth and non-truth without hypothe-
sizing either of the two. Zen masters' responses to the same or similar questions are frequently contradicting one another, destabilizing the meaning of
given answers. The end result is a constant dismantling of the construction
of a coherent conceptual frame. Case number thirty of *The Gateless Gate*
records:

> Damei asked Mazu, "What is the Buddha?"
> Mazu said, "The very mind itself is Buddha."[37]

The essence of Zen Buddhism which claims that everybody's mind is itself
Buddha is clearly declared in this case. However, the declaration is immediately refuted in case number thirty-three, in which Mazu offers an answer
opposite to this to the same question.

> A monk asked Mazu, "What is Buddha?"
> Mazu said, "Not mind, not Buddha."[38]

The negation of the existence of either the mind or the Buddha is further
emphasized in case twenty-seven:

> A monk asked Master Nanquan, "Is there a truth not spoken to people?"
> Nanquan said, "There is."
> The monk asked, "What is the truth not spoken to people?"
> Nanquan said, "It is not mind, it is not Buddha, it is not a thing."[39]

Case twenty-nine, on the other hand, reinstates the existence of the mind
as the cause of our perception:

> Once when the wind was whipping the banner of a temple, the Sixth Patriarch
> of Zen witnessed two monks debating about it. One said that the banner was
> moving, one said the wind was moving.

They argued back and forth without attaining the principle, so the Patriarch said, "This is not the movement of the wind, nor the movement of the banner; it is the movement of your minds."
The two monks were both awestruck.[40]

Case forty-one likewise confirms both existence and non-existence of the mind:

> As the founder of Zen faced a wall, his future successor stood in the snow, cut off his arm, and said, "My mind is not yet at peace. Please pacify my mind."
> The founder said, "Bring me your mind, and I will pacify it for you."
> The successor said, "I have looked for my mind and cannot find it."
> The founder said, "I have pacified your mind for you."[41]

A certain logical strategy of Zen *gong'an* dialogue is emerging here. This logic is comparable to what Derrida would call a "super oscillation." The *gong'ans* are not simply oscillating two poles of affirmation and negation of the existence of mind; they "[oscillate] between two types of oscillation: the double exclusion (neither/nor) and the participation (both this and that)."[42] Derrida's statement was given in the context of his discussion of *chora* (*khōra*; space, placing, site, or topos), which Plato proposes as the in-between state between the intelligible and the sensible worlds.[43] The betweenness of *chora* refutes the logic of non-contradiction as Derrida states:

> what Plato in the *Timaeus* designates by the name of *khōra* seems to defy that "logic of noncontradiction of the philosophers". . . One cannot even say of it [*khōra*] that it is *neither* this *nor* that or that it is *both* this *and* that. It is not enough to recall that *khōra* names neither this nor that, or that *khōra* says this and that. The difficulty declared by Timaeus is shown in a different way: at times the *khōra* appears to be neither this nor that, at times both this and that, but this alternation between the logic of exclusion and that of participation . . . stems perhaps only from a provisional appearance and from the constraints of rhetoric, even from some incapacity for naming.[44] (Emphasis in the original.)

The *chora* refutes any type of paradigm to categorize it; it rejects the logic of the logos and violates the logic of noncontradiction and of naming. *Gong'an* dialogues rely on the same logic, the origin of which can be traced to the silence of the Buddha. Based on our discussions on *gong'ans* from the *Gateless Gate* and the *Blue Cliff Record*, we can categorize *gong'an* episodes into three clusters.

The first group contains dialogues that plainly declare the identity of the provisional and ultimate levels of truth. These dialogues emphasize that the awakening or truth is not different from one's daily activity. Zhaozhou's "Wash Your Bowl" and Nanquan's "The Ordinary Mind is the Way" belong to this category. These *gong'an* episodes, however, entail their own limits, both philosophically and soteriologically. As Zhaozhou in the above *gong'an* asks, if the provisional and ultimate truths are expressed in the same way, how does one distinguish between the two? How does one understand the difference between the finger raising by the apprentice and that by the Zen master? One answer to this question can be found in the *gong'ans* we group together below as the second category.

The second category employs a linguistic imbalance that brings a shocking effect to the reader. The visible discrepancy in the question and answer violates commonsense logic. *Gong'ans* in the second group are the most well-known, probably because of the unfamiliar logic involved in these stories. "Zhaozhou's Dog" (*The Gateless Gate*, case 1), "Dongshan's Three Pounds" (*The Gateless Gate*, case 18; *The Blue Cliff Record*, case 12), or "Yunmen's Turd" (*The Gateless Gate*, case 21) all contains the exchanges between Zen masters and disciples in a manner which exceeds commonsense logic. As Chinul expounds, *gong'ans* are not truth as they are; they have a function of facilitating a transition from the hermeneutical to the existential in the reality of the subject. The gap between the question and the answer generates a situation in which the habitual exercise of the subject's understanding faces a dead-end.

The third category employs the narrative of violence. Derrida's identification of three forms of violence offers a neat paradigm to interpret the meaning of violence in this group. Derrida identifies three types of violence. Violence begins with articulation; or violence is inscribed in our capacity to use language that makes distinctions through a linguistic system. The first layer of violence in the form of naming opens a door for the second layer of violence arising from the institutionalized system such as moral codes, social regulations, and social laws. Out of this second layer of violence emerges empirical and physical violence. The use of violence in Zen literature can be read as a drastic measure to destabilize the proper name. From Derrida's and Continental postmodern thinkers' perspective, the first-level violence has real impact in history, which is as much physical as metaphorical.[45] When postmodern thinkers launch a critique of modernity and modernist enlightenment philosophy for its totalitarian tendency, they are also concurring with Derrida about the close relationship among the three layers of the violence outlined above.

Like the symbolic demonstration of one's attachment to a fixed concept of truth through Nanquan's killing of a cat, Huike's cutting of his arm symbolizes the cutting off of one's attachment; likewise chopping off the apprentice's finger reveals the dangerous border between the truth real and fake. The use of violence in Zen literature then is a metaphoric rendering of the violence that is involved in the fixed mode of thinking, which Zen Buddhism considers as the major problem one needs to overcome in order to attain the ultimate reality.

Chapter Six

Violence Institutionalized: The Social Dimension of Zen Language

1. Zen Language of Heterogeneity and its Social Dimension

A question might arise as to the reality of violence we discussed in the previous chapter. Does the Zen metaphor of violence, whose origin we traced to our mode of thinking, have any potential to be transformed into empirical violence, to which we usually restrict our use of the term violence? Well-equipped with the idea that no-killing is the first precept of Buddhism, we refuse to consider the possibility of empirical violence in the story of Nanquan's cat. We are ready to be complacent with the idea that the action is only symbolic: not only was there no actual killing of a cat in a monastery—since that is impossible to imagine—, but no social or public domain can be extracted from this figurative action in Zen literature. We would be happy to think that killing of a cat, slicing off of an arm, and chopping off of a finger—these are all a figure of speech, emphasizing the importance of cutting off one's attachment and desire in Zen Buddhist practice. By quarantining the reality of violence in the realm of a symbolic discourse in this manner, we mitigate the force of violence involved in these actions, and thus come to characterize Zen discourse as exotic stories on the one hand and as subjective idealism on the other. However, if we stop limiting the scope of violence in Zen literature to a metaphoric function, we might be able to see a different dimension of Zen Buddhist philosophy which we can identify as a social dimension of Zen language. In this way, we can also identify the different layers of violence that exist both in philosophical discourse and in our society.

We can begin our thought experiment on our premise that the metaphor of violence in Zen literature could be a symptom of potential empirical violence in the life-world with the following questions. In the literature of early Buddhism, the Buddha did not use a radical metaphor of violence. Why is it the case that Zen Buddhism uses the metaphor of violence extensively? Does it suggest that violence has a function in Zen tradition other than a literary trope?

The claim that the figurative violence appearing in Zen literature actually has its status in our life-world is not far from the discussion we had regarding Zen *gong'an* language. In our discussion of Chinul's *huatou* meditation, we identified subjectivity as a major obstacle to an individual's pursuit of ultimate freedom, or enlightenment. The enslavement by subjectivity in one's understanding of Buddhist texts and teaching is another way of understanding the case of "dead words," in which the subject maintains a clearly distanced position from the contents of teaching in a text. The subject understands the passage, but the linguistic expression remains as an object of the subject's scrutiny, and thus its contents fail to be the reality of the subject. This problem is relevant to what is known as the Zen rejection of language. Language's capacity to create a self-sufficient theoretical framework without connecting itself with the subject who is the receiver of the articulated product led the Zen tradition constantly to disqualify language as a medium delivering the message that the subject intends to embody. Pointing out the limits of linguistic expression, however, did not begin with the Zen school in Buddhism. The silence of the Buddha is one representative case in which Buddhist tradition demonstrates the limits of the existing linguistic practice as well as the limits of language itself. The Buddha claimed that he kept silent on the questions asked by his students because they were based on either annihilationism or eternalism. This was also Huineng's position when he advised his student to explore two extremes when using language.

In order to problematize the substantive nature of language and substantive mode of thinking, the Buddha, as well as Vimalakīrti, employed silence as an antidote to the substantialization of linguistic practice. Silence in these cases is itself language in the sense that it does not indicate a mere lack of sound or response, but imparts its message of disapproval and the limits of existing linguistic structure. The Zen Buddhist tactic was to act out silence and use language to represent this silence, and the tradition did so by using language against itself. *Gong'an* language, in which we encounter seemingly nonsensical dialogues, presents to the subject the limit of one's linguistic capacity and of the self-closure of normative language. This demands us to ask the question: how is it possible to use language against itself to begin with? Is the language used against itself language or not? If it is language, how is this language different from normative language? Is there a specific function of this non-normative, or performative, form of language?

The underlying assumption of these questions is that language and one's capacity to use language already entail the capacity to create a non-normative form of language. This awareness further develops into an insight that normative language is neither the only form of language nor its only "legitimate" form. Normative language is constructed through diverse participatory elements whose nature can be traced back to different sources related to social, political, and cultural arenas. This understanding of the position of normative language raises a question as to the relationship between language and power: who has the authority to decide the boundary of normative language, the normative way of thinking, and the norms in a society?

Let us examine the following *gong'an* encounter dialogue to place it in the context of the questions we posed above. The case number nine of the *Blue Cliff Record* contains the following dialogue:

> A monk asked: "What is Zhaozhou?"
> Zhaozhou answered: "East gate, west gate, south gate, north gate."[1]

Like other encounter dialogues, the above case is characterized by a gap between the question and the answer. We would not know, at least at this point, what the "correct" answer for the question could be, but it seems clear that the answer given by Zhaozhou is not an expected answer. What could have been the correct answer? Whatever the correct answer might be, the response given in this dialogue failed to offer that answer. Does that mean that the answer was wrong? Our answer will be negative. What is the difference between the answer which failed to provide the expected answer and the wrong answer?

Case number nine, which is basically a question about the identity of Zhaozhou, ends with Zhaozhou's witty word play. The inquisitor asked about the identity of the Zen master Zhaozhou and Zhaozhou answered by describing the city named Zhaozhou. By playing on homophones, Zhaozhou could have intended to debunk the questioner's desire to make Zhaozhou define his identity. However, Yuanwu Keqin (1063-1135), the commentator of the *gong'ans* collected in the *Blue Cliff Record*, criticizes this interpretation by saying that such a reading of the *gong'an* would be destroying the Buddha's teaching itself:

> Later people said this was "Chan of no-concerns' [C. *wushi Chan*], cheating quite a few people. What was their reason? When the monk asked about Chao Chou [Zhaozhou], Chao Chou answered, "East gate, west gate, south gate, north gate"; therefore (these people say) he was just answering about the other Chao Chou (i.e., the city). If you understand in this fashion, then any rustic from a village of three families understands more about the Buddha Dharma than you do. Such an interpretation destroys the Buddha Dharma. It's like comparing a fish eye to a bright pearl; in appearance they are alike, but actually they are not the same. As I said, if it's not south of the river, then it's north of the river. But is the Way to have concerns or not to have concerns? This does indeed require you to be thoroughgoing before you understand. (Translation modified.)[2]

Yuanwu's interpretation of the *gong'an* leads us to a new dimension in our interpretation of this *gong'an*. The original question demanded the identity of the Zen Master Zhaozhou. Zhaozhou turned it around by answering it with the description of the city named Zhaozhou. Yuanwu criticizes those people who understand this mismatching of the question and the answer as performed by Zhaozhou as a teaching of Zen's "not-concern" of anything. The Zen master Zhaozhou and the city Zhaozhou are all part of the world, people would say, and not making any distinction between a person and a city (since everything is dependently co-arising) will lead one to enlightenment. Yuanwu says that this is a misleading interpretation of the *gong'an* and any one who interprets the *gong'an* in this manner is destroying the Buddha's vision. The question of one's identity, which Zen Master Zhaozhou answered by replacing it with the identity of his environment (i.e., the city Zhaozhou), turns out to be another incident of Nanquan's cat and the search for the one truth. Yuanwu, in his comments, cites a dialogue between the Buddha and his inquisitor to make this point:

> There was an outsider who came to question the World Honored One holding a sparrow in his hand. He said, "Tell me, is this sparrow in my hand dead or alive?" The World Honored One then went and straddled the threshold and said, "You tell me, am I going out or coming in?" . . . The outsider was speechless; then he bowed in homage. This story is just like the main case; . . . 'The question is where the answer is, the answer is where the question is."[3]

Answering with the identity of the city Zhaozhou in response to the question asking the identity of Zen master Zhaozhou requires a capacity to break oneself free from the normative form of a question and an answer. However, even when one is able to break the distinction between the identity of a city and that of a person, the fundamental frame involved in this question and answer has not been changed because it is still addressing the issue of identity, the essence of an entity. As Jacques Derrida states, unless the whole format of questioning which asks "what is . . . " is broken down, one cannot free oneself from the substantive mode of thinking and its corollary. Derrida states, "One cannot get around that response [of identifying a sign with its formal essence, and thus of its presence], except by challenging the very form of the question and beginning to think that the sign is that ill-named thing, the only one, that escapes the instituting question of philosophy: 'what is . . .?'"[4] Derrida's statement reverberates the Buddha's silence, and what we defined as the problem of the ill-formed question. A certain underlying philosophical position in Zen *gong'an* literature then can be identified by now. Nanquan's cat, Chinul's dead words, and Zhaozhou's four gates—all problematize ossification in one's mode of thinking, and Zen *gong'an* claims that the process of ossification is especially relevant with the way language functions in our thought system.

How is it possible to reach this hermeneutical conclusion out of Zhao-zhou's simple answer, "East gate, west gate, south gate, north gate"? Why should following the meaning structure in our linguistic convention necessarily create constraints and what do these constraints entail? We can answer these questions by identifying two different aspects of language, the nature of which seem contradictory to each other. That is, language has the power to legitimate and consolidate the existing norms as norms with its basic function of making distinctions and giving substantive identity to separate entities; at the same time, language has the power to dissolve the identity it has endorsed. The former has been relatively well recognized in our philosophizing of language, whereas the latter has not. However, without such a dual function of language, language itself cannot survive. That which we call descriptive and prescriptive languages is one of the indicators of the legitimating and dispersing functions of language.

Changes within an entity, including language, are facilitated by its own other as much as outside conditions. Without outside stimuli, the other inside an entity might not be aroused; but if the other were not within one's identity to begin with, changes would not occur when external conditions are presented. Without considering the vulnerability of the identity of an entity to changing environments, Zen *gong'an* cannot function as *gong'an*. At the same time without considering the existing normative language, Zen *gong'an* cannot be *gong'an* either. The mutual indebtedness of the normative and anti-normative aspects of language that makes *gong'an* possible in Zen Buddhism recapitulates the existential and ontological position of the Buddhist doctrine of no-self. The identity of an entity is always already based on inter-subjectivity, and the self is from its inception heterogeneous.

Language is supposedly a tool for communication, and, in that context, language's capacity to create a normative communicative environment could be considered as a social function of language. In the case of Zen language, the reverse seems to be the case. Both the social and linguistic dimensions of Zen language lie in its capacity to disintegrate the seemingly consolidated meaning structure endorsed by a society. *Gong'an* language primarily demonstrates the linguistic practice which defies the normative format of linguistic structure. The resonance created by the ill-fitting nature of *gong'an* dialogue opens a space that makes the subject face a situation in which the normative language fails to produce meaning. The failure of normative language, however, does not terminate the role of language in this case, because the failure will gradually be transformed into an introduction to another form of language. The well-known Zen tripartite phrases neatly sum this up: "Rivers are rivers, mountains are mountains; rivers are not rivers, mountains are not mountains; rivers are rivers, mountains are mountains."[5] When one reads these passages without considering the different layers involved in the subject's relation with language, the passage could be none other than tautological and logically ill-formed phrases. It could even be deciphered as an expression of Zen Buddhism's non-concern about any distinctions in the phenomenal world. Yuanwu criticizes such an attitude as the mistake of "Chan of no-concern." Yuanwu states in the spirit of the above tripartite phrases:

> Some people say, "Fundamentally there isn't the slightest bit of anything, but when we have tea we drink tea, and when we have rice we eat rice." This is big vain talk; I call this claiming attainment without having attained, claiming realization without having realized. Basically since they haven't bored in and penetrated through, when they hear people speaking of mind and nature, of the mysterious or the abstruse, they say, "This is just mad talk; fundamentally there isn't anything to be concerned with." This could be called one blind man leading many blind men. They are far from knowing that before the Patriarch came, people scarcely called the sky earth or called mountains rivers; . . . It is all [a matter of] judgements of intellectual consciousness; when the feelings of judgements of intellectual consciousness are ended, only then can you see through. And when you see through, then as of old, sky is sky, earth is earth, mountains are mountains, rivers are rivers.[6]

Yuanwu here is similar to Chinul in saying that Zen practice does not offer a new theory or doctrines. Zen Buddhism does not make mountains into rivers or vice versa. What does Zen do then? Like Chinul, Yuanwu identifies the function of Zen discourse as pointing out the problem of subjectivity, which is also the problem of normative language.

Yuanwu specifies this issue with the problem of "the feelings of judgments of intellectual consciousness." Like the discourse on Zen Buddhism's relationship to language, this frequently appearing passage of Zen Buddhism's critical stance of rationalization and theorization could mislead the reader of Zen literature to the assumption that Zen refutes reason and thought. However, as Huineng articulated in his explanation of the meaning of "no-thought," no-thought does not mean not thinking; by the same token, identifying the problem involved in "the feelings of judgements of intellectual consciousness" does not indicate that Zen negates the function of intellect per se or any types of rational thinking. As the Sixth Patriarch Huineng writes:

> In this teaching of mine, from ancient times up to the present, all have set up no-thought as the main doctrine. . . 'No' is the 'no' of what? 'Thought'—what is this? 'No' is the separation from the dualism of all activities. True Suchness is the body of thought; thought is the function of True Suchness. If one's nature gives rise to thoughts, even when one sees, hears, and realizes it, one is not constrained by outside conditions and thus is always free.[7]

Through his own hermeneutical work, Huineng in this passage separates two Chinese characters of no-thought into "no" and "thought" so that the expression becomes a compound of negation ("no") and affirmation ("thought"), instead of the negation of thinking ("no-thought"). Huineng explains that "no" is the negation of the prevalent mode of thinking which Huineng identifies as the dualistic mode of thinking; "thought" is the activity of one's nature, which Huineng describes as True Suchness, that is, things as they are in the context of conditionally caused reality.[8] Like the silence of the Buddha, which negates the substantialist presupposition of his inquisitors, the "no" in Huineng's no-thought negates dualism as the most commonly shared pre-supposition in one's thinking practice. No-thought understood in this manner, which became possible by violating a syntactic norm, comes to mean different thinking activities instead of negation of thinking per se. In a passage prior to this citation, Huineng explains the problem of dualism as follows:

> Successive thoughts do not stop; prior thoughts, present thoughts, and future thoughts follow one after the other without cessation. If one instant of thought is cut off, the Dharma body separates from the physical body, and in the midst of successive thoughts there will be no place for attachment to anything. If one instant of thought clings, then successive thoughts cling; this is known as being fettered. If in all things successive thoughts do not cling, then you are unfettered. Therefore, non-abiding is made the basis.[9]

Thoughts arise in a constant interaction with stimuli produced inside and outside oneself. When the process of thought is interrupted, the activities of thinking become isolated; the interruption creates stagnation, and stagnated ideas are the symptom of one's clinging or attachment to the contents of that specific thought. This is also the instance when the subjectivity develops and consolidates its own system. By fragmentizing the thought out of the context in which it was originally created and further substantiating the separated thought, dualism is constructed. Chinul's "dead word" is the instance when thinking becomes stagnated and influenced by the subject's mode of thinking, whereas the "live word" indicate the context in which the subject engages herself/himself through the language presented, which Chinul evaluates as the state of the freedom: the subject frees herself/himself from the limits created by her/his own mode of thinking.

Liberation obtained in this manner cannot be limited to the subject's private domain but inevitably should be extended into the social dimension of one's existence. In this context, the socially engaged Korean Buddhist thinker Pŏpsŏng writes in his meditation on Zen *huatou* language[10]: "Language is a reflection of reality as well as a human construction of reality. To mystify formal logic which is a reflection of the totality of reality or to suppress the total reality of things through the fixation of formal logic is an attitude which fails to realize the dependent co-arising of language and reality."[11] He further states: "*Huatou* language reveals the dependently co-arising nature of things by negating falsehood and unreality; it is also the reality of existence revealed through such activities in our mode of thinking. Practicing *huatou*, seen from this perspective, is not a training to achieve a complete and holy self as many idealist Zen masters would like to think;. . . instead, it is a practice of re-cognizing things anew every time in the midst of nothing to cognize mystically." [12] Pŏpsŏng thus declares *huatou* as "a question-in-action which one asks oneself with regard to the situation at hand."[13]

Pŏpsŏng's emphasis on the renovating function of *huatou* language in the life-world is also voiced by Yŏ Ikku, another Korean engaged Buddhist thinker. In his outline of engaged Buddhist philosophy, Yŏ criticizes Mahāyāna Buddhist schools, claiming that they turned Buddhism into idealism by emphasizing the subjective aspects of mind and consciousness as opposed to the early Buddhism whose practice was focused on discipline. Despite his critical stance against Mahāyāna Buddhism, Yŏ suggests that the Zen Buddhist tendency for challenging the status quo and authority needs to be acknowledged and could make a contribution to conceptualize the social function of Buddhism. Zen *gong'ans*, Yŏ contends, "destroy the pitfalls of authority, idolized fixation, and ideological dogma to which people so easily become prey."[14] Yŏ further emphasizes, "If such a revolutionary philosophy of Zen Buddhism could have been connected with revolutionary thought of liberals, instead of having been employed as an ideology by the ruling class for the sake of their idealism, Zen thought could have functioned as a focal point of revolutionary movement anchored in the dynamic model of early Buddhism during the time of the Buddha. This remains as a challenge for those who practice and study Zen Buddhism to definitely keep in mind for the future."[15]

Here we are dealing with different layers of institutions in different arenas in our life-world, into which the dismantling power of the non-normative mode of thinking will be disseminated. On the first layer of institution we find the subject's mode of thinking that is constructed through normative language and formal logic. The second layer of institution includes socially constructed concepts such as gender, ethnicity, or social class. On the third layer one finds more tangible institutions such as nation-states or laws which maintain social categories. By noting these different layers of institutionalization in an individual's life, one can claim that liberation of an individual from the fettered mode of thinking cannot but be related to the liberaion from the other layers of institutions. The institutionality of these institutions, which we can identify as grounded in the centripetal force, is also being constantly undermined by the centrifugal force of language.

An institution, by definition and from the Zen Buddhist perspective, cannot but be violent, because an institution is constructed through the provisional seizure of otherwise fluctuating constituents of the structure. The centripetality, the power and the justification for the creation and maintenance of an institution, demands the unification in the form of commonly shared identity, goal, and signification, which offer meaning through the construction of a sense of a coherent whole in an individual, in a community, or in a meaning structure. The construction of such a whole inevitably entails the suppression and exclusion, which makes the process itself violent. To be noted, however, is the delicate fact that such an institutionalized violence, be it linguistic and conceptual, social and ethical, or political and legal, cannot but be also, in its turn, violated, or encroached by that which has been excluded in the construction of the coherent whole. Encroachment in this case might not be as visible as physical invasion but visible enough to make us aware of the unstable state of seemingly self-sufficient systems. The encroachment could take the form of a discomfort, alienation, or uncanny feeling in an individual, or a disturbance or commotion in a society. It could also develop into an awakening or a revolution.

This line of argument brings us close to what contemporary Continental philosopher Julia Kristeva defines as the revolutionary function of the poetic language. The revolution in this case includes all three levels of institutions we have identified: that is, mental, social, and political. Kristeva's discussion on the relation of three tiers of revolution through the signifying process is much relevant to Korean engaged Buddhist Pŏpsŏng's or Yŏ's interpretation of the social function of Zen language in the context of life-world. Let us briefly look into Kristeva's paradigm regarding the relationship among the three layers of institution before we further move on to our discussion of the social dimension of Zen *huatou* language.

2. Poetization and the Language of Revolution

In explaining the synergy of how our linguistic practice is related to the revolution of both the private realm of mind and the public realm of social discourse, Kristeva introduces a formulation that she identifies as the semiotic and the symbolic and investigates their relation to our mode of thinking. Revolution, by definition, suggests an entity's capacity to be its other. A revolution, however, is not simply a change. When milk is changed into cream, we do not call it a revolution. Revolution is a rupture; it is a sudden and radical discrepancy between the states before and after. A revolution also includes a belief that the changed status will drastically ameliorate and improve the condition of existence. For Kristeva, a revolution represents a rupture of heterogeneity that the unifying system of a society has suppressed. Kristeva calls the totality of the unifying and normative social system "the symbolic." Representative of the symbolic is language. Language, in this case, is not limited to a tool for communication facilitated by linguistic norms; it includes the act of differentiating, naming, and defining things by allotting space for a separate entity to emerge from the undistinguished stream of thought. The symbolic projects a transparent and scientific language in which the relation between the signifier and signified is rigidly set.

As opposed to the symbolic, the totality of that which is regulated, differentiated, defined and often suppressed by the symbolic is named "the semiotic." The semiotic in this sense is the "nonexpressive totality."[16] The semiotic for Kristeva—which is to be distinguished from the semiotic in semiotic theory or semiosis—is neither a sign nor even a signifier; it exists before the differentiation of the linguistic system. Another name Kristeva employs to identify the semiotic is *chora* (topos or place), borrowing the term from Plato's *Timaeus*.

Chora in *Timaeus* is proposed by Plato as a "third kind" of category in addition to his two categories of the world. There is the world of the intelligible or "that which always is and has no becoming," and there is the world of the sensible or "that which is always becoming and never is."[17] Plato writes, "That which is apprehended by intelligence and reason is always in the same state, but that which is conceived by opinion with the help of sensation and without reason is always in the process of becoming and perishing and never really is."[18] Unlike these two worlds of the form and of the imitations of the form, the exact nature of this third kind is not clearly articulated in the *Timaeus*. As Derrida suggests, the lack of a clear definition of this third kind could be the very nature of this "third kind." That is so, because the state of in-betweenness, by nature, defies a clear categorization, hence, the problem of identity follows. Plato first identifies the "third kind" by saying, "it is the receptacle, and in a manner the nurse, of all generation."[19] Plato further explains the third kind as follows: "the mother and receptacle of all created and visible and in any way sensible things is not to be termed earth or air or fire or water, or any of their compounds, or any of the elements from which these are derived but is an invisible and formless being which receives all things and in some mysterious way partakes of the intelligible and is most incomprehensible."[20] Hence, for Plato there are three kinds of world: "being and space [*chora*] and generation."[21] The question Plato attempts to deal with by introducing the third-kind, or *chora,* is the indefinable state of an entity. Plato reflects on the situations that "what we just now called water, by condensation, . . . becomes stone and earth, and this same element, when melted and dispersed, passes into vapor and air."[22] Plato contends that for those things that continually change, one should not identify them by naming, but indicate their instability through expressions like "such-ness." The space that holds the changing intermediate states of an entity is the receptacle that is "the recipient of all impressions" without itself being changed.

Reminiscent of Plato's *chora*, Kristeva's semiotic *chora* is mobile as opposed to static and provisional instead of definite. Kristeva also describes the semiotic *chora* through Freudian libido or life energy. If the semiotic *chora* is not a sign, but a state before signification, how do we know of its existence? Any attempt to explain the semiotic *chora* is already a meaning-giving-act and, thus, violates the nature of the semiotic itself, for it requires us to bring this non-linguistic dimension to the structure of language. In a strict sense, then, one cannot describe the semiotic. Kristeva readily admits this. Even though we talk about the semiotic as if it existed as an independent entity, this is only a provisional speculation about that which cannot present itself without first being subject itself to the rules of language. When we talk about the semiotic, the non-linguistic semiotic is already being combined with the linguistic.

This brief outline of the semiotic and the symbolic might generate an impression that they are dualistic or in a binary relationship: non-verbal versus verbal, mobility versus stasis, energy charges versus law, spontaneity versus continuity, and differentiation versus totality. However, Kristeva's device of the semiotic and the symbolic serves to demonstrate that no signifying system can be exclusively semiotic or exclusively symbolic; instead it is marked by indebtedness to both. The symbolic is a linguistic stage; however, signification takes place only when the symbolic interacts with and, thus, subjects the all-encompassing semiotic *chora* to the regulation of the symbolic. The semiotic "precedes and underlies figuration and thus specularization."[23] The semiotic is a precondition of the symbolic; but again, since the semiotic is a pre-linguistic state, it defines itself only through the signifying practice, which is a result of the transgression of the symbolic.

In discussing the semiotic *chora* and the symbolic, Kristeva calls attention to the asymmetrical function between these two in our use of language. Once the symbolic transgression takes place, the semiotic (or the drive charge) subjects itself to the rules of language. The symbolic defines, regulates, and asserts its rule. In this procedure, distinction creates a gap among the things that are distinguished, and naming cannot contain the whole of what is named. This is the limitation imposed on the symbolic by its own structure, determinations, and motivations. This limitation, however, is frequently ignored and an environment is created in which the symbolic dominates as if it were a self-sufficient system. To Kristeva, patriarchy, stratified class society, and monotheistic religion are examples of the situation when the dominance of the symbolic reaches extremes.

Kristeva's discussion of the semiotic and the symbolic and their relation to the power structure in the life-world explains the synergy between heterogeneity of existence and its homogenous manifestations. The relation between the two is neither equal nor voluntary. As for other postmodern thinkers, for Kriseva, understanding of human existence is linked to finding a social mechanism and its process of suppression as well as the contents of the suppressed. Once the validity of the transcendentality of ego or a priori conditions, which could have guaranteed the uniformity and consensus among humans, is put into question, there is no legitimate channeling system to generate and validate a regulating practice in a society.

When the Buddha declares his vision as the middle path, like the in-between state of Plato's *chora*, the problem of articulation and signification appears and remains throughout the evolution of Buddhism. Sometimes the issue comes at the fore of Buddhist discourse, as in the case of Zen Buddhism, and at other times it becomes almost oblivious, as in the case of folk Buddhism or new Buddhist movements at the beginning of the twentieth century in Asia. The postmodern awareness of the relation between the signifying process, theories of language, and those of subject, in this sense shares the common root with Buddhism.

By postulating the semiotic *chora* as a pre-verbal totality, Kristeva offers a linguistic presentation of the non-linguistic state of signifying process. The postulation of the semiotic *chora* as a precondition for the symbolic signification makes any coherent meaning structure provisional; a coherent whole is possible only through the temporary seizure of motility of the semiotic. In order to avoid the dualistic understanding of the two, instead of understanding the idea of *chora* as a "precondition" of the symbolic chronologically, one might want to borrow Derrida's idea and consider the "anachronic" postulation of the semiotic *chora*. [24] In his essay "Khōra," Derrida states: "The *khōra* is anachronistic; it 'is' the anachrony within being, or better: the anachrony of being. It anachronizes being."[25] As Huineng states, the expression darkness is possible, because there is light there; without light, darkness cannot obtain its position within the signification process. By the same token, the expression darkness becomes possible only when its indebtedness to light and non-darkness aspects becomes suppressed. In the expression darkness is included different shades of light and darkness. The symbolic expression darkness functions as a linguistic sign by being pregnant with its others, heterogeneous semiotic *chora*, but at the same time by suppressing the others. The signification in this sense takes place through self-denial by denying certain aspects that are inevitable constituents of its identity. Meaning construction of a linguistic system functions through the negation of the invisible aspect of the signified of the signifier. The dual operation of indebtedness to others and, at the same time, negation of others that are intrinsic parts of identity formation is indispensable in the signifying process. Homogeneity of linguistic expression is always already embedded within the suppressed heterogeneity. Heterogeneity in this case is not a precondition that exists before the signifying process of the symbolic. When the symbolic takes place, so does the semiotic; the semiotic and the symbolic give identity to each other simultaneously.

The semiotic *chora* helps us to clarify the nature of the centrifugal forces. Centrifugality, with its Latin origin *centrifugus*, a compound of *centr-* and *fegere* (to flee), is a tendency to proceed in a direction away from the center or axis. Centripetality, with the Latin word *centripetus*, *centr-* and *petere* (to seek), is a force moving toward the axis. When used together with centripetality as we do here, centrifugality might give the impression that it is a force that systematically and coherently moves toward the circumference, as centripetality does toward the axis. However, when we conceptualize centrifugality together with the semiotic *chora*, we understand that centrifugality is a state of diffusion rather than a force with direction. In the state of diffusion, there is no center; centrifugality understood as diffusion demystifies the concept of a center. This already indicates the politics involved in the concepts of the center and margins, understood from the perspective of centripetality and centrifugality. Margins are margins only when the center is declared and exercises its power. The seemingly clear division between the center and margins becomes problematic once we open up the question of boundary: where does one locate the boundary between the center and margins? By placing the ideas of the centripetal and centrifugal forces side by side with the concepts of the center and margins, one can visualize the suppression that takes place in the construction of the center. The idea of a center is always already an institutionalized concept, whose authority cannot but come from itself. This is the incident that Derrida describes as the "self-legitimation" in which one draws authority only from oneself.[26] For Derrida, metaphysical foundation is the absolute form of self-legitimation. It is the case of the center centering itself.

By introducing the semiotic *chora* as a non-foundational precondition for the linguistic signifying process, Kristeva brings our attention to the regulatory force of a linguistic system in a similar way that Zen *gong'an* language evokes the limits of normative language in the practitioner of *gong'an*. Kristeva's interest in this context lies in revealing how an institution, by the very fact of its non-naturalness, entails the rupture of the other, how the rupture exposes the suppression of the non-center, and how eventually the process frees the subject from the reified concept of identity.

Our daily use of language is a discourse in which the semiotic is relatively at peace with the symbolic, or the semiotic fully complies with the symbolic law. Poetry, according to Kristeva, is an explicit confrontation between socio-symbolic regulation and semiotic flow. In a normative discourse, the semiotic is subject to the ordering system of the symbolic. In poetry, the semiotic *chora* overflows the confines of the symbolic order, and the position between the semiotic and the symbolic runs in the opposite direction toward a "semiotization of the symbolic." When poetic language shakes up the stagnated meaning structure in normative discourse, linguistic practice is not the only area that is being challenged. The semiotic rupture can take place and dismantle any system that anchors itself on the illusory concept of a certain underlying totalizing power, be it a linguistic system, monotheistic religion, or patriarchal law.

The semiotic is a hypothesized state of pre-linguistic dimension whose status is functional but not existential. The symbolic is all types of regulatory systems, most representative of which is the linguistic system, but which also includes social customs, rules, and laws in a society. Once we admit that the relationship between the semiotic and the symbolic is characterized by mutual indebtedness, it is not difficult to see that the signification process inevitably involves suppression, and suppression is violence. Such suppression and violence indicates that signification is always already pregnant with rupture. Kristeva's outlining of the revolutionary resonance by bringing back the suppressed heterogeneity in linguistic expression and its social and political dimension can be paralleled with the function of *gong'an* language and Zen awakening in relation to linguistic and social dimensions. The fixed mode of thinking and rules and regulations that normative discourse has endorsed cannot but be affected. What Kristeva has tried to explain through a kinetic relationship of the semiotic and the symbolic is what Pŏpsŏng identifies as a dependent co-arising of language and reality.

Reminiscent of Chinul's distinction of the dead word and the live word, Kristeva identifies two types of text according to their function. The "genotext" organizes the space "in which the subject will be *generated* as such by a process of facilitations and marks within the constraints of the biological and social structure."[27] As opposed to the genotext, the "phenotext" denotes "language that serves to communicate, which linguistics describes in terms of 'competence' and 'performance'."[28] Text for Kristeva is "a practice that could be compared to political revolution: the one brings about in the subject what the other introduces into society."[29] Eventually, the political dimension in a society and literary practice is not separable, because "'incomprehensible' poetry . . . underscore[s] the limits of socially useful discourse and attest to what it represses: the *process* that exceeds the subject and his communicative structures."[30] The same can be said of Zen Buddhist employment of language, especially in the form of *gong'an* dialogues.

The engaged Buddhist thinkers like Pŏpsŏng and Yŏ Ikku tried to expand Zen *gong'an* language or the revolutionary spirit of Zen into the social dimension. Likewise, constant interplay of the semiotic and the symbolic reveals for Kristeva a close connection between language and socio-political reality. The Russian thinker Mikhail Bakhtin explains this issue through the dialogism of the centripetal and centrifugal forces of language. Bakhtin writes: "A unitary language is not something given [dan] but is always in essence posited [zadan]—and at every moment of its linguistic life it is opposed to the realities of heteroglossia."[31] For Bakhtin, "verbal discourse is a social phenomenon,"[32] and should not be reduced into an abstract discussion without a consideration of the social contexts that produced the discourse. What he calls the "unitary language," what Chinul calls "the dead word," or what Kristeva calls the "phenotext," "gives expression to forces working toward concrete verbal and ideological unification and centralization, which develop in vital connection with the processes of sociopolitical and cultural centralization."[33] The point to be made is that "the centripetal forces of the life of language, embodied in a 'unitary language', operate in the midst of heteroglossia."[34]

If distinctions are to be made among the three thinkers we brought together here in the demonstration of the social dimension of linguistic practice, we can arrange them in the following scale. At one end of the scale, we locate Chinul's Zen *gong'an* language in which the relation between the live and the dead word takes more existential tones; at the other end shall be located Bakhtin's unitary language and heteroglossia of social historical dimension of language, and Kristeva's semiotic and symbolic shall take the mid-point. All three cases demonstrate the mutual indebtedness of the two opposing forces in the signifying process.

3. Centrifugality and the Forms of Self-Legitimation

By postulating the mutual indebtedness of the semiotic and the symbolic, Kristeva wished to offer a philosophical paradigm which explained the suppression of femininity by the patriarchal system and create an androgynous vision. By the same token, if we envision the social dimension of Zen language as an integral part of the mental revolution outlined in Zen practice, and thus understand it to function as a challenge to the status quo, that aspect should be reflected in someway in Zen Buddhism's encounter with the life-world. However, contrary to such a positive evaluation of Zen philosophy, scholars have doubt about the possibility of Zen Buddhism's function in a society as an antidote to the existing authority. Instead of challenging authoritative voices in a society and thus offering itself as a subversive force to ameliorate problems in the life-world, Zen Buddhism seems to have remained ignorant of social problems or even intentionally stayed away from them, exclusively emphasizing the importance of religious practice or awakening. In an investigation of Zen Buddhism's relation to society, Christopher Ives points out this odd relationship of Zen and society as follows:

> Zen Buddhists usually treat the 'universal' religious predicament in virtual isolation from particular social situations. They tend to speak in ideal terms, usually

arguing that a human being can awaken in any time and place, regardless of the circumstances. This emphasis on the possibility of Awakening in any time or place drives a wedge between the overarching religious concern and specific social concerns. As a result, social suffering is either ignored or, if considered by Zen, relegated to a distant secondary position. Historically, monastic Zen has not studied, analysed, or responded self-critically to the full range of suffering in the social world. This lack of a critical spirit has contributed to problematical support of the status quo, whether the aristocracy, samurai dictators, militarists, or certain large corporations.[35]

From Ives's perspective, the exclusive focus of Zen Buddhism on an individual's enlightenment creates an ironic negation of the universality of the ontic or social level of suffering in the emphasis on the universality of ontological or existential suffering. The frustration Ives expressed here regarding Zen Buddhism's incompetence in dealing with social issues has been shared by those who wanted to understand the tradition in the broader milieu of the life-world and thus consider Zen Buddhism's position in social ethics.

When Minjung Buddhists of Korea criticized Zen and other forms of Mahāyāna Buddhism for the idealistic perspectives— as we briefly discussed in the case of Yŏ Ikku—, the Minjung criticism aimed at the Mahayanist tradition's exclusive focus on the individual's religious goals at the expense of its social dimension. As noted by both Yŏ and Ives, Zen Buddhism failed to call attention to the public dimension of one's life and religious practice, thereby defeating its own philosophical promise of universal enlightenment. As a result of this failure, the tradition has contributed to the authoritarian vision in the society. When such an authoritarian and asocial aspect of Zen Buddhism reaches its extreme, one finds Zen militarism, to which some scholars of Japanese Buddhism have recently paid close attention. According to the study of these scholars, instead of being a power detrimental to the status quo of a society, Zen Buddhism was an active collaborator for the militant imperial nationalism in modern Japan. In this context, Robert Sharf demonstrated how Zen Buddhism—especially in the form that became familiar to the Western practitioners and scholars of Zen Buddhism in the twentieth century—was closely related to and even a result of Japanese nationalism during the first half of the twentieth century.[36] Brian Victoria also has brought our attention to Zen Buddhism's involvement with Japanese militarism during World War II, raising doubts about Zen Buddhism's capacity as an ethical discourse. In two volumes, *Zen at War* (1997/2006) and *Zen War Stories* (2003), Victoria documents stories that demonstrate how Japanese Zen Buddhism (ab)used the Zen Buddhist doctrine of no-self to bolster patriotism during the late-nineteenth and early-twentieth centuries. Victoria states, "The 'selflessness' of Zen meant absolute and unquestioning submission to the will and dictates of the emperor."[37] One of many passages Victoria cites from the militant Japanese

Zen includes a statement made by Zen Master Harada Sōgaku who wrote, "[If ordered to] march: tramp, tramp, or shoot: bang, bang. This is the manifestation of the highest Wisdom [of Enlightenment]. The unity of Zen and war of which I speak extends to the farthest reaches of the holy war [now under way]."[38] In Japanese militant Zen, the Zen Buddhist emphasis on moving beyond the egoistic small self into the larger concept of self was interpreted literally to mean death, sacrificing one's self to the greater cause, which meant to "serve the State" and "serve the Emperor."[39] In these incidents, one finds that the figurative violence represented by the 'Nanquan's cat' episode has transformed into an actual violence in society and history. The emptiness of entity and identity which the *gong'an* addresses through the rhetorical violence in the *gong'an* "Nanquan Cuts the Cat in Two" became the theoretical ground for the actual violence of Zen involvement with imperialism, war, and nationalism.[40] In this history on Zen and war, the relationship between violence and Zen discourse takes a form which is completely opposite to what we have previously discussed. Instead of challenging the violence created by an institution, such as language or a normative mode of thinking, Zen Buddhism itself becomes an institutionalized violence. How do we explain the discrepancy between Zen Buddhism as a challenge to the institutionalized violence and Zen Buddhism as institutionalized violence?

One possible interpretation of this conflicting position of Zen Buddhism in its relation to institution, violence, and authority appears in a study that historically examines the formation of Zen *gong'an* narrative. John R. McRae, in this context, offers the explanation that the spontaneity involved in Zen *gong'an* was inscribed into the narrative when *gong'ans* were written down during the Song dynasty, instead of being actually performed by Zen masters during the Tang dynasty. McRae states: "Chan encounter dialogue derived not (or perhaps not solely) out of *spontaneous* oral exchanges but (perhaps only in part) out of *ritualized* exchanges."[41] McRae thus contends: "Given arguments already made by other scholars that spontaneity is merely 'inscribed' within the heavily ritualized context of Song-dynasty Chan, this interpretation allows us to wipe out the distinction between the 'classical' age of Tang-dynasty Chan when encounter dialogue was spontaneous and the subsequent ritualization of dialogues within Song-dynasty Chan."[42] The implication, especially in the context of our discussion, is that what we considered as the Zen Buddhist challenge to institutionalized authority and violence, which appears in the form of spontaneity and ill-formed linguistic dialogue in *gong'an* literature, was not there to begin with other than in the format which was inscribed in Zen texts with the purpose of reinforcing the institution as Zen. Bringing the reader's attention to the claim that "*there was never any such thing as an institutionally separate Chan 'school' at any time in Chinese Buddhist history*" (italics original),[43] McRae further employs historical contexts as support for his statements: "During the Song dynasty, Chan monks became abbots of most of the great monastic establishments in China, moving by imperial invitation from one position to the next, often carrying imperially bestowed titles and purple robes along the way."[44] This argument connects to Dale Wright's claim that Zen *gong'an* language is a "Zen monastic language game," the mastery of which brings power to the practitioner within the monastic community.[45] Both Wright and McRae suggest a certain linguistic structure embedded in encounter dialogue, which not only the Zen community shared, but which each member of the community was *trained* to master in order to be a member of that community. In Wright's reading of Zen encounter dialogue, the qualitative mastery of Zen language was rewarded with authority and power among those who share the language game. Zen encounter dialogue, in this sense, not only has its social dimension, but functions as a tool for group identity. McRae's and Wright's interpretation of the function of Zen *gong'an* language in the history of Chinese Zen Buddhism seems to demonstrate that *gong'ans* were a means for Zen Buddhists to consolidate power both in and outside monasteries. Does this indicate that the anti-authoritarianism of Zen spirit did not exist other than being employed for the purpose of consolidating the power of the school?

Another way of interpreting the seeming gap between the Zen philosophy of anti-authoritarianism and the school's failure to transfer this philosophy into the social life-world is to resort to the conventional idea of the breach between theory and practice. In other words, one can argue that the Zen Buddhist challenge to authority and an institutionalized mode of thinking was the original intention of Zen teaching, but when it was practiced by individuals, it became distorted, and thus individual practitioners remained in the hierarchical system of human group identity or fell short of moving beyond the individual level of religious emancipation. However, what we call the disparity between theoria and praxis has been a poor designation for finding the real cause of the gap. If there exists a chasm between theory and practice, the cause of that problem must be embedded within the theory itself, instead of being something that newly emerged in the process of the theory's encounter with the social life-world. If Zen Buddhism has demonstrated the authoritarian tendency, Zen authoritarianism must be a manifestation of a certain form of authoritarianism that is embedded in Zen literature and Zen philosophy, instead of a mere by-product that was generated by the gap between theory and practice. By identifying the philosophical foundation of the dual identity of Zen as a challenge to institutional authority and violence on the one hand and Zen itself as an institutional violence on the other, we might be able to address the issue to which the historicist approaches were not sensitive.

To put it in more concrete terms, even when we admit that the Zen rhetoric of spontaneity or the philosophy of subversion was retroactively inscribed into Zen literature and thus served the function of consolidating the social position of the school as the historicist approach to Zen Buddhism has claimed, the question still remains why the tradition chose to inscribe spontaneity and subversion of existing authority instead of inscribing something else. Zen Buddhism could have been openly supportive of the existing status quo in its process of consolidating its power and social position, and thus joined the rhetoric of social norms, claiming that Zen Buddhism can make contributions to the creation of social order and security for everybody. One might argue that the rhetoric of liberation—the aim of the Zen discourse of subversion— was a more effective tool to consolidate power in a given situation than the rhetoric of conformity. This claim, in order to earn full validity, requires the historical analysis of the context in which the Zen rhetoric of liberation becomes more effective than the rhetoric of conformity. What we call historical contexts, however, are not something "out there" for historians, or anybody else for that matter, to lift up and employ in order to evaluate the efficiency of a certain philosophical paradigm. More importantly, a text is never a closed system. A text here denotes not only printed texts which contain a particular discourse but philosophical systems and social contexts. A text generates its own effect, which cannot be limited to the intention of the author or the aim anticipated by the interest group. A discourse of liberation, subversion, and challenge to the status quo, even when it has been produced for the purpose of consolidating power within a group, cannot but engender, even in a dormant form, the effect of subversion, thus even undermining its own enterprise *if* the sole goal of such discourse was to consolidate the power of the group.

A similar but delicately different issue to consider in our interpretation of the social dimension of Zen Buddhism is the intrinsic self-contradiction a text comes 'to be born with' in the process of its generation. A text is a product of different layers of meaning structure and these constituents of a text not only can sometimes include claims that are contradictory to each other, but in the ultimate sense cannot but give rise to self-contradiction. This is so because a text is itself an institution created through the suppression and manipulation of the heterogeneity of its constituents, a heterogeneity which needs to be curtailed in order to produce the intended meaning of the text. In addition, in the context of non-substantialist philosophy, by which I categorize Buddhism in general and Zen Buddhism in particular, self-contradiction is an inevitable stage. This is the case because of two reasons: philosophizing and language. A philosophical text contains a philosophical system in language. The non-substantialist mode of thinking, with its rejection of any type of institution because of the latter's substantializing tendency, cannot but make self-contradictory claims in the attempt to establish its own philosophy. The radical use of language in Zen literature is one device Zen employed to resolve this tension between the non-substantialist philosophy of Zen Buddhism and the institutionalization of meaning in language and a discourse.

To rearticulate this idea in the context of the relationship between centripetality and centrifugality, we can formulate the self-embedded authoritarianism of Zen Buddhism as follows: centrifugality cannot exist without creating its own form of centripetal force in order to give legitimacy to centrifugality. As much as metaphysics relies on the transcendental conditions to anchor itself, the a-metaphysical mode of thinking needs to create its own center to authorize the validity of the discourse. The inevitability and burden of creating a self-authority, auto-legitimacy, and self-foundation exist in a non-substantialist mode of thinking as much as in the substantialist and traditional concept of the metaphysical mode of thinking. Zen Buddhism is no exception.

We noted that in the case of the silence of the Buddha, despite the Buddha's refusal of metaphysical and substantialist modes of thinking which he identified with eternalism and annihilationism, the Buddha himself had to universalize his experience of the dependently co-arising nature of existence. In the case of Zen Buddhism, Zen philosophy emphasized the non-substantiality of the mind, language, and eventually, of the Buddha and enlightenment. However, the authenticity of such non-substantialist philosophy had to be endorsed in some way for it to claim its own validity. The irony that non-reliance itself needs to rely on some ground, and that non-conformity itself has to create a certain form of conformity of its own to be valid, suggests the possibility that a non-substantialist system can resort to a strictly authoritarian form of self-legitimatization because the validation comes by way of defeating its own logic. The forms of self-legitimation most visibly employed in Zen tradition include the authority of the patriarch and that of the text.

These two forms of auto-legitimation seem to be in a contradicting relationship. One finds these two forms of authority alternatively employed in the process of self-legitimation of a particular Zen sect or a text since the beginning of the school. As the rhetoric of non-reliance on linguistic expression becomes stronger, the patriarchal authority also becomes fortified; in the relative lack of the emphasis on patriarchal authority, textual authority regains its power.[46] The *gong'an* encounter dialogue is a good example of this chiasmic relationship of the patriarchal and textual authorities in Zen Buddhism's auto-legitimation. As a performance and speech act, the *gong'an* encounter dialogue cannot function without the authority of the Zen master who offers a seemingly illogical answer to the question. The radical challenge to the existing mode of thinking which constitutes the content of *gong'an* discourse is framed within the unquestionable authority of the Zen master who presides over and conducts the *gong'an* dialogue. The centripetal force concretized in the Zen master's authority facilitates the dismantling ability of centrifugal power in a *gong'an* episode. To claim that the latter is a mere foil to consolidate the former seems to oversimplify the power structure and signifying process involved in *gong'an* discourse in particular and discourse in general. The balance might tilt: at a certain point, the patriarchal authority might overpower the subversive character of a *gong'an* dialogue, and at other times, the radical message of a *gong'an* episode could weaken the patriarchal authority as the frame enabling the dialogue. The case of Zhaozhou's 'wu' seems to belong to the category of the former, whereas 'Nanquan's cat' belongs to the latter. The distribution of power, however, could be based more on the context in which a certain *gong'an* is accessed by the practitioner.

When the spontaneity and thus the subversive nature of the *gong'an* episode is denied and their retroactive inscription into the *gong'an* text is emphasized (as is claimed by the historicist approach to *gong'an* literature), the relationship between the authority of the patriarch and that of the text enters into a new dimension. In this case, the authority of the patriarch is generated not by negating the authority of the text but *through* the text. Even though the act of producing the written texts of *gong'an* episodes was to promote and enhance the power of Zen masters, in this case, the Zen masters relied on the existence of texts, which is itself the evidence of textual power. Outwardly, the authority of the patriarch increased with the production of written texts; in reality, the authority of texts outwitted that of patriarchs.

Gong'ans are arguably the most subversive device that the Zen Buddhist tradition has generated. Because of the non-confirmative nature of *gong'ans*, their contribution to the establishment of internal power structures and authority seems less visible than that in the other form of auto-legitimation which Zen tradition has employed. A more visible form of self-promotion appears with the interplay of patriarchal authority and exclusive veneration of a specific text as the most authentic form of imparting the Buddhist teaching. A good example is Huineng's *Platform Sūtra*. In the *Platform Sūtra*, Huineng repeatedly emphasizes non-abiding as the keynote of his teaching. The *Sūtra* ends with Huineng's statement: "Among all, non-abiding was transmitted; even our minds do not abide."[47] The non-abiding nature of things, which is also another way of explaining non-substantiality or the selflessness of entities, served as a doctrinal foundation for Huineng's subitist claim of sudden enlightenment. The sudden enlightenment was endorsed as the "correct" way of practicing the Buddha's teaching in the *Platform Sūtra* first through the well-known poetry competition between Huineng and Shenxiu; it was again endorsed as the very teaching transmitted to Huineng by the Fifth Patriarch Hongren; and at the end of the book, in a deathbed conversation with his disciples, Huineng further endorses it as the teaching transmitted from the Seven Buddhas to Śākyamuni Buddha and all the way down to Huineng himself, as we read:

Fa-hui asked: "From the very beginning up to now, how many generations have there been in the transmission of the doctrine of the Sudden Enlightenment teaching?"

The Master said: "The first transmission was from the Seven Buddhas [of the past], and Śākyamuni was the seventh. Eighth was Kāśyapa, ninth Ānada, tenth Madhyāntika, . . . as of now I am the fortieth to have received the Law."[48]

What is known as the dharma-lineage of Zen Buddhism is once again confirmed here by Huineng to authenticate the identity of the sectarian teaching of sudden enlightenment. This process of self-legitimation becomes completed with the consecration of the text itself. Huineng states: "When [in the future] this Dharma is to be handed down, it must be attained by a man of superior wisdom, one with a mind of faith in the Buddha dharma, and one who embraces the great compassion. Such a person must be qualified to possess this *Sūtra*, to make it a mark of the transmission, and to see that in this day it is not cut off."[49] Huineng's case demonstrates how the teaching of non-abiding earns its validity through self-legitimation of the sectarian identity of sudden teaching.

Non-reliance on language by definition assumes the existence of language; without language, one cannot consider non-reliance on language. Buddhist literature has been keenly aware of this issue. The famous Vimalakīrti's silence, or the statement that the Buddha did not say a word during his forty-five years' teaching, could be representative of such an awareness. But the fact of the matter is that the Buddha did speak and so did Vimalakīrti, and thus they could not free themselves from the problem of self-authorization. In this context, Chinul offers to us a profound statement regarding the self-contradiction involved in human beings' activities of thinking, articulating, and meaning-making. At the very end of his work *Pŏpchip pyŏrhaeng nok chŏryo pyŏngip sagi* (*Excerpts from the Dharma Collection and Special Practice Record with Personal Notes*), after he introduced the Ten Diseases of practicing *huatou* meditation,[50] Chinul writes:

If you are truly an outstanding person, you will not be pressured by words and speech or by intellectual knowledge and conceptual understanding. Then, throughout the twelve periods of the day, whether you are in contact with sense-objects or involved with conditions, you will neither disseminate mundane truths nor formulate theoretical notions about the Buddha-dharma. If you do find the living road, you will naturally see the mistakes of all the Buddhas of the three time periods, and the mistakes of the six generations of patriarchs, and the mistakes of all the masters of this generation."[51]

Despite the speech act performed by the Buddha through his silence as well as that of Vimalakīrti and of Zen Buddhist *gong'an* dialogue, the act of meaning production, which is an inevitable portion of philosophizing, cannot but create its own limits. As Chinul notes here, even the Buddhas and patriarchs cannot be exempted from the limits involved in these activities.

If the self-legitimation process is an inevitable part of non-substantialist philosophy as much as it is the foundation of substantialist metaphysics, what would be the benefit of distinguishing the two? Are the differences merely a matter of degree or do they involve the nature of legitimation to the extent that they take us to a new dimension in our understanding of the function and meaning of legitimation? Our deliberation on the mutual indebtedness of the centripetal and centrifugal forces can be helpful to clarify this point. The proposal that centrifugality cannot exist without centripetality, nor revolution without institutionalization, does not amount to negating the differences between the two. This is so because the forms of legitimations and their functions within a discourse vary. It is through the consideration of different modes of self-legitimation, and not with the dream of a complete removal of legitimation itself, that one might approach a new mode for the legitimation process. The new mode can arise by considering a constant and consistent tension between the centripetal and centrifugal forces.

Part Three

THE TENSION: BUDDHISM AND THE POLITICS OF POSTMODERNITY

Chapter Seven

Modernity, Postmodernity, and the Question of Legitimation

1. Modernity, Postmodernity, and the Question of Legitimation

The problem of legitimation has rarely been a topic in the history of Buddhist thought. When the Buddha legitimated the validity of his claim that dependent co-arising is the basic structure of the world, the claim was grounded in his experience: the Buddha understood the reality of the world during his meditations, and the reality he experienced was that the world is dependently arising and that no being is endowed with its own independent self-nature. Hence, experience legitimates the Buddha's claim, which becomes one of the sources of the odd relationship between Buddhism and language throughout the history of Buddhism.

Legitimation comes to the fore in philosophical discussion when a discourse begins to separate itself from the metaphysical foundation. Once the given in a discourse is challenged and understood as a retroactive imposition through the process of universalization of the local truth, the question of legitimation emerges as the most urgent and defining factor in the construction of truth and the power which sets the parameter for the truth to exercise its validity. The production of meaning, which is one main goal of an articulation, is related to an issue of legitimation. Meaning-production in a given narrative is not a free-flowing activity, but an action performed within the existing constraints. The rules of games, in this case, also mean the rules of those who have power. A postmodern critique of modernity, both in cultural modernism and modernist philosophy, offers a way of considering how differing approaches to legitimation bring about changes in our way of understanding beings and the world.

In the discussions of modernity and postmodernity, the two have been frequently contrasted as if they were exclusive of each other: the modernist viewpoint is perceived as totalitarian in social, cultural, and philosophical discourses, and postmodernism is understood as yet another promise of liberation. However, the relationship between what we call the modern and the postmodern exceeds the simplistic projection of a binary opposition. Instead, like centripetal and centrifugal forces, they are mutually influencing: they are in a relationship of tension.

Jean-François Lyotard defines the postmodern turn as "incredulity toward metanarratives."[1] The modern period is characterized by "any science that legitimates itself with reference to a metadiscourse . . . making an explicit appeal to some grand narrative."[2] As opposed to the modern metanarrative, Lyotard characterizes postmodernism in reference to its acknowledgements of small discourse (or little narrative; *petit récit*). The modern metanarrative includes "the dialectics of Spirit, the hermeneutics of meaning, the emancipation of the rational or working subject, and the creation of wealth."[3] Lyotard contends that it shares as a narrative the assumed consensus between the sender of the message and its receiver. In modern grand narrative, "the rule of consensus between the sender and addressee of a statement with truth-value is deemed acceptable if it is cast in terms of a possible unanimity between rational minds: this is the Enlightenment narrative, in which the hero of knowledge works toward a good ethico-political end-universal peace."[4] As opposed to modern belief in the certainty of knowledge and its function as a creator of ethics and justice, postmodernism begins with the question: "Who decides what knowledge is, and who knows what needs to be decided?"[5]

The dream of a metanarrative in the manifestation of modernity is noticeable in various fields of human sciences: man-centered Ego-Cogito in the modern Continental metaphysical tradition, the emergence of the artist-creator in modernist art and literature, and imperialism and colonialism in modern politics. Underlying these discourses is an attempt to erase "others" in an effort to establish the "the subject" at the center. The name of the game is universal emancipation, which is believed to become possible by the human heroes who are equipped with knowledge earned through the rational thinking. Behind the tendency to create meta-narratives through human heroes in the modernist odyssey lies the human desire to seize reality. The struggle between the human desire and the reality of the world, which is, by nature, inhuman, constitutes the story of the modern period. The nature of the world is inhuman, and the inhuman, in this case, needs to be distinguished from the concept of the inhuman we are familiar with.

Lyotard in this sense clarifies two types of inhuman-ness: "The inhumanity of the system which is currently being consolidated under the name of development (among others) must not be confused with the infinitely secret one of which the soul is hostage."[6] Hence, Lyotard asks, "What if human beings, in humanism's sense, were in the process of, constrained into, becoming inhuman . . . ? And . . . what if what is 'proper' to humankind were to be inhabited by the inhuman?"[7] Needless to say, there exists a significant distance between the "inhuman" in the former and the "inhuman" in the latter. Humans are not at the center of the world and the world as it is does not have to be designed for the benefit of humanity. This also does not need to be understood as the universe being basically hostile to humans. Rather, Lyotard understands it as "the infinite secret of soul." Jacques Derrida would also join Lyotard in his understanding of the reality of existence as the "secret."[8] The "secret" for Derrida denotes the inexhaustibility of the context in which each event takes place. It is the totality of contextuality of one's existence, whose boundaries can never be reached because of their indeterminacy.

Human efforts to create institutions reflect human being's desire to decode and dissect the secret of human existence. Institutions in this case are not limited to the forms of commonly recognized entities, such as nation-states or governments, but also include those which are usually not thought of as institutions, including philosophy, arts, or literature; and there exist even more subtle forms of institutions, such as language, normative forms of emotions, and ethics. For some postmodern thinkers and critics of modernist projects, modernism, both as a historical period and a cultural philosophical manifestation, is the apex of the human dream to "humanize" the world.

Lyotard declares: "Modernity, in whatever age it appears, cannot exist without a shattering of belief and without discovery of the 'lack of reality' of reality, together with the invention of other realities."[9] In modern architecture, specific topographies are flattened and, thereby, erased, only to be re-created in the name of functionalism.[10] In a similar manner, modernist artists expressed their despair at the loss of a theocentric world, which, however, was eventually replaced by another order in which art and artists assumed the position of the surrogate God.[11] At the axis of this transformation from the disruption of the traditional world to the creation of a new world stands the artist. For modernist writers, "the world, reality, is discontinuous till art comes along . . . but within art all become vital, discontinuous, yes, but within an aesthetic system of position."[12] Time and history, as well as humans, regain their positions within the system created by the artists: a new order is established. The human-centered world created by modernist thinkers and artists, however, soon becomes the object of gloomier meditation on its nature before the postmodern era launches its full-scale criticism of modernist projects. The predecessors of the postmodern critique of the modernist Enlightenment project diagnose the exclusivist rationalism of modern philosophy and its projects as the principal cause of the very limit of the modernist vision.

In this context, Max Horkheimer and Theodor Adorno remind us of what has been forgotten in the midst of the promotion of reason and universal emancipation in the Enlightenment thinkers' project of philosophical modernity. Despite the promise to eliminate superstition and break down the collective powers of myth through the exercise of the rational capacity of each individual, the projects of Enlightenment and modernity have turned out to be relapses into mythic power. Modernity has become its own victim in terms of creating and believing the myth of a universal emancipation of human "selfhood." The authors of *Dialectic of Enlightenment* thus write: "Myth is already enlightenment; and enlightenment reverts to mythology."[13] Here, one finds another occasion in which mythos and logos, fiction and truth, overlap in one's attempt to create a desired reality.[14]

The chain of substitutions is characteristic of this project of humanization of the world. The theocentric world is replaced by an anthropocentric world; the omnipotent God is replaced by the Cartesian thinking subject and the artist-creator; the power of the man-centered world is generated by a "myth" which will become a reality in the future. Lyotard thus writes:

> These narratives [of modernity] are not myths in the sense that fables would be (not even the Christian narrative) myth. Of course, like myths, they have the goal of legitimating social and political institutions and practices, laws, ethics, ways of thinking. Unlike myths, however, they look for legitimacy, not in an original founding act, but in a future to be accomplished, that is, in an Idea to be realized. This Idea (of freedom, "enlightenment," socialism, etc.) has legitimating value because it is universal. It guides every human reality.[15]

The promise of universal emancipation justifies universal control. Both historical modernism in arts and the technocratic functionalism of social modernization share the desire to control. Horkheimer and Adorno thus declare: "Enlightenment is totalitarian."[16] Horkheimer writes: "This mentality of man as the master (which was the essence of the Enlightenment view) can be traced back to the first chapter of Genesis."[17] As a secular version of Christian belief, the project of modernity states: "Man dominates nature and the world." To Horkheimer, Enlightenment has "always taken the basic principle of myth to be anthropomorphism,"[18] and its tendency of domination reflects "the entire spectrum of Western thought."[19]

The desire for dominance constitutes the core of modern culture. Julia Kristeva identifies such instances in the monotheism of Judeo-Christian tradition, the phallo-centrism of patriarchal society, and the capital-monopoly of capitalism.[20] Jacques Derrida provides us with a list of traditions which are characterized by the dominance of central powers over the margins which he names as: logocentrism, egocentrism, phonocentrism, phallocentrism, and ethnocentrism.[21] In this spectrum of monotheism in religion, philosophy, the economic system, and gender and racial politics, those who are on the periphery are subject to the logic of the center. The East, women, people of color, and the have-nots are controlled by the center, which renders the peripherals to be mortified and, eventually, silenced.

The postmodern criticism of the modern, for its tyranny of reason, cannot be understood as a literal criticism of the human being's rational capacity, per se. Be it reason, emotion, intuition, or whatever faculty of human beings, be they Caucasian males or Asian women, the self-closure of a system separating its parameters of power from its environments and consolidating its center, shall be duly subject to the postmodern charge of modern totalitarianism. Once the relationships of the center and margins in the modernist project become identified, we begin to recognize another type of silence, which is similar in its source but different in nature from that of the Buddha and Vimalakīrti. For the sake of convenience, we will call it postmodern silence, not in the sense that postmodernity has caused the silence, but in that it begins to recognize this type of silence as silence.

2. The Buddha's Silence and Différend

Silence is a charged language in Buddhist tradition. The silence of the Buddha and that of Vimalakīrti have been recognized as prime messages that the truth which Buddhism tries to expound is beyond linguistic expression and that the ultimate truth is always ineffable. The incompatibility between the ultimate truth and language in this context has been repeatedly addressed by Buddhist scholars. What also needs to be recognized, however, is the fact that both the Buddha and Vimalakīrti did speak. Their silence was language as charged with signification as any verbal communication. Mañjuśrī thus acknowledged Vimalakīrti's silence as being the best form of expressing non-duality, and the Buddha articulated his silence through the doctrine of the middle path. Both in the Buddha's and Vimalakīrti's cases, silence demonstrates the limits of existing linguistic and philosophical structures. In understanding their silence, then, we need to move one step further and consider the situation in which the different modes of thinking put the under-represented subject into actual silence. In this case, the silence does not signify a challenge to the existing linguistic expression nor is it another form of communication that is more elevated than articulation itself. The silence, in this case, represents none other than a complete lack of communication in which the subject loses all the means to express itself.

The two types of silence, that is, the silence of the Buddha and the postmodern silence, are caused by similar contexts. The subject either refuses or fails to conform to the existing means of articulation which include not only linguistic conventions but norms of the dominant mode of thinking in a given community. When the subject refuses to follow the norm, as in the case of the Buddha and Vimalakīrti, to keep silence takes the form of a subversive act. However, when the silence is forced on the subject, instead of being the subject's speech act, the silence does nothing but confirm the subject's invisible existence. In a more nuanced and politicized understanding of silence as invisibility, Lyotard explicates it by employing the concept *"différend."* Borrowed from the context of litigation, *différend*, in the way Lyotard uses the term, refers to the situation when the plaintiff "is divested of the means to argue and becomes for that reason a victim."[22] It is a "case of conflict, between (at least) two parties, that cannot be equitably resolved for lack of a rule of judgment applicable to both arguments."[23]

One memorable example of *différend* that Lyotard offers is a case regarding the existence of a gas chamber. Plaintiff *A* claims that the gas chamber was used to kill people, and, that once placed inside, no one survived. Defendant *B* demands evidence of this, and the only evidence s/he would take is testimony from an eyewitness. Since nobody has survived the gas chamber, *A* cannot provide any eyewitnesses. But, if there were someone who could testify to this, *A*'s claim that the gas chamber was used to kill people and that nobody survived it could not be sustained. Either way, *A* fails to make his/her case and is at the mercy of the opponent to prove his/her claim. The case is characterized by the fact that "the 'regulation' of the conflict . . . is done in the idiom of one of the parties while the wrong suffered by the other is not signified in that idiom."[24] On a surface level, *différend* is a linguistic problem in which the speaking subject fails to find proper language to express his/her situation. On a deeper level, it carries the complexity of the social, historical, and philosophical context which occurs when a dominant discourse in a society deprives other parties of their right to take different positions and the right to tell the story on their own.

The insight that postmodern discourse brings into this situation marks the limit of legitimacy as well as its conditionality. Postmodernity does not simply contend that the truth or legitimacy exercised in a given situation at a given time by a particular agency is either illegitimate or wrong. Instead, the problem to recognize, from the postmodern perspective, is the fact that "[o]ne side's legitimacy does not imply the other's lack of legitimacy."[25] By the same token, one side's logical argument does not, by default, guarantee the other's lack of logicality. The binary and hierarchical model on which modernist discourse has anchored itself is not something that can be thrown away off-handedly; instead, the fundamental ambiguity and ambivalence which a discourse contains within itself should be manifested once parties involved in a discourse begin to receive due attention. To approach *différend* as a problem of narrative and legitimacy, instead of a searching for one truth and its legality, reflects the nature and orientation of postmodern discourse and its position in ethical and political domains.

The postmodern investigation begins with the concern, as Lyotard puts it, "How do you prove the proof?"[26] The most common responses to this question, especially in philosophical investigations, are of two types: either one falls into the infinite regression of searching for the origin of the origin ad infinitum; or one stops the flow of this regression at one point and turns it into one's own transcendental foundation. The former has been categorized as a part of nihilism, as the latter is a tendency generally found in a metaphysical tradition. An alternative to these two responses, one which has been unduly neglected, is to rephrase the question itself. That is, one can ask how one can still create meaning and continue the activity of searching for truth without proving the proof. Both Buddhism and the postmodernist turn in Continental philosophy can be understood as attempts to utilize this third option. When the Buddha refuses to answer the questions posed by Māluṇkyāputta or Vatsa, and later proposes his response to the questions as the middle path, the Buddha is not suggesting that the speculative issues on philosophical discourse are irrelevant to his philosophy. The Buddha's silence is not a refusal to discuss the issues presented by Māluṅkyāputta, but is his way of problematizing the metaphysical mode of narrative. The issue to consider in reference to the Buddha's silence is not so much *what* as *how*. By presenting the middle path as the core of his philosophy, the Buddha repudiates both annihilationism and eternalism in understanding the identity of self. The former is a corollary of nihilism, as the latter is of metaphysics. One cannot generalize that all different Buddhist schools and theories share the third alternative proposed here. However, one can contend that our discussions of Zen *gong'an* language and its social dimension, and Zen *huatou* meditation and its potential as a subversive power, proffer us a clue to map out a Buddhist-postmodern paradigm of continuing to search for truth without closure.

The modern asserts its "meta-narrative," the all-encompassing world of the one-theory and one-paradigm, in an attempt to control particularities in the phenomenal world. Unlike the modern meta-narrative which subjugates and assimilates others to the discourse of the powerful under the logic of consensus, the postmodern turn is characterized by its recognition of "small discourses." As a constant reminder of the existence of different narratives, postmodernity begs us to examine conditions for the possibility of the co-existence of small discourses without hierarchy. Postmodern small discourses take diverse forms. Women will tell their versions of stories alongside the long-reigning meta-narrative of patriarchal tradition; Asians, African descendents, and other ethnic minorities will raise their voices against the centuries-long discrimination of ethnocentrism. Speak they will, but what kind of language will they speak? Mute for so long, speakers of small discourses are strangers to their own language because their language has forgotten them. Narratives of small discourses have stories, but no idiom, no logic, and no language in which to tell the story—another moment of postmodern silence. Understood in this perspective, postmodernism, a time for small discourses, cannot take place by simply letting small stories be told; it puts up with their muteness, waits for them to find their phrases, and links them together so that *différends* find their own voices.

For some people, the idea of letting different groups in a society raise their voices could be a scary thought. The inability to seize reality and to leave the multitudes to their own hands without properly regulating them could cause anxiety and make some worry. Charles Newman expresses his worries that the postmodern "inflation of discourses"[27] possibly fosters "cultural incoherence of the most destructive sort,"[28] and Fredric Jameson characterizes postmodern hostility toward the center and regulating power as "schizophrenic."[29] Further, postmodernism has been blamed for creating an anything-goes culture, and conservative intellectuals in the United States have even accused postmodernism of having caused the decline of liberal education in American academia.[30]

For those who are discontent with the postmodernism of heterogeneity, Jürgen Habermas's interpretation of postmodernism can be an appealing alternative to the Lyotardian proposal.[31] For Habermas, postmodernity is another attempt to accomplish the original goal of the Enlightenment so as to complete the "incomplete" project of modernity. Habermas contends that postmodernity calls one's attention to the harmony of reason and imagination. Postmodernity is an attempt to combine the Weberian sub-divisions of science, morality, and art into the realm of the life-world by employing them in the service of everyday life.

With Habermas, the Frankfurt school's criticism of the modernity project following the Weberian line takes a positive turn. This turn anchors itself on what Habermas calls communicative action based on communicative reason. For Habermas, the problem entailed in modernity is not rooted in rationalization as such, but in the unbalanced development of different dimensions of reason. Accordingly, from this viewpoint, both Weber (who reads rationalization explicitly as the dominance of the instrumental form of reason) and Horkheimer and Adorno (who deny any trace of reason in the structures and institutions of modern life) are making the mistake of dismissing "the selectivity of capitalist rationalization." Whereas Weber sees no possibility of reconciliation between substantial and instrumental reason, Habermas explicitly calls for their balance as a way back to the aim of the Enlightenment project to be continued in the future. For Habermas, the project of postmodernity is to revoke the assertion of separation and autonomy in Weber's divisions of reason back to the hermeneutics of everyday communication.[32] Doing so would complete the incomplete project of modernity. This Habermasian blueprint of postmodernity is grounded on his belief in rationalization. The "rationalization of everyday practice," Habermas suggests, should increase the possibility of communication reached via rational understanding-agreement, and this should further enhance the structures of inter-subjectivity in the life-world.[33]

For Lyotard, however, consensus is "a horizon that is never reached."[34] Lyotard argues that consensus, even when it is obtained through discussion, cannot find legitimacy if the heterogeneity and diversity of small discourses of the postmodern world are to be fully recognized. For Lyotard, the Habermasian call for consensus is none other than a remnant of totalitarian philosophy. The back-to-the-future plan proposed by Habermas only reinforces another form of meta-narrative, in which the logic of *we* overrules the logic of *them*. From Lyotard's viewpoint, the failure of such a meta-narrative of universality, the promise of the project of modernity, was already inscribed into its inception. Here, the specific reference for Lyotard is the Declaration of the Rights of Man, in which the promise of free citizenship for all is overshadowed by the emphasis on its author-ship: "We, the French People."[35] The door to universalism was already closed at the beginning of modernity. The meta-narrative of universal emancipation was liquidated with Auschwitz, which Lyotard characterizes as "the crime opening postmodernity."[36] Auschwitz, Lyotard announces, is the "paradigmatic name for the tragic 'incompletion' of modernity."[37] The modernist dream of humanizing history by creating order and regulating diversity, Lyotard suggests, justified the logic of exclusion. Hence, Lyotard declares: "We have paid a high enough price for the nostalgia of the whole and the one, for the reconciliation of the concept and the sensible, of the transparent and the communicable . . . Let us wage a war on totality; let us be witnesses to the unpresentable; let us activate the *différends* and save the honor of the name."[38]

One might ask how postmodern tolerance for heterogeneity validates itself without defeating its own claim. If truth is contingent upon the conditions of truth, and the conditions are set by those who have power to set the rules for the conditions, as much as modernist meta-narrative, the postmodern small discourses shall also be subject to the self-legitimating tendency of a discourse. In the process, small discourses themselves will create hierarchy, make them another form of meta-narrative, and turn the trend back to the modernist paradigm. How should one be convinced that small discourses will remain appreciative of the horizontally layered heterogeneity of their identities? Why should small discourses refuse to turn themselves into another meta-narrative, since any narrative—regardless of the number of people affected by the discourse—can turn itself into a totalitarian vision of a meta-narrative by universalizing its local values? Even in postmodernity, there is the subject who lives life and makes decisions in each and every moment. In postmodern small discourses, as in the modernist meta-narrative, there should be "we" who become members of each small discourse. Lyotard even declared that "we" should wage a war against the modernist desire for totality. Who could be this "we" through whom a war against the logic of "we" shall be waged? Is this "we" different from the modernist logic of "we" against "them"?

Lyotard responds to this potential criticism against the postmodern "we" by defining the "we" in postmodernism as an "affair of linking phrases."[39] Lyotard contends that the construction of "we" in postmodernism is only provisional; there is no universalizing "we" that can create the totalitarian meta-narrative, hence, the postmodern "we" is like linking of fragmented phrases. In order to indicate the provisional nature of the postmodern "we" as opposed to the modern "we," Lyotard sometimes uses "we" with a question mark in parenthesis "we(?)," a technique analogous to Heidegger's "b̶e̶i̶n̶g̶". This "we" is that which "is never *we*, never stabilized in a name for *we*, always undone before being constituted, only identified in the non-identity between *you*—the unnameable one, who requests—and me, the hostage."[40] Like Kristeva's concept of the "subject-in-process," the postmodern "we" for Lyotard is never a fixed entity. The identity is always already non-identity, and subjectivity is possible only by being inter-subjectivity.

3. Legitimating Small Discourses

Modernity is a tendency to create a center, order, and unity, and thus foregrounds homogeneity; whereas postmodernity reveals the limits of the modernist project and demonstrates that the creation of order is possible only through the humanization of inhuman reality. Lyotard explains the relationship as follows: "A work can become modern only if it is first postmodern. Postmodernism thus understood is not modernism at its end but in the nascent state, and this state is constant."[41] Unlike the commonsense postulation that post-modernism, with its prefix *post-*, designates what comes after modernism, Lyotard reveals that modernism is our reaction to the conditions that we eventually identify as the postmodern. Without the initial awareness of the diversity of the world, one does not have to attempt to create a coherent system out of diverse existence in life. Also, unless one is exposed to the differing values, universalism would not emerge as a way to regulate differences. This explains why the postmodern mode of thinking rejects the linear and teleological time concept of metaphysics and projects a concept of time that considers the present only as a retroactive construction. Lyotard explains this nature of a non-teleological time line in postmodernism through the expression, "the paradox of future anterior."[42]

What would it mean to say that an incident is understood as the paradox of "future anterior," or that the signification of the present is possible only as an afterthought? The a-linear and a-teleological mode of thinking is not (or not just) about time but about the nature of reality. From this perspective, reality exceeds the frame of references that are available at a given moment, and that is because, for Lyotard, an interpretation or a discourse can happen any number of incommensurable ways. The idea rejects the modernist subject that is at the center of meaning-giving action as well as modernist universalism as the regulating factor of values and norms. As opposed to the organizing subject, the postmodern mode of thinking admits incommensurability amongst heterogeneous language games. No one interpretation can be universal enough to encompass all the significations with which a discourse or an event is pregnant. Thus, each event is unique. Lyotard explains this uniqueness of each event, which defies any regulation by ready-made interpretations, with the concept of *happening*. That is, once postmodern sensitivity puts into question the legitimacy of meaning-giving action, each discourse and event in the postmodern is understood as just an *occurrence*.

The postmodern warning signal calls for alertness. The meaning-giving-act through which humans try to control reality cannot be suspended. Situations already 'happen' before being regulated by logic, and the awareness of such a nature of situations is to be practiced. Lyotard writes: "Just occurrence . . .. That it happens 'precedes' . . . the question pertaining to what happens . . . The event happens as a question mark 'before' happening as a question. *It happens* is rather 'in the first place' *is it happening, is this it, is it possible?*"[43] It should not be difficult to note in Lyotard's postmodern interrogative form the echo of the logic that Zen Buddhism employs in its *gong'an* encounter dialogue, especially in the form of *huatou* meditation. Like Zen *huatou* meditation, which employs the interrogative spirit to create a space for a practitioner to move beyond the commonsense logic, Lyotard's postmodern questioning suspends the ready-made interpretation of an event. As Merleau-Ponty expounds clearly, interrogation is an effort through which both the subject who is interrogating and the object that is being interrogated meet in the chiasmic realm of middle point. Interrogation in the *gong'an* mode of thinking and Merleau-Ponty's philosophy represents the openness of being, as opposed to the seizure of reality in a declarative form of narrative, and so does Lyotard's postmodern interrogation.

The sensitivity to the mutually penetrating effect of time radically challenges the metaphysical concept of time characterized by teleological linearity. That the time and event exist as a future anterior does not imply a reversibility of time and meaning. The present will always be in the form of the future anterior, which amounts to saying that the grasping of present moments, and, by the same token, those of the past and future, is not possible without an intentional and artificial construction of the concept of past, present, or future. The postmodern understanding of events as the future anterior, which refuses to resort to that point in time where one encounters the 'present', is to be understood, then, as a manifestation not of time but of the unpresentability of events, whose boundaries always already exceed the existing signifying system. [44] The postmodern awareness of the *incommensurable* reality, according to Lyotard, refines "our sensitivity to differences," and thus "reinforce[s] our ability to tolerate the incommensurable."[45]

In the whole process of the Lyotardian discussion of postmodernism and its juxtaposition with modernism, on the one hand, and with the Habermasian model of postmodernism on the other, one might feel that there is a missing link. To put it in a nutshell, would it be possible to completely break up with what is represented by the spirit of modernity, its concept of the subject at the center of meaning giving act, and its desire for universalism? Can consensus as proposed by Habermas be completely dismissed in postmodern endorsement of small discourses and indeterminacy? The postmodern for Lyotard is a break with the modernist universalist dream; it is a break-up without nostalgia, Lyotard contends.[46] However, an emphasis on postmodern diversity and heterogeneity with a desire to completely separate from the modernist centralizing power could be a symptom of the return of the modern. As much as the exclusive promotion of homogeneity in the case of modernity generates totalitarianism, a dream of *pure* heterogeneity can produce the same effect.

Homogeneity is indebted to both regulating and dispersing forces, and so is heterogeneity. The exclusive elevation of postmodern diversity with an emphasis on a complete break with modernity can render the position of postmodern small discourses ambiguous. It raises the question of the validity as to the grounds of the postmodern claim that one needs to pay attention to small discourses and bear witness to the *différends*. Where does this responsibility or obligation come from when the transcendental foundation is denied? The consideration of the ambiguous position of small discourses raises questions about the ethical stance of postmodern discourse. In a situation when all and any legitimating foundation is negated, if no regulatory guide can be validated, and consensus is a horizon that can never be reached, how does even a small discourse validate its own existence? One goal of postmodern discourse has been to deconstruct the self-imposed substantiality of modernist discourse. When a discourse is understood as an independent entity, it brings with it a certain form of power; meta-narrative is another name for the omnipotence of the power of a narrative and of those who control it. Subversive forces inevitably consolidate their power to subvert, which cannot but repeat the logic of "we" standing against the logic of "them." How would the Lyotardian paradigm of postmodernity avoid being a part of the power structure which it criticizes? Some have already raised the issue of whether small discourses are another grand-narrative.[47] Others claim that this paradox itself makes the postmodern.[48] These doubts regarding the nature of the small discourse and small discourse's relation to grand narrative ask us to reconceptualize and clarify the position of small discourses in postmodernity.

The modernist idea of meta-narrative and the postmodern concept of small discourses is a variation of one of the perennial themes in philosophy, which can be categorized under a general rubric of the *one* and the *many*. In philosophical discourses, the issue has been discussed under the categories of universality and particularities, or unity and diversity. In the postmodern discourse, the expressions have been frequently replaced with the center and margins, fully charged with the social and political implications of this theme. One can also understand the relationship between the two poles in connection with the paradigm of centripetality and centrifugality. Different philosophical trends offer different visions as to the relationship between the two. As postmodernism refutes the possibility of a metaphysical foundation, it shows the tendency to completely dismiss the role of noumenon (or the unifying principle) which underlies phenomena. The point to consider, however, is that, despite the seeming bipolar positions drawn from the linguistic renderings of the two poles under our consideration, the rapport between the two is rather subtle and complex in the sense that one cannot separate the two completely. This suggests us that a certain form of underlying principle might be possible without setting itself as a *prima causa* and thus exercising its privilege as it does in the metaphysical paradigm. This foundation which is not founding is the *one*, but the oneness is possible by being not the one but the many. One might already detect here the echo of Zen philosophy as in the Zen *gong'an* "All things return to one and to where does the one return?" Zen Buddhism constantly disperses the desire for the one truth but does not completely negate the existence of the one. This rather counterintuitive relationship between the one and the many, or noumenon and phenomena, is elaborately explored and systematized in an of East Asian Buddhist School known as Huayan Buddhism.

In the following chapter, we shall explore the status of postmodern small discourses in connection with Huayan Buddhist philosophy on the phenomenal world. On the one hand, the way in which Huayan philosophy presents the relationship between noumenon and phenomena is comparable to the relationship between the modern and the postmodern as outlined in Lyotard's postmodern philosophy. On the other hand, the nature of noumenon in Huayan Buddhism maintains a distance from the way in which modernist metaphysics envisioned the noumenal reality. In this combination, one might be able to find a paradigm which will better suit the nature and position of the small discourses in postmodernity.

Chapter Eight

Postmodern Small Discourses and the Huayan World of Mutually Non-interfering Phenomena

1. The Huayan Fourfold Worldview and Mutually Non-interfering Phenomena

As a culmination of the doctrinal synthesis of Chinese Buddhism, Huayan Buddhism has been best known by its fourfold worldview (or fourfold realm of reality; C. *sifajie*), which was first conceptualized by Dushun (557–640), and later systematized by Chengguan (738–840). The paradigm neatly theorizes the Huayan version of the theory of dependent co-arising, as explained through the relationship between noumenon and phenomena or the universal and the particular.[1] The fourfold worldview is a four layered hermeneutical proposition and does not have four different matching ontological states. In other words, the fourfold worldview does not claim the actual existence of four different levels of existence; it is a hermeneutical device to explain the nature and structure of existence by illuminating the relationship between noumenon and phenomena. The fourfold worldview consists of the reality realm of phenomena (C. *shifajie*), the reality realm of noumenon (C. *lifajie*), the reality realm of the non-interference between noumenon and phenomena (C. *lishi wuai fajie*), and the reality realm of the non-interference among phenomena (C. *shishi wuai fajie*).

The "reality realm of phenomena" designates the world of concrete reality in which diverse particularities co-exist. The "reality realm of noumenon," the second layer of the vision, conceptualizes an overarching principle which encompasses the diversity that is present in the phenomenal world; in the third level, since each and every phenomenon in the world commonly shares noumenon which pervades individual entities in the phenomenal world, the relationship between noumenon and phenomena is understood as non-interfering. As an extension of the third level, all the particular phenomena in the world, being illustrations of noumenon, are understood as existing without obstructing one another. This fourth level of "the reality realm of non-interference among phenomena" (or "the reality realm of mutually non-interfering phenomena") has been promoted as a culmination of Huayan Buddhist philosophy, the hallmark by which Huayan Buddhism claims the superiority of Huayan thought over other Buddhist schools, as the tradition identifies itself as the "complete teaching" or "perfect teaching" (C. *yuanjiao*).

The four layers of the fourfold worldview of Huayan Buddhism have too often been cited without critical evaluations of significant ramifications the vision entails. Seemingly simple on its surface level, a close look at the paradigm evokes questions that do not seem clearly articulated by the major thinkers of Huayan Buddhism during its inceptive period. Even though the fourth level of the fourfold worldview characterizes the world as "mutually non-interfering," this cannot indicate that Huayan Buddhism does not recognize the conflicts existing in the world. On the contrary, Chengguan, the Fourth Patriarch of the school, acknowledges, "phenomena basically obstruct each other, being different in size and so forth."[2] If the conflicts in the phenomenal world are to be admitted, as Chengguan does in this passage, how should we interpret the hallmark statement of Huayan Buddhism which postulates a world in which particularities in the phenomenal realm co-exist without conflict? The question is quite relevant to our concern with postmodern small discourses: why should we assume that small discourses co-exist without conflicts and without eventually expanding their local value into a universal one?

Francis H. Cook claims that one of the major achievements of Huayan Buddhism lies in the fact that phenomenal diversity regained respectability in Huayan teaching, after it had been marginalized in the Mahāyāna Buddhist schools preceding Huayan Buddhism. In this context, Cook evaluates characteristics of Huayan Buddhism with the following three aspects which he considers as distinguishing the school from Indian Buddhism:

> First of all, it is a universe in which phenomena have been not only restored to a measure of respectability, but indeed, have become important, valuable, and lovely. Second, to accept such a worldview would entail a radical overhauling of the understanding of traditional Buddhist concepts such as emptiness and dependent origination. Finally, it would have meant that many of the important dogmas of Indian Buddhism would have to be abandoned, such as the belief in gradual self-purification, the difference between the noumenal and phenomenal orders, and the distinctions of the stages of progress.[3]

Cook's evaluations of Huayan Buddhism in this passage raise further questions: (1) What would it mean to restore phenomena in Buddhist discourse? (2) What is the nature of the radical reconceptualization of emptiness and dependent co-arising in Huayan philosophy? and (3) What is the implication of abandoning, if that actually took place in Huayan Buddhism, gradualism of practice and self-purification, together with the differences between noumenon and phenomena? Needless to say, all three questions are tightly interconnected with the construction of the Huayan Buddhist paradigm. In order to answer these questions, let us reiterate the basics of the fourfold worldview.

On the surface level, the phenomenal world consists of diverse entities. Huayanists look into the seemingly fragmented existence of each phenomenon and expound that, on its noumenal level, the structure of existence is identical. Be it a stone, a cat, or a human, the underlying principle of existence cannot differ. Another way of articulating this view is to say that the phenomenal world exists as a manifestation of noumenon or principle (*li*). These two statements, even though they seem to express the same view, could represent two significantly different philosophical standpoints. In the first statement—different entities in the phenomenal world exist with the same underlying existential structure—the phenomenality of each existence is sustained and its noumenal structure is expounded. In the second statement—different entities in the phenomenal world are the reflection of noumenon—noumenon is the initiator of the different entities in the phenomenal world, and, as a result, the phenomenality of different entities is negated. The former explicates the relationship between phenomena and noumenon without privileging either, whereas, in the latter, noumenon has a priority since it is the ground for the existence of phenomena. Depending on one's hermeneutical position regarding the complex presentations offered in the major corpus of Huayan Buddhism, the school invites both interpretations. In the case of former, Huayan Buddhism can be understood, as Cook did, as a paradigm to vindicate the equal position of diverse entities in the phenomenal world. In the latter, Huayan philosophy can lead a totalitarian vision in which the principle of the one subjugates the many in the name of noumenon.

The totalitarian interpretation of Huayan Buddhism and its application to political power has been noted by Korean historians in their assessment of the role of Buddhism in the historical context of Korea. The establishment and flourishing of Huayan (Hwaŏm) Buddhism in Korea corresponds to the unification of the Korean peninsula by the Unified Silla dynasty during the seventh century. In this context a claim has been made that the Huayan doctrine of the fourfold worldview offered a philosophical foundation for the establishment of a centralized authoritarian monarchy:

Among these [various Buddhist sects] it was the Avantamsaka (Hwaŏm; Chinese: Hua-yen) that was accorded the most devout adherence by aristocratic society when Silla was in full flourish. Hwaŏm taught the doctrine of all encompassing harmony, that the one contains the multitude and that the multitude is as one, a concept that sought to embrace the myriad of sentient beings within the single Buddha mind. Such a doctrine was well suited to a state with a centralized power structure under an authoritarian monarchy and this surely was one reason why the Hwaŏm teaching was welcomed by the ruling elite of Unified Silla's aristocracy.[4]

We will not dwell on the social and historical aspects of this evaluation of Huayan Buddhism but take this as one concrete example of a totalitarian reading of the Huayan paradigm. What is most relevant to our discussion in this context is the affinity between the centripetal and centrifugal forces or between totalitarian and dispersing powers that a thought system is pregnant with. As in the case of Zen Buddhism, in which Zen Buddhism's radical challenge to authoritarianism and its self-generated authoritarianism co-exist, Huayan Buddhist philosophy can also be interpreted either as an endorsement of diversity or that of totalitarianism.

What is the nature of the principle or noumenon in Huayan Buddhism? The *li* is characterized by the basic Buddhist doctrine of dependent co-arising, especially in the form of emptiness as elaborated in the Mādhyamika school of Buddhism. Buddhist tradition claims that entities, by nature, lack the self-nature that sustains an entity in separation from other existence. Huayan Buddhism also subscribes to this position. Existence, in this sense, is understood as inter-relationship, and subjectivity, as intersubjectivity. No entity contains its self-nature or independent essence of its own, but exists in conjunction with other beings.

If Huayan Buddhism shares with Mādhyamika Buddhism in its understanding of noumenon as the Buddhist concept of emptiness, Huayan Buddhism diverges from Mādhyamika Buddhism in that it pays close attention to noumenon's manifestation in each phenomenon. In this context, a series of hermeneutic tools are introduced in order to explain the intrinsic non-identity of a being and, thus, the mutual dependency of things. One set of such hermeneutical device Huayan Buddhism employs includes the concepts of "mutual identity" (C. *xiangji*) and "mutual containment" (C. *xiangru*). The latter is also translated as "mutual pervasion," "mutual penetration," or "mutual interpenetration," which we will use interchangeably, depending on the context. The ideas of mutual identity and mutual containment are well articulated in the Huayan signature expression: *the one is the many and the many are the one.* The basic position here is that the one attains its identity through the many, and vice versa. Because there is the one, the many become possible, and since the one attains its identity by being accepted by the many, the one becomes the many. The one and the many are not only closely related, but cannot be separated, which is called *mutual identity*. The one and the many are separate concepts but their identities are established by the existence of the other side.

For example, the identity of the number "one" in the numerical system cannot have its meaning without all of the non-number-one elements in the system. The ironic corollary of this mode of thinking is that each individual number in the system, as it is, represents the entire numerical system, since, without each individual number, the system itself cannot be the whole. The whole in this sense is not a mere collection of individual parts as our commonsense logic would like to hold; instead, each individual part, itself, represents the whole. This mode of thinking is also distant from the idea that a whole is more than an accumulation of individual entities as proposed by the theory of social organism. Whereas the theory of the social organism views a society as a whole—that is, an organism—and individual entities in a society as a part of an organism (and thus functioning only as a part), the Huayan vision of mutual penetration offers a radical endorsement of the individuality of each existence. Such radical endorsement is simultaneously subsumed into the radical negation of individuality since the identity of an individual entity is possible only through its relation to the whole. Huayan Buddhism explains this relationship between a part and the whole through the concept of "the same body and the different body" (C. *tongti yiti*): the part and whole are the same in the sense that the part is, itself, reflecting the whole, and the whole cannot exist without the part; but, at the same time, the part and the whole are different as they are, and, in this sense, they are different bodies.

The ideas of mutual identity and mutual containment are also explained through the concepts of "simultaneous arising" (C. *tongshi dunqi*) and "simultaneous containment" (C. *tongshi hushe*), respectively. Take the example of the letter "A." The letter "A" cannot have meaning outside of a larger picture called "alphabet"; it belongs to a language named "English," and then a category called "language." When one says "apple," each letter, "a," "p," "p," "l," and "e," exists within the structure of the English linguistic system. An "a" cannot exist by itself, nor does it have any intrinsic meaning. Hence, when the word "apple" is articulated, an "a" or a "p" and other letters in this word have the same value, which Huayan Buddhism calls "mutual identity": the identity of "a" makes possible the identity of "p" and vice versa; the identities of "a" and "p" arise simultaneously through mutual indebtedness. At the same time, "a" contains "p," "l," "e," the meaning "apple," and the English linguistic system as well at a given moment when a speaker articulates an "apple," with the intention of communicating the meaning of an "apple." The whole "apple" does not exist in separation from each individual letter of the linguistic system, meaning structure, and so on and so forth. All of the elements which contribute to the meaning-giving action of "apple," *ad infinitum,* simultaneously arise at the moment the word "apple" is articulated. At the moment that "apple" is articulated, "a" is an apple, English, and a linguistic system. Hence the Huayan dictum: "one particle of dust contains the entire world."

To further examine the Huayan doctrine of the relationship between the part and the whole, let us consider the relationship between a part of one's body and the entire body. The common sense understanding takes it granted that when we put each part of a body together, they create the whole called the body. Huayan Buddhism claims that one specific part of one's body is the sole cause of the entire body in a given moment for a given reference, and the same is the case with any part of the body, that is, eyes, fingers, and so on. Several indications are involved in this claim. First, the Huayan paradigm challenges the essentialist view of identity by blurring the demarcation between differing identities. A simple question illuminates the issue at hand in this case: where does one draw the line between one's nose and non-nose parts in one's face? To claim that different parts of one's body constitute parts of a whole, and, thus, a whole is a collection of these parts, assumes a separate existence of each part of one's body. This approach claims that the nose is an independent entity as much as an individual self. However, as the attempt to draw a dividing line between a nose and a non-nose part of one's face makes us aware of the intrinsic ambiguity involved in this action, so does the division between the self and non-self. The non-self elements of one's existence, such as a room where one places one's physical entity at each moment, or a group such as one's family to which one belongs, emerge as fundamental components of one's identity.

When Huayan Buddhism asserts that a part—the nose, for example—is the sole cause of a whole—the body—at a given moment, it does not suggest that a nose is *exclusively* the only supreme cause of the existence of the body. A nose is the sole cause of a body at a given moment for a given referential purpose, and so is each section in the rest of one's body.

Fazang (643–712), to whom the Huayan hermeneutic devices have been attributed, expounds on the issue in detail in his *Wujiao zhang* (Treatise on the Five Teachings). In chapter ten of the book, Fazang explains the differences between Huayan Buddhism and other Buddhist schools, as follows:

> In the perfect causation of the one vehicle of Samanthabhadra [Huayan Buddhism], the inexhaustible dependent co-arising with the complete activities of intersubjectivity is the stage of ultimate wisdom. The concepts of emptiness and existence make mutual identity possible; the concepts of function and non-function make mutual interfusion possible. The concepts of reliance and non-reliance on origination [dependent co-arising] make the same and different bodies possible. Based on these ideas, it is possible to put the entire world into the follicle of a hair.[5]

The passage succinctly summarizes the Huayan Buddhist phenomenology. In this passage, the possibility of seemingly counterintuitive concepts of mutual identity and mutual containment, which culminate in the idea of "putting the entire world into the follicle of a hair," is explained through the co-existence of opposite natures in an entity: that is, coexistence of emptiness and existence in the case of the mutual identity, of function and non-function in the case of mutual containment, and of reliance and non-reliance on dependent co-arising for the concept of the same and different bodies. The Buddha's logic of the middle path which constructs itself through the violation of the logic of non-contradiction and which dominates Zen *gong'an* literature once again offers the ground for the Huayan paradigm for understanding the phenomenal world. In his elucidation of the above three concepts, Fazang employs the relationship of the individual numbers in counting them from one through ten, which we have briefly discussed. Ten is the number that Huayan thinkers consider to be the perfect number; like Huayan Buddhism, which the school's patriarchs envision as the "perfect and complete teaching," Huayan thinkers contend that in the number ten is inscribed the perfection they envision. In this sense, it was not a random choice that Fazang chose to use the example of the relationship between numbers one and ten to expound his doctrine of the Huayan theory of the interpenetration of parts and the whole.

In the structure of numbers one through ten, one is a part and ten is its whole. Since one and ten are different, they are "different bodies" (C. *yiti*). In the identity of one and ten, their relationship is characterized by their "reliance on dependent origination." Neither one nor ten exists by itself, for one is one by virtue of the existence of the rest of numbers in the one-to-ten system, and ten is ten by virtue of the existence of the other nine numbers. This relationship is explained by Fazang with the co-existence of emptiness and existence. Number one exists as number one in separation from the other nine numbers, hence existence; but number one, as explained so far, becomes number one only when there are the other nine numbers; hence, its identity is empty. Because an entity contains the nature of both existence and emptiness, or identity and non-identity, this is called mutual identity. The identity of one is possible because of the co-existence of number ten and the other nine numbers, and the same can be said for all other numbers in the system; therefore, their identities are mutually the same. Another way of explaining this inter-subsumption of existence and emptiness, of identity and non-identity, and of function and non-function at work in Huayan paradigm of identity construction is by virtue of mutual containment. One exists as one, and, thus, functions as one in the numeric system of one-to-ten. However, the function of being one is possible only when the rest of the nine numbers function as they are; the function of being one is possible through its non-function as one, that is, its subsuming non-one-functions of other nine numbers. The end result is that one functions as one, both by virtue of its function as one and through its non-function as one.

The concept that one and ten are the "same bodies" (C. *tongti*) in the context of mutual identity and mutual containment can be explained through the same logical ramifications. The major difference to be noted is that, in the approach of the "same bodies" in understanding the relationship between one and ten, one is explained as being a part of a series of one to ten, whereas, in the concept of the "different bodies," one is explained in its relationship with the rest of the nine numbers. Since one is already within the number ten in the concept of "the same bodies," this is called "non-reliance on dependent co-arising" (C. *budaiyuan*). Non-reliance on dependent co-arising does not imply that an entity has its own independent substance which is immune from external stimuli and conditions; if this were the case, the theory would be directly contradicting the basic Buddhist doctrine of non-existence of self-nature in an entity. The non-reliance on dependent co-arising indicates that the cause is included within the entity; hence, there is no outside to construct dependency *between* or *among* entities. The concepts of the "same body" and "non-reliance on the dependent co-arising" are important in understanding the Huayan Buddhist conceptualization of what is known as "nature-origination" (C. *xingqi*), to which we will come back.

Huayan Buddhism has been known as the culmination of the doctrinal sophistication of Chinese Buddhism. The doctrinal elaboration of Huayan Buddhism, however, is not achieved at the expense of reality. The habit of contrasting theory (doctrine) with practice frequently interprets Huayan Buddhism as an abstruse theorization that ignores the practical level of Buddhism. However, Huayan Buddhism, in terms of its ultimate goal, is an effort to articulate Buddhist doctrine at the level of immediate reality, which is the world of phenomena, and by doing so, leads the practitioner to understand each and every phenomenon as an occasion to realize the nature of the world. Huayan Buddhism, in this sense, paves a path for Buddhism to return to the phenomenal world, as Cook pointed out, after a series of doctrinal elaborations in Mahāyāna Buddhism. Dushun, the retroactively appointed First Patriarch of the Huayan school, confirms the idea in his *Huayan wujiao zhiguan* (Cessation and Contemplation in the Five Teachings of Huayan).

In this essay, Dushun explains, "The scripture states, 'linguistic rendering is different from practice. Truth is divorced from words.' Hence, noticing such phenomena as our eyes' seeing and our ears' listening and so forth is [the very way of] entering into the midst of the dependent co-arising of the realm of reality [*dharmadhātu*]."[6] In other words, each and every phenomenon is to be understood as the unfolding of the underlying noumenon of the phenomenon. However, the ultimate confirmation of noumenon becomes possible only through the actual happening of each phenomenon. In this sense, Huayan Buddhism emphasizes that the Buddhist noumenon of interdependence is not a separate entity or an abstract concept that can exist beyond reality, but that which is taking place each and every moment in this world, here and now. Any one phenomenon is a manifestation of the conditional nature of all things in the universe. This vision of simultaneous arising of each individual phenomenon as a manifestation of the entire whole and, at the same time, each individual entity's inter-subsumed identity, is well described in the signature image of Huayan Buddhism known as Indra's net. Dushun writes:

> . . . the celestial jewel net of Kanishka, or Indra, Emperor of Gods, is called the net of Indra. This imperial net is made all of jewels: because the jewels are clear, they reflect each other's images, appearing in each other's reflections upon reflections, ad infinitum, all appearing at once in one jewel, and in each one it is so—ultimately there is no going or coming. Now for the moment let us turn to the southwest direction and pick a jewel and check it. This jewel can show the reflections of all the jewels all at once—and just as this is so of this jewel, so it is of every other jewel: the reflection is multiplied and remultiplied over and over endlessly. These infinitely multiplying jewel reflections are all in one jewel and show clearly—the others do not hinder this. If you sit in one jewel, then you are sitting in all the jewels in every direction, multiplied over and over. Why? Because in one jewel there are all the jewels. If there is one jewel in all the jewels, then you are sitting in all the jewels too. And the reverse applies to the totality if you follow the same reasoning. Since in one jewel you go into all the jewels without leaving this one jewel, so in all jewels you enter one jewel without leaving this one jewel.[7]

The image of Indra's net has been employed as a representative of the Huayan Buddhist vision of the relationship between the part and the whole or of phenomena and noumenon. Indra's net is the ultimate example of the infinite inter-subsumption of beings (C. *chongchong wujin*), in which the idea of "mutual identity" and "mutual containment" is fully exercised.

2. Mutually Conflicting Phenomena and Totalitarian Noumenon

Indra's net has been understood as representing the egalitarian vision of Huayan Buddhism with its ultimate declaration of the mutually non-interfering phenomena. The image, however, needs to be used with caution if we are to understand the image of the net with the reality of the world in mind. As Chengguan admitted, "phenomena basically obstruct each other, being different in size and so forth." The phenomenal world is charged with conflicts, and the vision offered by the image of Indra's net does not seem to consider the conflicts existing in the phenomenal world. How is Chengguan's acknowledgement of conflict among phenomena represented either in the image of Indra's net or Fazang's elaboration of the non-substantialist identity of each phenomenon? Does this indicate that Huayan Buddhism promotes its vision of noumenon at the expense of phenomenal reality?

Let us consider the issue with the following examples. Suppose a person X had shrimp scampi for his dinner. On a pragmatic level, between the person X and the shrimp the person consumed for his dinner, there exists an inevitable conflict, even when X was not directly involved in the catching and killing of those shrimp. X is a predator, and shrimp are victims of human beings' activities of profiting from trading the shrimp, taking their lives for their nutritional value, or just to subdue one's hunger. One might assume that, based on our discussion of the mutually non-interfering phenomena, from the Huayan perspective, no conflict between the person X and shrimp should exist. This interpretation further contends that as individual entities, neither the shrimp nor a person X can interfere with the other because both of them lack self-nature; since no subjectivity that can construct objective reality can exist, the construction of interference is not possible. This logic leads us to the non-obstruction among phenomena as the ultimate vision of the fourfold worldview of Huayan Buddhism. Can this be the implication of the fourth level of the fourfold worldview?

Let us consider another scenario. Suppose a person Y tripped over a branch on a mountainside, hit his forehead against a nearby rock, and suffered an open wound. The existence of the branch, the rock, and Y are obviously in a conflicting relationship, even if this non-intentional occurrence were to have taken place between an animated organism and inanimate objects. Once again one might assume that, from the perspective of the Huayan fourfold worldview, there cannot be any conflict among the constituents of the incident, for none of them has self-nature. One might also contend that the first and second examples cannot be put into the same category because the former involves humans' intentional actions whereas, in the latter, no intentionality is involved. The seemingly clear border of the presence or absence of intentionality in these two examples becomes nebulous with our third example.

In the natural world, a tiger will eat a rabbit. Like the person X who consumed shrimp for his meal, a tiger consumes a rabbit for its meal. What would, from the Huayan perspective, be the position of the conflict between the rabbit and the tiger? Is there an intentionality involved in a tiger's consumption of a rabbit? If this relationship between a tiger and a rabbit does not involve intentionality and is considered the result of a food chain of entities which simply follows the natural environmental setting of the world, one should ask where we draw the line between "naturalness" and "intentionality." Is nature devoid of conflict because of the simple fact that it is natural? The relationship between X and the shrimp in the earlier example can be expanded to any types of relationship between a predator and its victims or the exploiter and the exploited in our society, which takes the issue into a broader context of ethical implications of the Huayan fourfold worldview. The questions we raise here have multilayered significance. First of all, the investigation questions the ethical relevance of the Huayan Buddhist world. If both the predator and its victim can be put in the same value structure because of the fact that both lack self-nature, does this amount to saying that Huayan Buddhism does not have a moral and ethical system? Does Huayan Buddhism neutralize the obvious conflict and its discriminating reality in our society and even promote the idea that one should be complacent with the conflict in the phenomenal level by nullifying it with the egalitarian reality on the noumenal level? Secondly, this investigation raises a hermeneutical question: What would be the Huayan interpretation of the existence of clear conflicts on the phenomenal level, regardless of their ethical evaluation? The third layer of this question involves a pragmatic and soteriological dimension: How would the Huayan Buddhist paradigm help individuals deal with reality which is obviously charged with conflicts?

In order to answer these questions, let us revisit the fourfold worldview, or four *dharmadhātu*, which we have examined, and we will do so by beginning with the Huayan definition of the term *dharmadhātu* (C. *fajie*), which we have translated as "worldview," or "the realm of reality." In an essay on *dharmadhātu*, Kang-nam Oh succinctly sums up how the meaning of the term has gone through evolution in the course of Buddhist history. As a Sanskrit compound of *dharma* and *dhātu*, the term literally conveys a variety of meanings, including "dharma-element," "the reality of dharma," "the essence of reality," and "ultimate reality," among others.[8] Oh explains that in the *Dīgha–nikāya*, one of the texts in early Buddhism, the term is employed to denote the "principle of truth" or "the causal nature of things."[9] In the *Saṃyutta–nikāya*, another of the early Buddhist texts, *dharmadhātu* is listed as the seventeenth out of the eighteen *dhātus*, in which "*dhātu* is regarded as the object of the mind (*manas*), in the same way as color is the object of the eye or sound is the object of the ear."[10]

More relevant to our discussion of the Huayan concept of *dharmadhātu* is Oh's evaluation of the contrasting views of *dharmadhātu* in the Mādhyamika philosophy and the Yogācāra system. Oh claims that in Nāgārjuna's Mādhyamika thought, because of his prioritization of the ultimate reality, Nāgārjuna employs expressions such as emptiness (*śūnyatā*), reality (*dharmatā*), or suchness (*tathatā*), instead of *dharmadhātu*. On the other hand, in the Yogācāra tradition, Oh contends, *dharmadhātu* is used as one of the designations of the Absolute. Especially in the *Laṅkāvatāra-sūtra*, *dharmadhātu* is synonymous with *ālayavijñāna*, *tathāgatagarbha* and *citta*, and, thus, "is invested with positive significance."[11] The discussion of the relationship between the ultimate and conventional realities in the Mādhyamika philosophy, as well as the issue of a positive or negative signification of *dharmadhātu* in Yogācāra, is still very much debatable, to say the least. However, this brief survey of the differing concepts of *dharmadhātu* in different Buddhist schools suggests that the concept of *dharmadhātu* in a Buddhist school reflects the school's view of the ultimate reality and its location. In Oh's interpretation, Nāgārjuna's elevation of the ultimate reality into the status beyond the conventional realm together with his tendency to consider the conventional realm as falsity results in the depreciation of *dharmadhātu* in the Mādhyamika school, whereas, in the Yogācāra school, *dharmadhātu* is identified as the reality itself, that is, the matrix of Tathāgata. In both cases, however, *dharmadhātu* is understood as separated from the phenomenal world. Comprehending the Huayan concept of the *dharmadhātu* in this context, we can better understand Francis Cook's evaluation in our earlier citation that Huayan Buddhism brought respectability back to phenomena.

In his essay, *Huayan fajie xuanjing* (Mirror of the Mysteries of the Realm of Reality of Huayan), Chengguan explains the meaning of *dhātu* (C. *jie*) by drawing a distinction between the *dhātu* (or realm) in the *dharmadhātu* of noumenon and that in phenomena:

> In naming a phenomenon a "realm," by "realm" we mean "division"—referring to phenomena in terms of the divisions of infinite differentiations. In naming noumenon a "realm," by "realm" we mean "nature" [C. *xing*], because infinite phenomena have the same unitary nature. The reality-realm of noninterference contains both the sense of division and nature. Without destroying phenomena and noumenon, there is still no interference between them; therefore the fourth level of the reality-realm also contains both meanings, because nature merges phenomena but individual phenomena do not lose their forms—in accord with nature they merge, multiplied and re-multiplied without end.[12] (Translation modified.)

Seminal aspects of the Huayan view of ultimate reality, its location, and its relation to the phenomenal world can be identified in this passage. Huayan Buddhism applies the term *dharmadhātu* to both noumenal and phenomenal realms. In doing so, Chengguan makes a distinction of the meaning of *dhātu* in the former and in the latter, without forgetting to emphasize that they cannot be separated. The individuality of phenomena remains as it is, for division is what characterizes the phenomenal world of entities; however, the division and distinction of each entity does not negate the underlying noumenal reality of each entity, which Chengguan identifies as the unifying nature. That is, Huayan Buddhism understands phenomenal reality in connection with noumenon, bringing the phenomenal world back into the Buddhist discourse. That said, if we look into the nature of this phenomenal world which is described by Dushun and Chengguan, there is something unclear in the way in which Huayan Buddhism deals with the world of phenomena. Like each jewel in Indra's net, each entity exists in division, but its characteristics as an individual entity seem completely erased in their 'belonging togetherness' with the totality of the net. The phenomenality of each entity is affirmed only to be negated. As a result, the diversities in the phenomenal world simply become reflections of the noumenal. If this is the case, can the school still claim the mutually non-interfering phenomena as its hallmark?

The non-obstruction in the level of phenomena in the way it is described by the Huayan patriarchs seems possible only through noumenon. If that is the case, one can argue that in the Huayan fourfold worldview, the individuality of phenomena or even the phenomena themselves exist only nominally. In this context, one can draw the following reinterpretation of the example of the person Y's flipping over a branch. Each constituent involved in this incident has both phenomenal and noumenal levels: a protruded branch on the ground, Y's foot flipping over it, the rock, and the action of bumping his forehead against the rock, the rock itself, Y's frustration about the event, anger and pain due to the open wound—all exist as momentary phenomena whose nature is all the same, empty; the non-reality of each entity is derived from the fact that each of the constituents of the event lacks self-nature and does not and cannot obstruct the others. The same can be said about the conflict between the shrimp and the person X, or that between the predator tiger and its victim rabbit.

The non-obstruction among phenomena in the fourfold worldview, then, is possible only as an inference drawn from the contemplation of noumenon. Huayan Buddhism justifies this vision of phenomena as a reflection of noumenon with its claim that the final stage of the fourfold worldview is the world seen by the Buddha when he was in the deep samādhi of oceanic reflection. The vision of the non-obstructing world of phenomena is not the world experienced by un-enlightened individuals, but a postulation for the future as a promise to be realized once one attains enlightenment. Here, we are once again reminded of Chinul's criticism of Huayan Buddhism for its elevation of the ultimate goal, or the state of enlightenment, without properly offering to the practitioner a means to reach this realm.

Modern Buddhist scholarship has also been keenly aware of Huayan Buddhism's tendency of privileging noumenon and negating phenomena. A claim has been made that, despite the Huayan promotion of the fourth level of "mutually non-interfering phenomena" as its ultimate teaching, Huayan patriarchs were in fact more interested in the third level of mutual inter-penetration between noumenon and phenomena, and thus contradicted the basic promise of the school's doctrine. This contradiction was identified as a "hermeneutic problem" within Huayan Buddhist philosophy.[13] In this vein, it has been noted that Fazang's writings reveals a conflict between the third level (non-interference between noumenon and phenomena) and the fourth level (non-interference among phenomena), and that the Fourth Patriarch Chengguan emphasizes the third level of the fourfold worldview over the fourth level. This claim earns support if we look into these thinkers' exposition of Huayan teaching.

In his *Mirror of the Mysteries of the Realm of Reality of Huayan*, Cheng-guan openly admits the importance of noumenon in understanding the nature of phenomena. In this work, Chengguan suggests five pairs to identify the relationship between noumenon and phenomena: "first, the pair of noumenon and phenomena pervading each other; second, the pair of noumenon and phenomena completing or making each other; third, the pair of noumenon and phenomena destroying each other; fourth, the pair of noumenon and phenomena identifying with each other; fifth, the pair of noumenon and phenomena denying each other."[14] Immediately after this categorization, Chengguan adds, "These five pairs all explain noumenon first, since noumenon is considered important."[15] Throughout the essay, which has been noted as the seminal piece elaborating the Huayan fourfold worldview, Chengguan addresses the status of phenomena only as an inference from noumenon. Even in the section examining the phenomenal, Chengguan's discussion still focuses on the relationship between noumenon and phenomena. Hence it has been asked: If the school is to prefer the third level and is more interested in the function of noumenon in the phenomena, why does the school insist on the fourth level as its signature? The question is not only valid but it contains a key to understanding Huayan phenomenology.

Despite the constant emphasis on noumenon by Huayan thinkers, Huayan Buddhism has identified its teaching and the validity of its superiority with the fourth level of mutually non-interfering phenomena, not the third level of noninterference of noumenon against phenomena. In addition, the tradition following the major patriarchs in the formative stage of the school has continued to emphasize the fourth level of non-interfering phenomena as the signature of the school, the evidence of the superiority of Huayan Buddhism over other Buddhist schools. This gives us a reason to re-consider the relationship between noumenon and phenomena in Huayan Buddhism and contemplate different hermeneutic possibilities. In other words, the seemingly clear gap between the school's official emphasis on the fourth level and the patriarchs' interest in the third level is the indication that the relationship between noumenon and phenomena in the Huayan fourfold worldview begs us to consider a further hermeneutic endeavor, instead of dismissing the paradigm as merely containing a logical flaw. In the following section, we will examine the possibility of different interpretations of the Huayan understanding of the phenomenal world and the relationship of phenomena to noumenal reality.

3. Phenomena, Noumenon, and the Ethical Dimension of the Huayan Fourfold Worldview

In his book *Selfless Persons: Imagery and Thought in Theravāda Buddhism*, Steven Collins states that "in the Theravāda tradition [the denial of ātman] has been of most importance in the ethical and psychological dynamics of spiritual education, while in other traditions, especially the Mahāyāna schools, it has been much developed as a topic of epistemology and ontology under the general name of 'Emptiness.'"[16] This is an insightful statement which succinctly offers basic differences in the orientation of Theravāda and Mahāyāna Buddhism. This understanding of the difference between the two schools has also served the basis in postulating Mahāyāna Buddhism's position with regard to ethics. In the context of understanding Huayan Buddhism, Collins's characterization of Mahāyāna Buddhism, with its primary concern for the epistemological and ontological reality of emptiness, accords with the claim that Huayan Buddhism's promotion of the phenomenal level is only nominal, and, in reality, the noumenal reality of emptiness was the major concern of Huayan masters. However, once we begin to reconceptualize the relationship between noumenon and phenomena in Huayan Buddhism, we reach the point at which the function and the synergy between the ethical, soteriological, epistemological, and ontological cannot be very different in Theravāda and Mahāyāna Buddhism. As much as the ontological and epistemological understanding of no-self theory sets the ground for ethical behaviors and religio-spiritual betterment in the Theravāda school, the understanding of the underlying reality of emptiness offers the philosophical foundation for an ethical and soteriological dimension in the Mahāyāna tradition. The combination of the two sides in Collins's distinctions—the ethical, on the one hand, and the epistemological and ontological, on the other—is the way in which Huayan thinkers explain the relationship between the noumenal and the phenomenal.

The seeming prioritization of noumenon over phenomena in the discussions of Huayan Buddhism results in the nebulous position of Huayan Buddhism in relation to ethical discourse. However, as we shall see, Huayan Buddhism does not fail to combine the ontological and epistemological implications of the wisdom of the noumenal level into the compassion of the ethical and soteriological dimensions. To examine the position of phenomenal diversity, as well as the ethical implications of the Huayan Buddhist paradigm, we will consider the following four issues: first, the evolution of the theory of the fourfold worldview from Dushun to Chengguan; second, Fazang's vindication of the significance of phenomena in the Huayan paradigm; third, the implication of the journey of Sudhana in the "Entering the Realm of Reality" chapter of the *Huayan jing*; and fourth, the function of wisdom and compassion in respect to noumenal and phenomenal realities.

The foundation of the Huayan fourfold worldview is already well developed in Dushun's *Fajie guan* (Contemplation of the Realm of Reality), the existence of which is known about only through its appearance in the commentaries by Huayan scholars after him. In this essay, Dushun identifies three types of contemplation in relation to practicing the realm of reality in Huayan Buddhism. They are: (1) contemplation of true emptiness (C. *zhenkong guan*); (2) contemplation of non-obstruction between noumenon and phenomena (C. *lishi wuai guan*); and (3) contemplation of universality and inclusion (C. *zhoubian hanrong guan*). The Huayan fourfold worldview is Chengguan's reworking of this threefold contemplation of Dushun. To reiterate them, the fourfold worldview consists of: (1) the realm of phenomena; (2) the realm of noumenon; (3) the realm of non-interference between noumenon and phenomena; and (4) the realm of non-interference among phenomena. Even though the fourfold worldview is a reiteration of Dushun's Threefold Contemplation, there exist delicate differences between Dushun's original proposal and Chengguan's interpretation. These differences have rarely been addressed; however, they merit our attention for us to get a better understanding of the ethical implication of the fourfold worldview. As Dushun emphasizes, in presenting the relationship between noumenon and phenomena, Huayan Buddhism underscores the importance of "contemplation." Whether contemplation is related to noumenon, to phenomena, or to the relationship between the two, in Dushun's paradigm, the basic position requires one to understand the existential structure of the fragmented world of actuality; only then, one is able to perceive the underlying meaning-structure of the physical reality. This does not imply that the ultimate reality exists in separation from the fragmented world of actuality. Nor does it claim that authentic understanding of the realm of reality is available only to the enlightened mind. Instead, Dushun contends that contemplation is the mode through which one encounters the objective reality without being disturbed by subjectivity. That should be the case in all three tiers of his Threefold Contemplation of noumenon (emptiness), of the relationship between noumenon and phenomena, and of the phenomena. In this sense, Dushun's paradigm is soteriologically oriented in its basic nature. When Chengguan reformulates this "contemplation" about the realms of reality into a paradigm of the fourfold realm of realities, the paradigm asserts itself as a fact; it is postulated without consideration of the subject's relation to the factual world. The dismissal of the subjective position in the understanding of reality is a path to universalize the given paradigm or mode of thinking. The implication resulting from the transformation of *contemplation* of the phenomenal world into the *reality* of the phenomenal world is significant. From the perspective of Dushun's paradigm of "contemplation" of the threefold realm of reality, the non-interference either between noumenon and phenomena or among phenomena is an awareness obtained through the subject's mental cultivation so as to be able to realize the underlying structure of reality, whereas, from Chengguan's paradigm of the fourfold worldview, the non-interference becomes factual reality itself.

The fourth level of non-interference of phenomena cannot denote that conflicts do not exist amongst each phenomenon. As Chengguan acknowledges, the phenomenal world, by nature, contains obstructions because of the sheer fact of its tangible reality, not to mention the more complex issue of the intentionality of the subjective agency. Chengguan, thus, states, "if we see only in terms of phenomena, then they obstruct one another; if we see only in terms of noumenon, there is nothing which can mutually obstruct. Now in this case, merging phenomena by noumenon, phenomena are therefore without obstruction—therefore it says that phenomena, in conformity with noumenon, merge."[17] Hence, the fourth level of the fourfold worldview should be read as "non-interference among phenomena seen from the perspective of noumenon." This is exactly what Dushun suggests in the third layer of his Threefold Contemplation, identified as "contemplation of universality and inclusion." This line of argument could be viewed as another confirmation of the Huayan paradigm privileging noumenon. However, a subtle difference needs to be noted here: that is, Chengguan did not deny the existence of conflict on the phenomenal level, as we have noted. Our task, then, is to unravel how Huayan Buddhism draws its vision of the mutually non-interfering phenomena despite its awareness of the inevitably mutually obstructing nature of phenomena.

The continued emphasis of Huayan patriarchs in reference to the fourth level of the non-interference among phenomena as the signature of Huayan Buddhism is another demonstration of the fact that the relationship between noumenon and phenomena in Huayan Buddhism is rather complex. Fazang describes the differences between the "three vehicles" and the "one vehicle" as located in the Huayan views on phenomena. In the eighth section of his *Treatise on the Five Teachings*, Fazang identifies ten aspects by which Huayan Buddhism (or the "one vehicle") distinguishes itself from other Buddhist schools preceding it (that is, "the three vehicles"). The tenth difference is identified as "Differences in [Understanding] Things":

> The tenth is the difference of things. All such things as dwellings, forests, rivers, land, mountains, and so on are dharma talks. They may be practices, or stages, or teachings and their meanings, yet, [individual phenomenal] entities are not harmed. Consequently, each particle of dust possesses all the different things in the realm of reality [*dharmadhātu*]. They form the subtle interrelationships of the realm of Indra. All things arise as one thing does. The "three vehicles" and so on are not the same. They merely say "It is empty," or "It is suchness [*tathatā*]," which cannot be the same [as the teachings of the "one vehicle" of Huayan Buddhism]. Even if they used the inconceivable power of supernatural penetration and made it [the theory] appear momentarily in the phenomenal world, this is not the same as the self-nature of dharma (things) in the "one vehicle."[18] (Translation modified.)

In this passage, Fazang criticizes other Buddhist schools for privileging noumenon. Fazang contends that other Buddhist schools project the totality of noumenon, such as "emptiness" or "suchness," to the nature of the world, but are not concerned with how noumenon might be related to the concrete reality of phenomena in which one lives. As opposed to the single-handed promotion and even hypostatization of noumenon in other Buddhist schools (or in the "three vehicles"), Fazang considers the value of Huayan Buddhism to be its capacity to incorporate and acknowledge the doctrine of "emptiness" or "suchness" (or "tathatā") in each and every existence in the phenomenal world. Fazang's argument, then, directly contradicts the criticism of Huayan Buddhism privileging noumenon over phenomena. Francis Cook comments on Fazang's passage as follows:

> All things can be contained within a single thing without destroying its integrity as that particular thing; thus even the factual, phenomenal things in the *dharma-dhātu* [the realm of reality] are pregnant with the reality which is the object of the Bodhisattva's quest. Because any one thing contains the functions of all other things as a result of the infinitely repeated interrelationship of primary and secondary, all things arise when one thing arises. This is the inexhaustibility of the arising from conditions of the *dharma-dhātu*. For this reason, the one vehicle does not stop at a single characteristic, such as emptiness or *tathatā* [suchness]. This relationship of primary and secondary is the property of the Hua-yen; in the three vehicles, such a relationship is only temporarily possible, as when Vimalakīrti includes Mt. Sumeru in a grain of mustard. In the one vehicle, however, this is the very nature of the universe.[19]

Both Fazang's description and Cook's interpretation, with which I concur, emphasize the importance of phenomena as a major characteristic distinguishing the school from other Buddhist teachings. Fazang's emphasis on the importance of phenomena in the Huayan paradigm is well-articulated in one of the chapters of the *Huayan jing* (Flower Garland Scripture).

"Entering the Realm of Reality" (*Rufajie pin*) is one of the most well-known chapters in the *Huayan jing*. In the chapter, a young truth-searcher named Sudhana asks Mañjuśrī about how to practice bodhisattva paths. Mañjuśrī sends Sudhana to a monk named Maghśri, who turns out to be only the first out of the fifty-three dharma-teachers who this truth-searcher is to meet during his pilgrimage. What distinguishes Sudhana's search for truth in this chapter is the diversity in terms of the characters of the dharma-teachers who he meets during his journey. Other Buddhist *sūtras* usually take Buddha's disciples as their main characters. *The Heart Sūtra*, for example, is told to Sāriputra, the wisest among the Buddha's disciples. The *Diamond Sūtra* is recounted to Subhuti, who is known as the best among the Buddha's disciples on the teaching of emptiness. In the *Lotus Sūtra,*

Sāriputra, Mahākāśyapa, Subhuti, and Ananda appear, along with numerous bodhisattvas. The characters in Mahāyāna scriptures are dominated by arhats, bodhisattvas, or a super-human figure, such as the lay Buddhist Vimalakīrti, in order to demonstrate the superiority of Mahāyāna teaching over Theravāda. All of them have already reached significant levels in their spiritual journey when they appear as characters in a *sūtra*. Sudhana's dharma-teachers in the *Huayan jing,* however, are neither Mahākāśyapa nor Subhuti nor Sāriputra. Among the teachers who Sudhana is led to meet are monks, nuns, laymen, and laywomen. They also include sages, kings, a heretic, an incense seller, and a seaman. The diversity in their occupations and social positions symbolically demonstrates the *Sūtra*'s agenda. Each of these dharma-teachers has mastered a certain degree of Buddhist teaching, along with the mastery of her/his occupation. The incense seller, for example, has learned how to use various incenses to cure diseases, to dispel evil, and to cut off attachments and defilements. The seaman, in turn, has completely mastered various features of ships, of the ocean, and high and low tides; he helps people to enjoy safe voyages through the ocean, while, at the same time, offering Buddha's teachings to them. Even the heretic has learned various ways to deal with people in his village who have various wrong views. Each character Sudhana encounters in his journey has learned how to practice Buddhist teachings by perfecting his or her own occupation. Each of them, however, denies having attained the perfection of the bodhisattva path, and refers this pilgrim to yet another dharma-teacher.

In order to develop an idea of how each of the diverse phenomena has its own importance in the "Entering the Realm of Reality" chapter, let us read some passages from a section on the mariner Vaira, who is the twenty-second *dharma* teacher who Sudhana meets in his pilgrimage to learn the bodhisattva path. The mariner Vaira speaks to Sudhana:

I live in this coastal metropolis of Kutagara, purifying enlightening practice characterized by great compassion. . . . With this thought in mind I roam this city on the edge of the ocean. Thus committed to the welfare and happiness of the world, I know all the treasure islands in the ocean. I know all the deposits of precious substances, all the types of precious substances, and all the sources of precious substances. I know how to refine, bore out, extract, and produce all precious substances, and I know all precious vessels, tools, and objects, and the light of all precious substances. I know the abodes of all water spirits, the agitations of all water spirits, the abodes of all spirits, the agitations of all spirits, the abodes of all goblins, how to alleviate the danger of goblins, the abodes of all ghosts, and how to put an end to obstacles caused by ghosts. I know how to avoid all the whirlpools and billows, and I know the colors and depths of all the waters. I know the cycles of the sun, moon, stars, and planets, and the lengths of the days and nights. I know when to travel and when not to;

I know when it is safe and when it is dangerous. I know the performance and soundness of the hull and rigging of ships. I know how to control and steer ships, I know how to catch the wind, I know where the winds rise from, and I know how to direct the ship and how to turn it around, I know when to anchor and when to sail.

With this knowledge, always engaged in working for the benefit of beings, with a sturdy ship, safe, peaceful, without anxiety, I convey merchants to the treasure islands of their choice, pleasing them with spiritual conversation. Having enriched them with all kinds of jewels, I bring them back to this continent. And I have never lost a single ship."[20]

We need to keep in mind that this is a talk given by a spiritual teacher to a pilgrim. One can read the passage as a symbolic statement. In fact, immediately after this passage, Vaira changes the tone of his expression and use the "ocean" as a metaphor. For example, those people who were on board his ship "become aware of the knowledge of how to go into the ocean of omniscience, they learn how to evaporate the ocean of craving, they are illumined with the knowledge of the ocean of past, present, and future, they become capable of annihilating the ocean of minds of all sentient beings."[21] Vaira's description of his knowledge of the ocean and navigation, however, cannot be read as merely metaphoric expressions, because Vaira is not the only person who offers vocational knowledge as a spiritual teaching to Sudhana.[22] The fifty dharma teachers out of fifty-three, in their own ways, speak of issues related to their vocations as spiritual teachers to Sudhana. The basic position of phenomena endorsed by Dushun is repeatedly reconfirmed in this chapter of the *Huayan jing*. As Dushun states, the noumenal truth of dependent co-arising or emptiness can be realized in an event as insignificant as the twinkling of an eye.

As important to note as the endorsement of diversity of phenomena in the "Entering the Realm of Reality" chapter is the message that no one phenomenon can completely represent the entirety of truth. This statement might sound as if it is contradicting the signature Huayan concept that one particle of dust contains the entire universe. On a closer reading, one finds that both statements represent the Huayan understanding of the "inexhaustibility" (C. *chongchong wujin*) of the realm of reality. Like Lacan's sliding subject, the articulation of the ultimate truth, or the ultimate truth of bodhisattva path in the Huayan paradigm, is constantly deferred to the next dharma teacher, as Sudhana moves on to meet fifty-three teachers to accumulate the truth on top of each. At the last stage of his pilgrimage, the boy Shrisambhava and the girl Shrimati, who are the fiftieth dharma teachers Sudhana meets in his journey, offer him the teaching of the inexhaustibility of the reality and of the bodhisattva path. In response to Sudhana's question of how to practice the bodhisattva path, they respond:

You should not develop just one virtue, nor concentrate on clarifying just one doctrine, nor be satisfied with just one practice, nor concentrate on carrying out just one vow, nor take up just one instruction, nor rest in completion, nor think of attaining the three tolerances as ultimate, nor rest upon fulfillment of the six transcendent ways, nor stop on attainment of the ten stages, nor vow to encompass and purify a finite Buddha-land, nor be content with attendance on a limited number of spiritual benefactors [*dharma* teachers].

Why? Because a bodhisattva should gather infinite roots of goodness, assemble infinite provisions for enlightenment, produce infinite bases of aspiration for enlightenment, learn infinite principles, extinguish the afflictions of an infinite number of sentient beings, penetrate the minds of an infinite number of sentient beings, know the faculties of an infinite number of sentient beings, work for the emancipation of an infinite number of sentient beings, be aware of the conduct of an infinite number of sentient beings, create guidance for an infinite number of sentient beings, be aware of the conduct of an infinite number of beings, ...[23] (Translation modified.)

The problem of the "one Truth" that repeatedly appears in the *gong'an* literature echoes here. (Rather, it is the *gong'an* literature which echoes the problem of the one truth articulated here, given the historical time-line.) If there existed one Truth or one Law that is the foundation of the world, the mastery of that one Truth or observance of that one Law will guarantee an individual the mastery of the truth of the world. In the Huayan world, in which a truth-searcher goes through different *dharma* teachers who continue to defer him to the next teacher, there is no one Truth or one Law to reveal the truth of the world. If there existed only one ultimate truth that a bodhisattva needed to master in order to understand the truth of the world, through which the bodhisattva could offer help to sentient beings, a bodhisattva-apprentice such as Sudhana would not need to go through fifty-three different *dharma* teachers only to learn that there would be no ending of learning. That Sudhana meets fifty-three teachers does not indicate that there are only fifty-three teachers; instead, the search for truth for Sudhana, and in that sense, for any individual, will continue inexhaustibly, because that is the nature of the world and entities from the Huayan Buddhist perspective. Each *dharma* teacher has perfected in her/his own way the truth in her/his context, but it always falls short of being the one universally perfect truth. And that is the nature of truth: truth is always already conditioned and limited by its own context, and context is inexhaustible in Huayan Buddhism because beings, by nature, exist through interaction.

From the soteriological perspective, the diverse reality which Sudhana has experienced reflects the boundlessness of the bodhisattva path as repeatedly emphasized in the *Sūtra*. The bodhisattva path, the *Sūtra* suggests, cannot be realized by practicing just one good behavior, one ultimate way, or through one vow, however supreme that behavior, that way, or that vow might be.

What Sudhana's pilgrimage symbolically articulates is the intrinsic diversity of the world. Sudhana's journey and various bodhisattva paths represented by diverse characters in the *Sūtra* affirm the phenomenal diversity, instead of negating it.

Sudhana is told that mahasattvas (or great-beings) need to plant boundless goodness and to collect boundless tools and causes for wisdom. Bodhisattvas (or wisdom-beings) should learn about the countless minds, countless roots, countless behaviors, and countless practices of sentient beings. Nothing can be excluded in this world in which countless diverse existences, behaviors, and events are taking place, and the bodhisattva path begins as one embraces all of these as the very happening of dependent co-arising and emptiness.

The radical endorsement of diversity in the phenomenal realm in the "Entering the Realm of Reality" chapter of the *Huayan jing* and the meaning of such an endorsement for the bodhisattva path and one's search for enlightenment suggest both the soteriological and ethical function of the Huayan emphasis on phenomena. One might argue that to interpret the "Entering the Realm of Reality" chapter as negating the one ultimate truth contradicts the Huayan concept of noumenon which is the all encompassing underlying reality of infinitely diverse phenomena. However, one should consider the nature of the noumenon in Huayan Buddhism. Noumenon, or the principle, in Huayan Buddhism does not subscribe to substantial essence. Like the "one" in the Zen *gong'an*, "All the things in the world return to one; where does the one return to?," the one-ness of noumenon does not stand as the one and only truth, but is immediately dispersed into the phenomena because the essence of noumenon is essencelessness.

As Chengguan acknowledged, phenomena by nature conflict with one another and only when the phenomenal world is viewed from the noumenal point of view does the emptiness of conflict lead to the understanding of the non-interfering phenomena. What is still not clear in this Huayan paradigm of the "mutually non-interfering phenomena" is the question of how the conflicting nature of phenomena is endorsed without being regulated or hierarchically stratified. In presenting various people's lives as spiritual teachings, Sudhana's journey does not take into account the idea that the differences existing in the life-world might create conflict between them. That none of Sudhana's *dharma* teachers claims that her/his truth is "the ultimate truth" could be an indirect acknowledgement that Sudhana's journey implies potential conflict among phenomena, since conflict is a symptom of finite beings who are characterized by boundaries and limitations. In the "Entering the Realm of Reality" chapter, the possibility of conflict is suggested, but the chapter does not openly discuss the issue of potential conflicts.

At the final stage of his journey, Sudhana meets Maitreya, who puts Sudhana into the great samādhi at the tower of Vairocana, the Buddha of Light.

The ultimate vision which Sudhana experiences at the tower has been interpreted as the symbolic manifestation of the harmony of the world of diversity, and the harmony in this case means the noumenal reality as discussed in the fourfold worldview. The two major events in this chapter "Entering the Realm of Reality,"—meeting dharma-teachers in various occupations, on the one hand, and experiencing the harmony of the world at the tower of Vairocana, on the other,—symbolically articulate one of the major themes of Huayan Buddhism. By presenting fifty-three *dharma* teachers who represent various aspects in the life-world, the *Huayan jing* advocates the world of diversities, which is the world of every man and woman. The vision of the Vairocana tower suggests that the diverse realities in the life–world share the underlying structure of existence about which Huayan Buddhism takes pains to explain through its theory of the fourfold worldview. This interpretation reconfirms the idea that Huayan Buddhism privileges the world of noumenon, despite its emphasis on the diverse phenomenal world. Does this imply that the world of every man and woman represented by the fifty-three dharma-teachers eventually becomes negated in the all-encompassing noumenal world of the Vairocana Buddha? We will consider an answer which is distant from the reading of Huayan Buddhism as a sweeping endorsement of harmony.

In his *Mirror of the Mysteries of the Universe of the Hua-yen*, Chengguan writes, "contemplating phenomena involves compassion [in addition to wisdom] whereas contemplation of noumenon is [related to] wisdom."[24] Chengguan does not elaborate on the meaning of this insightful passage; after this statement, he goes back to discussing the importance of noumenon in understanding phenomena. However, this short passage offers a clue to decipher another aspect of the Huayan position as to the relationship between noumenon and phenomena. Huayan patriarchs took pains to expound the nature of noumenon and its importance in understanding the phenomenal diversity; however Chengguan's statement reveals that, in the ultimate sense, phenomena cannot be fully understood if approached only with the quality that is required to understand noumenon. To deal with phenomena, one needs an additional feature which Chengguan finds in the Buddhist concept of compassion. Understanding the non-interfering reality of the noumenal world requires only wisdom, whereas, in order to understand the mutually non-interfering and at the same time mutually interfering world of phenomena one needs to exercise both wisdom and compassion.

From Gautama Śiddhartha, the Buddha, to the Dalai Lama in our time, compassion has been emphasized as a major concept in the Buddha's teaching. Simple as it might sound, the logic of how compassion functions in Buddhism has yet to be fully investigated. What does the Buddhist concept of compassion actually entail? Is it sympathy, emotion, or moral capacity? Is compassion an obligation or is compassion a natural overflow of an enlightened individual? The Huayan vision of compassion is completely anchored in the understanding of noumenon, which is defined as the emptiness of an entity. Compassion, understood in this manner, cannot be a simple empathy for other beings in a predicament. Instead, compassion becomes possible when one becomes aware of the absolute dependent co-arising of reality. The first of the Buddhist Four Noble Truths is suffering, and, in this case, suffering does not denote suffering or pain as we use the term in our daily conversation. Likewise, compassion, in the way Buddhism employs the term, cannot be a mere emotional response to a situation. In a strict sense, compassion is neither virtue nor an emotional quality nor an intuitive response to a given situation. Nor can compassion be exercised with a sense of obligation. Instead, compassion is another expression of ultimate irony or even the aporia—as Derrida notes—which characterizes human existence and experience.[25]

When the young Gautama Śiddhartha faces the existence of death for the first time in his adventure into the world outside his palace and experiences compassion, as the legend goes, the compassion he encounters cannot be a mere sense of pity for fellow living beings who would eventually turn into ashes like those in his hand. It is an encounter with the ultimate absurdity of existence itself. Compassion, in this sense, is an exercise of one's courage to accept the limits of human beings' capacity to understand existence through the existing logical frame of reference. When all of the referential points which make possible meaning-giving acts of an individual agency become exhausted, there, one faces what Buddhism calls compassion.

Compassion as an encounter with one's existential reality is not far removed from the compassion arising from one's awareness of the suffering in life. Compassion arises when loving-kindness (metta) meets the suffering of beings. And loving-kindness is the general attitude of kindness and caring arising from one's realization that existential reality is always already a differential notion without a substantial entity on which to ground it. Suffering, the first noble truth of Buddhism, is not an individualized pain or feeling of discomfort, but the pain which has universal cause in the sense that it applies to the basic structure of existence, not to incidents occurring in isolation. An individual incident could serve as an occasion to enable one to understand suffering, but, as it is, it is not the foundation of the suffering per se.

Allow me for a moment to borrow what modern Japanese thinker Nishida Kitarō identifies as characteristics of the religious worldview, which, it seems to me, has a strong affinity with the structure of Buddhist compassion that I am trying to articulate here. In his discussion of religion and the religious worldview, Nishida challenges some of the familiar conceptions about religion. To put it briefly, religion, for Nishida, is not about subjective belief because religious faith contains "something objective, some absolute fact of the self."[26] Religion, for Nishida, is not about morality because morality is socially constructed, whereas religion is about the "absolute overturning of values."[27] Nishida contends that the religious worldview arises when an individual realizes the absolute contradictory self-identity, whereas moral values emerge when one erases such ambiguity in one's existence. Religion, for Nishida, is not about mysterious experiences because the religious worldview emerges when one "becomes aware of the bottomless self-contradiction of one's own self," which cannot, in any mysterious way, be resolved. And religion is not about the peace of mind; instead, religious consciousness arises, according to Nishida, when an individual realizes the existential predicament. Enlightenment understood in this context does not mean "to see anything objectively." Instead, for Nishida, it is "an ultimate seeing of the bottomless nothingness of the self that is simultaneously a seeing of the fountainhead of sin and evil."[28]

Like Nishida's religious worldview, Buddhist compassion cannot be fully explicated if we approach it as a subjective emotion or a mystical experience or an activity which ensues from the practitioner's peace of mind. Nor can it be understood as an individual's moral capacity which enables the individual to exercise ethical obligation. Instead, compassion comes to pass when an individual realizes the ultimate absurdity of existence itself. Absurdity, in this case, does not need to be understood in a negative sense. To use the Huayan Buddhist terminology, compassion arises when one realizes the inexhaustibility of the context of each incidence as one considers the dependently arising nature of being. Huayan Buddhism's emphasis on the noumenal world, in this context, is an apt preparation for the practitioner to become awakened to the existential reality which is conducive to the exercise of compassion on the phenomenal level.

When Huayan Buddhism repeatedly employs the counterintuitive expression that in a particle of dust is included the entire world, the statement, obviously, is to be understood symbolically. That is, the existence of each entity is always in the net of excess which defies the existing referential system of the subject. This excess is called, in Huayan Buddhism, the inexhaustibility (C. *chongchong wujin*) of the realm of reality. This inexhaustibility of context is the reality of each entity in the phenomenal world, like each jewel in Indra's net. From the Huayan perspective, it does have an ethical implication. Ethics, in this case, is not just related to moral laws or moral obligation.

Let us go back to the example of the conflict between the person X and the shrimp consumed by the person, and consider the ethical stance of Huayan Buddhism, based on the "inexhaustibility" of each phenomenon in the realm of reality. According to the third level of the fourfold worldview, no conflict in the ultimate reality can be detected between X and the shrimp because neither of them has self-nature to create conflict. On the phenomenal level, the shrimp was killed and eaten by X, and the conflict, from the Huayan perspective as well, is acknowledged. What the Huayan Buddhist does not subscribe to is the idea that the exact structure of a conflict can be known to us. Conflict, by definition, requires competing parties. Parties involved in a conflict need to be identified, together with their contentions, in order to identify the structure of the conflict. Conflict resolution generally goes through the process in which each party weighs the benefits and disadvantages involved in the contents of conflict, and based on those evaluations, each party will take its position. However, if we consider the Huayan concept of an individual identity explained through "mutual identity" and "mutual penetration," the structure of a conflict will be revealed only in the form of constant deferral.

An important point to note is that the impossibility of offering a clear structure of conflict in the phenomenal world does not negate or dismiss the conflict itself; instead, the subject is required to approach the phenomenal conflict from a perspective which is different from a commonsense logic. This is what Chengguan indicates with his statement that with wisdom alone, the phenomenal world, which is charged with conflicts, cannot be fully understood; the activation of one's compassion, in addition to wisdom, is required. "Understanding," in this context, does not have to mean agreement; it might not even include acceptance of the position of the other parties involved in the conflict. Here, we are reminded of Lyotard's claim that a consensus from the postmodern perspective is a horizon that can never be reached, once the diversity of the language game is recognized.

Efforts to resolve or minimize a conflict, from the Huayan perspective, are not based on a logically identified structure of a conflict and subsequent evaluations of the role of each component involved in the occurrence of the conflict, which will further result in the action of eliminating what is identified as evil and promoting what is identified as good. The first step in the acknowledgement and resolution of a conflict arises from the realization that to draw a complete picture of the structure of conflict is not possible, because an event, and a conflict as well, occurs through differing factors which are intricately interwoven with one another.

The example of the conflict between a shrimp-eater and the shrimp might sound too simple to assert our claim that a conflict should be resolved through compassion and that compassion is initiated through the awareness that to obtain the ultimate structure of conflict is not possible. But the logic still holds in this seemingly too naive situation. Suppose one claims that the shrimp eater was wrong and responsible for the creation of the conflict between himself and the shrimp by devouring the poor helpless shrimp. Based on what protocol and rules can one claim that it is wrong to eat shrimp? On what ground does one contend that shrimp, in this case, are innocent victims? As much as humans devour shrimp, shrimp also consume microscopic organisms, and so on. If one becomes aware that there exists conflict between a shrimp eater and shrimp that are eaten, and if the person has decided to stop eating shrimp in order to resolve that conflict, the action, from the Huayan perspective, cannot be based on a certain rule stating that one should not eat shrimp, nor is it based on the logic that it is outright wrong to eat shrimp. Rather, it shall be based on the realization that the killing involved in the action of eating shrimp causes suffering and pain to other organisms. In other words, compassion, or resolution of conflict in the Huayan Buddhist sense, does not arise because one feels sorry for the victims of conflict, but because the very existence of conflict itself is aporia, the impossibility of fully exhausting the causes and constituents which have made a contribution to the occurrence of the conflict.

That Buddhist compassion cannot be a condescending action of feeling pity for others is well articulated in the various discourses on the bodhisattva path. The paradoxical passages in the *Diamond Sūtra* are superb examples. The *Sūtra* explains that a bodhisattva's activities are to be performed with "the mind detached from any formal notions [or phenomenal appearances]."[29] That is so because bodhisattvic activities are not those which could be exercised by the subject upon objects, but are activities performed in a state of no-boundaries. In other words, bodhisattvic activities are to be done with no subjective intentionality involved in them. At the very beginning of the *Diamond Sūtra*, the Buddha characterizes bodhisattva activities as non-abiding:

> All living creatures of whatever class, . . . are caused by me [Tathāgata] to attain unbounded liberation nirvāna. Yet when vast, uncountable, immeasurable numbers of beings have thus been liberated, verily no being has been liberated. Why is this Subhūti? It is because no bodhisattva who is a real bodhisattva cherishes the idea of an ego entity, a personality, a being, or a separated individuality.[30]

In an ultimate sense, then, the concept of responsibility, which has always been at the center of moral and ethical discourse, will take a new turn in the Huayan Buddhist ethical paradigm. At the center of the Huayan ethical paradigm lays the interpretation of the nature of noumenon identified as emptiness and of its manifestation in phenomena through diverse entities. Ethics in this paradigm does not arise by negating the diverse phenomena and emphasizing all encompassing noumenon. Instead, ethics begins with the realization of the tension between the two. Like centripetal and centrifugal forces, two aspects of the Huayan vision, that is, the principle and particularities, noumenon and phenomena, are in a relationship of constant tension, instead of a hierarchical relationship of one subjugating the other. The tension in this case does not indicate conflict that needs to be resolved. Tension denotes, among other things, a state of awareness and this state is to be constant. The unobstructed inter-penetration of noumenon and phenomena as represented by the harmony at the tower of Vairocana, and the endless bodhisattva path represented by Sudhana's *dharma* teachers in the *Huayan jing* are mutually reinforcing, instead of a movement heading from one to the other. The world of harmony is not the teleological goal to be reached when the diversity in the phenomenal world is regulated into one: the one and the many co-exist. By understanding noumenon and phenomena as being in a state of tension, we can also envision the relationship between wisdom and compassion which has been at the core of the discussion of Zen Buddhist position in the ethical discourse.

To remember Chengguan's statement again, understanding the noumenal reality requires wisdom, and the phenomenal diversity requires both wisdom and compassion. Compassion cannot be exercised without the attainment of wisdom, but the attainment of wisdom is not possible without compassion to engage in the phenomenal diversity, since noumenon does not exist in separation from phenomena in the Huayan world. In this context, one can say that Huayan offers a philosophical paradigm for Zen Buddhism, especially in conceptualizing Zen Buddhist ethics, and Zen offers a paradigm to actualize the contents of Huayan Buddhism. In the following chapter, we will look into this issue more in detail, by examining Chinul's dialectical employment of Zen and Huayan Buddhism.

Chapter Nine

Envisioning Zen Ethics through Huayan Phenomenology

1. Zen Buddhism in the Discourse of Ethics

Since Zen Buddhism's entry into the Western world, the ethical stance of Zen Buddhism has become one of the most discussed topics. In this context, a claim has been made that Buddhism in general, and Zen Buddhism in particular, needs to offer a clearer blueprint on social issues and thus demonstrate its viability as an ethical discourse in order for the tradition to survive in the West. James Whitehill, for example, claims, "Buddhism must begin to demonstrate a far clearer *moral form* and a more sophisticated, *appropriate ethical strategy* than can be found among its contemporary Western interpreters and representatives, if it is to flourish in the West" (emphasis original).[1] In a similar context Daniel Palmer argues, "If Buddhists cannot develop dialogical responses to these concerns [for social issues], then Buddhism in all likelihood will remain on the periphery of Western cultural practices, representing only an exotic curiosity and not a vital resource."[2] It is debatable whether ethics will be "the" factor for the survival and prosperity of Buddhism in the West. However, the importance of considering the ethical paradigm of Zen Buddhism cannot be denied, given our discussions on Zen Buddhism in previous chapters. Among different Buddhist schools, Zen Buddhism has been frequently singled out for its problem with ethics. What is the ground of the commonly held view that Zen Buddhism by nature is at odd with ethics? In order to conceptualize Zen ethics, let us begin our discussion by situating Zen Buddhism in the general discussion of ethics and identify issues that could be considered problematic from the perspective of normative ethics.

The basic premise of Zen Buddhism states that the sentient being is the Buddha. The fundamental oxymoron involved in this statement—that is, a sentient being is the Buddha and at the same time is a sentient being—

189

becomes the ground of subsequent problems that Zen Buddhist tradition has to deal with in facing normative ethics. The source of this oxymoronic existential reality of a sentient being is more often than not identified by the mind of the sentient being. This is especially the case with Chinul's Zen Buddhism. At the beginning of *Encouragement to Practice: the Compact of the Samādhi and Prajñā Community* (*Kwŏnsu chŏnghye kyŏlsa mun* 1190), Chinul states, "When one is deluded about the mind and gives rise to endless defilements, such a person is a sentient being. When one is awakened to the mind and gives rise to endless marvelous functions, such a person is the Buddha. Delusion and awakening are two different states but both are caused by the mind. If one tries to find the Buddha away from this mind, one will never find him."[3] In *Secrets on Cultivating the Mind* (*Susimkyŏl* 1203-1205), Chinul states, "If one wants to avoid transmigration, the best way is to search for the Buddha. Though I said 'search for the Buddha,' this mind is the Buddha. The mind cannot be found in a distant place but is inside this body" (*HPC* 4.708b). Also in *Straight Talk on the True Mind* (*Chinsim chiksŏl*, around 1205), Chinul advises that the role of patriarchs is "to help sentient beings look at their original nature by themselves" (*HPC* 4.715a).

By identifying the mind, the Buddha, and one's original nature, Chinul joins many other Zen masters for whom the identity between the Buddha and the sentient being in her/his original state marks the basic premise of the school. Chinul further characterizes the original state of a sentient being as a state of liberation and, thus, advises his contemporary practitioners:

> Why don't you first trust that the mind is originally pure, the defilement empty. Do not suspect this, but practice by relying on this. Outwardly observe precepts, and forget about binding or attachment; inwardly practice *samādhi*, which, however, should not be suppression. When one detaches oneself from evil, there is nothing to cut off, and when one practices meditation, there is nothing to practice. The practice without practice, the cutting off with nothing to cut off, can be said to be real practice and real cutting off. (*HPC* 4.700b)

Through such paradoxical statements as "the practice without practice" or "the cutting off with nothing to cut off," Zen Buddhists, including Chinul, emphasize that the ultimately realized liberated state of enlightenment is none other than the original state of a being. Chinul describes such a state of the mind as the original mind of both the Buddha and sentient beings. In the *Secrets on Cultivating the Mind*, Chinul clarifies this non-existence of the differences between the Buddha and sentient beings through his emphasis on "the mind of marvelous knowing" (K. *yŏngchi chisim*) which is empty and quiet (K. *kongjŏk*). Chinul states, "The deluded thoughts are originally quiet, and the outside world is originally empty; in the place where all dharmas are empty the marvelous knowing exists, which is not dark. This mind of marvelous knowing, which is empty and quiet, is your original face. This is also the dharma-recognition that has been mysteriously transmitted through all the Buddhas in the three worlds and all the patriarchs and dharma teachers" (*HPC* 4.710a).

The emptiness and quietness are the ontological reality of being, whereas marvelous knowing is the epistemological ground for the being's awareness of the empty and quiet nature of her/his existence. Chinul further elaborates on the quiet and marvelous mind by pointing out that neither an entity (an individual) nor the action of the entity—both physical and mental—has one identifiable control center. Both an entity and its actions are empty. Their source, which Chinul describes as one's own nature (K. *sŏng*), is empty, and thus, cannot have a shape. Chinul states:

> Since there is no shape, how can it be either big or small? Since it is neither big nor small, how can there be limits? There being no limits, there is neither inside nor outside; there being neither inside nor outside, there is neither far nor close; there being neither far nor close, there is neither this nor that; there being neither this nor that, there is neither going nor coming; there being neither going nor coming, there is neither life nor death; there being neither life nor death, there is neither past nor present; there being neither past nor present, there is neither delusion nor awakening; there being neither delusion nor awakening, there is neither the secular nor the sacred; there being neither the secular nor the sacred, there is neither purity nor impurity; there being neither purity nor impurity, there is neither right nor wrong; there being neither right nor wrong, all the names and sayings cannot explain it. (*HPC* 4.710c)

The statement succinctly sums up the logical development of the ontological status of a being, its implications for religious practice, and its position in ethical discourse. The non-discriminative nature of one's being negates the secular distinctions of binary opposites, and this has been identified as a major obstacle that Zen Buddhism needs to deal with in order to make it viable as an ethical system. For the sake of convenience, let us identify this as the first problem of Zen Buddhist ethics: the ambiguity of ethical categories in Zen Buddhist discourse.

Despite the non-existence of a binary distinction between the Buddha and sentient beings, in reality, a gap still exists, between the two. Chinul explains the bound state of sentient beings on three levels: the first involves being bound through external phenomena; the second, through inner desire; and the third, through the desire for enlightenment. One can identify them as epistemological, psychological, and religio-teleological bondages respectively. These are the bound states that individuals have to get over in order to fully realize their original nature.

Liberation from external phenomena becomes possible through one's realization of the nature of the relationship between an individual and the outside world. In this encounter, the disturbance of the mind by the phenomenal world indicates that the practitioner is bound by the characteristics of the object of her/his perception. Whether the object is a thing or an event, the disturbance of the mind by an external phenomenon gives evidence that the subject takes the phenomenon as an entity with a closed identity, and this perceptual illusion, according to Chinul, is created through the function of the mind. By understanding the phenomenon as if it had a substantial nature, the mind not only mistakes the nature of the object of perception, but misunderstands the subject's own nature by imposing sustained qualities on the object. In this process, both the mind and the phenomenon turn into substances, creating a dualistic structure of the subject and the object, and binding both of them to imaginary substances.

The second and the third instances of bondage—that is, bondage through an inner desire (or psychological binding) and bondage through the teleological idea (or religio-teleological binding)—can be explained through the same logic. Emotional reactions to the outside world such as greed, anger, or pleasure become problems only when the subject considers them to be fixed entities with substantial nature in and of themselves. Once the subject realizes that emotions and thoughts are subject to conditioned causality like any other things in the world, the subject moves to free her/himself from stagnated emotions. In this case, the reality of greed, anger, or pleasure is admitted, but at the same time their provisional status is recognized. The realization of the first and second instances of bondage opens a way to liberation from the third, for a logical conclusion indicates that, from the beginning, there is nothing that the practitioner frees her/himself from. Searching for a goal, that is, enlightenment per se, turns out to be the practitioner's illusion. At this point, the original state of the practitioner is confirmed as the state of full liberation and that of wisdom.

This brief analysis of the status of sentient beings in bondage reflects the inward movement in Zen Buddhism's understanding of an individual's reality and the subject's realization of innate wisdom. The bondage begins with one's mind and so does the liberation from the bondage. The subjective and individualistic nature of one's realization of original nature, as demonstrated in the above process, can be addressed as another potential problem in the construction of Zen Buddhist ethics. We will identify this as the second problem of Zen ethics: subjectivitism of Zen practice.

The identity of difference and difference of identity between the enlightened and unenlightened leads us to the third potential problem in Zen ethics: the issue of the ethical agent. In his discussion of Chinul's Buddhism, Korean philosopher Hyŏnghyo Kim introduces the idea of existentiality (K. *siljonsŏng*) and essentiality (K. *ponjilsŏng*) of the self-nature (K. *chasŏng*). Characterizing Chinul's Buddhism as a "metaphysics of the self-mind [K.

chasim],"[4] Kim defines the meaning of awakening in Chinul as follows: "As the mind becomes calm in the process of its acceptance of the self-nature, the existential mind experiences a metaphysical acceptance of the self-nature; such acceptance is the awakened mind [K. *osim*]."[5] The existential mind is the unenlightened aspect of the mind, whereas the self-nature is the mind in its original state; the former is bound to various aspects of the worldliness of an individual, whereas the latter is free from such bondages. When the existential mind becomes one with the essence of the self-nature, the existential mind turns into the true mind (K. *chinsim*). Kim's philosophical rephrasing of Chinul's Zen thought elaborates on the problem of ethical agency in Chinul's thought. Is it the essential (enlightened) mind that is the ethical agent or is it the existential (unenlightened) mind? On a theoretical level, they cannot be separated. On the other hand, it is true that there exists a gap between the two in the real world.

The three issues that we have identified as potential problems in Zen ethical discourse from the perspective of normative ethics—that is, ambiguity of ethical categories, subjectivism of practice, and ambiguity in the identity of the ethical agent— are not separate issues, but closely related. As the fourth entry in this list, we also need to consider the public dimension of Zen awakening. Supposing that the original nature is an awakened state, how does it enable an individual to practice virtuous actions? Why does the ontological recovery of one's original state facilitate moral behavior and bodhisattvic activities? The former occurs within the domain of the subject, whereas the latter takes place in the subject's shared realm with others. How are they connected to each other?

The Zen Buddhist tradition has offered at best a vague response to this issue. Examine the following statement by Chinul from his *Encouragement to Practice*:

> Vain are all phenomena. [When you encounter phenomena] search for the body in a calm state, firmly close the castle of your mind, and make more efforts to concentrate. You will find a quiet returning place, which is comfortable and without discontinuity. In that situation, the mind of love or hatred will *naturally* disappear; compassion and wisdom will *naturally* become clearer as your evil karma will be *naturally* cut off and meritorious behavior will *naturally* be advanced (emphasis mine). (*HPC* 4.699b)

In this passage, the correction of perceptual illusion is directly connected with moral activities. In other places in the same text, Chinul quotes a gāthā which runs: "Dhyāna is the armor of diamond. It is capable of fending off the arrows of defilement; Dhyāna is the storehouse of wisdom; it is the field of all kinds of meritorious virtues" (*HPC* 4.701a). In this gāthā, meditation leads one to virtuous behavior. Not only is there no explanation of why that should be the case, but Chinul does not explain the nature of this meritorious behavior either. Do they have to do with social engagement or is the fact that one is free from all illusionary thoughts itself virtuous behavior?

Chinul's "naturalist" position exposed above seems a good example of what James Whitehill criticizes as a "transcendence trap" of the romanticized version of Zen Buddhist ethics. Whitehill writes: "The trap misleads them [interpreters of Zen] and us into portraying the perfected moral life as a non-rational expressiveness, something natural, spontaneous, non-linguistic, and uncalculating."[6] The claim that enlightenment, identified as the recovery of the original mind, will "naturally" condition ethical behaviors is challenged by an incident related to the founder of Buddhism, the Buddha. The Buddha's awakening was not immediately transformed into compassionate activities. After attaining enlightenment, the Buddha hesitated as to whether he should share the contents of his awakening with fellow human beings. If the Buddha attained awakening, he must have fully embodied wisdom. But still he hesitated before he made up his mind to exercise his compassion to help fellow human beings.

According to the "Brahmā Sutta" in the *Saṃyutta-nikāya*, the Buddha needed outside help to reach the conclusion that he should share the content of his awakening. The "Brahmā Sutta" begins with the Buddha's doubt about the possibility of being understood, if he imparts the content of his enlightenment:

> Thus have I heard:—The Exalted One was once staying at Uruvelā, on the banks of the river Nerañjarā, beneath the Goatherd's Banyan, and he had just attained full enlightenment. Now as he was privately meditating, the thought arose in him: 'I have penetrated this Norm, deep, hard to perceive, hard to understand, peaceful and sublime, no mere dialectic, subtle, intelligible only to the wise. But this is a race devoting itself to the things to which it clings, devoted thereto, delighting therein. And for a race devoting itself to the things to which it clings, devoted thereto, delighting therein, this were a matter hard to perceive, to wit, that this is conditioned by that—that all that happens is by way of cause. This, too, were a matter hard to discern, to wit, the tranquillization of all the activities of [worldly] life, the renunciation of all substrates of rebirth, the destruction of natural cravings, passionlessness, cessation Nibbāna. And now I only might teach the Norm, and others might not acknowledge me: this would be wearisome to me, this would be hurtful to me.[7]

When the Buddha was speculating like this, knowing the Buddha's thinking, Brahmā-Sahampati comes to exhort the Buddha to preach his teaching for those who were yet to completely succumb to the defilements of the worldly life. Brahmā-Sahampati thus states, "Lord! Let the Exalted One preach the Norm! Let the Blessed One preach the Norm! There are souls whose eyes are hardly dimmed by dust; they are perishing from not hearing the Norm. They will come to be knowers of the Norm."[8] The Buddha concedes to the advice and turns the wheel of the dharma. How do we contend, with this example of the Buddha, that the full realization of wisdom will be, immediately and naturally, and without mediation, transformed into compassion? In addition, if Zen ethics is possible only in the state of enlightenment when an individual has fully recovered her/his original wisdom, what is the status of ethical behaviors of sentient beings who are yet to attain the state of pure awakening and wisdom?

It is true that Zen Buddhism has not been eager to provide a clear answer to these questions, but a close examination of Chinul's texts indicates that Chinul is in fact keenly aware of this problem and constantly emphasizes the gap between the sentient being and the Buddha as much as he confirms the identity between the two. The co-existence of the identity and the differences between the Buddha and sentient beings can confuse practitioners and cause a theoretical conflict in Chinul's Buddhism. However, binary postulations in the Zen tradition, including the Buddha and the sentient being, wisdom and compassion, the unenlightened and the enlightened, awakening and cultivation, should be understood not as a bipolarization for either/or but as in a relationship of constant tension. In Chinul's Zen Buddhism, the structure of this tension is concretized through the paradigm of subitism and gradualism.

2. The Dialectic of Zen and Huayan

The dialectics of subitism and gradualism, like that of wisdom and compassion, lie at the core of the Zen Buddhist basic thesis of the sentient being qua the Buddha. In the *Excerpts from the Dharma Collection and Special Practice Record with Personal Notes*, Chinul discusses the four Zen schools of China as they appear in the *Special Dharma Records* of Guifeng Zongmi (780-841) and connects them with the theory of subitism and gradualism. In his commentaries, Chinul states that the doctrinal school spreads out teachings and that Zen makes a selection and, thus, simplifies. Chinul summarizes the simplified teachings of Zen Buddhism with the following two aspects: "With regard to the *dharma*, there are absolute (K. *pulbyŏn*) and changing (K. *suyŏn*) aspects; with regard to humans, there are sudden awakening (K. *ton'o*) and gradual cultivation (K. *chŏmsu*)" (*HPC* 4.734c). The absolute and changing aspects of the dharma are not two separate phenomena but different aspects of the same dharma. Likewise, for Chinul, sudden awakening and gradual cultivation are not in the relationship of either/or, but represent two aspects of the same phenomenon. Chinul further elaborates on the relationship between awakening and cultivation and, thus, wisdom and compassion, as follows:

Practitioners in our time often say, "if one is able to look into one's Buddha-nature clearly, the vow and altruistic behavior will naturally be realized." I, Moguja, do not think that this is the case. To see clearly one's Buddha-nature is to realize that sentient beings and the Buddha are equal and that there is no discrimination between 'me' and others. However, I worry that if one does not make the vow of compassion, s/he will stagnate in the state of calmness. The *Exposition of the Avatamsaka Sūtra* says: "The nature of wisdom being calm, it needs to be guarded by the vow." Therefore in the deluded state before the awakening, the strength of the mind is dark and weak, and thus is unable to realize the vow. However, once one experiences [the initial] awakening, one will be able to sympathize with the suffering of the sentient beings through one's discriminative-wisdom, and thus exercise one's compassion and make a vow, and practice the bodhisattva path according to one's capacity, which will gradually complete one's awakened-behavior. How could this not be joyful? (*HPC* 4.755b)

In this passage Chinul emphasizes that a mere awareness of wisdom cannot be directly connected to compassionate activities. This claim of non-natural transition from wisdom to compassion could be understood as contradicting the remark in the *Encouragement to Practice* in which Chinul emphasizes the natural flow from the former to the latter. However, the relationship of wisdom to compassion, like that of the sentient being and the Buddha, takes the oxymoronic state in Zen Buddhism: wisdom and compassion are one, and at the same time, different. We can interpret the situation by employing twofold approaches following Sung Bae Park who makes a distinction between the realm of faith and the realm of practice in understanding the sudden-gradual paradigm in Chinul. In terms of the realm of faith, practitioners believe that their minds are the original Buddha; thus, enlightenment should be sudden. In the realm of practice, however, the realization of the innate Buddha-nature requires a constant cultivation.[9] In a similar context, Korean Buddhist scholar Kŏn'gi Kang states that sudden awakening is the realization of wisdom, as gradual cultivation is the exercise of compassion.[10] Pŏpchŏng, another scholar of Korean Buddhism, moves one step further in his interpretation of the relationship between wisdom and compassion in the soteriological structure of sudden-awakening-and-gradual-cultivation in Chinul, and claims: "In the case of Śākyamuni Buddha, awakening under the bodhi trees represents sudden enlightenment, whereas forty-five years' activities of guiding numerous sentient beings represents gradual cultivation. This also represents the two wings in Buddhism: wisdom and compassion."[11]

This view of sudden awakening and gradual cultivation, especially in our exploration of Zen Buddhist ethics, suggests that the seemingly exclusive dominance of the inward movement of the practitioner in understanding Zen practice needs reconsideration. Unlike the common assumption that Zen practice is exclusively dominated by introspective subjectivism, Chinul contends that even though introspection facilitates one's awakening, awakening should also accompany social activities of compassion to reach its perfection. For Chinul, compassionate activities are manifestations of wisdom. This is an important point because, unlike the romanticized version of Zen practice that envisions a "natural" activation of compassion upon the realization of wisdom, Chinul is claiming that compassion *is* wisdom; that is, wisdom per se, without compassionate actions, cannot be obtained. The commonly accepted movement from wisdom to compassion, then, is reversed here.

In discussing Chinul's view on sudden awakening and gradual cultivation, Robert Gimello proposes to understand the sudden-gradual paradigm in Chinul as a reflection of the tension within Zen Buddhism between the radical challenge to the existing status quo and the necessity of ethical concern and responsibilities.[12] Gimello suggests that sudden awakening reflects the very promise of Zen Buddhism, whereas gradual cultivation meets the ethical dimension required for the maintenance of religious practice. Gimello's interpretation can also be applied to the seeming conflict between acquiring wisdom and the exercise of compassion. Chinul further consolidates the social and ethical dimension of Zen practice by bringing together the Huayan doctrine of the dependent co-arising of the realm of reality and Zen meditation.

For Chinul, the mind of the practitioner is a microcosm of Indra's net. Chinul adopts Fazang's Huayan idea of the "dependent co-arising of the realm of reality" (C. *fajie yuanqi*; K. *pŏpkye yŏn'gi*) as another expression of the mind of sentient beings. Since the realization of one's mind is equivalent to realizing the dependent co-arising of the realm of reality, the Zen practice of the mind is directly related to the practitioner's awareness of her/his relation with others in the objective world. On the other hand, Chinul also follows the interpretation of Huayan Buddhism by the lay Buddhist scholar in Tang China, Li Tongxuan (635–730), who emphasizes the mind of sentient beings in relation to the doctrine of "nature-origination" (C. *xingqi*; K. *sŏnggi*). This enables Chinul to criticize the limits of Fazang's Huayan Buddhism for its lack of connection with the practitioner's reality. Dominant scholarship on Chinul has understood Chinul's position on Huayan Buddhism as opposing the "orthodox" Huayan theory of Fazang's dependent co-arising of the realm of reality and preferring the nature-origination of Li Tongxuan.[13] It is true that, from the beginning of the *Treatise on the Attainment of Buddhahood*, Chinul cites Li Tongxuan as the textual ground for his thoughts on Huayan doctrines and takes a critical stance against Fazang apropos of his treatment of the theory of the dependent co-arising of the realm of reality. However, it is also true that Chinul employs Fazang to support his own theory that Zen meditation is not a subjective solipsist practice by identifying the mind of the sentient being with the dependent co-arising of the realm of reality.

In the *Treatise on the Complete and Sudden Attainment of Buddhahood*
(*Wŏndon sŏngbul ron*), Chinul relies on Li Tongxuan's interpretation and
identifies the Buddha nature as the revelation of the "Buddha of the Unmoving Wisdom" (K. *pudongji Pul*), with which every sentient being is equipped.
Enlightenment is possible because everybody is already enlightened and,
thus, existence itself is the occurrence or appearing of the Buddha nature.
The Buddha of the Unmoving Wisdom is also described as the "original wisdom of universal bright light" (K. *kŭnbon po 'gwangmyŏngji*), which Chinul
identifies with the true nature of sentient beings. Since every sentient being
already has this wisdom, enlightenment is sudden. Asked about whether
Zen is not one-sided, with its emphasis on the noumenal aspect (K. *sŏng*),
and lacking the domains of form (K. *sang*) and function (K. *yong*), Chinul
responds by saying, "In the experience of awakening to the original nature
[of one's mind in Zen school], one realizes that within the mirror of one's
mind exists the inexhaustible world of the multi-layered net of Indra" (*HPC*
4. 728 a). Chinul resolves the problem of subjectivism of Zen meditation by
identifying the inner world of the subject in Zen with the objective world of
Indra's net: the inside is the outside.

Commenting on the beginning section of the *Hymns of the Dharma Nature (Pŏpsŏng ke)* in which Ŭisang (625–702), the First Patriarch of Korean
Huayan (K. Hwaŏm) Buddhism, describes the world of interpenetration
among things, Chinul writes:

> Only if one reflects upon the pure, clear, and enlightened nature of one's mind,
> myriad images will appear on the transparent mind from which delusions have
> been exhausted. It is just like seawater that is transparently clear: there are no
> images that are not reflected. Hence it is called the ever-abiding function of the
> ocean-seal of all phenomena in the universe. We thus know that the function
> of the round and bright self-reliant realm of reality as well as the unobstructed
> interpenetration among phenomena in three pervasions is not different from the
> clear and transparent enlightened nature [of an individual] (*HPC* 4.729b).

In this passage, Chinul emphasizes the importance of recovering the
"pure, clear, enlightened nature of one's mind." Also, in this section of the
text, Chinul repeatedly uses the expression "reflecting upon (looking back
upon) one's mind" as the very way to attain Buddhahood. The final stage of
the Huayan vision is identified with the "clear and transparent enlightened
nature" of an individual. The result of such an amalgamation of the Huayan
vision of the unimpeded interpenetration of things in the phenomenal world
and Zen emphasis on the mind-qua-Buddha is to confirm that Zen awakening is only possible for Chinul through the practice of "reflecting upon
one's mind" (K. *panjo*), and that awakening is, as it is, the realization of the
mutually non-interfering phenomena, the ultimate vision of Huayan Bud-

dhism. The movement saves Zen from the criticism of internal solipsism, about which Chinul agonized.

Chinul's employment of Huayan thought in his discussion of Zen Buddhism does not stop here. As much as Chinul emphasizes the sameness in theory between Huayan and Zen Buddhism, Chinul also strongly asserts the superiority of Zen over Huayan Buddhism. This position of Chinul constitutes another aspect of Chinul's thought: Chinul contrasts Zhiyan-Fazang's understanding of the dependent co-arising of the realm of reality and nature-origination against the Li Tongxuan-Chinul version of nature-origination. In order to clarify this position, we need to briefly survey the evolution of the concept of the dependent co-arising of the realm of reality and nature-origination in the evolution of the Buddhist doctrine of dependent co-arising.

The Huayan concept of nature-origination can be understood as the ultimate stage of the Buddhist tenet of conditioned causality which has been at the center of Buddhist philosophy since the beginning of the tradition. The theory of causality appears in early Buddhism in the texts of the Chinese Āgama and Pāli canon as the idea of the twelve links of dependent co-arising. In this format, one's ignorance (C. *wuming*) is identified as the original cause of the chain of dependently arising entities. The Abhidharma literature takes pain to identify the conditions in which a dharma arises. Dependent co-arising is understood in connection with various impersonal categories, through which the theory of no-self is expounded. The Mādhyamikans make it their task to demonstrate that the impersonal categories are empty themselves; hence, the famous declaration by Nāgārjuna that "Whatever is dependently co-arisen/ That is explained to be emptiness."[14] Sinification of Buddhism adds new dimensions to the Buddhist theory of dependent co-arising.

The theory of dependent co-arising of the realm of reality of Huayan Buddhism expands the dependently arising nature of things to the entire universe, as the simile of Indra's net suggests. Nature-origination takes one step beyond the theory of dependent co-arising of the realm of reality. Conceptually and linguistically speaking, the idea of dependent co-arising presupposes entities that are dependently arising. When we say the one is the many, we are already assuming this one, whose identity is non-identity. Fazang painstakingly elaborates on the identity of non-identity of this one in his *Treatise on the Five Teachings* through the conceptual frames such as mutual identity and mutual penetration. However, mutual identity or mutual penetration itself cannot be conceived without first designating the identity which creates the mutuality. The idea of nature-origination attempts to resolve this problem. Its logic can be explained as follows: even though we speak of dependent co-arising, in the ultimate sense, there are no independent entities that are depending on others to arise; if entities are non-entities, then, co-airsing (C. *yuanqi*) in the ultimate sense is no-arising (C. *buqi*); hence, it is called nature-origination (C. *xingqi*).

The question naturally arises as to what is referred to here by the "nature" in nature-origination. What is the nature of nature?

In *Hymns of the Dharma Nature*, Ŭisang refers to the image of the jewels in Indra's net, and states, "In one particle of dust/ is contained the ten directions [the entire world]/all other particles of dust/are the same [in their relation to others]."[15] Ŭisang further explains:

> In the teaching of the great dependent co-arising, if there is no "one," the "many" cannot be established. [Practitioners] should be well aware of this nature. What is called the "one" is not the "one" by its self-nature. [By the same token] what is known as the "ten" is not the "ten" by its self-nature; the "ten" comes to be known as the "ten" by its relation to others [or by dependent co-arising]. All the beings produced out of dependent co-arising do not have definite marks nor a definite nature. Since there is no self-nature, beings do not exist independently, which suggests that birth actually means no-birth. No-birth means no need to abide, and no abiding means the middle path.[16]

The first part of this passage reveals similarity with Fazang's explanation of the numbers one through ten in the context of the doctrine of the dependent co-arising of the realm of reality. In the second half, Ŭisang further expands the discussion and identifies the nature in nature-origination as the non-abiding, the middle path. Since things do not have an independent substantial essence of their own, the "co-arising" in the theory of dependent co-arising, in its ultimate sense, is "no-arising." This idea of the no-arising of co-arising is explained in the *Huayan jing* as the reality of the world of the Buddha or the Tathāgata. The nature in nature-origination refers to the nature of the Buddha (or Tathāgata). The nature of the Buddha being non-substantial, nature-origination is another way of articulating dependent co-arising of entities.

In his exposition of the tenets of Huayan Buddhism, Chinul repeatedly emphasizes that the mind, body, and thought of the sentient being are the same as the mind, body, and thought of the Buddha. Chinul concurs with Li Tongxuan in interpreting the Mahāyāna Buddhist pantheon as a symbolically rendered state of sentient beings. In Li Tongxuan's and Chinul's reading, the various figures appearing as celestial Buddhas and bodhisattvas in Mahāyāna Buddhism turn into symbolic statements of different aspects of sentient beings' activities of benefiting others:

> If one attains this dharma [of the sameness between the mind of the sentient being and that of the Buddha] and benefits sentient beings universally with this dharma, it is the practice of Samantabhadra. If one discerns, according to the sublime wisdom which is devoid of mind, nature, and principle, the one vehicle, the three vehicles, and the causes and results of human and deva existence, the person is named Mañjuśrī. Practicing together tirelessly, using discriminative

wisdom to benefit sentient beings while being aware of their faculties, the person is named Samantabhadra. To vow to rescue all sentient beings through great compassion is named Avalokiteśvara. To cultivate these three types of mind simultaneously is named Vairocana Buddha (*HPC* 4.725b; translation modified).[17]

The implication is that the nature in nature-origination in Chinul's Huayan Buddhism cannot presuppose any transcendental being of 'essence'. After all, as Chinul emphasizes, the Buddha exists only in the mind of the sentient being.

Despite this identification between nature-origination and the dependent co-arising of the realm of reality, Chinul makes a movement to distinguish his exposition of nature-origination from that of Fazang. Chinul contends that in Fazang's theory of the "nature-origination qua dependent co-arising of the realm of reality," the relationship between the Buddha and sentient beings is like jewels in Indra's net: they are separate. In Chinul's own theory of the "nature origination qua dependent co-arising of the realm of reality," Indra's net is the mind of sentient beings: the Buddha and sentient beings are identical. In this manner, Chinul criticizes that in Fazang's version of Huayan Buddhism, there is no connection between sentient beings and the ultimate reality of the world. However, Chinul does not completely dismiss the idea that Fazang actually negated this relationship between the Buddha and sentient beings. To make this claim, Chinul resorts to Fazang's essay *Xiu Huayan aozhi wangjin huanyuan guan* (Cultivation of Contemplation of the Inner Meaning of the Huayan: The Ending of Delusion and Return to the Source), and comments:

According to the explanation given here by Hsien-shou [Xianshou], the quality of unimpeded interfusion which universally pervades the *dharmadhātu*. . . arises from the pure, perfectly bright essence of the self-nature within the minds of sentient beings. If, as the Hwaŏm [Huayan] sect explains, this one, true, unobstructed *dharmadhātu* and the original enlightenment of pure nature in the minds of sentient beings are different in their nature, the Patriarch Hsien-shou would be a deceitful liar luring the blind and the deaf with such statements" (HPC 4.729 a; translation modified).[18]

For Chinul, the original nature implies "the pure and perfectly bright essence of the self-nature within the minds of sentient beings" (*HPC* 4.729a). This nature is the same with both the Buddha and the sentient beings, and its appearance in the phenomenal world is called the dependent co-arising of the realm of reality, and its microcosm is the minds of sentient beings. For Chinul, the final stage of mutually non-interfering phenomena in the Huayan fourfold worldview is possible only when each individual is in a state of his/her original nature, without being deluded by the concepts of self, person, and so forth.

By incorporating the Huayan fourfold worldview into his philosophy of mind, Chinul is able to present the Zen practice of mind as that which is equivalent to understanding and getting involved with the phenomenal world. Here we find a juncture in which the Zen Buddhist theory of mind and practice, Huayan phenomenology, and the postmodern claim of heterogeneity come together in sharing their problems in confronting normative ethical discourse.

3. Identifying the Problematics

We have proposed four categories as potential problem areas for understanding Zen Buddhism in the context of ethical discourse: (1) ambiguity of ethical categories, (2) subjectivism of practice, (3) ambiguity in the identity of the ethical agent, and (4) the relationship between awakening and altruistic action. These seemingly apparent problems are not irreparably negative markers for Zen Buddhist ethics. Instead, a serious consideration of Zen Buddhism's position in ethical discourse can revalorize the tradition itself in the sense that Rita Gross claims that the feminist re-reading of Buddhism is a revalorization of the tradition.[19] At the same time, considering the nature of Zen Buddhist ethics also challenges traditional normative ethics and demands a new ethical mode in our time. In the section below, I will briefly discuss why this is the case.

First, the subjectivist nature of Zen meditation has been understood as an anti-social aspect of Zen Buddhism. Chinul's incorporation of the Huayan vision of non-obstructive inter-penetration among phenomena in Zen practice of mind indicates that for Chinul Zen awakening does not limit itself to the personal level of the individual practitioner, but encompasses the diverse reality of the phenomenal world. Historically Zen tradition per se has not developed exclusively as a meditation oriented school, nor have Zen masters exclusively focused on solipsistic meditational practices in seclusion. In another place, I demonstrated this aspect of Zen Buddhism through the case example of Korean Zen Master T'oe'ong Sŏngch'ŏl (1912-1993).[20] S'ŏngch'ŏl has been well known for his relentlessly strict views in relation to both Zen practice and Zen theory. In terms of theory, he challenged Chinul's sudden-enlightenment-gradual-cultivation paradigm as a heretic teaching of Zen Buddhism. He criticized Chinul's Zen Buddhism with a derogatory term "Huayan Zen." In his own practice, he undertook, for eight years, the practice of 'never lying down' (K. *changjwa purwa*) and, for ten years, the practice of seclusion (K. *tonggu pulch'ul* 1955-1965). He was also obstinate in his belief that practitioners should lead a life of isolation on a mountainside without becoming involved in worldly affairs. However, in his dharma talk to Buddhist practitioners, S'ŏngch'ŏl relies on Huayan thought and brings special attention to the practice of Samantabhadra-bodhisattva in the *Huayan jing*. In the *Sūtra*, the truth searcher Sudhana comes to hear Samantabhadra bodhisattva's great vows, in which Samantabhadra explains the dharma-offerings as follows:

> [Dharma-offerings means] making offerings to the Buddha by practice as taught by the Buddha: that is, by helping sentient beings; by respecting and embracing sentient beings; by emphasizing the suffering of sentient beings; by producing the root of goodness; by not deserting bodhisattvic activities; by not leaving the bodhisattvic mind. . . . Such utmost and universal offerings should be made until the empty sky becomes exhausted, until the world of sentient beings becomes exhausted, until the karmic result of the sentient beings and their defilements becomes exhausted. Only then, my offering-makings will come to an end, too. However, the empty sky and all of the above including the defilement of sentient beings cannot be exhausted, my offering-making cannot come to an end, either.[21]

Sŏngch'ŏl emphasizes that, among the above seven dharma-offerings, helping sentient beings is the marrow of the Buddha's teaching. He also cites the story from the same *Sūtra* that to offer a bowl of cold rice to a starving dog is a better way to make offerings to the Buddha than offering thousands of prostrations to the Buddha.[22]

Secondly, the relationship between the subjective mind and objective phenomenal world is realized in the paradigm of the sudden and gradual practice and this clarifies the relationship beween awakening (wisdom) and altruistic activities (compassion) in Zen Buddhism. The awakening to the nature of one's mind is sudden, but its actualization in the phenomenal world is gradual. Chinul emphasized that awareness of one's wisdom does not naturally translate into activities of compassion, and that one should constantly make efforts for altruistic behavior as one makes offerings to the Buddha.

Thirdly, the ambiguity of ethical categories and the identity of the ethical agent are not so much a problem of Zen Buddhism per se, but rather arise when one views the Zen Buddhist value system from the perspective of normative ethics. If the metaphysical concept of ethics is grounded in the belief that humans as rational beings are capable of distinguishing between right and wrong or good and bad, then Zen Buddhist ethics cannot follow the mode of normative ethics, for, from the Zen perspective, making a distinction itself creates delusion. This, however, does not mean that Zen cannot provide ethical guidelines, for ethics begin with the acceptance that such distinctions are possible only after appropriation and, thus, suppression in decision-making. One name for such an appropriation is bias; Zen Buddhism calls it delusion. This suggests that one cannot create Zen Buddhist ethics simply by appropriating Zen theories into the format of existing normative ethics; instead, Zen Buddhist ethics demands a new direction in our understanding of ethical categorization itself.

Zen Buddhism is not alone in demanding a new form of ethics that radically challenges normative ethics with metaphysical postulations. Through the negation of totalizing metaphysical power and endorsement of a non-substantialist mode of thinking, postmodern philosophy has also faced problems similar to thoes of Zen Buddhist ethics. In this context, a consideration of the nature of Zen Buddhist ethics can align with postmodern ethical thinking. In order to consider Zen Buddhist ethics in its full scope, a new ethical paradigm to which both postmodern philosophy and Zen Buddhism can contribute, should emerge as an alternative to normative ethics.

Chapter Ten

The Ethics of Tension:
Toward Buddhist-Postmodern Ethics

1. Ethics and Tension

In his book *Step Back: Ethics and Politics after Deconstruction,* David Wood characterizes postmodern forms of ethics as a "step back": "The step back marks a certain shape of philosophical practice, one that does not just resign itself to, but affirms the necessity of, ambiguity, incompleteness, repetition, negotiation, and contingency."[1] What Wood identifies as the characteristics of deconstructive ethics—that is, ambiguity, incompleteness, repetition, negotiation, and contingency—stands opposite to the general characteristics of normative ethics and moral philosophy. Normative ethics becomes possible through a clear cut judgment between binary opposites, whereas Wood's statement is characterized by a refusal to provide such a definitive mode in our ethical imagination. Instead of offering a ready-made recipe to answer our ethical questions, Wood suggests the ethical as a state of suspension. He explains this suspension by using John Keats' famous expression "negative capability," which Keats defines as a state "when man is capable of being in uncertainties, Mysteries, doubts, without any irritable reaching after fact and reason."[2]

Wood's description is reminiscent of the way Lyotard describes postmodern knowledge: "Postmodern knowledge is not simply a tool of the authorities; it refines our sensitivity to differences and reinforces our ability to tolerate the incommensurable."[3] We are also reminded of Chinul's teaching that *huatou* is neither a presentation of truth nor a cure of the practitioner's diseases. It is in the way a *huatou* interacts with the practitioner that a *huatou* becomes a *huatou,* and the reality to which a *huatou* leads the practitioner is the Huayan world of the unobstructed interpenetration of phenomena, or the world of inexhaustibility of beings.

Doubts and the ensuing state of uncertainty are inevitable stages that the practitioners of *huatou* meditation have to deal with as they confront the aporia that sentient beings are Buddhas just as they are. Does Zen Buddhism offer a final resolution to this paradox of sentient being-qua-Buddha? The paradigm of subitism and gradualism suggests that this is not the case. Counterintuitive as it might sound, a sentient being does not "become" a Buddha in the Zen Buddhist paradigm; instead, a sentient being "is" the Buddha. The Buddha and sentient beings are "non-dialectizable aporia," as Derrida would have it.

What kind of ethics can we envision in this context? Simon Critchley, the author of *Ethics of Deconstruction: Derrida and Levinas*, discusses the nature of the ethics of deconstruction as follows: "an ethical moment is essential to deconstructive reading and that ethics is the goal, or horizon, towards which Derrida's work tends."[4] However, Critchley warns the reader that this does not imply that "an ethics can be derived from deconstruction."[5] Critchley contends, "deconstruction 'is' ethical, or . . . deconstruction takes place (*a lieu*) ethically." Critchley relies on Levinas's concept of the ethical in order to illustrate deconstructive ethics. The validity of such a move is questionable, given that Derrida has criticized in his early works Levinas's absolute other, or the face of the other, as still hovering in the domain of the identity principle.

Wood makes a similar move as he refers to Levinas in his discussion of the ethical mode in deconstruction and describes it through a spatial concept. Wood notes that Levinas's idea of ethics as a first philosophy is removed from the normative concept of ethics, which is rule-bound, and states, "for Levinas, the ethical is the space of infinite responsibility for the other man. . . . For Derrida, this responsibility takes on a more general openness to the sites at which otherness—and not just other man—is occluded in our thinking and writing."[6] Both Wood and Critchley counterbalance deconstructive ethics arising in the space with the rule-bound ethics of metaphysics. What could it mean to say that the ethical arises in this space? The idea demands that we re-conceptualize the very definition of ethics. I would like to place the space for Buddhist deconstructive ethics in the tension between the centripetal and centrifugal forces.

The ethics of tension, as a potential form of Buddhist-postmodern ethics, has some similarities with Wood's proposition of openness. Tension, as a form of ethical awareness and a paradigm, does not denote a conflict that is subject to a final resolution. Like Lyotard's postmodern resistance to consensus, the ethics of tension represents an inevitable heterogeneity existing in the identity of an entity, be it individual, cultural, social, or philosophical. The ethics of tension reflects what Derrida calls undecidability, which rises from the inexhaustibility of context. The tension is also reminiscent of the

Buddha's silence, which is his acting out of the middle path. Like Derrida's undecidability, the Buddha's silence is the expression of the non-identity of an entity, the impossibility of making a once-and-for-all demarcation. What should be noted in understanding the concepts of heterogeneity and undecidability is that they are anchored in the concept of homogeneity and decision-making (i.e. decidability). Ironic as it may be, without the idea of homogeneity and the need for a decision, heterogeneity and undecidability cannot earn their meaning. As Chinul emphasizes, the Buddha is the Buddha in the mind of sentient beings. Without the discriminating mind of sentient beings, the Buddha does not exist. The very tension between the two, instead of a naïve inflation of either side—be it heterogeneity, undecidability, or the Buddha on the one hand, and homogeneity, decision-making, or sentient minds on the other—facilitates the space for the ethical.

Tension has taken various forms in our philosophical discussion. Just to name a few, in Kristeva, the tension appears as that between the semiotic drive, energy, and source of life and the symbolic designation of language, social norms, and the law. In Heidegger, this tension is revealed through metaphysics and the violation of metaphysics and logic through the imagination of the nothing, the nothing that exists before negation. In *Prajñāpāramitā* literature, this tension is expressed through the alternating use of affirmation and negation of the nothing. In Huineng's *Platform Sūtra*, the tension appears between his teaching of the non-abiding and the self-legitimization of his own teaching of subitism. In Zen *gong'an* dialogue, the tension is between commonsense logic of linguistic conventions and their deviations. In Chinul, the tension is imbedded in the relationship between sudden enlightenment and gradual cultivation. In the context of Zen Buddhism, tension can also be identified as that between wisdom and compassion, and in the context of deconstruction, tension exists between the two poles in the binary postulations existing in our linguistic-philosophical framework.

In the history of philosophy, a generic form of acknowledging the two poles out of which tension emerges has various names: the transcendental and the empirical, the noumenal and the phenomenal, universality and particularity, the Buddha and sentient beings, the mind and the world, the subject and the object, the one and the many, the ontological and the ontic, the Truth and its dissemination, sudden enlightenment and gradual practice. For the purposes of our discussion, we have identified this as that which falls between centripetal and centrifugal forces. The former denotes the attempt to identify a unified and orderly logic of the world and being whereas the latter refers to the inevitable disseminating, dispersing, and diffusing nature of existence, which both Buddhism (especially Zen and Huayan versions of it) and postmodernism (if not the Habermasian version of it) consider the nature of an entity. When we approach these poles without a final resolution on the horizon, the mutually enforcing relationship between the two becomes one of excess, the overflow of an existing signifying system. This excess or overflow marks the limits of rule-bound ethics, and in the space of that marking, what is called the ethical emerges.

To acknowledge 'tension' as a form of ethics is an effort to prevent closure in reading texts and contexts. In accordance with this spirit, we have discussed the tension between the centrifugal force of the self-legitimation of the Zen text/tradition and the centripetal force of Zen Buddhism's challenge to the reifying mode of human minds, including the different types of authorities in life, whether linguistic, social, or religious. By acknowledging both sides of the Zen tradition, and by identifying their relationship as one of tension (instead of eliminating one as an authentic form of the tradition, while ostracizing the other as false), our discussion moves beyond the desire to make a final decision.

In our discussion of Huayan Buddhism as well, we have paid attention to the co-existence of the centripetal and centrifugal forces in Huayan philosophy and its self-presentation. We examined the force represented by the early Huayan masters' emphasis on noumenon (the all-encompassing one) and at the same time noted the centrifugal force of recognizing phenomenal diversity as the tradition continues to claim the mutually non-interfering phenomena (the world of diversity) as the signature of the school. Instead of treating their co-existence as a hermeneutic problem, we have proposed understanding this tension between the two as part of the message that is Huayan Buddhism.

In the spirit of the modernist thinking and scholarship, to search for a unity in a text, in a discourse, or in an individual's life has been linked with identifying its value. Consistency and coherency were understood as generating meaningful logic whereas conflict and gap in a discourse were stigmatized as defects. Postmodernity questions the rules to which the unity and consistence anchor themselves. To repeat Lyotard, once we raise questions as to who decides the rules for the existence of a coherent unity, and from whose perspective coherence will be tailored, we come to realize that there is not one or two coherent themes in a discourse, but as many coherent interpretations of a text as there are different views—without any guarantee that these individually (and seemingly coherent) interpretations will not contradict one another.

Can we ever know which interpretations are authentic, valuable, and even legitimate readings of a text, and which ones are by-products of the reader's poorly trained reading skills? One might argue that the invitation to entertain heterogeneity in a text is an invitation to chaos and the loss of quality in our lives, and some people criticize postmodernity with this argument. However, we should note that the question itself is posed in the modernist spirit to find one right answer instead of acknowledging differences and heterogeneity.

Here once again we are reminded of the undeclared thesis of the Buddha in which the questions are posed in a way that the other party's possibility to respond to the questions is foreclosed. In this sense, Lyotard states that the principle of postmodern knowledge "is not the expert's homology, but the inventor's paralogy."[7] Lyotard's paralogy denotes the multiple-localized centers that make a value judgment depending on the context. What makes our knowledge and value judgments a local truth instead of a universal one is the mutually enforced tension between the centripetal and centrifugal forces.

2. *Aporia, the Ethical, and the Logic of Compassion*

The tension between the universal (or unconditionality) and the particular (or conditionality) of an event becomes a theme of Derrida's discussion of hospitality which frequently appears in Derrida's discussion of ethics in his later works. Hospitality by definition means being hospitable: it is a generous, cordial and welcoming reception of others, one's guests, to one's residence. This relationship between the host/hostess and the guests can be expanded to include different levels ranging from an individual's invitation to one's friends, a community's invitation to non-community residents, or a nation's reception of non-citizens of the nation. Kant explores the idea in his 1795 essay "Perpetual Peace," in which he argues that hospitality is a basis for a nation-state's hosting of foreigners, whether they are temporary visitors to that country, immigrants, asylum seekers, or refugees. Still on an abstract level, hospitality is one's relation to the other, the subject's reception of what the subject considers its non-identity. Since hospitality is a reception of the other and the relationship is based on one's willingness and aspiration to maintain a good relationship with others, hospitality for Derrida co-exists with ethics.

What is at stake in Derrida's discussion of hospitality is the very aporia that the concept of hospitality carries with it. On the one hand, hospitality means one's opening of one's space to guests, foreigners, and visitors whole-heartedly and without condition; hence conceptually, hospitality is pure and unconditional. On the other hand, hospitality in reality cannot but be limited by reality. No one can just open their home unconditionally even when they are welcoming their guests with their whole heart. This is not because one receives guests with an unwelcoming mind, but because no matter how much one opens one's door to a commitment to hospitality, appropriation is inevitable in the actualization of hospitality.

The conditionality of hospitality becomes a more serious issue when it comes to a nation's acceptance of foreigners. No nation—at least in our time—can accept foreigners unconditionally without contradicting its responsibility to protect its citizens. Further, one cannot fully conceptualize unconditional hospitality, because it is unconditional. As Derrida notes, "this concept of pure hospitality can have no legal or political status. No state can write it into its laws."[8] The point, however, is not that unconditional hospitality cannot be performed in reality; but that one cannot simply dismiss it because of its impracticality and its ineffability and choose conditional hospitality. Derrida writes, "No state can write it into its laws. But without at least the thought of this pure and unconditional hospitality, of hospitality itself, we would have no concept of hospitality in general and would not even be able to determine any rules for conditional hospitality."[9] Anyone who falls in love dreams of unconditional and pure love—pure and unconditional love in which one can open oneself to and love the other party, no matter what. However, pure love, because of its purity and unconditionality, cannot be actualized; when it is actualized, one needs to put it in a concrete form, which inevitably involves the process of appropriation. The love, which is always conditioned and conditional, cannot be separated from the concept of pure and unconditional love. Derrida writes:

> Unconditional hospitality, which is neither juridical nor political, is nonetheless the condition of the political and the juridical. . . . Paradox, aporia: These two hospitalities are at once heterogeneous and indissociable. Heterogeneous because we can move from one to the other only by means of an absolute leap, a leap beyond knowledge and power, beyond norms and rules. Unconditional hospitality is transcendent with regard to the political, the juridical, perhaps even to the ethical. But—and here is the indissociability—I cannot open the door, I cannot expose myself to the coming of the other and offer him or her anything whatsoever without making this hospitality effective, without, in some concrete way, giving something determinate. This determination will thus have to re-inscribe the unconditional into certain conditions.[10]

The logic Derrida employs in this passage is reminiscent of our discussions of Zen Buddhism—especially its identification of Buddha and sentient beings and the functioning of wisdom and compassion—and Huayan Buddhism's exposition of the noumenal and the phenomenal. In our approach to Zen Buddhism, there has always been a certain attachment to enlightenment. The idea that enlightenment should be explained once and for all represents the mentality that is accustomed to linear temporality and the teleological paradigm. What if the Buddha's enlightenment were not the end of his enlightenment? And surely his enlightenment under the bodhi tree cannot be the end or completion of his enlightenment. But how else could we conceive of the Buddha's enlightenment? According to Vimalakīrti, enlightenment is "the eradication of all marks. Enlightenment is free of presumptions concerning all objects. Enlightenment is free of the functioning of all intentional thoughts. Enlightenment is annihilation of all convictions."[11] Note the absolutist postulation reflected in Vimalakīrti's articulation of enlightenment.

In a seemingly different expression, but within the same boundary of understanding, one finds a modern version of the definition of enlightenment. Nishida Kitarō states, "enlightenment is . . . an ultimate seeing of the bottomless nothingness of the self that is simultaneously a seeing of the fountainhead of sin and evil."[12] Chinul repeatedly emphasizes that in the ultimate sense, all obstacles to enlightenment are enlightenment just as they are. As another variation of presentation of enlightenment, we are reminded of the story of Mazu and Shuiliao which we discussed earlier. In this famous Zen *gong'an*, Mazu is not bothered with Shuiliao when the latter breaks out into loud laughter after Mazu hits him. These diverse expressions of enlightenment address the issue of how to inscribe this pure concept of enlightenment into the conditioned and conditional existence of a being. A similar question can be asked about the Huayan view of the noumenal and the phenomenal. In the Huayan fourfold worldview, if we understand the noumenal as the unconditional that cannot be inscribed into reality "as it is" because of the very fact that it is unconditional, but at the same time, noumenon cannot be completely dissociated from the phenomenal reality, then we begin to understand Chengguan's insightful statement: the noumenal is to be approached with wisdom and the phenomenal both with wisdom and compassion.

Let us try to apply this concept of heterogeneity between the unconditional and the conditional—and their indissociability—to concrete examples. I will provide two traumatic episodes from the history of the twentieth century, and I will demonstrate how they can be explained using our concept of the tension between the unconditional and conditional or between the centripetal and centrifugal forces.

The first example is related to the conflict between Tibet and China. Victor Chan, the co-author of *The Wisdom of Forgiveness: Intimate Conversations and Journeys,* describes his first encounter with the Dalai Lama as follows:

> As you remember . . . in my first audience with you back in 1972, the question uppermost in my mind was whether you hated the Chinese. You told me you don't hate them; you told me you have truly forgiven them. Your holiness, this was just thirteen years after you'd lost your country. I was very surprised at your magnanimity." "That's Buddhist training," the Dalai Lama replied. "Not something unique in my case. . . Forgiveness and compassion are important parts of practice." [13]

The second example deals with the conflict between the Jews and the Nazis. January 27, 2005 marks the sixtieth anniversary of the liberation of Auschwitz-Birkenau in Poland. As many as 1.5 million people were gassed or shot to death in this camp in rural southern Poland. Dick Cheney, Vice-

President of the United States, attended the ceremony and was reported to have commented on the occasion: "The story of the camps reminds us that evil is real and must be called by its name and confronted."[14] Vice-President Cheney's determination to confront evil is in stark contrast to a statement made by a woman who survived Auschwitz. Her name is Eve Mezes Kor. She was one of 7,000 people left behind by the Nazis when the Nazis abandoned the camp. She was only ten years old at the time and had been abused by Dr. Joseph Mengele, Auschwitz's head physician, who conducted gruesome medical experiments on humans. Since the liberation, Eve Kor had returned to the camp several times. In an interview marking the sixtieth anniversary of the liberation of the camp, she was quoted as saying, "I know most people won't understand this, but I have forgiven the Nazis. I have forgiven Mengele, I have forgiven everybody. I no longer carry the burden of pain. I have given myself the gift of forgiveness."[15]

Atrocities at Auschwitz and in Tibet are two of the most well-known mass-events in the history of the twentieth century which have left behind traumatic memories of the "unforgivable." Despite the extreme cruelties the historical situation had created for them, the Dalai Lama and Eve Mezes Kor expressed forgiveness as the ultimate way for them to make peace with history and their traumatic memories. When forgiveness is expressed as the ultimate way of reconciling with the conflict one experiences, what do people forgive? Do people forgive unconditionally or are there conditions for forgiveness?

In his essay "On Forgiveness," Derrida draws our attention to the pervasiveness of "asking for forgiveness" on the international scene since the Second World War. In that context, he asks why the Abrahamic tradition of asking for forgiveness is so pervasive even in nations, such as Korea, China, or Japan, whose dominant tradition is not based on Abrahamic religions. He further states, "The proliferation of scenes of repentance, or of asking 'forgiveness', signifies, no doubt, a *universal urgency* of memory: it is necessary to turn toward the past; and it is *necessary* to take this act of memory, of self-accusation, of repentance', of appearance [*comparution*] at the same time beyond the juridical instance, or that of the Nation-State" (emphasis original).[16] As we have already noticed in the statement by the Dalai Lama, Derrida was not completely correct in assuming that to compromise the history of traumatic memory through the exercise of "forgiveness" was an exclusive part of the Abrahamic tradition. However, his meditation on the meaning of forgiveness provides us with an important question to consider from a Buddhist perspective.

In his discussion of forgiveness, as in the case of hospitality, Derrida brings our attention to the question of whether conditionality is possible in the act of forgiving and of asking forgiveness. By asking forgiveness, one is searching for an ultimate way to reconcile with a conflict from the past. The urgency involved in the act of forgiveness requires that the action should be done unconditionally. Derrida observes that this urgency of reconciling with a history of traumatic memory is frequently charged with its conditionality. When forgiveness is brought up, an individual, a society, or a nation-state tends to use the act of asking for forgiveness as a means to move beyond that act. For example, between two nations, the normalization of their relationship is frequently an expected end result of the act of asking for forgiveness. If an individual, the head of a society, or the head of a nation state says, "'I' ask for your forgiveness so that we can normalize our relationship", does this statement actually mean that individual is asking for forgiveness? If the other party in this act of asking forgiveness and of forgiving responds with, "'I' will forgive you on the condition that you do this and that," is the act of forgiving actually taking place?

Conditional forgiveness, by its very nature, creates a debt; with an outstanding debt to pay back, forgiveness cannot be an ultimate resolution. What we are witnessing in this case is an exchange of benefits through forgiveness. Forgiveness, in this case, has conditions—the fulfillment of which will result in the expected profits or gains of that action. The exchange of values as a reward or a cost of one's action is a familiar discourse in our capitalist society. However, if forgiveness can be on the horizon only within that context, is forgiveness actually taking place? Derrida thus asks whether forgiveness can have finality and is exchangeable:

> each time forgiveness is at the service of a finality, be it noble and spiritual (atonement or redemption, reconciliation, salvation), each time that it aims to re-establish a normality (social, national, political, psychological) by a work of mourning, by some therapy or ecology of memory, then the 'forgiveness' is not pure—nor is its concept. Forgiveness is not, it *should not be*, normal, normative, normalizing. It *should* remain exceptional and extraordinary, in the face of the impossible: as if it interrupted the ordinary course of historical temporality.[17]

In this statement, Derrida places the act of forgiveness in the context outside of "historical temporality." To consider the act of forgiveness an atemporal action without imposing on it any supreme being such as God or an Absolute Spirit means that one should be able to confront the impossible, since there is no being who will offer a resolution of the atemporal nature of forgiveness within the temporal frame of history. Put another way, from Derrida's perspective, if forgiveness takes place as forgiveness, without being subjugated by the logic of exchange or conditionality, the act as well as the concept of forgiveness is an aporia. That is, to forgive means to forgive even the unforgivable. Because if we forgive only that which is forgivable, what do we actually forgive? The unforgivable by nature means that which cannot be forgiven. However, to forgive means to for-*give* unconditionally, which should include for-*giving* the unforgivable. Here is the aporia: the full scope of the activation of forgiveness demands forgiving the unforgivable and forgiving unconditionally. As in the case with unconditional hospitality, one might feel that Derrida's contention of unconditional forgiveness forgiving the unforgivable outside historical time is too outwardly idealistic, or even naïve. What is at stake in Derrida's discussion on forgiveness is not that one should make the aporia of forgiving the unforgivable happen; instead, we should ask: what would it mean to think about forgiveness without a condition?

In *The Wisdom of Forgiven*ess, the Dalai Lama explains the two wings of Buddhist philosophy as compassion and interdependence. These are also what he identifies as two foundations of the act of forgiveness. In explaining how forgiveness is and should eventually be a natural and logical way of reacting to situations one encounters in life, the Dalai Lama gives an example of a Chinese boy who was beaten to death by a Chinese soldier because the boy's father was a counterrevolutionary. From our (Western) perspective, we might be ready to feel outraged by the cruelty of the Chinese soldier. On the other hand, from the viewpoint of the Communist party, the soldier could be a faithful follower of the party line. Is the Chinese soldier immoral and unethical because he killed the innocent boy for the behavior of his father? Or is his action justifiable as being faithful to the party line, which condemns counterrevolutionaries? Depending on the position from which one approaches the situation, one can evaluate the Chinese solider either as a villain or a patriot. By considering the two different interpretations of the Chinese soldier's action, the nature of whose action might be obvious to many people, we are already entering into the realm of what Derrida calls double-binding. The Dalai Lama states:

> The officer's action depends on his motivation; his motivation depends on propaganda. Because of propaganda, the counterrevolutionary father is seen as evil. Elimination of evil is something positive. That kind of faith—wrong faith. You can't blame that person. . . . Interdependence gives you the whole picture: this happens because of that, and that happens because of this . . . .. We have to oppose bad action. But that does not mean we against [sic] that person, actor. Once action stopped, different action come [sic], then that person could be friend. That's why today Chinese is enemy; the next day, there's always the possibility to become friend. And that's why I have no problems forgiving the Chinese for what they've done to my country and people.[18]

As the Dalai Lama explains, the theoretical grounds of Buddhist forgiveness is the idea of interdependence, and thus of the emptiness of the self. A being, or an actor, is not an entity having a substance which can be reified either as good or bad, but rather is a result of multilevel causations. The act of beating a child for the crime committed by his father cannot be fair. But the Chinese soldier who performed that action is also a result of his historical situation as much as the child beaten by that soldier is a result of *his* situation, according to the Dalai Lama.

In keeping with the way the Dalai Lama interprets the situation, we note the same logic Huayan Buddhism develops through the fourfold worldview. The episode puts together the Huayan concepts of noumenon and phenomena and the activation of wisdom and compassion in the form of forgiveness. The understanding of inexhaustible contextuality makes it impossible to know the whole picture of an event, but the very recognition of the inexhaustibility of context, or what Buddhists call wisdom, opens a door toward one's exercise of compassion. Actions and entities do not have their own essence, hence they are empty; however, this does not indicate that there are no conflicts on the phenomenal level. On the phenomenal level, there is a conflict between revolutionary and counterrevolutionary ideologies, and thus a conflict between the child-beating soldier and the child beaten for his father's action, which results in the death of the boy. From the Buddhist perspective, the act of forgiveness is possible because of one's understanding of this intertwining of events that constitutes the world. With this realization comes the overcoming of that history, because forgiveness in this case "interrupt[s] the ordinary course of historical temporality"—not in the sense that one moves beyond the world of causation or history itself, but in the sense that one's view of history moves beyond the segmented view of the events constituting history. The act of forgiveness in this case cannot be a part of a transaction, but an act of unconditional forgiveness.

Here comes a question regarding the ethical stance of unconditional forgiveness. Does forgiveness in this case suggest that no justice can be done in any way? If we separate the actor from the action, and excuse the actor from the responsibility of her/his actions based on the theory of interdependence, how do we achieve justice and maintain a society? In several places in the *Wisdom of Forgiveness*, the Dalai Lama emphasizes the importance of emptiness in Buddhism. For example, he states, "According to Buddhist belief, unless you meditate on and experience emptiness thoroughly, directly, it is very difficult to eliminate your destructive emotions."[19] The Dalai Lama further states, "Emptiness does not mean nothing exists. Things exist but the way they exist, we cannot find. Therefore empty."[20] He further elaborates on the concept by using an example of a flower vase: "So emptiness means this vase, . . . it exists, but it is the way of existence that we cannot find. Therefore empty. Empty nature."[21] In a similar way, Lyotard understands the world as postmodern sublime or the unpresentable.

Buddhists have been keen to the reality of the world, which always already exceeds the frame of reference created by the human mind. This excess, however, does not presuppose a super-natural or transcendental being; instead, in Buddhist tradition, the excess itself is the nature of the existence of beings when one sees the world as structured through multi-layered causations of dependent co-arising. The structure of conditioned causality is such that one cannot fully separate each entity which has made contribution to the occurrence of each event in the phenomenal world. This is what Fazang calls the inexhaustibility (C. *chongchong wujin*) of the dependent co-arising of the realm of reality in the Huayan Buddhist understanding of the phenomenal world. By the same token, Derrida explains this excessiveness in the structure of the world through the concept of the inexhaustibility of the context. Derrida states:

> there is a context but one cannot analyse it exhaustively; the context is open because 'it comes' [*ça vient*], because there is something to come [*il y a de l'avenir*]. We have to accept the concept of a non-saturable context, and take into account both the context itself and its open structure, its non-closure, if we are to make decisions and engage in a wager—or give as a pledge—without knowing, without being sure that it will pay off, that it will be a winner, etc.[22]

To be aware of the inexhaustibility of the context, the non-saturability of a context is possible only when human beings give up their desire to domesticate the world by imposing a value created by individual minds. Once one accepts that the world is beyond the domestication of human minds, the end result is, as Derrida states, the awareness of "non-closure" or the "openness" of the context. To realize the emptiness of a being is to be aware of the openness of being and the situation. To understand emptiness as the insaturability of the context of our existence, and thus the inevitable openness of one's perspective, leads us to the ethical implication of the act of forgiveness. To forgive does not mean that we will be ignorant of justice, fairness, or the law. But how then is justice realized in the act of forgiveness, when forgiveness is to be understood not as an act of transaction but of forgiving even the unforgivable? The Dalai Lama states:

> In my own case, in Tibet, all this destruction, death, all happened. Painful experiences. But revenge . . . creates more unhappiness. So, think wider perspective: revenge no good, so forgive. Forgiveness does not mean you just forget about the past. No, you remember the past. Should be aware that these past sufferings happened because of narrow-mindedness on both sides. So now, time passed. We feel more wise, more developed. I think that's the only way.[23]

The exercise of forgiveness, instead of revenge, can produce positive results. But is justice actually realized in this act of forgiveness? Revenge cannot be the only alternative to forgiveness. As our daily expression, 'to bring (someone to) justice' tells us, to judge an event at hand and treat it justly only seems fair. To answer this question, let us return to Derrida and consider his understanding of the relationship between justice and forgiveness. In the aforementioned essay, Derrida asks whether the act of the forgiveness goes together with the realization of justice. Thus Derrida writes, "We can imagine that someone, a victim of the worst, himself a member of his family, in his generation or the preceding, demands that justice be done, that the criminals appear before a court, be judged and condemned by a court—and yet in his heart forgives. The inverse, of course, is also true. We can imagine, and accept, that someone would never forgive, even after a process of acquittal or amnesty. The secret of this experience remains."[24]

Derrida's statement raises the question as to whether one can talk about the completion of the act of forgiveness and that of justice as well. When does the act of forgiveness reach its completion? When does an individual or a society absolutely make peace with history? The Dalai Lama himself also makes a statement which echoes the questions posed here when he describes the situation of the Chinese boy beaten by a Chinese soldier because of his father's counterrevolutionary activities. After stating that he has forgiven the Chinese for what they have done to his country and his people, the Dalai Lama also says, "But if I was on the spot and meet the Chinese soldier, the officer who beat that boy . . . If I was there, and I have gun, then I don't know. . . . Such moment, I may shoot the Chinese."[25] The Dalai Lama did not elaborate on this issue except to say, "Sometimes, thinking comes later. Action comes first."[26] But both Derrida's thoughts on the relationship between justice and forgiveness and the Dalai Lama's confession about the possibility of being controlled by the situation suggest that forgiveness is not an action that has finality.

That forgiveness cannot have finality is something closely related to what Derrida calls the unconditional forgiveness. By unconditional forgiveness Derrida does not simply mean that the forgiver demands nothing in exchange. If forgiveness is granted with a condition, like normalization, the act of forgiveness stops when the conditions of forgiveness are satisfied. In the case of Eve Mezes Kor or the Dalai Lama, if they have forgiven as they mention they have, the act of forgiveness cannot come to an end. It is an ongoing process. This is why, as Derrida states, forgiveness cannot be related to the signing of a contract, normalization, or a promise of permanent return to a normalcy. Instead, it requires a constant effort to realize the emptiness of reality from a Buddhist perspective and the insaturability of context from a Derridean deconstructive perspective.

Finality is a foreign concept for both Buddhism and Derridean deconstruction, for finality by its very definition and in its spirit anchors itself on the closed concept of identity. If forgiveness is understood in the context of an openness of being, then justice is also an open concept, which we can describe as "justice to be done"[27] in line with Derrida's concept of "the democracy to come" (*la démocratie à venir*).[28] This "to come" (*à venir*) is not "a *future* reality but . . . that which will always retain the essential structure of a promise and . . . that which can only arrive as such as *to come* [*à venir*]."[29] The intrinsic incomplete nature of justice and democracy in this sense is not contingent upon time or history for its completion. The openness of the world and its unfathomability demands of us, from both the Buddhist view of the world and from the deconstructionist perspective, constant reappropriations of our position. Such an effort is necessary so that we do not subjugate justice or forgiveness to the power of sovereignty and of the subject.

The democracy to come or justice to be done is not a middle stage that moves toward its completion through a linear and teleological time scheme. Democracy, in order to be democratic, is always democracy-to-come as much as justice or forgiveness, to be truthful to its spirit, is always yet to be complete. Hence, the democracy to come and the justice to be done share the spirit of the Zen Buddhist sudden-gradual paradigm, which we can even refer to as "enlightenment to come."

In the *Huayan jing*, after the meeting of the fifty-three dharma-teachers, in the final stage, the pilgrim Sudhana is sent back to Mañjuśrī, who was the first dharma teacher Sudhana met. Li Tongxuan interprets it as an indication that the final stage of practice is already in the first stage. What does it mean that the completion is already encompassed in the initial stage of the practice? Completion itself does not have finality; perfection can never be perfect. The very capacity to deal with the openness of the world is what Buddhists call compassion. As the Dalai Lama has stated, dependent co-arising and compassion go hand-in-hand in Buddhism. And as Chengguan notes, the phenomenal world cannot be understood only through wisdom. The emptiness of the noumenal reality of each phenomenon does not prevent mutual conflicts, and the full picture of the structure of the conflict is not available to human beings. The ambiguity in that sense is the basic condition of our daily existence. The logic of compassion anchors itself in the awareness of this ambiguity of existence itself.

3. Buddhism, Postmodernity, and the Ethics of Tension

In his essay "On Cosmopolitanism," Derrida addresses the special meaning of hospitality in its relation to ethics. He declares, "*ethics is hospitality*"[30] (emphasis original). He reiterates, "ethics is so thoroughly coextensive with the experience of hospitality."[31] The limits and perversion of our practice of hospitality is, from Derrida's perspective, the very limits of the ethics we practice.

Why is ethics hospitality? Because ethics, like hospitality, begins with one's relationship with others. Ethics, like hospitality, begins with one's desire to have a favorable, good, and right relationship with others; like hospitality, in one's attempt to be fair, be right, and be good, ethics always gets caught in the double-bind of the impossibility of making decisions without appropriation. To mark the instability of the existing ethics and our decision-making is itself deconstructive ethics. It is thus the interruption and intervention in our ethical mode of thinking that constitutes deconstructive ethics. From Derrida's perspective, the function of ethics does not lie in merely offering precise rules for our decision-making. Rather, deconstructive ethics functions by displacing the existing moral codes and thus reviving and bringing back from suppression the trace and forgetfulness of the exclusion. Ethics, from a deconstructive perspective, reminds us of the question of appropriation and domestication involved in our thinking, decision-making, and action-taking processes.

Deconstructive ethics is possible in our awareness of something to come or to happen. This event of the future anterior in turn reveals our awareness of the non-saturability of contexts in which we live. The impossibility of exhausting the contexts of our reality makes ethics a humble endeavor to remind us of the limitations of human beings. If the metaphysical concept of ethics grounds itself in the human rational capacity to distinguish between right and wrong or good and bad, deconstructive ethics begins with the acceptance that such distinctions are possible only after appropriation and thus suppression of the unfavored side in the decision-making process.

The non-saturability, inexhaustibility, and thus inconceivability, of the full scope of our reality contain the secret that every moment of life and every being retain within. By the same token, Huayan/Zen Buddhist ethics begins with our awareness of the non-closure of an entity. The non-identity of identity emphasized as the reality of being through the noumenal level of the Huayan fourfold worldview opens up the space for the ethical in the phenomenal world as entities constantly get involved in conflicts. The fact that the whole scope of the conflict cannot be known because of the openness of reality results in one of the existential conditions of one's being, and that is the first step toward compassion. The Zen Buddhist challenge to authority and institutions is a constant reminder against the reification of the human mind.

Deconstructive operations do not deny the fact that decisions should be made in our daily lives, and especially in the public and political realms. Conversely, the fact that decisions are there to be made each and every moment of our personal and public lives does not mean that the excluded part in the process of the decision-making should also be forgotten. Excluded parties and suppressed ideas are always there, as invisible traces, in the marking of the decision made. Only when we are constantly reminded of suppression and exclusion will democracy function as democracy. Hence to Derrida, democracy is always "democracy to come"; "it is necessary also in politics to respect the secret, that which exceeds the political or that which is no longer in the juridical domain. This is what I would call the 'democracy to come'."[32]

The ethical in the Derridean sense demands a consideration of the excess of conventional morality and conventional ethics. Deconstructive ethics provides us with the possibility of considering the ethical without resorting to the metaphysical grounding that frequently functions as a foundation for ethical value judgments. It demonstrates that ethics is not just about making distinctions, and that ethics is also possible by realizing the impossibility of making the final decision. The idea of indecidability and the double-bind, which Derrida sees at the core of a being and a being's relationship with the other, reveals the limits of any decision-making and thought process that are based on clear distinctions. However, the awareness of this indecidability does not negate the possibility of ethical discourse. Instead, it provides a non-substantialist mode of ethical thinking.

One might consider that the way ethics is outlined in Derridean deconstruction and Zen and Huayan Buddhism is not ethics. Or if it is ethics, it is non-functioning, or at least an impractical form of ethics, which amounts to saying that deconstructive Buddhist ethics does not exist. If ethics is not practical, what is ethics for? Here we need to step back and ask ourselves what we mean by "practical"; if we are able to define this term, we should ask ourselves whether ethics has ever been practical. I am posing this question not to say that ethics consists of empty words, but to say that no theory is practical as it is—that we put it into practice. To problematize impracticality of a theory is more often than not a way to evade the difficulty involved in understanding and practicing the theory because of its radical break with habitualized modes of thinking and behaviors. Both deconstructive-postmodern ethics and Buddhist ethics, especially in the form I propose here, undoubtedly demand a radical departure from the conventional concept of ethics itself and because of this fact, it is subject to the criticism of being impractical. If we look into the grounds of such a claim, we may, in fact, find that deconstruction's and Buddhism's refusal to offer any final solution makes many feel insecure. But if we "step back" and think about it, we realize that life itself is a continuation without final resolution. Wood puts it in such a simple way as he defines deconstructive ethics as a way to step back: "the interminable need to 'step back' is not the Sisyphean 'bad infinity' but rather the ongoing persistence of life, and our contemplation of it. It is no more a sign of failure that this movement must be repeatedly undertaken than that we cannot eat the breakfast to end all breakfasts, or say 'I love you' in a way that would never need repeating."[33] Just as our body needs nutrition through the continuous activities of intake and excretion and the constant movement of our muscles and respiratory organs, so too does our mind require incessant thinking. By the same token, an ethical decision needs constant recontextualization with our awareness of tension between parties involved in an event.

In a similar context, commenting on the meaning of the sudden enlightenment of *huatou* meditation in Chinul's *Treatise on Huatou Meditation*, Pŏpsŏng explains the ethical and practical dimension of the Huayan concept of the realm of reality in connection with the subitist-gradualist paradigm. That is, subitism and gradualism do not address which one is superior so that one can make a choice between the two, nor are they in a linear relationship, allowing us to move from the one to the other. Instead, Pŏpsŏng explains their relationship as the reality of life in the sense that life goes on. Subitism represents the reality of life understood through a horizontal slice whereas gradualism represents the idea that one lives life through physical temporality. The physical, clock time temporality in this case, does not include a teleological paradigm; linearity is present in the sense that there is a yesterday, a today, and a tomorrow in our calendar, but this linearity is not connected to a grand finale. Thus Pŏpsŏng states:

. . . gradual activities can be defined as social practice or Samanthabhadra activities, rather than practices to achieve enlightenment. In *Huayan jing*, Samanthabhadra activities are defined as the "action of being with," which cannot but be persistent as far as there exist the alienation of sentient beings and the fetters of history. If we understand cultivation in this context of "activities of being with" in the total horizon of reality (that is, the realm of phenomena), then, sudden awakening followed by sudden cultivation comes to mean that when one immediately awakens to the reality as phenomenon-qua-principle, then, the practice which is not stagnated within the mechanical causality will suddenly be realized in an individual's life, then, the closed form of life of an individual will be transformed into the socialized and historicized bodhisattvic activities of Samanthabhadra. [34]

When Zen Buddhist discourse problematizes the discriminating mind and challenges the traditional ethical category, this does not necessarily indicate a symptom, as some people argue, that Zen cannot have an ethical project of its own. Nor does this mean that Zen Buddhism needs to redirect itself to early Vinaya codes in order to create Zen ethics. Instead, as in the case of deconstructive ethics, Zen ethics proposes a new paradigm in thinking the ethical without foregrounding the categorical division of the good or the right that has characterized metaphysical ethics.

Ethics more often than not locates itself on the border between abstract conceptualization and concrete institutionalization. Institutionalization by nature goes against the non-substantialist stance of both deconstructive and Zen Buddhist ethics. As Derrida testifies, no thought system is intact from the reification resulting from its use of the institution called language. The ever-renewed deconstructive modes in the use of language that mark the history of Zen Buddhism demonstrate Zen Buddhism's efforts to challenge the reifying mind of human beings. When institutionalization suppresses the capacity to destabilize its own system, the non-substantialist mode of thinking turns itself into a totalitarian vision, as we witnessed in Zen militarism and Zen authoritarianism. Institutionalized Zen leads to Zen militarism, because institutionalization deprives the non-substantial mode of thinking of its capacity for destabilization.

A deconstructive paradigm of ethics is the result of the deconstructive mode of thinking based on the non-substantialist nature of the world and being. Likewise, Zen ethics, as I have proposed here, is the ethical mode that reflects Zen thought which has radically challenged any reification in our understanding of the world and beings. Similar to deconstructive ethics, Zen Buddhist ethics is made possible by "marking" (in the Derridean sense of the word) the border of the traditional ethical categories, including the subject and the object. The impossibility of delineating this division—and the division at the ultimate level between right and wrong, good and bad—functions as an ethical beginning point in the non-substantialist thought system. Unlike the convention in normative ethics, paradox, aporia, and antinomianism do not have to be an antidote to ethics; instead, they open a room for a new vision of the ethical. The ethics of tension is our proposal to identify the new ethical paradigm that should emerge from the shared realm of Buddhist and postmodern philosophy.

Notes

Introduction

1. Daisetz Teitaro Suzuki, trans., *The Laṅkāvatāra Sūtra: A Mahāyāna Text* (Delhi: Motilal Banarsidass Publishers, 2003), p. 11.
2. Suzuki, *The Laṅkāvatāra Sūtra: A Mahāyāna Text*, p. 35.
3. Steven Heine, "Zen Buddhist Rights and Wrongs," a paper presented at the Eastern Division Annual Meeting of the American Philosophical Association. December 28, 2006. Washington, DC.
4. John R. McRae, *Seeing through Zen: Encounter, Transformation, and Genealogy in Chinese Chan Buddhism* (Berkeley, CA: University of California Press, 2003), p. xix.
5. Jean-François Lyotard, *The Differend: Phrases in Dispute* (1983), trans. by Georges Van Den Abbeele (Minneapolis, MN: University of Minnesota Press, 1988), p. xi.
6. Jacques Derrida, *Of Grammatology* (1967), trans. by Gayatri Chakravorty Spivak (Baltimore and London: Johns Hopkins University Press, 1976), p. 112.
7. Charles W. Mills, "Non-Cartesian *Sums*: Philosophy and the African-American Experience," in *Blackness Visible: Essays on Philosophy and Race* (Ithaca, NY: Cornell University Press, 1998), p. 17.

Chapter One: The Silence of The Buddha

1. Henri de Lubac, *La rencontre du bouddhisme et de l'Occident* (Paris: Éditions Montaigne, 1952), p. 151. On the initial encounter between Buddhism and European intellectuals, see especially chapter IV "Les premières controverses," pp. 151–202.
2. Lubac, *La rencontre du bouddhisme et de l'Occident*, p. 151.
3. Stephen Batchelor, *The Awakening of the West: The Encounter of Buddhism and Western Culture* (Berkeley, CA: Parallax Press, 1994), p. 244.
4. For discussions of the Western encounter with the Eastern world and Buddhism before the mid-nineteenth century, see Lubac, *La rencontre du bouddhisme et de l'Occident*, pp. 9-131; Batchelor, *The Awakening of the West*, pp. 3–183; Frédéric Lenoir, *La rencontre du bouddhisme et de l'Occident* (1999) (Paris: Éditions Albin Michel, 2001), pp. 27–77. For a historical survey of the Western acceptance of Buddhism, see

J. W. de Jong, *A Brief History of Buddhist Studies in Europe and America* (New Delhi, 1983); William Peiris, *The Western Contribution to Buddhism* (Orient Book Distributors, 1973); On this topic in the Zen Buddhist tradition, see Bernard Faure, "Chan/Zen in the Western Imagination," *Chan Insights and Oversights: An Epistemological Critique of the Chan Tradition* (Princeton, NJ: Princeton University Press, 1993), pp. 15–51.

5. Roger-Pol Droit, *Le culte du néant, Les philosophes et le Bouddha* (Éditions du Seuil, 1997), p. 189. English translation by David Streight and Pamela Vohnson, *The Cult of Nothingness: The Philosophers and the Buddha* (Chapel Hill and London: University of North Carolina Press, 2003), p. 131.

6. Guy Richard Welbon, *The Buddhist Nirvāna and Its Western Interpreters* (Chicago, IL: University of Chicago Press, 1968), p. 73.

7. See Andrew P. Tuck, "Nineteenth-Century German Idealism and Its Effect on Second-Century Indian Buddhism," *Comparative Philosophy and the Philosophy of Scholarship: On the Western Interpretation of Nāgārjuna* (New York: Oxford University Press, 1990), pp. 31–53.

8. Eugène Burnouf, *Papiers d'Eugène Burnouf conservés à la Bibliothèque Nationale* (Paris: n.p., 1899), quoted in Guy Richard Welbon, *The Buddhist Nirvāna and Its Western Interpreters*, p. 62.

9. Cited in Welbon, *The Buddhist Nirvāna and Its Western Interpreters*, p. 62.

10. Peiris, *The Western Contribution to Buddhism*, p. 167–168.

11. Tuck, *Comparative Philosophy and the Philosophy of Scholarship*, p. 35.

12. René Descartes, *Discourse on the Method*, bilingual edition, trans. by George Heffernan (Notre Dame: University of Notre Dame Press, 1994), p. 47.

13. Descartes, *Discourse on the Method*, p. 51.

14. René Descartes, *Meditations on First Philosophy*, trans. by Donald A. Cress (Indianapolis: Hackett Publishing Company, 1993), p. 19.

15. Descartes, *Discourse on the Method*, p. 53.

16. Descartes, *Meditations on First Philosophy*, p. 9.

17. Descartes, *Discourse on the Method*, pp. 57–59.

18. Blaise Pascal, *Pensées*, trans. by A. J. Krailsheimer (Penguin Books, 1966), p. 355.

19. "Jianyujing" in the *Zhong ahan jing* (The Middle Length Āgamas), *T* 1.26.804a. Throughout this book, all translations from Korean and Classical Chinese are mine, unless noted otherwise. For English translation from the Pāli version, see "Cūla-Māluṅkya-sutta," no. 63, *Majjhima-nikāya* (*The Collection of the Middle Length Sayings*), vol. II, trans. by I. B. Horner (London: Luzac & Company, Ltd, 1957), p. 97. Discussions of the Āgamas in this chapter are based on the Chinese Āgamas. Whenever corresponding suttas are found in the Pāli Nikāya, I will note them in the endnotes. The ten undeclared questions in the Māluṅkyāputta sutta are further elaborated into thirty-six categories in "Qingjing jing" (*Chang ahan jing* [Longer Āgama-sūtra] vol. 12, *T* 1.1.75c–76b) and into sixty-two categories in "Fandong jing" (*Chang ahan jing* vol. 14, *T* 1.1.88b–94a).

20. *Zhong ahan jing*, *T* 1.26. 805b.

21. For example, see Nagamura Hajime, *Wŏnsi Pulgyo* (Primitive Buddhism), trans. by Chŏng T'aehyŏk (Seoul: Tongmunsŏn, 1993), p. 64.

22. John Hick, *Disputed Questions in Theology and the Philosophy of Religion* (New Haven, CT: Yale University Press, 1993), p. 108. Hick repeats the discussion in his *Fifth Dimension: an Exploration of the Spiritual Realm* (Oxford: Oneworld, 2004), pp. 225–234.

23. Hick, *Disputed Questions in Theology and the Philosophy of Religion*, p. 108.

24. For a survey discussion of the treatment of the "undeclared" thesis in the history of Buddhism, see Yi Chungp'yo, *Aham ŭi chungdo ch'egye* (The System of the Middle Path in the *Āgamas*) (Seoul: Pulgwang ch'ulp'ansa, 1991), pp. 25–35; For discussions of the Buddha's silence, see Troy Wilson Organ, "The Silence of the Buddha," *Philosophy East and West* 4, no. 2 (July 1954): 125–140.

25. David J. Kalupahana, *Buddhist Philosophy: A Historical Analysis* (Honolulu: University of Hawaii Press, 1976), p. 156.

26. *Za ahan jing, T* 2.99.245b.

27. *Za ahan jing, T* 2.99.86a.

28. Steven Collins, *Selfless Persons: Imagery and Thought in Theravāda Buddhism* (Cambridge: Cambridge University Press, 1982), p. 132.

29. This interpretation of the Buddha's silence places him in the same context of what Jean-François Lyotard defines as *différend*. See chapter 7 for discussion.

30. Kalupahana in this sense states that the Buddha denied metaphysics but not philosophy itself.

31. *Zhong ahan jing, T* 1.26.805b.

32. *Zhong ahan jing, T* 1.26.805b. English translation of the Pāli canon version "Cūla- Māluṅkya-sutta," no. 63, *Majjhima-nikāya* (*The Collection of the Middle Length Sayings*), vol. II, p. 101.

33. Yi, *Aham ŭi chungdo ch'egye*, p. 28.

34. *Za ahan jing, T* 2.99.85c-86a. Equivalence in the Pāli text: "The Kaccāyana" *Samyutta-nikāya*, vol. II, no. 15. English translation of the Pāli version, *The Book of the Kindred Sayings*, trans. by Mrs. Rhys Davids (Oxford: The Pali Text Society, 1999), p. 12–13.

35. *Za ahan jing, T* 2.99.102 b.

36. Henry Cruise, "Early Buddhism: Some Recent Misconceptions," in *Philosophy East and West* 32, no. 2 (April 1983): 149–166, p 163.

37. In this sense, Dan Lusthaus claims that Buddhism itself was "a type of phenomenology" from its beginning. See Dan Lusthaus, *Buddhist Phenomenology: A Philosophical Investigation of Yogacara Buddhism and the Ch'eng Wei-shih Lun* (London: Routledge, 2002), p. viii.

38. *Za ahan jing, T* 2.99.85b.

39. Yi, *Aham ŭi chungdo ch'egye*, p. 32.

40. T. R. V. Murti, *The Central Philosophy of Buddhism: A Study of the Mādhyamika System* (London: George Allen and Unwin Ltd., 1960), p. 37.

41. Murti, *The Central Philosophy of Buddhism*, p. 47.

42. Murti, *The Central Philosophy of Buddhism*, pp. 8–9.

43. Kalupahana, *Buddhist Philosophy*, pp. xiii–xiv.

44. Kalupahana, *Buddhist Philosophy*, p. 161.

Chapter Two: Hegel and Buddhism

1. G. W. F. Hegel, *Phenomenology of Spirit*, trans. by A.V. Miller (London: Oxford University Press, 1977), pp. 410–478, §§672–787.

2. G. W. F. Hegel, *Lectures on the Philosophy of Religion*, 3 vols., edited by Peter C. Hodgson, trans. by R. F. Brown, P. C. Hodgson, and J. M. Stewart with the assistance of H. S. Harris (Berkeley, CA: University of California Press, 1995), vol. II, p. 304. Quotations from the *Lectures on the Philosophy of Religion* will be marked in the text with the abbreviation *LPR* followed by volume and page numbers.

Given that Hegel's lectures on the philosophy of religion were posthumously published and Hegel had made radical changes in his interpretations of Buddhism in the course of his three lectures, one's understanding of Hegel's interpretation of Buddhism can markedly vary, depending on which editions one uses, and which lectures one is following. Historically Hegel's *Lectures on the Philosophy of Religion* were edited twice: first, in 1832 by Philipp Marheineke and the second, in 1840 by Philipp Marheineke and Bruno Bauer. I have used Peter C. Hodgson's English translation of the German version edited by Walter Jaeschke, *Lectures on the Philosophy of Religion*, which put Hegel's four lectures of the philosophy of religions together.

3. Peter C. Hodgson, the editor of the *Lectures on the Philosophy of Religion*, writes in a footnote in the section on Buddhism of the 1824 lectures: "On Hegel's own terms, Buddhism should not be considered under the general category of 'the religion of magic', since we are no longer dealing with formal but with actual objectification of the divine object, and have arrived for the first time at religion in the proper sense as distinguished from magic" (*LPR* II, 303, n.183).

4. G. W. F. Hegel, *Vorlesungen über die Philosophie der Religion*, hrsg. von Georg Lasson (Hamburg: Felix Meiner, 1966), p. 124–125.

5. See Hegel, *Vorlesungen über die Philosophie der Religion*, p. 125.

6. Hegel, *Vorlesungen über die Philosophie der Religion*, p. 128.

7. Hegel considers it inappropriate to use the expression "pantheism" to refer to the collective reality of God. In order to distinguish his concept of pantheism from the wrong use of the term, he claims that Spinoza's philosophy is not "pantheism" but the "philosophy of substantiality" (Philosophie der Substanzialität). Hegel argues that God in Spinoza is not collectivity (*Allesheit*) but universality (*Allemeinheit*). See Hegel, *Vorlesungen über die Philosophie der Religion*, p. 129.

8. See Droit, *Le culte du néant*, pp. 91–108; *The Cult of Nothingness*, pp. 59–72.

9. Yi Dong-hee, "Hegel ŭi Pulgyo ihae" (Hegel's Understanding of Buddhism), *Hegel yŏn'gu* (Hegel Studies) (1997): 108–141, pp. 109, 118, and 119. Yi also claims that Hegel included Buddhism in his lectures on the philosophy of religions because of his increasing interest in the Oriental world (See pp. 113 and 115).

10. Peter Hodgson states in the Introduction: "The Oriental and Near Eastern religions are no longer considered under the general category of 'nature religion' but in terms of distinctive phases of the dialectics of consciousness. While this is an important gain, new and unresolved problems are created for the appropriate treatment of Jewish and Roman religion" (*LPR* II, p. 72). He points out that such problems

with Jewish and Roman religions in the 1831 lectures suggest that Hegel was yet to complete his system in 1831 and "was still in process of refining and expanding his interpretation of the history of religions when he died."

11. Jacques Derrida, *Positions*, trans. by Alban Bass (Chicago, IL: University of Chicago Press, 1981), p. 44.

12. G. W. F. Hegel, *The Philosophy of History*, trans. by J. Sibree (Buffalo: Prometheus Books, 1991), p. 171.

13. Hegel, *The Philosophy of History*, p. 18.

14. Hegel, *The Philosophy of History*, p. 103.

Chapter Three: The Logic of Nothing and A-Metaphysics

1. Martin Heidegger, "What is Metaphysics?" (1929) in *Martin Heidegger: Basic Writings*, edited by David Farrell Krell (San Francisco: Harper Collins Publishers, 1993), 89–110, p. 107. Subsequent citations from this essay will be marked with "WM?" in the text followed by page numbers.

2. Martin Heidegger, *An Introduction to Metaphysics* (1935/1953), trans. by Ralph Manheim (New Haven, CT: Yale University Press, 1959), p. 2.

3. Reinhard May, *Heidegger's Hidden Sources: East Asian Influences on His Work* (1989), trans. by Graham Parkes (London: Routledge, 1996), p. 21. See especially Chapter 3, "Nothing, emptiness, and the clearing," pp. 21–34.

4. S. J. Paluch, "Heidegger's 'What is Metaphysics?'," *Philosophy and Phenomenological Research* 30, no. 4 (June, 1970): 603–608, p. 604.

5. Michael E. Zimmerman, "Heidegger, Buddhism, and Deep Ecology," in *The Cambridge Companion to Heidegger*, edited by Charles B. Guignon (Cambridge: Cambridge University Press, 1993), 240–269, pp. 240 and 241.

6. Stephan Käufer, "The Nothing and the Ontological Difference in Heidegger's 'What is Metaphysics?'," *Inquiry* 48, no. 6 (December 2005): 482–506.

7. John Steffney, "Man and Being in Heidegger and Zen Buddhism," *The Eastern Buddhist* XIV, no. 1 (Spring 1981): 61–74, p. 72.

8. See Jacques Derrida, *De la grammatologie* (Paris: Les Éditions de Minuit, 1967), pp. 31–64.

9. To note the similarities between Heidegger's philosophy and Asian thought is no longer an alien topic in the field of comparative philosophy. Especially valuable in this context is Reinhard May's *Heidegger's Hidden Sources: East Asian Influences on His Work,* from which I have already cited. Graham Parkes, the translator of the book, suggests that "Heidegger's direct contact with East Asian thought dates back at least as far as 1922, when he made the acquaintance of the second most eminent figure (after Nishida Kitarō) in twentieth-century Japanese philosophy, Tanabe Hajime" (p. viii). However, as Parkes notes, it was not until the 1950s that Heidegger came to mention anything about East Asian thought. The later Heidegger, with emphasis on the clearing, open, and so on, reflects more of the East Asian concept of nothing or non-being. On the issue of Heidegger and Asian thought, see also *Heidegger and Asian Thought*, edited by Graham Parkes (Honolulu: University of Hawaii Press, 1987/1990); Veronique Foti, "Heidegger and the Way of Art: The Empty Origin and Contemporary Abstraction," *Continental Philosophy Review* 31 (1998): 337–351;

Elisabeth Feist, "Martin Heidegger and the East," *Philosophy East and West* 20, no. 3 (1970): 247-263; Matthew Kapstein, "The Trouble with Truth: Heidegger on Aletheia, Buddhist Thinkers on Satya," *Journal of Indian Council of Philosophical Research* 9, no. 2 (1992): 69–85; Peter Kreeft, "Zen in Heidegger's 'Gelassenheit'," *International Philosophical Quarterly* 11 (1971): 521–545; John Steffney, "Transmetaphysical Thinking in Heidegger and Zen Buddhism," *Philosophy East and West* 27, no. 3 (July 1977): 323–335, and "Man and Being in Heidegger and Zen Buddhism," *Philosophy Today* 25 (1981): 46–54; Takeshi Umehara, "Heidegger and Buddhism," *Philosophy East and West* 20, no. 3 (1970): 271–281; Michael Zimmerman, "Heidegger, Buddhism, and Deep Ecology," in *The Cambridge Companion to Heidegger*, edited by Charles B. Guignon (Cambridge: Cambridge University Press, 1993), 240–269; Steven Heine, *Existential and Ontological Dimensions of Time in Heidegger and Dōgen* (Albany: State University of New York Press, 1983); Kim Chonguk, *Haidegŏ wa hyŏngi sanghak, kŭrigo Pulgyo* (Heidegger, Metaphysics, and Buddhism) (Seoul: Ch'ŏrhak kwa hyŏnsil, 2003)

10. Martin Heidegger, "Postscript," in "The Quest for Being," in Walter Kaufmann, *Existentialism from Dostoevsky to Sartre* (New York: New American Library, 1975), 257–264, p. 259.

11. Heidegger, "Postscript," p. 259.

12. In this context, Kim Hyŏnghyo's reading of Heidegger's concept of "anxiety" in connection with Buddhist awakening further illuminates this relationship. In his book, *Haidegŏ wa maŭm ŭi ch'orhak* (Heidegger and the Philosophy of Mind) (Seoul: Ch'ŏnggye, 2000), Kim interprets Heidegger's "anxiety" in the context of the Buddhist concept of impermanence. Heidegger's anxiety suggests to Kim that "man as Dasein, in order to obtain existential realization or awakening, performs the solitary action, the singular event, in which one deviates from one's worldliness—that familiar world and the rules taught by the world—, and through which Dasein recovers its original existential state" (p. 200).

The anxiety in this case is not only different from worries, or fear, but distinguishes itself from uncomfortable feeling, since it is the original state of the mind. For Kim, the anxiety Dasein experiences is "not the feeling that occurs easily to everybody. This is an experience of a precious moment which takes place when Dasein turns the direction of its mind to the original state of self-awakening" (p. 202). This precious feeling, to Kim, is Dasein's experience of its existential reality which becomes possible when a being realizes the impermanence of existence though nihilation of nothing. Heidegger's nothing, nihilation, and anxiety, for Kim, do not have negative implications, but offer a radical moment when a being (or Dasein) encounters the original state of its existence. In this context, Kim contends that for Heidegger "anxiety, uncanny feeling, quiet peacefulness, and nothing have the same value in their meaning" (p. 206). Dasein's encounter with nothing is understood to Kim as a moment when an entity, or a sentient being, realizes the impermanence and changeability which is the basic structure of existence in Buddhism. Since this encounter enables an entity to realize its ontological ground, Dasein's encounter with the nothing is described as an experience of peacefulness. Kim's interpretation of Heidegger's nothing can be one example which demonstrates how Heidegger's concept of the nothing distances itself from the existing Western metaphysical tradition. This also indicates the difficulty that Heidegger's discussion of the nothing encountered in Western philosophical circles.

13. *Daban niepan jing* (*The Nirvāna Sūtra*), *T* 12.375.819b. Earlier in the same text, it was also stated: "the Buddha nature is neither inside, nor outside, both inside and outside, therefore it is called the middle path" (*T* 12.375.819b).

14. Se Geun Jeong (Se'gŭn Chŏng), "Mu ŭi kamŭng" (Empathy of Nothing), in *Noja esŏ terida kkaji: to'ga ch'ŏrhak kwa sŏyang ch'ŏrhak ŭi mannam* (From Laozi to Derrida: the Encounter between Daoist and Western Philosophy), edited by Han'guk to'ga ch'ŏrhakhoe (Seoul: Yŏmun sŏwŏn, 2001), 245–264, p. 245.

15. Jeong, "Mu ŭi kamŭng," p. 248.

16. *Panruo boluomiduo xinjing*, *T* 8.251.848c. All the citations from the *Heart Sūtra* are from the same page.

17. Wŏnch'ŭk, *Pulsŏl Panya paramilda simgyŏng ch'an* (Commentaries on the *Heart Sūtra* Expounded by the Buddha), *HPC* 1.1a–15a, p. 3 a.

18. The God of the philosopher, an "infelicitous hybrid of religious faith and of rational thought," as Etienne Gilson puts it (*God and Philosophy* [New Haven, CT: Yale University Press, 1941], p. 89), has no longer any personal reality for man, since his function becomes limited to a guarantor of the harmony existing among the different monads or between human reason and the external world. In rationalist thinking, this God becomes a general and universal rule that guarantees man's right to free himself from any external authority and to follow where his strength and reason may guide him. He neither judges man, nor demands obedience; he leaves man alone in the face of a static world of things and individuals.

19. In this context, Walter Jaeschke states, "Hegel's philosophy begins by pronouncing the death of God, and ends with the insight into the end of religion" ("Philosophical Theology and Philosophy of Religion," in *New Perspectives on Hegel's Philosophy of Religion*, edited by David Kolb (Albany: State University of New York Press, 1992), 1–18, p. 1.

20. Philippe Lacoue-Labarthe, "The Fable," in *The Subject of Philosophy*, edited by Thomas Trezise (1979) (Minneapolis, MN: University of Minnesota Press, 1995), p. 1.

21. Dalia Judovitz, "Derrida and Descartes: Economizing Thought," in *Derrida and Deconstruction*, edited by Hugh J. Silverman (New York: Routledge, 1989), 40–58, p. 52.

22. Judovitz, "Derrida and Descartes," p. 57.

23. Paul de Man, "Phenomenality and Materiality in Kant," in *The Textual Sublime: Deconstruction and Its Differences*, edited by Hugh J. Silverman and Gary E. Aylesworth (Albany: State University of New York Press, 1990), 87–108, p. 104.

24. de Man, "Phenomenality and Materiality in Kant," p. 104.

25. Rowan Williams, "Hegel and the Gods of Postmodernity," in *Shadow of Spirit: Postmodernism and Religion*, edited by Philippa Berry and Andrew Wernick (New York: Routledge, 1992), 72–80, p. 75.

26. Williams, "Hegel and the Gods of Postmodernity," pp. 75–76.

27. Lacoue-Labarthe, "The Fable," p. 7.

28. Lacoue-Labarthe, "The Fable," p. 7.
29. Lacoue-Labarthe, "The Fable," p. 5.

Chapter Four: Language and Thinking:
Subjectivity and Zen Huatou Meditation

1. Daisetz Teitaro Suzuki, trans., *The Laṅkāvatāra Sūtra: A Mahāyāna Text* (Delhi: Motilal Banarsidass Publishers, 2003), pp. 123–124. The *Sūtra* emphasizes the issue again with the statement: "From the night of enlightenment till that of Nirvana, I have not in the meantime made any proclamation whatever" (p. 125). D. T. Suzuki adds a footnote to the passage, "The Zen masters frequently refer to this important declaration" (p. 125).

2. The eighteenth-century historian Louis Moreri states in his *Grand Dictionnaire historique* in the section of *"Fê* (ou *Fo*, ou *Foé*, idole de la Chine)": " . . . at the age of seventy-nine years, sensing his death is approaching, he declared to his disciples that, during the forty years he had preached to the world, he had not told them the truth at all, that he had hidden it under the veil of metaphors & figures, but that it was the time to de-clare the truth: that is, he said, there is nothing to search, nor is there anything on which one can place one's hope, other than nothing and void, which is the primary principle of all the things." Louis Moreri, *Grand Dictionnaire historique ou Mélange curieux de l'histoire sacrée et profane* (Paris, 1725). Cited in Droit, *Le culte du néant*, p. 97.

3. Bernard Faure, *The Rhetoric of Immediacy: A Cultural Critique of Chan/Zen Buddhism* (Princeton, NJ: Princeton University Press, 1991), p. 27.

In line with the statement of the Buddha's not having uttered a word, Florin Giripescu Sutton also sees the *Laṅkāvatāra Sūtra* as one in the series of dialectical movements in the evolution of Buddhism beginning with the silence of the Buddha in early Buddhism through Mādhyamika and Zen Buddhism (*Existence and Enlight-enment in the Laṅkāvatāra-sūtra: A Study in the Ontology and Epistemology of the Yogācāra School of Mahāyāna Buddhism* [Albany: State University of New York Press, 1989], p. 160–161).

4. Burton Watson, trans., *The Vimalakirti Sutra* (New York: Columbia University Press, 1997), pp. 110-111.

5. Roland Barthes, *The Empire of Signs* (1970), trans. by Richard Howard (New York: Hill and Wang, 1982), pp. 74-75.

6. Arthur Koestler, *The Lotus and the Robot* (New York: Macmillan Press, 1961), p. 58.

7. Mark Lawrence McPhail, *Zen in the Art of Rhetoric: An Inquiry into Coher-ence* (Albany: State University of New York Press, 1996), p. 6. Also see pp. 113–129 of this book and Carl Olson, *Zen and the Art of Postmodern Philosophy* (Albany: State University of New York Press, 2000).

8. Dale S. Wright, "Rethinking Transcendence: The Role of Language in Zen Experience," *Philosophy East and West* 42, no. 1 (1992): 113–138; Also see Dale S. Wright, "Kōan History: Transformative Language in Chinese Buddhist Thought," in *Zen Kōan: Texts and Contexts in Zen Buddhism,* edited by Steven Heine and Dale S. Wright (New York: Oxford University Press, 2000), 200–212.

9. Wright, "Rethinking Transcendence," p. 123.

10. Wright, "Rethinking Transcendence," p. 123.

11. Bernard Faure, *Chan Insights and Oversights: An Epistemological Critique of the Chan Tradition* (Princeton, NJ: Princeton University Press, 1993), p. 196. Also see pp. 195–216.

12. Sigmund Freud, "The Dissection of the Psychical Personality," in *The Standard Edition of the Complete Psychological Works of Sigmund Freud,* edited and trans. by James Strachey et al. (London: The Hogarth Press, 1952, 1974), vol. 22, p. 80. Jacques Lacan, *The Four Fundamental Concepts of Psycho-Analysis* (1973), trans. by Alan Sheridan (New York: W. W. Norton & Co., Ltd., 1981), p. 44.

13. Jacques Lacan, *Écrits: A Selection* (1966) (New York: W. W. Norton & Co. Ltd., 1977), p. 165. For a discussion of the Lacanian model of language, see Jean-Luc Nancy and Philippe Lacoue-Labarthe, *The Title of the Letter: A Reading of Lacan* (1973), trans. by François Raffoul and David Pettigrew (Albany: State University of New York Press, 1992), pp. 87–104.

14. Lacan, *The Four Fundamental Concepts of Psycho-Analysis,* p. 20.

15. Scholars have contended that the passages, instead of being a creation of Bodhidharma, had developed into the current format in the process of Zen Buddhism's attempts to create its own identity. The passage consisting of sixteen Chinese characters were not put together until the time when Zen Buddhism was established as an independent school, as Peter Gregory states: "These different lines were not subsumed together into a unified vision of the tradition as a whole until the end of the period with the writings of Tsung-mi (780-841)—but even that remained only another contending claim when it was put forth" (Peter Gregory and Daniel Gets, eds., *Buddhism in the Sung* [Honolulu: University of Hawaii Press, 1999], p. 4). According to Griffith T. Foulk, it was not until 1108 that all four lines appeared together (Griffith T. Foulk, "Myth, Ritual, and Monastic Practice in Sung Ch'an Buddhism," in *Religion and Society in T'ang and Sung China,* edited by Patricia Buckley Ebrey and Peter N. Gregory [Honolulu: University of Hawaii Press, 1995], p. 155 and endnote #16 on p. 199). Regardless of the historical accuracy of the author and composition of this definition of Zen Buddhism, one cannot deny the role the passage has played throughout the history of Zen Buddhism. The historical inaccuracy, hence, does not disqualify these four stanzas' function in the construction of Zen identity. John McRae discusses in detail about the interplay of historical factuality and mythopoetic narrative in Zen literature in his *Seeing through Zen: Encounter, Transformation, and Genealogy in Chinese Chan Buddhism* (Berkeley, CA: University of California Press, 2003).

16. Red Pine, trans., "Bloodstream Sermon," in *The Zen Teaching of Bodhidharma* (New York: North Point Press, 1987), p. 31.

17. Red Pine, trans., "Bloodstream Sermon," p. 65.

18. *The Diamond Sūtra (Jingang banruo buloumi jing),* *T* 8.235.749b

19. *T* 8.235.751a.

20. *T* 8.235.751 a-b.

21. *T* 8.235.751 c.

22. Huineng, *Nanzong dunjiao zuishang dasheng mahe panruo bolou mijing: Liuzu Huineng dashi yu Shaozhou Dafansi shifa tanjing* (The Great Perfection of

Wisdom Sūtra of the Best Mahāyāna Buddhism of the Sudden Teaching of the Southern School: the Platform Sūtra of the Sixth Patriarch Huineng of Dafan Temple in Shaozhou), *T* 48.2007.337a–345b, p. 343b.

23. Huineng, *T* 48.2007.343c.

24. Huineng, *T* 48.2007.343c.

25. Huineng, *T* 48.2007.343a.

26. The issue will be explored in detail in chapter 9.

27. The issue will be explored in detail in chapter 6.

28. Chinul's *Treatise on Huatou Meditation* has been considered the first major text on Kanhua meditation (K. Kanhwa Sŏn) in Korean Buddhism. In this text, not only does Chinul introduce the *kanhua* method, he also advocates its superiority over Huayan Buddhism, confirming that this approach is a shortcut way to enlightenment.

29. Chinul is believed to have had three incidents of awakening. For detailed description of these incidents, see Robert E. Buswell, Jr., trans. *Korean Approach to Zen: Collected Works of Chinul* (Honolulu: University of Hawaii Press, 1983), pp. 18–36.

30. Chinul, *Hwaŏmnon chŏryo* (Excerpts from the Exposition of the *Huayan jing*), *Han'guk Pulgyo chŏnsŏ* (Collected Works of Korean Buddhism), 4.767c–768b, p. 767c. All the citations from Chinul's works are from the *Han'guk Pulgyo chŏnsŏ*. Henceforth citations from Chinul's works will be marked in the text with *HPC* followed by page numbers. All translations are mine unless noted otherwise.

31. Questions and criticisms have been raised regarding the scholastic element in Chinul's Zen Buddhism. The time period that is described in the "Preface" (1185–1188) was still in the early stage of Chinul's career, but I believe that the doubt Chinul expressed in the "Preface" constitutes the core of the later development of Chinul's Buddhist thoughts. Chae Chŏngsu, for example, asks in his essay on Dahui's influence on Chinul why Chinul did not entirely focus on the practice of *huatou* meditation even after he read Dahui, which Chae conjectures to have taken place when Chinul was around forty. (Ch'ae Chŏngsu, "Taehye ŭi Sŏchang kwa Pojo Sŏn" [Dahui's Letters and Pojo Zen], *Pojo Sasang* 2 [November 1988]: 289–304, p. 298.)

32. Robert E. Buswell, Jr., *The Korean Approach to Zen*, p. 198. The discussion of Chinul's *Wŏndon sŏngbul ron* appears in chapter 9.

33. Kim Hosŏng, "Kanhwa kyŏrŭi ron yŏkchu: Hwaŏm kwa Kanhwa Sŏn ŭi pyŏnchŭngbŏp" (Translation, with Commentaries, of the *Treatise on Resolving Doubts about Huatou Meditation*: the Dialectic of Huayan and Kanhua Zen"), *Pojo sasang* 9 (1995): 137–172.

34. Most well-known is a criticism by T'oe'ong S'ŏngch'ŏl in his *Sŏnmun Chŏngro* (The Correct Path of Zen School) (Seoul: Pulgwang ch'ulp'ansa, 1981). In the section "Ta'mun chihae" S'ŏngch'ŏl criticizes Chinul's amalgamation of Zen and Huayan as a heretical approach to Zen Buddhism and attaches to Chinul's Zen the derogatory expression "Huayan Zen" (p. 209).

35. With this realization, Chinul confirms the Huayan Buddhist doctrine of "nature-origination" (K. *sŏnggi*; Ch. *xingqi*) as a philosophical and textual authority of the Zen claim of the mind qua the Buddha. Discussions of nature-origination and Huayan doctrine appear in chapter 9.

36. A discussion of the concept of *dharmadhātu* (the realm of reality) in Huayan Buddhism appears in chapter 8.

37. Chinul's five questions are asked with Fazang's five-level taxonomy of Buddhist schools in mind. In his classification of Buddhist teachings as elaborated in *Wujiao zhang* (Treatise on the Five Teachings *T* 45.1866.477a–509a.), Fazang categorizes Buddhist schools in the following ways: (1) Hīnayāna Teaching (C. *xiaochengjiao*); (2) Mahāyāna Inception Teaching (C. *dasheng shijiao*); (3) Mahāyāna Final Teaching (C. *dasheng zhongjiao*); (4) Sudden Teaching (C. *dunjiao*); and (5) Complete Teaching (C. *yuanjiao*). The Complete Teaching refers to the Huayan school, whereas the Zen school is included in the Sudden Teaching. Buddhist schools in China created their own doctrinal classifications, each putting its own school at the final stage in the evolution of the Buddha's teaching, thus self-legitimatizing its own authenticity and superiority as a Buddhist teaching. Huayan Buddhism was no exception.

Fully developed and articulated in Fazang's *Treatise on the Five Teachings*, the doctrine of the Five Teachings is already traceable in the writings of Dushun (557–640), the First Patriarch of the school. See Dushun, "Cessation and Contemplation in the Five Teachings of the Hua-yen" (*Huayan wujiao zhiguan, T* 45.1867.509a–513c). For an English translation of "Cessation and Contemplation in the Five Teachings of the Hua-yen" see Thomas Cleary, *Entry into the Inconceivable: An Introduction to Hua-yen Buddhism* (Honolulu: University of Hawaii Press, 1983/1994), pp. 43–68. For an English translation of Fazang's *Treatise on the Five Teachings*, see Francis Cook, "Fa-tsang's Treatise on the Five-Doctrines: An Annotated Translation," Ph. D. dissertation, University of Wisconsin, 1970. For the relation between the Flower Garland and Zen schools in Chinul, see Robert E. Buswell, Jr., "Chinul's Systematization of Chinese Meditative Techniques in Korean Sŏn Buddhism," in *Traditions of Meditation in Chinese Buddhism*, edited by Peter N. Gregory (Honolulu: University of Hawaii Press, 1986), pp. 199–242.

38. Dahui's influence on Chinul has been well noted. In the *Treatise on Huatou Meditation*, Chinul discusses his view of *huatou* meditation, extensively relying on Dahui. The discussion of the Ten Zen Diseases, with which Chinul opens the *Treatise*, is one of the instances in which one notes both the strong influence of Dahui on Chinul and at the same time Chinul's systematization of his own Zen *huatou* theory. The Ten Zen Diseases first appear at the end of Chinul's *Personal Records*, in which Chinul cites Dahui regarding the latter's teaching of how to practice Zhaozhou's *wu huatou*. Dahui's original discussion contains only eight wrong ways to practice Zhaozhou's *wu huatou*. Chinul added two new items to Dahui's list and created the Ten Zen Diseases (See *Pŏpchip pŏrhaengrok chŏryo pyŏngip sagi* [Excerpts from the Dharma Collection and Special Practice Record with Personal Notes], *HPC* 4.765 b-c).

39. The Ten Diseases are: "(1) Do not try to be decisive and say that the word [Zhaozhou's *wu* (or nothing)] means either yes or no; (2) Do not play with the idea that the no should imply the 'no' of the primordial non-being; (3) Do not try to conjecture based on logicality; (4) Do not try to infer relying on the meaning of linguistic expression; (5) Do not try to make meaning of *huatou* out of your master's gestures of raising eye brows or blinking; (6) Do not try to find a way out by relying on lin-

guistic meanings; (7) Do not pretend to work seriously while guarding yourself within
the shell of no-concern; (8) Do not try to find the meaning of *huatou* by bringing all
your attention to bear; (9) Do not try to find evidences from linguistic expressions
[scriptures]; (10) Do not wait for awakening while remaining in the state of foolish-
ness" (*HPC* 4.735a).

40. As cited in the *Treatise on Huatou Meditation*. The passage is originally from
the *Complete Enlightenment Sūtra, T* 17.842.917b.

41. *T* 17.842.917a.

42. The expression is also translated as "underdeveloped *dharmakāya*," by Robert
Buswell in *Korean Approach to Zen*, p. 241, "the *dharmakāya* which is pure but without form" by Pŏpsŏng in *Kanhwa kyŏrŭi ron kwahae* (Section-by-section Translations
and Commentaries of the *Treatise on Resolving Doubts about Huatou Meditation*)
(Seoul: K'ŭnsure, 1993), p. 24, and "original *dharmakāya*" by Hosŏng Kim in "Kanhwa kyŏrŭi ron yŏkchu," p. 151, and in *Pojo kuksa chŏnsŏ* (The Complete Works of
National Master Pojo), trans. by Taljin Kim (Seoul: Koryŏwŏn, 1987), p. 196.

43. *Dahui yulu* 14, *T* 47.1998.870b.

44. McRae, *Seeing through Zen,* p. 102. McRae begins his chapter "Zen and the
Art of Fund-Raising" by introducing a number of book titles which he considers as
representatives in this trend of "the Zen of Anything." The list includes: *Zen and
the Art of Motorcycle Maintenance* by Robert Pirsig, *Zen and the Art of Archery* by
Eugen Herrigel, *Zen and Japanese Culture* by D. T. Suzuki, and *The Way of Zen* by
Alan Watts. The list further includes titles like, *The Zen of International Relations,
The Zen Teachings of Jesus,* and *Zen and the Art of the Macintosh.* Whether one can
offhandedly claim that they are not Zen is a debatable issue, which is related to how
to define a certain philosophical and religious tradition. The point to be made here, as
McRae states, is: "Although undivided concentration and bare-bones simplicity are
legitimate messages of Chinese Chan as a mode of self-cultivation, the Chan tradition,
. . . involves far more than this" (P. 102).

45. McRae, *Seeing through Zen*, p. 102.

46. *Wumen guan, T* 48.2005.292c-299c, Case #37, p. 297c.

47. Chinul emphasizes this fact in several places in the text, making a distinction
between Zen *huatou* method and the Sudden Teaching, which Fazang put into the
same category in his five-layered classification. Throughout the *Treatise on Huatou
Meditation*, Chinul is sensitive to Fazang's taxonomy and takes much pain to emphasize that Zen Buddhism is not the same as the Sudden Teaching, despite Fazang's
attempt to treat them as the same.

48. Heinrich Dumoulin, *Zen Buddhism in the 20th Century*, trans. by Joseph S.
O'Leary (New York: Weatherhill, 1992), p. 126.

49. Sung Bae Park, *Buddhist Faith and Sudden Enlightenment* (Albany: State
University of New York Press, 1983), p. 66.

50. Maurice Merleau-Ponty, *Le Visible et l'invisible* (Paris: Édition Gallimard,
1964), p. 183 ; *The Visible and the Invisible*, trans. by Alphonso Lingis (Evanston, IL:
Northwestern University Press, 1968), p. 139.

51. Maurice Merleau-Ponty, *The Prose of the World* (1969), trans. by John O'Neill
(Evanston, IL: Northwestern University Press, 1973), p. 10.

52. Merleau-Ponty, *The Prose of the World*, p. 10.

53. Merleau-Ponty, *The Prose of the World*, p. 13.

54. Merleau-Ponty, *Le Visible et l'invisible*, p. 167; *The Visible and the Invisible*, p. 125.

55. *Dasheng qixin lun* (Treatise on the Awakening of Mahāyāna Faith), attributed to Aśvaghoṣa, *T* 32.1666.576a.

Chapter Five: Thinking and Violence: Zen Hermeneutics

1. Sohaku Ogata, trans., *The Transmission of the Lamp: Early Masters* (Wolfeboro, NH: Longwood Academic, 1990), p. 69.

2. *Linji lu*, *T* 47.1985.496b-506c, p. 500b ; Burton Watson, trans., *The Zen Teachings of Master Lin-chi* (Boston: Shambhala Publications, Inc., 1993), p. 52.

3. Watson, *The Zen Teachings of Master Lin-chi*, p. 64, footnote # 20.

4. *Wumen guan*, case # 3. *T* 48.2005.292a-299c, p. 293 b; *Unlocking the Zen Koan: A New Translation of the Zen Classic Wumenguan*, trans. by Thomas Cleary (Berkeley, CA: North Atlantic Books, 1997), p. 18.

5. The story of violence does not stop in classical Zen texts. For example, the modern Korean Zen tradition also inherited such a practice. Kyŏnghŏ Sŏng'u, who has been credited as the founder of modern Korean Zen tradition, has been recorded to have kept a sharp gimlet under his chin so that in case of dosing off while meditating with a *huatou*, he will be awakened by the gimlet.

6. *Wumen guan*, *T* 48.2005.294c. English translation mine. For other English translations, see Cleary, *Unlocking the Zen Koan*, p. 66; Thomas Cleary and J. C. Cleary, trans., *The Blue Cliff Record* (Boston and London: Shambhala, 1992), pp. 358-370; Katsuki Sekida, trans., *Two Zen Classics: Mumonkan* (*The Gateless Gate*), *Hekiganroku* (*The Blue Cliff Record*) (New York: Weatherhill, Inc., 1977), pp. 58–59, 319–321.

7. The absolutization of practice at the expense of logical and linguistic medium, when they are misunderstood and thus absolutized in Zen tradition, can be considered as another form of Zen violence, which is further related to Zen authoritarianism.

8. See Maurizio Ferraris, *History of Hermeneutics* (1988), trans. by Luca Somigli (New Jersey: Humanities Press, 1996); Richard E. Palmer, *Hermeneutics* (Evanston, IL: Northwestern University Press, 1969).

9. The assumption that meaning production in hermeneutics is especially related to textual analysis has created an impression that Zen Buddhism might be at odds with this discipline. Defying such a concern, Buddhist scholars demonstrated that Zen Buddhism provides a potential contribution to hermeneutics. See for example Robert E. Buswell, Jr. "Ch'an Hermeneutics: A Korean View," in *Buddhist Hermeneutics*, edited by Donald S. Lopez (Honolulu: University of Hawaii Press, 1988), 231–256. For a discussion of Buddhist hermeneutics see Donald S. Lopez, Jr. "Buddhist Hermeneutics: A Conference Report," *Philosophy East and West* 37, no. 1 (January 1987): 71–83; Ninian Smart, "Comparative Hermeneutics: An Epilogue about the Future," in *The Cardinal Meaning: Essays in Comparative Hermeneutics: Buddhism*

and Christianity, edited by Michael Pye and Robert Morgan (The Hague: Mouton and Co., 1973), 195–199.

10. Wŏnch'ŏl Yun and Inhae Kang, "Chonggyo ŏnŏ rosse ŭi kongan" (Gong'an as Religious Language), *Chonggyo wa munhwa* (Religion and Culture) 7 (2001): 59–79, pp. 65–72.

11. This approach to Zen *gong'an* as part of Wittgensteinian language game is comparable to Dale Wright's claim of Zen language as a "monastic language game."

12. *Biyan lu, T* 48.2003.181c, case number 45.

13. Yun and Kang, "Chonggyo ŏnŏ rosse ŭi kongan," p. 73.

14. Martin Heidegger, "The Origin of the Work of Art," in *Poetry, Language, Thought*, trans. by Albert Hofstadter (New York: Harper & Row, Publishers, 1971), 15-87, p. 51.

15. Heidegger, "The Origin of the Work of Art," p. 51.

16. Martin Heidegger, "The End of Philosophy and the Task of Thinking," *On Time and Being* (1964), trans. by Joan Stambaugh (New York, Hagerstown, San Francisco, London: Harper & Row, Publishers, 1972), p. 68.

17. Han Hyŏngjo, *Mumun'gwan, hogŭn, 'nŏ' nŭn nu'gu'nya'* (The Gateless Gate, or "Who Are You?") (Seoul: Yŏ'si'a'mun, 1999), p. 93.

18. The concept of self-philosophy does not indicate a philosophy emphasizing the self in the sense of ego-cogito. Instead, Kim's self-philosophy refers to the philosophy that concerns an individual's encounter with philosophical discourse. In self-philosophy, the theory of philosophy opens up an individual's praxis and, thus, in self-philosophy, the reader (self), the philosophical text, and thinking belong together as in the Heideggerian hermeneutical circle.

19. Hosŏng Kim, "Chŏja ŭi pujae wa Pulgyo haesŏkhak" (The Absence of the Author and Buddhist Hermeneutics), *Pulgyo hakpo* (Buddhist Studies) 35, no. 1 (1998): 187–206, p. 204.

20. Martin Heidegger, "A Dialogue on Language," in *On the Way to Language* (1957), trans. by Peter D. Hertz (New York: Harper San Francisco, 1971), 1–54, p. 29.

21. Richard E. Palmer, "Liminality of Hermes and the Meaning of Hermeneutics," *Proceedings of the Heraclitean Society: A Quarterly Report on Philosophy and Criticism of the Arts and Sciences* 5 (1980): 4–11.

22. Heidegger, "A Dialogue on Language," p.30.

23. Jay L. Garfield, trans., *The Fundamental Wisdom of the Middle Way: Nāgārjuna's Mūlamadhyamakakārikā* (New York and Oxford: Oxford University Press, 1995), p. 68.

24. Jacques Derrida, *De la grammatologie*, p. 33 ; *Of Grammatology*, p. 20.

25. Reihō Masunaga, *A Primer of Sōtō Zen: A Translation of Dōgen's Shōbōgenzō Zuimonki* (Honolulu: University of Hawaii Press, 1978), p. 9. Douglas K. Mikkelson develops his theory of Dōgen's views on moral action based on this passage. See "Who is Arguing about the Cat? Moral Action and Enlightenment according to Dōgen," *Philosophy East and West* 47, no. 3 (July 1997): 383–397.

26. Heidegger, "A Dialogue on Language," p. 29.

27. Derrida writes, "According to Hegel, philosophy becomes serious. . . only from the moment when it enters into the sure path of logic: that is, after having aban-

doned, or let us rather say sublated, its mythic form: after Plato, with Plato. Philosophical logic comes to its sense when the concept wakes up from its mythological slumber" ("Khōra," in *On the Name*, trans. by David Wood, John P. Leavey, Jr., and Ian McLeod [Stanford, CA: Stanford University Press, 1995], p. 100).

28. The discussion appeared in chapter 3.

29. Heidegger, "The Origin of the Work of Art," pp. 33–34.

30. Heidegger, "The Origin of the Work of Art," p. 38.

31. Heidegger, "The Origin of the Work of Art," p. 38.

32. Heidegger, "The Origin of the Work of Art," p. 36.

33. Jacques Derrida, "Restitutions," in *The Truth in Painting* (1977), trans. by Geoff Bennington and Ian McLeod (Chicago, IL: University of Chicago Press, 1987), 255–382, p. 259.

34. Maurice Merleau-Ponty, *Signs*, trans. by Richard C. McCleary (Evanston, IL: Northwestern University Press, 1964), p. 14.

35. *Wumen guan*, *T* 48.2005.293c; Cleary, *Unlocking the Zen Koan*, p. 39.

36. *Wumen guan*, *T* 48.2005.295b; Sekida, *Two Zen Classics*, p. 73

37. *T* 48.2005.296c; Cleary, *Unlocking the Zen Koan*, p. 144.

38. *T* 48.2005.297b; Cleary, *Unlocking the Zen Koan*, p. 155.

39. *T* 48.2005.296b; Cleary, *Unlocking the Zen Koan*, p. 129. ·

40. *T* 48.2005.296c; Cleary, *Unlocking the Zen Koan*, p. 141.

41. *T* 48.2005.298a; Cleary, *Unlocking the Zen Koan*, p. 181.

42. Derrida, "Khōra," p. 91.

43. A further discussion of *chora* appears in chapter 6.

44. Derrida, "Khōra," p. 89.

45. The issue will be discussed in detail in chapter 7.

Chapter Six: Violence Institutionalized:
The Social Dimension of Zen Language

1. *Biyan lu*, *T* 2003.48.149 a; English translation by Cleary, *The Blue Cliff Record*, p. 59.

2. *Biyan lu*, *T* 2003.48.149 b; Cleary, *The Blue Cliff Record*, p. 61.

3. *Biyan lu*, *T*. 2003.48.149c-150a; Cleary, *The Blue Cliff Record*, p. 64.

4. Derrida, *Of Grammatology*, p. 19.

5. *Xu chuangdeng lu*, vol. 22, *T* 51.2077.614c.

6. *Biyan lu*, *T* 2003.48.149c; Cleary, *The Blue Cliff Record*, p. 62.

7. *Tanjing*, *T* 48.2007.338.03c. For Yampolsky's translation, see *The Platform Sūtra of the Sixth Patriarch: The Text of the Tun-Huang Manuscript*, trans. with notes by Philip B. Yampolsky (New York: Columbia University Press, 1967), p. 139.

8. In this context, Yampolsky translated "True Suchness" as "True Reality."

9. *T* 48.2007.338.03c; Yampolsky, *The Platform Sūtra of the Sixth Patriarch*, p. 138.

10. "Engaged Buddhism" is the term first used by Vietnamese Zen Master Thich Nhat Hanh. In his *Vietnam: Lotus in a Sea of Fire* (1967), Thich Nhat Hanh discusses the role of Buddhism in connection with the suffering of Vietnamese people and

used the expression "engaged Buddhism." The expression is now used in a broader context as in *Engaged Buddhism: Buddhist Liberation Movements in Asia*, edited by Christopher S. Queen and Sally King (Albany: State University of New York Press, 1996). I will use the expression "engaged Buddhism" or "engaged Buddhists" to refer to socially conscious Buddhists without limiting the scope to Vietnamese Buddhism. In the context of Korean Buddhism, engaged Buddhists I discuss in this book are mostly related to Minjung Buddhism (Buddhism for the masses) who were active during the 1970s and 1980s.

11. Pŏpsŏng, "Kkaedarŭm ŭi ilsangsŏng kwa hyŏngmyŏngsŏng" (Commonality and Revolutionality of Awakening), in *Ch'angjak kwa pip'yŏng* (Creation and Criticism) 21, no. 4 (Winter 1993): 329-430, p. 331.

12. Pŏpsŏng, "Minjung Pulgyo undong ŭi silch'ŏnjŏk ipchang" (The Practical Standpoint of the Minjung Buddhist Movement), in *Chonggyo yŏn'gu* (Religious Studies) 6 (1990): 223-228, p. 223.

13. Pŏpsŏng, "Minjung Pulgyo undong ŭi silch'ŏnjŏk ipchang," p. 224.

14. Yŏ Ikku, *Minjung Pulgyo ch'ŏrhak* (Philosophy of Minjung Buddhism) (Seoul: Minjoksa, 1988), p. 126.

15. Yŏ, *Minjung Pulgyo ch'ŏrhak*, pp. 126–127.

16. Kristeva, *La révolution du langage poétique* (Paris: Éditions du Seuil, 1974), p. 23; English translation by Margaret Waller, *Revolution in Poetic Language* (New York: Columbia University Press, 1984), p. 24.

17. Plato, *Timaeus*, 27d, in *The Collected Dialogues of Plato*, edited by Edith Hamilton and Huntington Cairns (Princeton, NJ: Princeton University Press, 1989), p. 1161.

18. Plato, *Timaeus*, 27d-28a, *The Collected Dialogues of Plato*, p. 1161.

19. Plato, *Timaeus*, 49a-b, *The Collected Dialogues of Plato*, p. 1176.

20. Plato, *Timaeus*, 51a-b, *The Collected Dialogues of Plato*, p. 1178.

21. Plato, *Timaeus*, 52-d, *The Collected Dialogues of Plato*, p. 1179.

22. Plato, *Timaeus*, 49b-c, *The Collected Dialogues of Plato*, p. 1176.

23. Kristeva, *La révolution du langage poétique*, p. 24; *Revolution in Poetic Language*, p. 26.

24. One might ask whether Kristeva is proposing a metaphysical foundation of language by assuming the semiotic *chora* as a precondition of the symbolic linguistic stage. Kristeva would contend that such an interpretation is possible only when one understands the semiotic *chora* and the symbolic in a dualistic structure in which the two first exist separately and come to work together. However, for Kristeva, they are non-dual to begin with. Whether Kristeva's presentation of the semiotic and the symbolic is convincingly non-dual is a debatable issue. Criticisms have been raised that Kristeva's *chora* invokes certain primordial and ahistorical states. Relevant to our discussion, however, is the heterogeneity of psyche which Kristeva's *chora* reminds us of, the problem of homogeneous concept of language, and of the purity of logos.

For a brief survey of the criticism of Kristeva's *chora*, see Maria Margaroni's essay "'The Lost Foundation': Kristeva's Semiotic Chora and Its Ambiguous Legacy" (*Hypatia* 20, no. 1 [Winter 2005]: 78-98, pp. 78–79). As Margaroni points out, probably influenced by criticism, Kristeva has taken a distance from the use of the *chora* in her recent works. Margaroni's goal in the essay is to reinstate the original intention of Kristeva's *chora* project, which Margaroni identifies as embodying two issues: the first is an issue of the beginning, and the second is to explain the relationship between two seemingly contradictory entities, that is, an individual's desire and the social law. Critique of Kristeva's *chora* mostly goes on the first question, claiming that *chora* could posit certain ahistorical foundations. Our concern here lies with the second issue, as Margaroni puts it: "the *chora* constitutes an effort on her [Kristeva's] part to explore a mediating space that preserves the alterity of the entities engaged in the process of mediation" (p. 82).

25. Derrida, "Khōra," p. 94.

26. Jacques Derrida, "Privilege: Justificatory Title and Introductory Remarks," in *Who's Afraid of Philosophy? Right to Philosophy I*, trans. by Jan Plug (Stanford, CA: Stanford University Press, 2002), pp. 48 and 56.

27. Kristeva, *Revolution in Poetic Language*, p. 86.

28. Kristeva, *Revolution in Poetic Language*, p. 87.

29. Kristeva, *Revolution in Poetic Language*, p. 17.

30. Kristeva, *Revolution in Poetic Language*, p. 16.

31. Mikhail Bakhtin, *The Dialogic Imagination: Four Essays*, edited by Michael Holquist, trans. by Caryl Emerson and Michael Holquist (Austin: University of Texas Press, 1981), p. 270.

32. Bakhtin, *The Dialogic Imagination*, p. 257.

33. Bakhtin, *The Dialogic Imagination*, p. 271.

34. Bakhtin, *The Dialogic Imagination*, p. 271. For Bakhtin, the heteroglossia of verbal practice is the ground of the literary form novel, which he defines as a "poetic discourse, but one that does not fit within the frame provided by the concept of poetic discourse as it now exists" (p. 269). For Bakhtin, the novel is a literary genre that shows the rupture of the margins against the center, or of the centrifugal forces against the centripetal forces, through its dialogic imagination: "The novel can be defined as a diversity of social speech types (sometimes even diversity of languages) and a diversity of individual voices, artistically organized" (p. 262). Bakhtin further writes:

At the time when major divisions of the poetic genres were developing under the influence of the unifying, centralizing, centripetal forces of verbal-ideological life, the novel—and those artistic-prose genres that gravitate toward it—was being historically shaped by the current of decentralizing, centrifugal forces. At the time when poetry was accomplishing the task of cultural, national, and political centralization of the verbal-ideological world in the higher official socio-ideological levels, on the lower levels, on the stages of local fairs and at buffoon spectacles, the heteroglossia of the clown sounded forth, ridiculing all "languages" and dialects; there developed the literature of the *fabliaux* and *Schwänke* of street songs, folksayings, anecdotes, where there was no language-center at all, where there was to be found a lively play with the "languages" of poets, scholars, monks, knights and others, where all "languages" were masks and where no language could claim to be an authentic, incontestable face" (p. 273).

Bakhtin aptly explains here his theory of the novel in which the dispersing power of language is understood as challenges to the centralized monologue of a society and one's mode of thinking. This understanding of language in the context of the power structure in a society is comparable to the Zen *gong'an* use of language and its position with regard to normative narrative as well as Zen's relation to the traditional form of Buddhist literature.

35. Christopher Ives, *Zen Awakening and Society* (Honolulu: University of Hawaii Press, 1992), pp. 103–104.

36. Robert H. Sharf, "The Zen of Japanese Nationalism," in *Curators of the Buddha: The Study of Buddhism under Colonialism*, edited by Donald S. Lopez, Jr. (Chicago, IL: University of Chicago Press, 1995), 107–160, p. 107.

37. Victoria, Brian Daizen, *Zen at War*, 2nd Edition (Lanham, MD: Rowman and Littlefield, Inc., 2006), p. xiv.

38. Victoria, *Zen at War*, p. xiv.

39. Victoria, *Zen at War*, p. 60.

40. Admitting the importance of the study of Japanese Zen Buddhism's involvement with nationalism, imperialism, and militarism in our understanding of Zen Buddhism's capacity for social ethics, one should resist the temptation to generalize this phenomenon of "Japanese" Zen Buddhism as a characteristic feature of Zen in general. Japanese Zen militarism of the first half of the twentieth century reflects the history of Zen Buddhism in Japan, which is not shared by Zen Buddhism in other East Asian countries, namely China and Korea. From its early period, Japanese Zen Buddhism developed with a close connection with the warrior spirit and warrior class; the samurai's overcoming of the division between life and death found a philosophical, religious, and psychological support from Japanese Zen Buddhism. Any attempt to present Japanese Zen Buddhism's militarism as an incurable ethical pitfall of Zen Buddhism in general is misleading.

41. McRae, *Seeing through Zen*, p. 92.

42. McRae, *Seeing through Zen*, pp. 92–93. These arguments suggest that a consideration of the social dimension of Zen language enables us to open up a new reading of the tradition, which sometimes seriously challenges the so-far dominant claims about the tradition. For example, it has been claimed that Zen encounter dialogue took place "spontaneously," that the Tang dynasty was the "Golden Age" of Zen Buddhism when major Zen masters practiced encounter dialogues, and that the core of Zen lies in the non-linguistic nature of Zen language. These claims now confront the new claims that the spontaneity in Zen encounter dialogue was in fact "inscribed," that Zen Buddhism reached its climax during the Song period, instead of Tang, with the publications of *gong'an* texts, and that Zen enjoyed social power with the publication of *gong'an* texts. Identifying the Song period as the climax of Chinese Zen Buddhism, McRae writes: "By 'climax paradigm,' I mean a conceptual configuration by which Chan was inscribed in written texts, practiced by its adherents, and, by extension, understood as a religious entity by the Chinese population as a whole."

43. McRae, *Seeing through Zen*, p. 122.

44. McRae, *Seeing through Zen*, p. 121.

45. For the discussion of this, see chapter 4.

46. Huineng and Chinul offer us a good example of each incidence: Huineng is heavily based on the patriarchal authority, whereas Chinul relies more on the textual authority. In Chinul, all three occasions of his enlightenment experiences were en-

dorsed by the textual sources. Chinul's case was opposite to that of Huineng, in that Chinul did not have a specific teacher who endorsed his awakening. The lack of a patriarchal authority to endorse Chinul's awakening was complemented by textual authority. All awakenings were facilitated by texts: the first awakening took place when Chinul read a line from Huineng's *Platform Sūtra*, the second, with the *Huayan jing* and Li Tongxuan's *Exposition of the* Huayan Jing, and the third, with Dahui's *Yulu*. Even in Huineng's case, which is a supreme example of the rhetoric of the non-linguistic approach of the Zen school, his awakening was facilitated by the *Diamond Sūtra*. In fact, many major events in Zen history were accompanied by textual authority. Bodhidharma offers the *Lankāvatāra Sūtra* to Huike and advises him to transmit it to sentient beings. The well-known section in the *Transmission of the Lamp* describes that, after Bodhidharma chose Huike as his disciple to disseminate his teaching, offering him his "robe" and "bowl" as the symbols of the mind-to-mind transmission, Bodhidharma also offers Huike a text: "The Master further told him, 'I have with me the *Lankāvatāra Sūtra* in four scrolls which I will also give to you. This contains the essentials of the Tathāgata's spiritual doctrine and allows all sentient beings to develop enlightenment" (English translation by Sohaku Ogata, *The Transmission of the Lamp: Early Masters* [Wolfeboro, NH: Longwood Academic, 1990], p. 71). The subsequent replacement of the *Lankāvatāra Sūtra* with the *Diamond Sūtra*, and of the authority of Tathāgata with that of Zen patriarchs, is another intriguing issue that needs a further discussion to clarify the synergy between the text, patriarchal authority, and self-legitimation in the Zen tradition.

47. Yampolsky, *The Platform Sutra of the Sixth Patriarch*, p. 183.
48. Yampolsky, *The Platform Sutra of the Sixth Patriarch*, p. 179.
49. Yampolsky, *The Platform Sutra of the Sixth Patriarch*, p. 182.
50. For the discussion of the Ten Diseases, see chapter 4.
51. *HPC* 4.766b-c; Buswell, *The Korean Approach to Zen*, p. 339–340.

Chapter Seven: Modernity, Postmodernity, and The Question of Legitimation

1. Jean-François Lyotard, *The Postmodern Condition: A Report on Knowledge* (1979), trans. by Geoff Bennington and Brian Massumi (Minneapolis, MN: University of Minnesota Press, 1984), p. xxiv.
2. Lyotard, *The Postmodern Condition*, p. xxiii.
3. Lyotard, *The Postmodern Condition*, p. xxiii.
4. Lyotard, *The Postmodern Condition*, pp. xxiii–xxiv.
5. Lyotard, *The Postmodern Condition*, p. 9.
6. Jean-François Lyotard, *The Inhuman* (1988) (Stanford, CA: Stanford University Press, 1991), p. 2.
7. Lyotard, *The Inhuman*, p. 2.
8. See Jacques Derrida, "I Have a Taste for the Secret," in *A Taste for the Secret*, trans. by Giacomo Donis (Malden, MA: Blackwell Publishers, Inc, 2001), 1–92.
9. Jean-François Lyotard, "Answering the Question: What is Postmodernism?," trans. by Régis Durand, in *The Postmodern Condition*, 71-82, p. 77.

10. In *The Language of Post-Modern Architecture*, Charles Jencks marks the death of modern architecture as occurring on July 15, 1972, 3:32 p.m., when the Pruitt-Igoe Housing Project (1952–1955) in St. Louis was demolished with explosives. This was only twenty years after the modern building earned an award from the American Institute of Architects (Charles Jencks, *The Language of Post-Modern Architecture* [New York: Rizzoli, 1991], p. 23). The implication of this incident is as substantive as it is symbolic. Modern architecture was driven by the belief that efficiency and economy of functionalism could produce better environments. With a commitment to functionalism, modern architecture claimed that new and technocratically created buildings would replace the inefficacy of traditional structures, thus benefiting the entire society. Based on this concept, mass-produced housing projects, such as the Pruitt-Igoe, were proposed as solutions to social problems relating to housing. The limitations of attempts to mitigate human problems through rationally regulated and unified projects became clear very quickly, which led to the tragic ending of the building.

As Jencks describes it, the building consisted of "elegant slab blocks fourteen stories high with rational 'streets in the air' (which were safe from cars, but as it turned out, not safe from crime); . . . It had a separation of pedestrian and vehicular traffic, the provision of play space, and local amenities such as laundries, crèches and gossip centres,—all substitutes for traditional patterns. Moreover, its Purist style, its clean, salubrious, hospital metaphor, was meant to instill, by good example, corresponding virtues in the inhabitants. Good form was to lead to good conduct; the intelligent planning of abstract space was to promote healthy behavior . . . . such simplistic ideas, taken over from the philosophies of Rationalism, Behaviorism and Pragmatism proved as irrational as the philosophies themselves. Modern Architecture, as the son of the Enlightenment, was an heir to its congenital naiveté, too great and awe-inspiring to warrant refutation in a book on mere building" (pp. 23–4).

11. The desire to humanize the world and history is also found in literary modernism. Literary modernism has made efforts to express the disorder of the world by emphasizing the breakdown of traditional value systems, and, consequently, by highlighting a sense of alienation, despair, anarchy, and nihilism that modernists believe to be the fate of individuals in the modern world. The modernist world, in which the center has lost its power and disintegration has become rampant, has been represented through a stylistic device such as the stream of consciousness technique, in which one's sense of self, time, history, and memory become fragmented and discontinuous. The aesthetics of crisis—another name for modernism in the arts—however, has never lost its belief that fragmentation could not and should not remain fragmentary: gaps will be filled; bits and pieces of reality will be rearranged so that changes will find meaning within the universal goal of progress. In addition, disjointed time will recover its continuity within the introverted time of the writer's modernist narrative.

That the stream of consciousness technique captures the alinear, subjective, and disorderly time is only partially true, for the transgression of physical, linear time by internal, alinear, and subjective time is placed within the orderly time of the narrative. The stream of consciousness technique is, thus, double-edged: first, it "separates the presentation of consciousness from the chronological sequence of events"; then, it "enables the quality of a given state of mind to be investigated" so that "we do not need to wait for time to make the potential actual before we can see the whole" (David Daiches, *The Novel and the Modern World: Joseph Conrad, James Joyce, D. H. Lawrence, Virginia Woolf* [Chicago, IL: University of Chicago Press, 1960], p. 24). Further, the chaos of the world and the contingencies of history will find meaning in the newly created world of art. The breakdown of tradition will be replaced with the joy of the new technocratic world of the machine that one finds in the paintings of Italian Futurists and Russian Constructivists, among others.

12. Malcolm Bradbury and James McFarlane, "The Name and Nature of Modernism," *Modernism*, edited by Malcolm Bradbury and James McFarlane (Harmondsworth, England: Penguin, 1976), 19-55, p. 50.

13. Max Horkheimer and Theodor Adorno, *Dialectic of Enlightenment* (1944), trans. by John Cumming (New York: Continuum, 1993), p. xvi. See especially the first chapter, "Odyssey." Horkheimer further develops this idea in his *Eclipse of Reason* (New York, 1947), in which he demonstrates how little the world has become rationalized, despite a claim of "rationalization" in the philosophy of Enlightenment. Reason, as the title of his book suggests, is in eclipse. Also see Jürgen Habermas, "The Entwinement of Myth and Enlightenment: Max Horkheimer and Theodor Adorno," in *The Philosophical Discourse of Modernity: Twelve Lectures* (1985), trans. by Frederick G. Lawrence (Cambridge, MA: MIT Press, 1993), 106–130.

14. The reference here is to our earlier discussion of logos and mythos in chapter 2. Adorno and Horkheimer share Weber's criticism of the project of modernity, but distance themselves from his skepticism. They emphasize the importance of "objective reason," which balances out the one-sided ascendancy of instrumental, subjective reason. The two conceptions of reason, to Horkheimer, do not represent two separate and independent ways of the mind, although their opposition expresses antinomy. The task of philosophy is not to stubbornly play one against the other, but to foster a mutual critique in the intellectual realm and to prepare a reconciliation of the two in reality.

15. Jean-François Lyotard, *The Postmodern Explained* (1988), trans. by Don Barry, Bernadette Maher, Julian Pefanis, Virginia Spate, and Morgan Thomas (Minneapolis, MN: University of Minnesota Press,1992/1993), p. 18.

16. Horkheimer and Adorno, *Dialectic of Enlightenment*, p. 6.

17. Horkheimer, *Eclipse of Reason*, p. 104.

18. Horkheimer and Adorno, *Dialectic of Enlightenment*, p. 6.

19. Horkheimer and Adorno, *Dialectic of Enlightenment*, p. 286.

20. Julia Kristeva, *About Chinese Woman* (1974), trans. by Anita Barrows (New York: Marion Boyars, 1986), pp 11–33.

21. Derrida, *Of Grammatology*, see especially pp. 3–93.

22. Lyotard, *The Differend*, p. 9, #12.

23. Lyotard, *The Differend*, p. xi.

24. Lyotard, *The Differend*, p. 9, #12.

25. Lyotard, *The Differend*, p. xi.

26. Lyotard, *The Postmodern Condition*, p. 29.

27. Charles Newman, *The Post-Modern Aura: The Act of Fiction in an Age of Inflation* (Evanston, IL: Northwestern University Press, 1985), p. 10.

28. Newman, *The Post-Modern Aura*, p. 6.

29. Fredric Jameson, "Postmodernism and Consumer Society" (1982), in *The Anti-Aesthetic: Essays on Postmodern Culture*, edited by Hal Foster (Seattle: Bay Press, 1983), 111-125. In line with his emphasis on the fragmentary nature of postmodernism, Jameson also characterizes postmodernism as tending toward "pastiche."

30. See, for example, Dinesh D'Souza, *Illiberal Education: Political Correctness and the College Experience* (Ashland, OH: Ashbrook Publications, 1992); Arthur M. Schlesinger, Jr., *The Disuniting of America* (New York: W. W. Norton & Company, 1991).

31. The Lyotard-Habermas debate on the nature of postmodernism shows the scope of their difference in understanding the phenomenon called postmodernism. Lyotard's book, *The Postmodern Condition* (1979) represents a polemic against Habermas's *Legitimation Crisis* (1973, trans. by Thomas McCarthy [Boston: Beacon, 1975]); Habermas's concept of the postmodern in "Modernity-an Unfinished Project" (1980, re-titled as "Modernity versus Postmodernity," *New German* Critique 22 [Winter 1981]: 3-14) is criticized in Lyotard's "Answering the Question: What is Postmodernism?" (1982). Also see Richard Rorty, "Habermas and Lyotard on Postmodernity," in *Habermas and Modernity*, edited by Richard Bernstein (Cambridge, MA: MIT Press, 1985), 161-175, and Habermas' reply, "Questions and Counterquestions," in *Habermas and Modernity*, 192–216.

32. Habermas, "Modernity versus Postmodernity," pp. 8–9.

33. For Habermas's theory of postmodernism and communicative action, see *Legitimation Crisis* (1973), "Modernity versus Postmodernity," and *The Theory of Communicative Action: Lifeworld and System, A Critique of Functionalist Reason*, vol. II (1981), trans. by Thomas McCarthy (Boston: Beacon Press, 1987).

34. Lyotard, *The Postmodern Condition*, p. 61.

35. Lyotard, *The Postmodern Explained*, p. 35.

36. Lyotard, *The Postmodern Explained*, p. 19.

37. Lyotard, *The Postmodern Explained*, p. 18.

38. Lyotard, *The Postmodern Condition*, pp. 91–92.

39. Lyotard, "Discussions, or Phrasing 'after Auschwitz'," in *The Lyotard Reader*, edited by Andrew Benjamin (Cambridge: Basil Blackwell, 1989), 360-392, p. 360.

40. Lyotard, "Discussions, or Phrasing 'after Auschwitz'," p. 377.

41. Lyotard, "Answering the Question: What is Postmodernism?" p. 79.

42. Lyotard, "Answering the Question: What is Postmodernism?" p. 81.

43. Jean-François Lyotard, "The Sublime and the Avant-Garde," *The Inhuman*, p. 90.

44. Lyotard further expounds the characteristics of postmodernism as "the sublime," making reference to Kant's distinction between the beautiful and the sublime in his *Third Critique*. As opposed to the beautiful, which is bounded, the sublime is characterized by unboundedness, in Lyotard's term, "the unpresentable." The sublime is a feeling of the incommensurate, before which imagination's power of exhibition fails. When B. Newman titles his essay "The Sublime Is Now," which Lyotard discusses as an example of the postmodern sublime, this "now" is not that which one constitutes by consciousness. The "Sublime Is Now" should be understood as a question, 'Is it now?' or 'Is it happening?' (See Lyotard, "Newman: The Instant," in *The Inhuman*, pp. 78–88.)

45. Lyotard, *The Postmodern Condition*, p. xxv.

46. In this context, Derrida pays attention to Lyotard's desire to completely break up with modernity without "nostalgia." Nostalgia begins with the sense of loss. In our nostalgia, we read a desire for recuperation, along with a vague hope for the retrieval of what has been lost. Nostalgia, however, cannot be merely a matter of sentiment. At stake in our nostalgia is the issue of breaking: The breaking that is always in process, refusing to be a breaking up, the breaking that is an unfinished sentence. Nostalgia might be a badly regulated trace, but at issue is the question: Is a complete break-up possible? Derrida thus comments on Lyotard's style of "rupture with nostalgia (and with everything it brings or connotes) that is resolute," and, considers that this can be a symptom that, instead of breaking up with nostalgia, nostalgia is at work in Lyotard's efforts to completely break up with modernity (See Lyotard, "Discussions, or Phrasing 'after Auschwitz'," p. 388).

47. Madan Sarup, *An Introductory Guide to Post-structuralism and Postmodernism* (Athens, GA: University of Georgia Press, 1989), p. 133.

48. Linda Hutcheon, *A Poetics of Postmodernism: History, Theory, Fiction* (New York: Routledge, 1988), p. 20. Also see Linda Hutcheon, *The Politics of Postmodernism* (New York: Routledge, 1989), p. 14.

Chapter Eight: Postmodern Small Discourses and The Huayan World of Mutually Non-Interfering Phenomena

1. In the discussion of Huayan Buddhism, I translate *li* as noumenon and *shi* as phenomenon/phenomena following the translation of Thomas Cleary and Francis Cook. Noumenon and phenomena in this case have no relevance to Kantian philosophy. I will also occasionally use principle for *li* and particularities for *shi*.

2. Chengguan, *Huayan fajie xuanjing, T* 45.1883.672c; English translation by Thomas Cleary, "Mirror of the Mysteries of the Universe of the Hua-yen," in *Entry into the Inconceivable: An Introduction to Hua-yen Buddhism* (Honolulu: University of Hawaii Press, 1983), p. 74.

3. Francis H. Cook, "Fa-tsang's Treatise on the Five Doctrines: An Annotated Translation," Ph. D. Dissertation, University of Wisconsin, 1970, p. 2.

4. Carter J. Eckert, Ki-baek Lee, Young Ick Lew, Michael Robinson, and Edward W. Wagner, *Korea Old and New: A History* (Seoul: Ilcho'gak Publishers, 1990), pp. 50–51.

Ko Ikchin, a renowned scholar of Korean Huayan Buddhism, challenges this interpretation of historians, stating that the Huayan vision of the fourfold worldview is a purely religious paradigm and not a political theory. He claims that Huayan Buddhism's relationship with the authoritarian monarchy of Unified Silla should be understood through its religious dimension. The main Buddha in the *Huayan jing* is the Vairocana Buddha, the Buddha of Light. Koreans during the Silla, Ko contends, understood the Buddha of Light (Vairocana) as the God of the Sun, which in turn enables Koreans to identify Vairocana as the God of Heaven. The God of Heaven is a familiar figure to Koreans because of the similar figure existing in Shamanism, an indigenous religion of Korea. Ko also notes that the bodhisattva-king ideal in the *Huayan jing* made a great appeal to Silla kings who considered themselves as one of the bodhisattva-kings, who were also identified with the Sage King from the Heaven in the Shamanist tradition. Ko thus claims that "the world of Huayan gives a strong impression that it is a Buddhist version of the Shamanist world" and that this religious aspect of Huayan Buddhism was the central force for Silla Koreans to be attracted to Huayan Buddhism. See Ko Ikchin, "Pulgyo chŏk ch'ŭkmyŏn" (The Buddhist Aspects), in *Han'guk sasang sa taegye* (An Outline of the Intellectual History of Korea), vol. 1, edited by Ch'ŏrhak chonggyo yŏn'gusil (Sŏngnam, Korea: Han'guk chŏngsin munhwa yŏn'guwŏn, 1990), 177-202, pp. 191–192.

5. Fazang, *Wujiao zhang* T 45.1866.703 a; my translation here is somewhat different from that of Cook. For Cook's translation, see Cook, "Fa-tsang's Treatise on the Five Doctrines," p. 457.

6. Dushun, *Huayan wujiao zhiguan*, T 45.1867.512 b.

7. Dushun, *Huayan wujiao zhiguan*, T 45.1867.513a-b; Cleary, *Entry into the Inconceivable*, pp. 66-67. For Huayan thought in English, see Francis H. Cook, *Huayan Buddhism: The Jewel Net of Indra* (University Park, PA: Pennsylvania State University Press, 1977); Garma C. C. Chang, *The Buddhist Teaching of Totality: The Philosophy of Hwa Yen Buddhism* (University Park, PA: Pennsylvania State University Press, 1971/1991). Also see Robert M. Gimello, "Li T'ung-hsüan and the Practical Dimensions of Huayan," in *Studies in Ch'an and Huayan*, edited by Robert M. Gimello and Peter N. Gregory (Honolulu: University of Hawaii Press, 1983), 321–389.

8. Kang-nam Oh, "Dharmadhātu: An Introduction to Hua-yen Buddhism," *The Eastern Buddhist* 12, no. 2 (Oct 1979): 72-91, p. 73.

9. Oh, "Dharmadhātu," p. 74.

10. Oh, "Dharmadhātu," p. 74.

11. Oh, "Dharmadhātu," p. 77. For a discussion of the identification of *ālayavijñāna*, *tathāgatagarbha* and *citta* in the *Laṅkāvatāra-sūtra*, see Florin G. Sutton, *Existence and Enlightenment in the* Laṅkāvatāra-sūtra: *A Study in the Ontology and Epistemology of the Yogācāra School of Mahāyāna Buddhism* (Albany: State University of New York Press, 1991).

12. Chengguan, *Huayan fajie xuanjing*, T 45.1883.672c-673a; Cleary, "Mirror of the Mysteries of the Universe of the Hua-yen," pp. 74–75.

13. The problem became most noticeable in Zongmi (780-841), the Fifth Patriarch of Huayan. For a discussion of this issue in Zongmi, see Peter N. Gregory, "What Happened to the 'Perfect Teaching'? Another Look at Hua-yen Buddhist Hermeneutics," in *Buddhist Hermeneutics*, edited by Donald S. Lopez, Jr. (Honolulu: University of Hawaii Press, 1988), 207-230. See also a revised version in his book, *Tsung-mi and the Sinification of Buddhism* (Princeton, NJ: Princeton University Press, 1991), 154-170. Also see Liu Ming-Wood, "The Teaching of Fatsang: An Examination of Buddhist Metaphysics," Ph. D. dissertation, University of California at Los Angeles, 1979.

14. Chengguan, *Huayan fajie xuanjing*, T 45.1883.676 b; Cleary, *Mirror of the Mysteries of the Universe of the Hua-yen*, p. 91.

15. Chengguan, *Huayan fajie xuanjing*, T 45.1883.676 b; Cleary, *Mirror of the Mysteries of the Universe of the Hua-yen*, p. 92.

16. Collins, *Selfless Persons*, p. 116.

17. Chengguan, *Huayan fajie xuanjing,* *T* 45.1883.680ab; Cleary, "Mirror of the Mysteries of the Universe of the Hua-yen," p.111.

18. Fazang, *Wujiao zhang,* *T* 45.1866.474b; Cook, "Fa-Tsang's Treatise on the Five Doctrines," pp. 212–213.

19. Cook, "Fa-Tsang's Treatise on the Five Doctrines," p. 213.

20. English translation by Thomas Cleary, *The Flower Ornament Scripture: A Translation of the Avatamsaka Sutra* (Boston and London: Shambhala, 1993), pp. 1261–1262.

21. Cleary, *The Flower Ornament Scripture,* p. 1262.

22. Li Tongxuan, one of major commentators of the *Huayan jing* in the eighth century, offers a fully symbolic reading of the entire chapter. For example, in the section on the mariner Vaira, Li states, "The mariner Vaira in Chinese means 'self-reliant,' which indicates that he has come to be self-reliant; liberated from the ocean of life and death." Korean translation of the section by Chang Sunyong, *Sin Hwaŏm kyŏng ron* (The Exposition of the *Huayan jing* in the Eighty Fascicles), vol. 2 (Seoul: Tongguk yŏkkyŏngwŏn, 1997), pp. 417–422.

23. Cleary, *The Flower Ornament Scripture,* p. 1446.

24. Chengguan, *Huayan fajie xuanjing,* *T* 45.1883.676 b; Cleary, *Mirror of the Mysteries of the Universe of the Hua-yen,* p. 91.

25. A further discussion of aporia appears in chapter 10.

26. Nishida Kitarō, "Bashoteki ronri to shūkyōteki sekaikan," *Nishida Kitarō zenshū* (Complete Works of Nishida Kitarō), vol. 11 (Tokyo: Iwanami Shoten, 1975), p. 418; English translation, "The Logic of the Place of Nothingness and the Religious Worldview" in *Last Writings: Nothingness and the Religious Worldview*, trans. by David A. Dilworth (Honolulu: University of Hawaii Press, 1987), p. 85.

27. Nishida, "Bashoteki ronri to shūkyōteki sekaikan," p. 410; "The Logic of the Place of Nothingness and the Religious Worldview," p. 79.

28. Nishida, "Bashoteki ronri to shūkyōteki sekaikan," p. 411; "The Logic of the Place of Nothingness and the Religious Worldview," p. 80.

29. *Jingang banruo buloumi jing,* *T* 8.235.750b; *The Diamond Sutra and the Sutra of Hui-Neng,* trans. by A. F. Price and Wong Mou-lam (Boston: Shambhala, 1990), p. 33.

30. *Jingang banruo buloumi jing,* *T* 8.235.749a; *The Diamond Sutra and the Sutra of Hui-Neng,* p. 19.

Chapter Nine: Envisioning Zen Ethics Through Huayan Phenomenology

1. James Whitehill, "Buddhism and the Virtues," in *Contemporary Buddhist Ethics,* edited by Damien Keown (Richmond, Surrey: Curzon, 2000), 17-36, p. 17.

2. Daniel Palmer, "Masao Abe, Zen Buddhism, and Social Ethics," *Journal of Buddhist Ethics* 4 (1997): 112-137, p. 133–134.

3. *Kwŏnsu chŏnghye kyŏlsa mun* (Encouragement to Practice: The Compact of Samādhi and Prajñā Community), *HPC* 4.698a-708a, p. 4.698a.

4. Hyŏnghyo Kim, "Chinul sasang ŭi siljonsŏng kwa ponjilsŏng" (The Existential and Essential Dimensions in Chinul's Thought), in *Chinul ŭi sasang kwa*

kŭ hyŏndaejŏk ŭimi (Chinul's Thought and its Meaning in Our Time), edited by Han'guk chŏngsin munhwa yŏn'guwŏn (Pundang, Korea: Han'guk chŏngsin munhwa yŏn'guwŏn, 1996), 3-60, p. 8.

5. Kim, "Chinul sasang ŭi siljonsŏng kwa ponjilsŏng," p. 19.

6. Whitehill, "Buddhism and the Virtues," p. 21.

7. "The Brahmā Sutta," *The Book of the Kindred Sayings* (*Saṃyutta-nikāya*), vol. I, trans. by Mrs. Rhys Davids (Oxford: The Pali Text Society, 1999), pp. 171–172.

8. "The Brahmā Sutta," p. 173.

9. Sung Bae Park, "Ton'o tonsu ron" (The Theory of Sudden Awakening and Sudden Cultivation), *Paengnyŏn Pulgyo nonjip* 3 (1993): 201-254, pp. 217–224.

10. Kŏn'gi Kang, "Susimkyŏl ŭi ch'e'gye wa sasang" (The Structure and Thoughts in *Secrets on Cultivating the Mind*), *Pojo sasang* 12 (Feb 1999): 9-47, p. 43.

11. Pŏpchŏng, "Kanhaengsa" (A Statement upon Publication), *Pojo sasang* 1 (1987), p. 4.

12. Robert M. Gimello, "Songdae Sŏn Pulgyo wa Pojo ŭi ton'o chŏmsu" (Zen Buddhism during the Song Dynasty and Pojo's Sudden Awakening and Gradual Cultivation), trans. by Hosŏng Kim, *Pojo sasang* 4 (1990): 204-231, p. 231. Only the Korean translation (without the English original version) was published.

13. See Tŏkchin Yi, "Chinul ŭi sŏnggi sŏl e taehan ilgoch'al-Chungguk Hwaŏm kyohak kwa kwallyŏn hayŏ" (A Study of Chinul's Doctrine of Nature-Origination: in Relation to Chinese Huayan Teachings), *Pojo sasang* 13 (2002): 391-422; Sŏngyŏl Ch'oe "Pojo ŭi *Hwaŏm sin ron* yihae" (Pojo's Understanding of the *Huayan xin lun*), in *Chinul*, edited by Tŏkchin Yi (Seoul: Yŏmun sŏwŏn, 2002), 411-435; Chaeryong Sim, "Pojo kuksa Chinul ŭi *Wŏndon sŏngbul ron* sangsŏk" (An In-depth Interpretation of the National Master Chinul's *Wŏndon sŏngbul ron*), in *Chinul*, 436-464.

Robert M. Gimello offers an explanation of how Li Tongxuan's interpretation of the *Huayan jing* diverges from the Huayan philosophy of the early masters of Chinese Huayan Buddhism and considers why Li's exposition attained a recognition during the Song dynasty. See his "Li T'ung-hsüan and the Practical Dimensions of Huayan."

14. Jay L. Garfield, trans., *The Fundamental Wisdom of the Middle Way: Nāgārjuna's* Mūlamadhyamakakārikā (Oxford, New York: Oxford University Press, 1995), p.69, XXIV-18.

15. Ŭisang, *Hwaŏm ilsŭng pŏpkye to* (The Diagram of the Realm of Reality of the Huayan One Vehicle), *HPC* 2.1-8, p. 1a.

16. Ŭisang, *Hwaŏm ilsŭng pŏpkye to*, *HPC* 2.6b.

17. English translation by Buswell, *The Korean Approach to Zen*, p. 204-205.

18. English translation by Buswell, *The Korean Approach to Zen*, p. 216.

19. In her *Buddhism after Patriarchy: A Feminist History, Analysis, and Reconstruction of Buddhism*, Rita M. Gross writes:

> My primary task in this book is a feminist revalorization of Buddhism. In feminist theology in general, the task of "revalorization" involves working with the categories and concepts of a traditional religion in the light of feminist values. This task is double-edged, for on the one hand, feminist analysis of any major world religion reveals massive undercurrents of sexism and prejudice against women, especially in the realms of religious praxis. On the other hand, the very term "revalorization" contains an implicit judgment.

To revalorize is to have determined that, however sexist a religious tradition may be, it is not irreparably so. Revalorizing is, in fact doing that work of repairing the tradition, often bringing it much more into the line with its own fundamental values and vision than was its patriarchal form." ([Albany: State University of New York Press, 1993], p. 3.)

20. See my essay "Wisdom, Compassion, and Zen Social Ethics: the Case of Chinul, S'ŏngch'ŏl, and Minjung Buddhism in Korea," *Journal of Buddhist Ethics* 13 (2006): 1–26.

21. *Huayan jing*, *T* 10.293.845a.

22. Sŏngch'ŏl, *Chagi rŭl paro popssida* (Let's See Ourselves Clearly.) (Seoul: Changgyŏnggak, 1987), pp. 104–105.

Chapter Ten: The Ethics of Tension:
Toward Buddhist-Postmodern Ethics

1. David Wood, *The Step Back: Ethics and Politics after Deconstruction* (Albany: State University of New York Press, 2005), p. 4.

2. Wood, *The Step Back*, p. 1.

3. Lyotard, *The Postmodern Condition*, p. xxv.

4. Simon Critchley, *The Ethics of Deconstruction: Derrida and Levinas*, 2nd Edition (West Lafayette, IN: Purdue University Press, 1999), p. 2.

5. Critchley, *The Ethics of Deconstruction*, p. 2.

6. Wood, *The Step Back*, p. 5.

7. Lyotard, *The Postmodern Condition*, p. xxv.

8. Giovanna Borradori, *Philosophy in a Time of Terror: Dialogues with Jürgen Habermas and Jacques Derrida* (Chicago, IL: University of Chicago Press, 2003), p. 129.

9. Borradori, *Philosophy in a Time of Terror*, p. 129.

10. Borradori, *Philosophy in a Time of Terror*, p. 131-132.

11. Robert A. F. Thurman, trans., *The Holy Teaching of Vimalakīrti: A Mahāyāna Text* (University Park, PA: Pennsylvania State University Press, 1976/1994), p. 35.

12. Nishida, "Bashoteki ronri to shūkyōteki sekaikan," p. 411; Dilworth, "The Logic of the Place of Nothingness and the Religious Worldview," p. 80.

13. His Holiness the Dalai Lama and Victor Chan, *The Wisdom of Forgiveness: Intimate Conversations and Journeys* (New York: Riverhead Books, 2004), pp. 105-106.

14. *The Washington Post*, 27 January 2005. http://www.washingtonpost.com/ac2/wp-dyn/A40627-2005Jan27?langauge=printer. Visited on January 27, 2005.

15. *The Washington Post*, 27 January 2005. http://www.washingtonpost.com/ac2/wp-dyn/A40627-2005Jan27?langauge=printer. Visited on January 27, 2005.

16. Jacques Derrida, "On Forgiveness," in *Cosmopolitanism and Forgiveness*, trans. by Mark Dooley and Michael Hughes (London and New York: Routledge, 2003), p. 28.

17. Derrida, "On Forgiveness," p. 31-32.

18. The Dalai Lama and Chan, *The Wisdom of Forgiveness*, p. 111-112.

19. The Dalai Lama and Chan, *The Wisdom of Forgiveness*, p. 135.

20. The Dalai Lama and Chan, *The Wisdom of Forgiveness*, p. 135.

21. The Dalai Lama and Chan, *The Wisdom of Forgiveness*, p. 139.

22. Derrida, "I Have a Taste for the Secret," p. 13.

23. The Dalai Lama and Chan, *The Wisdom of Forgiveness*, p. 109.

24. Derrida, "On Forgiveness," p. 54-55.

25. The Dalai Lama and Chan, *The Wisdom of Forgiveness*, p. 112.

26. The Dalai Lama and Chan, *The Wisdom of Forgiveness*, p. 112.

27. Simon Critchley and Richard Kerney use the expression in the introduction to *On Cosmopolitanism and Forgiveness*: "We have to learn to forgive whilst knowing that true forgiveness only forgives the unforgivable. Justice must be restlessly negotiated in the conflict between these two imperatives. A justice that is always to be done" (p. xii).

28. Jacques Derrida, *Du droit à la philosophie* (Paris: Éditions Galilée, 1990), p. 41. English translation, *Who's Afraid of Philosophy?: Right to Philosophy I*, trans. by Jan Plug (Stanford, CA: Stanford University Press, 2002), p. 22.

29. Derrida, *Du droit à la philosophie*, p. 41; *Who's Afraid of Philosophy?*, p. 22.

30. Jacques Derrida, *Cosmopolites de tous les pays, encore un effort!* (Paris: Éditions Galilée, 1997), p. 42; English translation, "On Cosmopolitanism," in *On Cosmopolitanism and Forgiveness*, p. 17.

31. Derrida, *Cosmopolites de tous les pays, encore un effort!* p. 42; "On Cosmopolitanism," p. 17.

32. Derrida, "On Forgiveness," p. 55.

33. Wood, *The Step Back*, p. 2.

34. Pŏpsŏng, *Kanhwa kyŏrŭi ron kwahae,* p. 60.

Glossary of Chinese Characters

Banruo boluomiduo xinjing	般若波羅密多心經
Biyan lu	碧岩錄
budaiyuan	不待缘
buqi	不起
canju	參句
canyi	參意
ch'amgu (K)	參句
ch'amŭi (K)	參意
ch'ejunghyŏn (K)	體中玄
cha'gi ch'ŏrhak (K)	自己哲學
Chang ahan jing	長阿含經
changjwa purwa (K)	長座不臥
chasim (K)	自心
chasŏng (K)	自性
Chengguan	澄觀
chihae chip'yŏng (K)	智慧地平
chinsim (K)	眞心
Chinsim chiksŏl (K)	眞心直說
chŏmsu (K)	漸修
chongchong wujin	重重無盡
chŏnje (K)	全提
chosin (K)	祖信
Chuandeng lu	傳燈錄
chuch'ŭk (K)	周側
chŭksim chŭkpul (K)	卽心卽佛
Dabanniepan jing	大般涅槃經
Dahui	大慧
dasheng shijiao	大乘始敎
dasheng zhongjiao	大乘終敎

dunjiao	頓敎
Dushun	杜順
fa	法
Fada	法達
fajie guan	法界觀
fajie yuanqi	法界緣起
fajie	法界
Fandong jing	梵動經
Fazang	法藏
gong'an	公案
Guifeng Zongmi	圭峰宗密
hae'o (K)	解悟
Han'guk Pulgyo chŏnsŏ	韓國佛教全書
hoengjin pŏpkye (K)	橫盡法界
huatou	話頭
Huayan fajie xuanjing	華嚴法界玄鏡
Huayan jing	華嚴經
Huayan wujiao zhiguan	華嚴五敎止觀
Huayan	華嚴
Hua-yen	華嚴
huoju	活句
hwalgu (K)	活句
Hwaŏmnon chŏryo (K)	華嚴論節要
Hwaŏm (K)	華嚴
hyŏn (K)	玄
hyŏnjunghyŏn (K)	玄中玄
in'gong chinyŏ (K)	人空眞如
Jianyujing	箭喻經
jiaoxin	敎信
jie	界
Jingde chuandeng lu	景德傳燈錄
jue	覺
juzhongxuan	句中玄
Kanhwa kyŏrŭi ron (K)	看話決疑論
Kanhwa Sŏn (K)	看話禪
kongjŏk (K)	空寂
kujunghyŏn (K)	句中玄
kŭnbon po'gwang myŏngji (K)	根本普光明智
Kwŏnsu chŏnghye kyŏlsa mun (K)	勸修定慧結社文
kyŏnsŏng (K)	見性
Kyunyŏ (K)	均如
kyosin (K)	敎信
Li Tongxuan	李通玄
li	理
lifajie	理法界

Linji	臨濟
lishi wuai fajie	理事無碍法界
lishi wuai guan	理事無碍觀
Mazu	馬祖
Minjung Pulgyo (K)	民衆佛教
mongjung iryŏ (K)	夢中一如
niepan	涅槃
Nishida Kitarō	西田幾多朗
osim (K)	悟心
p'abyŏng (K)	破病
panjo (K)	返照
Pojo Chinul (K)	普照知訥
ponjilsŏng (K)	本質性
Pŏpchip pyŏrhaeng nok chŏryo pyŏngip sagi (K)	法集別行錄節要幷入私記
pŏpkong chinyŏ (K)	法空眞如
pŏpkye yŏn'gi (K)	法界緣起
Pŏpsŏng ke (K)	法性偈
pudongji Pul (K)	不動智佛
pulbyŏn (K)	不變
pulgong (K)	佛供
Qingjing jing	清淨經
rufajiepin	入法界品
sagu (K)	死句
samhyŏnmun (K)	三玄門
sang (K)	相
sanxuanmen	三玄門
shifajie	事法界
sifajie	四法界
siju	死句
shishi wuai fajie	事事無碍法界
shishi wuai	事事無碍
Shuiliao	水潦
sikjŏng (K)	識情
silch'ŏn chip'yŏng (K)	實踐地平
siljonsŏng (K)	實存性
sŏng (K)	性
sŏnggi (K)	性起
sŏngjŏng Pul (K)	性淨佛
Sŏnmun chŏngno (K)	禪門正路
sopŏpsin (K)	素法身
sujin pŏpkye (K)	竪盡法界
sungmyŏn iryŏ (K)	熟眠一如
Susimkyŏl (K)	修心訣
susun (K)	隨順
suyŏn (K)	隨緣

tizhongxuan	體中玄
T'oe'ong Sŏngch'ŏl (K)	退翁 性徹
tonggu pulch'ul (K)	洞口不出
tongjŏng iryŏ (K)	動靜一如
tongshi dunqi	同時頓起
tongshi hushe	同時互攝
tongti yiti	同體異體
tongti	同體
tonjŏmron (K)	頓漸論
ton'o (K)	頓悟
ton'o chŏmsu (K)	頓悟漸修
Wŏndon sŏngbul ron (K)	圓頓性佛論
wu huatou	無話頭
wuji	無記
Wujiao zhang	五敎章
wuming	無明
wushi Chan	無事禪
xiang	相
xiangji	相卽
Xianglin	香林
xiangru	相入
xiaochengjiao	小乘敎
xing	性
xingqi	性起
Xiu Huayan aozhi wangjin huanyuan guan	修華嚴奧旨妄盡還源觀
xuan	玄
xuanzhongxuan	玄中玄
yiti	異體
yong (K)	用
yŏngchi chisim (K)	靈知之心
yuanjiao	圓敎
Yuanjue jing	圓覺經
yuanqi	緣起
yulu	語錄
Za ahan jing	雜阿含經
Zhaozhou	趙州
Zhong ahan jing	中阿含經
zhoubian hanrong guan	周遍含容觀
zhenkong guan	眞空觀
zixing	自性
zuxin	祖信

Bibliography

Classical Sources

Banruo boluomiduo xinjing 般若波羅密多心經. *T* 8.251.848.

Biyan lu 碧巖錄. *T* 48.2003.139a-292a.

Chang ahan jing 長阿含經. *T* 1.1.1a-149c.

Chinsim chiksŏl 眞心直說. By Chinul 知訥. 1205. *HPC* 4.715c-723c.

Daban niepan jing 大般涅槃經. *T* 12.375.605a-852b.

Dahui yulu 大慧語錄. By Dahui 大慧. *T* 47.1998.811b-943a.

Dasheng qixin lun 大乘起信論. Attributed to Aśvaghoṣa. *T* 32.1666.576a.

Dafangguang fo huayan jing 大方廣佛華嚴經. Trans. by Śikṣānanda 實叉難陀. *T* 10.279.1b-444c.

Huayan fajie xuanjing 華嚴法界玄鏡. By Chengguan. 澄觀. *T* 45.1883.672c-673a.

Huayan wujiao zhiguan 華嚴五敎止觀. By Dushun 杜順. *T* 45.1867.509a-513c.

Hwaŏmnon chŏryo sŏ 華嚴論節要序. By Chinul 知訥. *HPC* 4.767c-768b.

Ilsŭng pŏpkyedo wŏnt'onggi 一乘法界圖圓通記. By Kyunyŏ 均如. *HPC* 4.1-39.

Jingang banruo buloumi jing 金剛般若波羅密經. *T* 8.235.748c-752c.

Jingde chuandeng lu 景德傳燈錄. By Daoyuan 道原. *T* 2076.51.196-467.

Kanhwa kyŏrŭi ron 看話決疑論. By Chinul 知訥. *HPC* 4.732c-737c.

Kwŏnsu chŏnghye kyŏlsamun 勸修定慧結社文. By Chinul 知訥. *HPB* 4.698a-708a.

Linji lu 臨濟錄. *T* 47.1985.496b-506c.

Liuzu tanjing 六祖壇經. Attributed to Huineng 慧能. *T* 48.2008.346a-362b.

Nanzong dunjiao zuishang dasheng mahe panruo bolou mijing: Liuzu Huineng dashi yu Shaozhou Dafansi shifa tanjing. 南宗頓教最上大乘摩訶般若波羅蜜經六祖惠能大師於韶州大梵寺施法壇經. Attributed to Huineng 慧能. *T* 48.2007.337a-345b.

Pŏpchip pyŏrhaeng nok chŏryo pyŏngip sagi 法集別行錄節要并入私記. By Chinul 知訥. *HPC* 4.741a-767b.

Pulsŏl panya paramilda simgyŏng ch'an 佛說般若波羅密多心經贊. *By Wŏnch'ŭk* 圓測. *HPC* 1.1a-15a

255

Sŏn'ga kuigam 禪家龜鑑. By Hujŏng 休靜. *HPC* 7.634c-646c.

Susim kyŏl 修心訣. By Chinul 知訥. *HPB* 4.708b-714a.

Wŏndon sŏngbul ron 圓頓成佛論. By Chinul 知訥. *HPC* 4. 724a-732b

Wujiao zhang 五教章. By Fazang 法藏. *T* 45.1866.477a-509a.

Wumen guan 無門關. By Wumen 無門. *T* 48.2005292a-299c.

Xin huayan jing lun 新華嚴經論. By Li Tongxuan 李通玄. *T* 36.1739.721-1007.

Xiu huayan aozhi wangjin huanyuan guan 修華嚴奧旨妄盡還源觀. By Fazang 法藏. *T* 45.1876.637a-641a.

Xu chuangdeng lu 續傳燈錄 *T* 51.2077.469a-714c.

Yuanjue jing 圓覺經 (Full title: *Dafangguang yuanjue xiuduluo liaoyi jing* 大方廣圓覺修多羅了義經). *T* 17.842.913a-922a.

Za ahan jing 雜阿含經. *T* 2.99.1a-373b.

Zhong ahan jing 中阿含經. *T* 1.26.421a-809c.

Modern and Contemporary Sources

Abe, Masao. *Zen and Western Thought.* Edited by William R. LaFleur. Honolulu: University of Hawaii Press, 1985.

———. *Zen and the Modern World: A Third Sequel to Zen and Western Thought.* Edited by Steven Heine. Honolulu HA: University of Hawaii Press, 2003.

Aitken, Robert, trans. *The Gateless Barrier: The Wu-men Kuan.* New York: North Point Press, 1997.

Bakhtin, Mikhail M. *The Dialogic Imagination: Four Essays.* Edited by Michael Holquist. Trans. by Caryl Emerson and Michael Holquist. Austin: University of Texas Press, 1981.

Barthes, Roland. *The Empire of Signs* (1970). Trans. Richard Howard. New York: Hill and Wang, 1982.

Batchelor, Stephen. *The Awakening of the West: The Encounter of Buddhism and Western Culture.* Berkeley, CA: Parallax Press, 1994.

Beardsworth, Richard. *Derrida & the Political.* London and New York: Routledge, 1996.

Bell, Daniel. *The Coming of Post-Industrial Society: A Venture in Social Forecasting.* New York: Basic Books, Inc., 1973.

Bennington, Geoffrey. *Interrupting Derrida.* London and New York: Routledge, 2000.

Bernstein, Richard, ed. *Habermas and Modernity.* Cambridge, MA: MIT Press, 1985.

Berry, Philippa and Andrew Wernick, eds. *Shadow of Spirit: Postmodernism and Religion.* London and New York: Routledge, 1992.

Borradori, Giovanna. *Philosophy in a Time of Terror: Dialogues with Jürgen Habermas and Jacques Derrida.* Chicago, IL: University of Chicago Press, 2003.

Bradbury, Malcolm and James McFarlane, eds. *Modernism.* Harmondsworth, England: Penguin, 1976.

Buswell, Robert E., Jr . "The 'Short-cut' Approach of K'an-hua Meditation: The Evolution of a Practical Subitism in Chinese Zen Buddhism." In *Sudden and Gradual:*

Approaches to Enlightenment in Chinese Thought, edited by Peter Gregory, 321–377. Honolulu: University of Hawaii Press, 1987.

———. "Chinul's Systematization of Chinese Meditative Techniques in Korean Sŏn Buddhism." In *Traditions of Meditation in Chinese Buddhism*, edited by Peter Gregory, 199–242.

———. "Ch'an Hermeneutics: A Korean View." In *Buddhist Hermeneutics*, edited by Donald S. Lopez, 231-256. Honolulu: University of Hawaii Press, 1988.

———, trans. *The Korean Approach to Zen: Collected Works of Chinul.* Honolulu: University of Hawaii Press, 1983.

Ch'ae Chŏngsu 채정수. "Taehye ŭi *Sŏchang* kwa Pojo Sŏn" 대혜의 <서장>과 보조선 (Dahui's *Letters* and Pojo Zen). *Pojo Sasang* 2 (November 1988): 289–304.

Chan, Wing-tsit, ed. *A Source Book in Chinese Philosophy.* Princeton, NJ: Princeton University Press, 1963.

Chang Kyehwan 장계환. "Chungguk Hwaŏm kyohak ŭi sŏnggi sasang yŏn'gu" 中國 華嚴教學의 性起思想 研究 (A Study of the Doctrine of Nature-Origination in Chinese Huayan Teachings). *Pulgyo hakpo* 30 (1993): 241–261.

Chang, Garma C. C. *The Buddhist Teaching of Totality: The Philosophy of Hwa Yen Buddhism.* University Park, PA: Pennsylvania State University Press, 1971/1991.

Ch'oe Sŏngyŏl 최성렬. "Pojo ŭi Hwaŏm sin ron yihae" 보조의 <화엄신론> 이해 (Pojo's Understanding of the *Huayan xin lun*). In *Chinul*, edited by Tŏkchin Yi, 411–435. Seoul: Yŏmun sŏwŏn, 2002.

Chŏn Haeju 全海住. *Ŭisang Hwaŏm sasangsa yŏn'gu* 義湘華嚴思想史研究 (A Study of the Intellectual History of Ŭisang's Huayan Thought). Seoul: Minjoksa, 1992.

Chŏng Sunil 鄭舜日. "Chiŏm ŭi Hwaŏm sŏnggi sasang" 智儼의 華嚴性起思想 (Zhiyan's Thoughts on Huayan Nature-Origination). *Han'guk Pulgyohak* 12 (1987): 99–128.

Clarke, J. J. *Oriental Enlightenment: The Encounter between Asian and Western Thought.* London and New York: Routledge, 1997.

Cleary, Thomas, trans. *The Flower Ornament Scripture: A Translation of the Avantamsaka Sutra.* Boston and London: Shambhala, 1993.

Cleary, Thomas, trans. *Unlocking the Zen Koan: A New Translation of the Zen Classic Wumenguan.* Berkeley, CA: North Atlantic Books, 1997.

———, trans. *Entry into the Inconceivable: An Introduction to Hua-yen Buddhism.* Honolulu: University of Hawaii Press, 1983.

Cleary, Thomas and J. C. Cleary, trans. *The Blue Cliff Record.* Boston: Shambhala, 1992.

Collins, Steven. *Selfless Persons: Imagery and Thought in Theravāda Buddhism.* Cambridge: Cambridge University Press, 1982.

Cook, Francis H. "Fa-tsang's Treatise on the Five Doctrines: An Annotated Translation." Ph. D. Dissertation. University of Wisconsin, 1970.

———. *Hua-yen Buddhism: The Jewel Net of Indra.* University Park, PA: Pennsylvania State University Press, 1977.

Critchley, Simon. *The Ethics of Deconstruction: Derrida and Levinas*, 2nd Edition. West Lafayette, IN: Purdue University Press, 1999.

Cruise, Henry. "Early Buddhism: Some Recent Misconceptions." *Philosophy East and West* 32, no. 2 (April 1983): 149–166.

D'Souza, Dinesh. *Illiberal Education: Political Correctness and the College Experience*. Ashland, OH: Ashbrook Publications, 1992.

Daiches, David. *The Novel and the Modern World: Joseph Conrad, James Joyce, D. H. Lawrence, Virginia Woolf*. Chicago, IL: University of Chicago Press, 1960.

Dalai Lama and Victor Chan, *The Wisdom of Forgiveness: Intimate Conversations and Journeys*. New York: Riverhead Books, 2004.

de Jong, J. W. *A Brief History of Buddhist Studies in Europe and America*. New Delhi, 1983.

De Man, Paul. "Phenomenality and Materiality in Kant." In *The Textual Sublime: Deconstruction and Its Differences*, edited by Hugh J. Silverman and Gary E. Aylesworth, 87–108. Albany: State University of New York Press, 1990.

Derrida, Jacques. *De la grammatologie*. Paris: Les Éditions de Minuit, 1967.

———. *Of Grammatology* (1967). Trans. Gayatri Chakravorty Spivak. Baltimore and London: Johns Hopkins University Press, 1976.

———. *Positions*. Trans. Alban Bass. Chicago, IL: University of Chicago Press, 1981.

———. "Restitutions." In *The Truth in Painting* (1978). Trans. Geoff Bennington and Ian McLeod, 255–283. Chicago, IL: University of Chicago Press, 1987.

———. *Du droit à la philosophie*. Paris: Éditions Galilée, 1990.

———. "Force of Law: The 'Mystical Foundation of Authority'." In *Deconstruction and the Possibility of Justice*. Edited by Drucilla Cornell, Michel Rosenfeld, and David Gray Carlson, 3–67. New York and London: Routledge, 1992.

———. *Aporias*. Trans. Thomas Dutoit. Stanford, CA: Stanford University Press, 1993.

———. "Khōra" (1993). In *On the Name*, edited by Thomas Dutoit, trans. by David Wood, John P. Leavey, Jr., and Ian McLeod, 87–127. Stanford, CA: Stanford University Press, 1995.

———. *Cosmopolites de tous les pays, encore un effort!* Paris: Éditions Galilée, 1997.

———. *Of Hospitality: Anne Dufourmantelle invites Jacques Derrida to respond* (1997). Trans. Rachel Bowlby. Stanford, CA: Stanford University Press, 2000.

———. *A Taste for the Secret*. Trans. Giacomo Donis. Malden, MA: Blackwell Publishers, Inc, 2001.

———. *On Cosmopolitanism and Forgiveness*. Trans. Mark Dooley and Michael Hughes. London and New York: Routledge, 2002.

———. *Who's Afraid of Philosophy? Right to Philosophy I*. Trans. Jan Plug. Stanford, CA: Stanford University Press, 2002.

———. *Ethics, Institutions, and the Right to Philosophy*. Edited and trans. by Peter Pericles Trifonas. Lanham, Boulder, New York, Oxford: Rowman & Littlefield Publishers, Inc., 2002.

Descartes, René. *Discourse on the Method*, bilingual edition. Trans. George Heffernan. Notre Dame: University of Notre Dame Press, 1994.

———. *Meditations on First Philosophy*. Trans. Donald A. Cress. Indianapolis: Hackett Publishing Company, 1993.

Droit, Roger-Pol. *Le culte du néant: Les philosophes et le bouddha*. Paris: Éditions du Seuil, 1997.

———. *The Cult of Nothingness: The Philosophers and the Buddha*. Trans. David Streight and Pamela Vohnson. Chapel Hill and London: University of North Carolina Press, 2003.

Dumoulin, Heinrich. *Zen Buddhism in the 20th Century*. Trans. Joseph S. O'Leary. New York: Weatherhill, 1992.

Eckert, Carter J. and Ki-baek Lee, Young Ick Lew, Michael Robinson, Edward W. Wagner. *Korea Old and New: A History*. Seoul: Ilcho'gak Publishers, 1990.

Fader, Larry A. "Zen in the West: Historical and Philosophical Implications of the 1893 Parliament of Religions." *The Eastern Buddhist* 15, no. 1 (Spring 1982): 122–145.

Faure, Bernard. *The Rhetoric of Immediacy: A Cultural Critique of Chan/Zen Buddhism*. Princeton, NJ: Princeton University Press, 1991.

———. *Chan Insights and Oversights: An Epistemological Critique of the Chan Tradition*. Princeton, NJ: Princeton University Press, 1993.

———. *Double Exposure: Cutting Across Buddhist and Western Discourses*. Trans. Janet Lloyd. Stanford, CA: Stanford University Press, 2004.

Feist, Elisabeth. "Martin Heidegger and the East." *Philosophy East and West* 20 (1970): 247–263.

Ferraris, Maurizio. *History of Hermeneutics* (1988). Trans. Luca Somigli. New Jersey: Humanities Press, 1996.

Foster, Hal, ed. *The Anti-Aesthetic: Essays on Postmodern Culture*. Seattle: Bay Press, 1983.

Foti, Veronique. "Heidegger and the Way of Art: The Empty Origin and Contemporary Abstraction." *Continental Philosophy Review* 31 (1998): 337–351.

Foulk, Griffith T. "Myth, Ritual, and Monastic Practice in Sung Ch'an Buddhism." In *Religion and Society in T'ang and Sung China*, edited by Patricia Buckley Ebrey and Peter N. Gregory, 147–208. Honolulu: University of Hawaii Press, 1995.

———. "Sung Controversies Concerning the 'Separate Transmission' of Ch'an." In *Buddhism in the Sung*, edited by Peter N. Gregory and Daniel A. Getz, Jr., 220-294. Honolulu: University of Hawaii Press, 1999.

Freud, Sigmund. "The Dissection of the Psychical Personality." P. 80 in *The Standard Edition of the Complete Psychological Works of Sigmund Freud*, edited and translated by James Strachey et al., Vol. 22. London: The Hogarth Press, 1952, 1974.

Garfield, Jay L. trans., *The Fundamental Wisdom of the Middle Way: Nāgārjuna's Mūlamadhyamakakārikā*. New York and Oxford: Oxford University Press, 1995.

Gilson, Etienne. *God and Philosophy*. New Haven, CT: Yale University Press, 1941.

Gimello, Robert M. "Li T'ung-hsüan and the Practical Dimensions of Huayan." In *Studies in Ch'an and Huayan*, edited by Robert M. Gimello and Peter N. Gregory, 321–389. Honolulu: University of Hawaii Press, 1983.

———. "Songdae Sŏn Pulgyo wa Pojo ǔi ton'o chŏmsu" 宋代 禪佛教와 普照의 頓悟漸修 (Zen Buddhism during the Song Dynasty and Pojo's Sudden Awakening and Gradual Cultivation). Trans. Hosŏng Kim. *Pojo sasang* 4 (1990): 204–231.

Gimello, Robert M. and Peter N. Gregory, eds. *Studies in Ch'an and Huayan.* Honolulu: University of Hawaii Press, 1983.

Gregory, Peter N. *Tsung-mi and the Sinification of Buddhism.* Princeton, NJ: Princeton University Press, 1991.

————, ed. *Traditions of Meditation in Chinese Buddhism.* Honolulu: University of Hawaii Press, 1986.

————, ed. *Sudden and Gradual: Approaches to Enlightenment in Chinese Thought.* Honolulu: University of Hawaii Press, 1987.

Gregory, Peter N. and Daniel A. Getz, Jr., eds. *Buddhism in the Sung.* Honolulu: University of Hawaii Press, 1999.

Habermas, Jürgen. *Legitimation Crisis* (1973). Trans. Thomas McCarthy. Boston: Beacon, 1975.

————. *The Theory of Communicative Action: Lifeworld and System, a Critique of Functionalist Reason,* vol. II (1981). Trans. Thomas McCarthy. Boston: Beacon Press, 1987.

————. "Modernity versus Postmodernity." *New German Critique* 22 (Winter 1981): 3–14.

————. *The Philosophical Discourse of Modernity: Twelve Lectures* (1985). Trans. Frederick G. Lawrence. Cambridge, MA: MIT Press, 1993.

Haeju sŭnim (Chŏn Haeju) 海住. *Hwaŏm ŭi segye* 화엄의 세계 (The World of Huayan). Seoul: Minjoksa, 1998.

Han Hyŏngjo 한형조. *Mumun'gwan, hogŭn, 'nŏ'nŭn nu'gu'nya'* 무문관, 혹은 너는 누구냐? (*The Gateless Gate,* or "Who Are You?"). Seoul: Yŏ'si'a'mun, 1999.

Harvey, Peter. *An Introduction to Buddhist Ethics.* Cambridge, UK: Cambridge University Press, 2000.

————. *Vorlesungen über die Philosophie der Religion.* Hrsg. von Georg Lasson. Hamburg: Felix Meiner, 1966.

————. *Phenomenology of Spirit.* Trans. A.V. Miller. London: Oxford University Press, 1977.

Hegel, G. W. F. *The Encyclopedia Logic.* Trans. T. F. Geraets, W. A. Suchting, and H. S. Harris. Indianapolis: Hackett, 1991.

————. *The Philosophy of History.* Trans. J. Sibree. Buffalo: Prometheus Books, 1991.

————. *Lectures on the Philosophy of Religion,* 3 vols. Edited by Peter C. Hodgson. Trans. R. F. Brown, P. C. Hodgson, and J. M. Stewart with the assistance of H. S. Harris. Berkeley, CA: University of California Press, 1995.

Heidegger, Martin. *An Introduction to Metaphysics* (1935/1953). Trans. Ralph Manheim. New Haven, CT: Yale University Press, 1959.

————. "A Dialogue on Language." In *On the Way to Language* (1957). Trans. Peter D. Hertz, 1–54. New York: Harper San Francisco, 1971.

————. "The Origin of the Work of Art." In *Poetry, Language, Thought.* Trans. Albert Hofstadter, 15–87. New York: Harper & Row, Publishers, 1971.

————. "The End of Philosophy and the Task of Thinking." In *On Time and Being* (1964). Trans. Joan Stambaugh. New York, Hagerstown, San Francisco, London: Harper & Row, Publishers, 1972.

————. *Martin Heidegger: Basic Writings.* Edited by David Farrell Krell. San Francisco: Harper Collins Publishers, 1993.

Heine, Steven. *Existential and Ontological Dimensions of Time in Heidegger and Dōgen.* Albany: State University of New York Press, 1983.

————. *Dōgen and the Kōan Tradition: A Tale of Two Shōbōgenzō Texts.* Albany: State University of New York Press, 1994.

————. "Zen Buddhist Rights and Wrongs." A paper presented at the Eastern Division Annual Meeting of the American Philosophical Association. December 28, 2006. Washington DC.

Heine, Steven and Dale S. Wright, eds. *The Kōan: Texts and Contexts in Zen Buddhism.* New York: Oxford University Press, 2000.

Heisig, James W. and John C. Maraldo, eds. *Rude Awakenings: Zen, the Kyoto School, and the Question of Nationalism.* Honolulu: University of Hawaii Press, 1994.

Hick, John. *Disputed Questions in Theology and the Philosophy of Religion.* New Haven, CT: Yale University Press, 1993.

————. *Fifth Dimension: an Exploration of the Spiritual Realm.* Oxford: Oneworld, 2004.

Horkheimer, Max. *Eclipse of Reason.* New York: Oxford University Press, 1947.

Horkheimer, Max and Theodor Adorno. *Dialectic of Enlightenment* (1944). Trans. John Cumming. New York: Continuum, 1993.

Hsieh, Ding-hwa Evelyn. "Yuan-wu K'o-ch'in's (1063-1135) Teaching of Zen Kung-an Practice: A Transition from the Literary Study of Ch'an Kung-an to the Practical K'an-hua Ch'an." *Journal of the International Association of Buddhist Studies* 17, no.1 (Summer 1994): 66–95.

Huh Woo Sung 허우성. "Chinul ŭi yulli sasang ŭi t'ŭksŏng kwa han'gye: Taehye Chonggo rŭl maegyero" 지눌의 윤리 사상의 특성과 한계-대혜 종고를 매개로 (Characteristics and Limitations of Chinulean Ethics: discussed in relation to Dahui Zonggao). In *Chinul ŭi sasang kwa kŭ hyŏndaejŏk ŭimi,* edited by Han'guk ch'ŏngsin munhwa yŏn'guwŏn, 123–192. Pundang, Korea: Han'guk chŏngsin munhwa yŏn'guwŏn, 1996.

Hutcheon, Linda. *A Poetics of Postmodernism: History, Theory, Fiction.* New York: Routledge, 1988.

————. *The Politics of Postmodernism.* New York: Routledge, 1989.

Ives, Christopher. *Zen Awakening and Society.* Honolulu: University of Hawaii Press, 1992.

Jaeschke, Walter. "Philosophical Theology and Philosophy of Religion." In *New Perspectives on Hegel's Philosophy of Religion,* edited by David Kolb, 1–18. Albany: State University of New York Press, 1992.

Jameson, Fredric. "Postmodernism and Consumer Society." In *The Anti-Aesthetic: Essays on Postmodern Culture,* edited by Hal Foster, 111-125. Seattle: Bay Press, 1983.

Jencks, Charles. *The Language of Post-Modern Architecture.* New York: Rizzoli, 1991.

Jeong Se Geun 정세근. "Mu ŭi kamŭng" 無의 感應 (Empathy of Nothing). In *Noja esŏ terida kkaji: to'ga ch'ŏrhak kwa sŏyang ch'ŏrhak ŭi mannam* 노자에서 데리다까지: 도가철학과 서양철학의 만남 (From Laozi to Derrida: the Encounter between Daoist and Western Philosophy), edited by Han'guk to'ga ch'ŏrhakhoe, 245–264. Seoul: Yemun sŏwŏn, 2001.

Jones, Ken. *The New Social Face of Buddhism: A Call to Action.* Boston: Wisdom Publications, 2003.

Judovitz, Dalia. "Derrida and Descartes: Economizing Thought." In *Derrida and Deconstruction,* edited by Hugh J. Silverman, 40–58. New York: Routledge, 1989.

Kalupahana, David J. *Buddhist Philosophy: A Historical Analysis.* Honolulu: University of Hawaii Press, 1976.

———. *Nāgārjuna: The Philosophy of the Middle Path.* Albany: State University of New York Press, 1986.

———. *A History of Buddhist Philosophy: Continuity and Discontinuities.* Honolulu: University of Hawaii Press, 1992.

———. *Ethics in Early Buddhism.* Honolulu: University of Hawaii Press, 1995.

Kang Kŏn'gi 강건기. "Susimkyŏl ŭi ch'e'gye wa sasang" 수심결의 체계와 사상 (The Structure and Thoughts in *Secrets on Cultivating the Mind*). *Pojo sasang* 12 (Feb 1999): 9–47.

Kang Kŏn'gi and Kim Hosŏng, eds. 姜健基, 金浩星. *Kkaedarŭm, ton'o chŏmsu in'ga ton'o tonsu in'ga* (Enlightenment: Is it Sudden Enlightenment with Gradual Cultivation or Is it Sudden Enlightenment with Sudden Cultivation?). Seoul: Minjoksa, 1992.

Kant, Immanuel. *Critique of Judgment* (1790). Trans. Werner S. Pluhar. Indianapolis: Hackett Publishing Company, 1987.

Kapstein, Matthew. "The Trouble with Truth: Heidegger on Aletheia, Buddhist Thinkers on Satya." *Journal of Indian Council of Philosophical Research* 9, no. 2 (1992): 69–85.

Kasulis, Thomas, P. *Zen Person Zen Action.* Honolulu: University of Hawaii Press, 1981.

———. *Intimacy or Integrity: Philosophy and Cultural Difference.* Honolulu: University of Hawaii Press, 2002.

Käufer, Stephan. "The Nothing and the Ontological Difference in Heidegger's 'What is Metaphysics?'" *Inquiry* 48, no. 6 (December 2005): 482–506.

Kaufmann, Walter. *Existentialism from Dostoevsky to Sartre.* New York: New American Library, 1975.

Keel Hee-Sung 길희성. "Minjung Pulgyo, Sŏn, kŭri'go sahoe yullijŏk kwansim" 민중불교, 선, 그리고 사회 윤리적 관심 (Buddhism for the Masses, Zen, and Socio-Ethical Concerns). *Chonggyo yŏn'gu* (1988): 27–40.

Keown, Damien. *The Nature of Buddhist Ethics.* London: Palgrave, 1999.

———. *Contemporary Buddhist Ethics.* Richmond, Great Britain: Curzon Press, 2000.

Kim Chonguk 김종욱. *Haidegŏ wa hyŏngi sanghak, kŭrigo Pulgyo* 하이데거와 형이상학, 그리고 불교 (Heidegger, Metaphysics, and Buddhism). Seoul: Ch'ŏrhak kwa hyŏnsil, 2003.

Kim Hosŏng. 김호성. "Chŏja ŭi pujae wa Pulgyo haesŏkhak" 저자의 부재와 불교 해석학 (The Absence of the Author and Buddhist Hermeneutics). *Pulgyo hakpo* 35, no. 1 (1998): 187-206.

————, trans. 김호성. "Kanhwa kyŏrŭi ron yŏkchu: Hwaŏm kwa Kanhwa Sŏn ŭi pyŏnjŭngbŏp" 간화결의론 역주: 화엄과 간화선의 변증법 (Translation with Commentaries of the *Treatise on Resolving Doubts about Huatou Meditation*: the Dialectic of Huayan and Kanhua Zen). *Pojo sasang* 9 (1995): 137–172.

Kim Hyŏnghyo. 김형효. "Chinul sasang ŭi siljonsŏng kwa ponjilsŏng" 지눌사상 의 실존성과 본질성. (The Existential and Essential Dimensions in Chinul's Thought). In *Chinul ŭi sasang kwa kŭ hyŏndaejŏk ŭimi*. 知訥의 사상과 그 현 대적 의미. (Chinul's Thought and Its Meaning in Our Time), edited by Han'guk ch'ŏngsin munhwa yŏn'guwŏn, 3–60. Pundang, Korea: Han'guk chŏngsin mun-hwa yŏn'guwŏn, 1996.

————. *Haidegŏ wa maŭm ŭi ch'ŏrhak* 하이데거와 마음의 철학 (Heidegger and the Philosophy of Mind). Seoul: Ch'ŏnggye, 2000.

————. *Haidegŏ wa Hwaŏm ŭi sayu* 하이데거와 화엄의 사유 (Heidegger and the Huayan Mode of Thinking). Seoul: Ch'ŏnggye, 2002.

Kim Pangryong 김방룡. "Kanhwa Sŏn kwa Hwaŏm, tanjŏl ŭl nŏmŏ hoet'ong ŭro" 간화선과 화엄, 단절을 넘어 회통으로 (Kanhua Zen and Huayan, beyond the Separation toward a Synthesis). *Pulgyo p'yŏngron* 24 (Autumn, 2005): 194–217.

————. *Pojo Chinul ŭi sasang kwa yonghyang* 보조지눌의 사상과 영향 (The Thoughts and Influences of Pojo Chinul). Seoul: Pogosa, 2006.

Kim Sangil 김상일. "Ŭisang kwa Pŏpchang ŭi Hwaŏm Pulgyo sasang pi'gyo" 의 상과 법장의 화엄불교사상 비교 (Comparative Study of Huayan Buddhist Thoughts of Ŭisang and Fazang). *Hansin nonmunjip* 6 (1989): 165–184.

Kim Talchin, trans. 金達鎭. *Pojo kuksa chŏnsŏ* 보조국사전서 (Complete Works of National Master Pojo). Seoul: Koryŏwŏn, 1987.

Ko Ikchin 高翊晉. "Pulgyo chŏk ch'ŭkmyŏn" 佛教的側面 (Buddhist Aspects [of Korean Thought]). In *Han'guk sasang sa taegye* 韓國思想史大系 (An Outline of the Intellectual History of Korea), vol. 1, edited by Ch'ŏrhak chonggyo yŏn'gusil, 177–202. Sŏngnam, Korea: Han'guk chŏngsin munhwa yŏn'guwŏn, 1990.

————, ed., trans. *Han'gŭl Ahamgyŏng* 한글 아함경 (Āgama in Korean). Seoul: Tongguk taehak ch'ulp'anbu, 1991.

Koestler, Arthur. *The Lotus and the Robot*. New York: Macmillan, 1961.

Kolb, David, ed. *New Perspectives on Hegel's Philosophy of Religion*. Albany: State University of New York Press, 1992.

Kongyŏn Mudŭk, trans. 空緣無得. *Hyŏnsu Pŏpchang Hwaŏmhak ch'egye-Hwaŏm o'gyojang*. 賢首法藏 華嚴學體系-華嚴五教章 (The System of Huayan Teachings by Xianshou Fazang-Treatise on the Five Teachings of Huayan Buddhism). Seoul: Uri ch'ulp'ansa, 1988.

Kopf, Gereon. *Beyond Personal Identity: Dōgen, Nishida, and a Phenomenology of No-self*. Richmond: Curzon Press, 2001.

Kreeft, Peter. "Zen in Heidegger's 'Gelassenheit'." *International Philosophical Quarterly* 11 (1971): 521–545.

Kristeva, Julia. *La révolution du langage poétique: L'avant-garde à la fin du XIXe siècle: Lautréamont et Mallarmé*. Paris: Éditions du Seuil, 1974.

————. *Revolution in Poetic Language*. Trans. Margaret Waller. New York: Columbia University Press, 1984.

————. *About Chinese Woman* (1974). Trans. Anita Barrows. New York: Marion Boyars, 1986.

Kyehwan 계환. "Hwaŏm ŭi pŏpkye yŏn'giron" 華嚴의 法界緣起論 (The Huayan Doctrine of the Dependent Co-arising of the Realm of Reality). *Pojo sasang* 17 (2002): 423–448.

Lacan, Jacques. *Écrits: A Selection* (1966). New York: W. W. Norton & Co. Ltd., 1977.

————. *The Four Fundamental Concepts of Psycho-Analysis* (1973). Trans. Alan Sheridan. New York: W. W. Norton & Co., Ltd., 1981.

Lacoue-Labarthe, Philippe. *The Subject of Philosophy* (1979). Trans. Thomas Trezise. Minneapolis, MN: University of Minnesota Press, 1995.

Lai, Whalen. "Chinese Buddhist Causation Theories and the Analysis of the Sinitic Mahayana Understanding of Pratitya-samutpada." *Philosophy East and West* 27, No. 3 (July 1977): 241–264.

Lee Kwang-Sae 이광세. *Tongyang kwa sŏyang: tu chip'ŏngsŏn ŭi yunghap* 동양과 서양: 두 지평선의 융합 (East and West: Fusion of Horizons). Seoul: Kil, 1998.

Lenoir, Frédéric. *La rencontre du bouddhisme et de l'occident* (1999). Paris: Éditions Albin Michel, 2001.

Levering, Miriam. "Lin-chi (Rinzai) Ch'an and Gender: The Rhetoric of Equality and the Rhetoric of Heroism." In *Buddhism, Sexuality, and Gender,* edited by José Ignacio Cabezon, 137–156. Albany: State University of New York Press, 1992.

————. "Is the *Lotus Sutra* 'Good News' for Women?" In *A Buddhist Kaleidoscope: Essays on the Lotus Sutra,* edited by Gene Reeves, 469–491. Tokyo: Kosei Publishing Co., 2002.

Li, Tongxuan 李通玄. *Sin hwaŏmgyŏng ron* 新華嚴經論 (The Exposition of the *Huayan jing* in Eighty Fascicles), 2 vols. Trans. Chang Sunyong, Seoul: Tongguk yŏkkyŏngwŏn, 1996.

Liu, Ming-Wood. "The Teaching of Fa-tsang: An Examination of Buddhist Metaphysics." Ph. D. dissertation. University of California at Los Angeles, 1979.

Lopez, Donald S., Jr. "Buddhist Hermeneutics: A Conference Report." *Philosophy East and West* 37, no. 1 (January 1987): 71–83.

————, ed. *Buddhist Hermeneutics.* Honolulu: University of Hawaii Press, 1988.

————, ed. *Curators of the Buddha: The Study of Buddhism under Colonialism.* Chicago, IL: University of Chicago Press, 1995.

Loy, David. *The Great Awakening: A Buddhist Social Theory.* Wisdom Publications, 2003.

————. "Indra's Postmodern Net." In *Buddhisms and Deconstructions*, edited by Jin Y. Park, 63–82. Lanham, MD: Rowman & Littlefield Publishers, Inc. 2006.

Lubac, Henri de. *La rencontre du bouddhisme et de l'Occident.* Paris: Éditions Montaigne, 1952.

Lusthaus, Dan. *Buddhist Phenomenology: A Philosophical Investigation of Yogācāra Buddhism and the Ch'eng Wei-shih Lun.* London: Routledge, 2002.

Lyotard, Jean-François. *The Postmodern Condition: A Report on Knowledge* (1979). Trans. Geoff Bennington and Brian Massumi. Minneapolis, MN: University of Minnesota Press, 1984.

————. "Presenting the Unpresentable: The Sublime." *Artforum* (April 1982): 64–69.

————. *The Differend: Phrases in Dispute* (1983). Trans. Georges Van Den Abbeele. Minneapolis, MN: University of Minnesota Press, 1988.

————. *The Inhuman* (1988). Stanford, CA: Stanford University Press, 1991.

————. "Discussions, or Phrasing 'after Auschwitz'." In *The Lyotard Reader*, edited by Andrew Benjamin. Cambridge: Basil Blackwell, 1989.

————. *The Lyotard Reader*. Edited by Andrew Benjamin. Cambridge: Basil Blackwell, 1989.

————. *The Postmodern Explained: Correspondence 1982–1985* (1988). Trans. Don Barry, Bernadette Maher, Julian Pefanis, Virginia Spate, and Morgan Thomas. Minneapolis, MN: University of Minnesota Press,1992.

Macy, Joanna Rogers. "Dependent Co-arising: The Distinctiveness of Buddhist Ethics." *The Journal of Religious Ethics* 7, no. 1 (Spring 1979): 38–52.

Magliola, Robert. *Derrida on the Mend*. West Lafayette, IN: Purdue University Press, 1984.

————. "French Deconstruction with a (Buddhist) Difference: More Cases from the *Gateless Gate* [*Wu-men-kuan*] and *Blue Cliff Record* [*Pi-yen-lu*]." *Studies in Language and Literature* 3, no. 1 (1988): 1–25.

————. "Differentialism in Chinese *Ch'an* and French Deconstruction: Some Test Cases from the Wu-Men-Kuan." *Journal of Chinese Philosophy* 17 (1990): 87–97.

————. *On Deconstructing Life-Worlds: Buddhism, Christianity, Culture*. Atlanta: Scholars Press, 1997; New York and London: Oxford University Press, 2000.

————. "Afterword." In *Buddhisms and Deconstructions*, edited by Jin Y. Park, 235–270. Lanham, MD: Rowman & Littlefield, Publishing, Inc., 2006.

————. "Hongzhou Chan Buddhism, and Derrida late and early: justice, ethics, and karma." In *Deconstruction and the Ethical in Asian Thought*, edited by Youru Wang, 175–191. New York: Routledge, 2007.

Majjhima-nykāya (The Collection of the Middle Length Sayings). Trans. I. B. Horner. The Pali Text Society. London: Luzac & Company, Ltd, 1957.

Margaroni, Maria. "'The Lost Foundation': Kristeva's Semiotic Chora and Its Ambiguous Legacy." *Hypatia* 20, no. 1 (Winter 2005): 78–98.

Masunaga, Reihō. *A Primer of Sōtō Zen: A Translation of Dōgen's Shōbōgenzō Zuimonki*. Honolulu: University of Hawaii Press, 1978.

May, Reinhard. *Heidegger's Hidden Sources: East Asian Influences on His Work* (1989). Trans. Graham Parkes. London: Routledge, 1996.

McNulty, Tracy. *The Hostess: Hospitality, Femininity, and the Expropriation of Identity*. Minneapolis, MN: University of Minnesota Press, 2007.

McPhail, Mark Lawrence. *Zen in the Art of Rhetoric: An Inquiry into Coherence*. Albany: State University of New York Press, 1996.

McRae, John R. *Seeing through Zen: Encounter, Transformation, and Genealogy in Chinese Chan Buddhism*. Berkeley, CA: University of California Press, 2003.

Merleau-Ponty, Maurice. "Eye and Mind" (1961). In *The Primacy of Perception and Other Essays*. Trans. James M. Edis. Evanston, IL: Northwestern University Press, 1964.

Merleau-Ponty, Maurice. *Signs*. Translated by Richard C. McCleary, p. 14. Evanston, IL: Northwestern University Press, 1964.

————. *Le Visible et l'invisible*. Éditions Gallimard, 1964.

————. *The Visible and the Invisible* (1964). Trans. Alphonso Lingis. Evanston, IL: Northwestern University Press, 1968/1980.

————. *The Prose of the World* (1969). Trans. John O'Neill. Evanston, IL: Northwestern University Press, 1973.

Mikkelson, Douglas K. "Who Is Arguing About the Cat?: Moral Action and Enlightenment According to Dōgen." *Philosophy East and West* 47, no. 3 (July 1997): 383–397.

Mills, Charles W. *Blackness Visible: Essays on Philosophy and Race*. Ithaca, NY: Cornell University Press, 1998.

Murti, T. R. V. *The Central Philosophy of Buddhism: A Study of the Mādhyamika System*. London: George Allen and Unwin Ltd., 1960.

Nagamura Hajime 中村元. *Wŏnsi Pulgyo* 原時佛教 (Primitive Buddhism). Trans. Chŏng Toehyŏk 정대혁. Seoul: Tongmunsŏn, 1993.

————. *Yongsu ŭi sam kwa sasang* 龍樹의 삶과 思想 (Nāgārjuna's Life and Thoughts). Trans. Yi Taeho. Seoul: Pulgyo sidaesa, 1993.

Nancy, Jean-Luc and Philippe Lacoue-Labarthe. *The Title of the Letter: A Reading of Lacan* (1973). Trans. François Raffoul and David Pettigrew. Albany: State University of New York Press, 1992.

Newman, Charles. *The Post-Modern Aura: The Act of Fiction in an Age of Inflation*. Evanston, IL: Northwestern University Press, 1985.

Nhat Hanh, Thich. *Vietnam: Lotus in a Sea of Fire*. New York: Hill & Wang, 1967.

Nishida Kitarō 西田幾多郎. "Bashoteki ronri to shūkyōteki sekaikan" 場所的　論理　と　宗教的　世界観 (The Logic of the Place and the Religious Worldview). *Nishida Kitarō zenshū* 西田幾多郎全集 (Complete Works of Nishida Kitarō), vol. 11, 371–468. Tokyo: Iwanami Shoten, 1975.

————. *Last Writings: Nothingness and the Religious Worldview*. Trans. David A. Dilworth. Honolulu: University of Hawaii Press, 1987.

Odin, Steve. *Process Metaphysics and Hua-yen Buddhism: A Critical Study of Cumulative Penetration vs. Interpenetration*. Albany: State University of New York Press, 1982.

Ogata, Sohaku. Trans. *The Transmission of the Lamp: Early Masters*. Wolfeboro, NH: Longwood Academic, 1990.

Oh, Kang-nam. "*Dharmadhātu*: An Introduction to Hua-yen Buddhism." *The Eastern Buddhist* 12, no 2 (Oct 1979): 72–91.

Olson, Carl. *Zen and the Art of Postmodern Philosophy: Two Paths of Liberation from the Representational Mode of Thinking*. Albany: State University of New York Press, 2000.

Organ, Troy Wilson. "The Silence of the Buddha." *Philosophy East and West* 4, no. 2 (July 1954): 125–140.

Palmer, Daniel. "Masao Abe, Zen Buddhism, and Social Ethics." *Journal of Buddhist Ethics* 4 (1997): 112–137.

Palmer, Richard E. *Hermeneutics*. Evanston, IL: Northwestern University Press, 1969.

————. "Liminality of Hermes and the Meaning of Hermeneutics." *Proceedings of the Heraclitean Society: A Quarterly Report on Philosophy and Criticism of the Arts and Sciences* 5 (1980): 4–11.

Paluch, S. J. "Heidegger's 'What is Metaphysics?'." *Philosophy and Phenomenological Research* 30, no. 4 (June 1970): 603–608.

Park, Jin Y. "Living the Inconceivable: Hua-yen Buddhism and Postmodern *Différend.*" *Asian Philosophy* 13, nos. 2/3 (July/November, 2003): 165–174.

———. "Zen Language in Our Time: The Case of Pojo Chinul's Huatou Meditation." *Philosophy East and West* 55, no. 1 (January 2005): 80-98.

———. "Wisdom, Compassion, and Zen Social Ethics: the Case of Chinul, S'ŏngch'ŏl, and Minjung Buddhism in Korea." *Journal of Buddhist Ethics* 13 (2006): 1-26.

——— 박진영. "T'oe'ong S'ŏngch'ŏl ŭi Pulgyo haesŏkhak kwa Sŏn Pulgyo yulli" 퇴옹성철의 불교해석학과 선불교 윤리 (T'oe'ong S'ŏngch'ŏl's Buddhist Hermeneutics and Zen Buddhist Ethics). In *T'oe'ong S'ŏngch'ŏl ŭi kkaedarŭm kwa suhaeng* 퇴옹성철의 깨달음과 수행 (T'oe'ong S'ŏngch'ŏl's Enlightenment and Cultivation), edited by Sungtaek Cho, 19-47. Seoul: Yemun sŏwŏn, 2006.

———. "'A Crazy Drunken Monk': Kyŏnghŏ and Modern Buddhist Meditation Practice." In *Religions of Korea in Practice*, edited by Robert E. Buswell, Jr., 130–143. Princeton, NJ: Princeton University Press, 2007.

———. "Transgression and Ethics of Tension: Wŏnhyo and Derrida on Institutional Authority." In *Deconstruction and the Ethical in Asian Thought*, edited by Youru Wang, 192–214. New York and London: Routledge, 2007.

———, ed. *Buddhisms and Deconstructions.* Lanham, MD: Rowman & Littlefield Publishing Inc., 2006.

Park, Sung Bae. *Buddhist Faith and Sudden Enlightenment.* Albany: State University of New York Press, 1983.

——— 박성배. "Ton'o tonsu ron" 頓悟頓修論 (A Theory of Sudden Awakening and Sudden Cultivation). *Paengnyŏn Pulgyo nonjip* 3 (1993): 201–254.

———. "Pŏpsŏng sŭnim ŭi tonjŏm nonjaeng pip'an e taehayŏ" 법성스님의 돈점논 쟁비판에 대하여 (In Response to Pŏpsŏng's Critique of the Subitist-Gradualist Debate). *Ch'angjak kwa pip'yŏng* 83 (Spring 1994): 401–408.

———. "Munja munhwa wa mumunja munhwa ŭi kaldŭng kwa Hwadu Sŏn" 문자 문화와 무문자 문화의 갈등과 화두선 (Huatou Zen and the Conflict between Letter Culture and Non-letter Culture). *Chonggyo wa munhwa* (1995): 5–16.

Parkes, Graham, ed. *Heidegger and Asian Thought.* Honolulu: University of Hawaii Press, 1987/1990.

Pascal, Blaise. *Pensées.* Trans. A. J. Krailsheimer. Penguin Books, 1966.

Peiris, William. *The Western Contribution to Buddhism.* Orient Book Distributors, 1973.

Pine, Red, trans. *The Zen Teaching of Bodhidharma.* New York: North Point Press, 1987.

Plato. *Timaeus. The Collected Dialogues of Plato*, edited by Edith Hamilton and Huntington Cairns. Princeton, NJ: Princeton University Press, 1989.

Pojo Chŏnsŏ 普照全書 (The Complete Works of Pojo). Songgwang sa, Chŏnnam, Korea: Puril ch'ulp'ansa, 1989.

Pŏmhu Cha'myŏng 범후자명. *Pojo Chinul ŭi Kanhwa Sŏn yŏn'gu* 普照知訥의 看話禪 研究 (A Study of Pojo Chinul's Kanhua Zen). Seoul: Sŏnhak yŏn'guwŏn, 1986.

Pŏpchŏng 法頂. "Kanhaengsa" 刊行辭 (A Statement upon Publication). *Pojo sasang* 1 (1987): 3–5.

————, trans. *Sinyŏk Hwaŏmgyŏng* 新譯華嚴經 (The New Translation of the *Huayan jing*). Seoul: Tongguk taehakkyo yŏkkyŏngwŏn, 1988.

Pŏpsŏng 法 性. *Almŭi haebang, salmŭi haebang-kŭnbon Pulgyo ŭi insik ron kwa silch'ŏn ron.* 앎의 해방 삶의 해방:근본불교의 인식론과 실천론 (Liberation through Knowledge, Liberation through Life: Epistemology and the Theory of Practice in Early Buddhism). Seoul: Hanmadang, 1989.

————. "Minjung Pulgyo undong ŭi silch'ŏnjŏk ipchang" 민중불교 운동의 실천 적 입장 (The Practical Standpoint of the Minjung Buddhist Movement). *Chonggyo yŏn'gu* 6 (1990): 223–228.

————. *Kanhwa kyŏrŭi ron kwahae* 간화결의론 과해 (The Section-by-section Translation and Commentaries of the *Treatise on Resolving Doubts about Huatou Meditation*). Seoul: K'ŭnsure, 1993.

————. "Kkaedarŭm ŭi ilsangsŏng kwa hyŏngmyŏngsŏng-Han'guk Pulgyo tonjŏm nonjaeng e puch'ŏ" 깨닳음의 일상성과 혁명성-한국불교 돈점(頓漸) 논쟁 에 부쳐 (The Commonality and Revolutionary of Awakening: in relation to the Sudden-Gradual Debate in Korean Buddhism). *Ch'angjak kwa pip'yŏng* 82 (Winter 1993): 329–430.

————. "Pulgyo sasang esŏ ŏnŏ wa silch'ŏn" 불교사상에서 언어와 실천 (Language and Practice in Buddhist Thought). *Ch'angjak kwa pip'yŏng* 84 (Summer 1994): 387–400.

Pŏpsŏng, et. al. 법성, 외. *Minjung Pulgyo ŭi t'amgu* 민중불교의 탐구 (Studies of Minjung Buddhism). Seoul: Minjoksa, 1989.

Pulgyo munhwa yŏn'guwŏn, ed. 佛教文化研究院. *Han'guk Hwaŏm sasang yŏn'gu* 韓國華嚴思想研究 (The Study of Huayan Thought in Korea). Seoul: Tongguk taehak ch'ulp'anbu, 1984.

Pulgyo munhwa yŏn'guwŏn, ed. 佛教文化研究院. *Han'guk Sŏn sasang yŏn'gu* 韓國禪思想研究 (The Study of Zen Thought in Korea). Seoul: Tongguk taehak ch'ulp'anbu, 1984.

Queen, Christopher S. and Sally King, eds. *Engaged Buddhism: Buddhist Liberation Movements in Asia.* Albany: State University of New York Press, 1996.

Rorty, Richard. "Habermas and Lyotard on Postmodernity." In *Habermas and Modernity*, edited by Richard Bernstein, 161–175. Cambridge, MA: MIT Press, 1985,

Rosemont, Henry, Jr. "Is Zen Buddhism a Philosophy?" *Philosophy East and West* 20 (1970): 63-72.

Samyutta-nikāya, The Book of the Kindred Sayings. Trans. Mrs. Rhys Davids. Oxford: The Pali Text Society, 1999.

Sarup, Madan. *An Introductory Guide to Post-structuralism and Postmodernism.* Athens: University of Georgia Press, 1989.

Schlesinger, Arthur M, Jr. *The Disuniting of America.* New York: W. W. Norton & Company, 1991.

Sekida, Katsuki, trans. *Two Zen Classics: Mumonkan and Hekiganroku.* New York: Weatherhill, Inc., 1977.

Sharf, Robert H.. "The Zen of Japanese Nationalism." In *Curators of the Buddha: The Study of Buddhism under Colonialism,* edited by Donald S. Lopez, Jr., 107–160. Chicago, IL: University of Chicago Press, 1995.

Silverman, Hugh J. *Textualities between Hermeneutics and Deconstruction*. New York: Routledge, 1994.

Silverman, Hugh J. and Gary E. Aylesworth, eds. *The Textual Sublime: Deconstruction and Its Differences*. Albany: State University of New York Press, 1990.

Sim Chaeryong 심재룡. "Han'guk Sŏn Pulgyo ŭi ch'ŏrhakchŏk yŏn'gu-Chinul ŭi Chungguk Sŏn yihae rŭl chungsim ŭro" 韓國禪佛敎의 哲學的研究: 知訥의 中國 禪 理解를 中心으로 (A Philosophical Study of Korean Zen Buddhism: focusing on Chinul's Understanding of Chinese Chan Buddhism). *Ch'ŏrhak non'gu* 13 (1985): 89–123.

————. "Pojo Kuksa Chinul ŭi *Wŏndon sŏngbul ron* sangsŏk" 보조국사의 <원돈성불론> 상석 (An In-depth Interpretation of the National Master Chinul's *Wŏndon sŏngbul ron*). In *Chinul*, edited by Yi Tŏkchin, 436–464. Seoul: Yemun sŏwŏn, 2002.

————. *Chinul Yŏn'gu* 지눌 연구 (A Study of Chinul). Seoul: Sŏul taehak ch'ulp'anbu, 2004.

Sim Chaeyŏl, trans. 沈載烈. *Haesŏl Pojo pŏbŏ* 解說普照法語 (The Annotated Translation of Dharma Talks by Pojo). Seoul: Posŏng munhwasa, 1995.

Smart, Ninian. "Comparative Hermeneutics: An Epilogue about the Future." In *The Cardinal Meaning: Essays in Comparative Hermeneutics: Buddhism and Christianity*, edited by Michael Pye and Robert Morgan, 195–199. The Hague: Mouton and Co., 1973.

Song Sŏkku 송석구. "Pojo ŭi Kanhwa kyŏrŭi ron so'go" 普照의 看話決疑論小考 (An Essay on Pojo's *Treatise on Resolving Doubts about Huatou Meditation*). *Tongguk sasang* 12 (1979): 21–34.

Sŏngch'ŏl 性徹. *Sŏnnum chŏngro* 禪門正路 (The Correct Path of the Zen School). Seoul: Pulgwang ch'ulp'ansa, 1981.

————. *Cha'gi rŭl paro popssida* 자기를 바로 봅시다 (Let's See Ourselves Clearly). Seoul: Changgyŏnggak, 1987.

Steffney, John. "Man and Being in Heidegger and Zen Buddhism." *Philosophy Today* 25 (1981): 46-54.

————. "Transmetaphysical Thinking in Heidegger and Zen Buddhism." *Philosophy East and West* 27 (1977): 323–335.

Streight, David and Pamela Vohnson, trans. *The Cult of Nothingness: The Philosophers and the Buddha*. Chapel Hill and London: University of North Carolina Press, 2003.

Sutton, Florin Giripescu. *Existence and Enlightenment in the Laṅkāvatāra-sūtra: A Study in the Ontology and Epistemology of the Yogācāra School of Mahāyāna Buddhism*. Albany: State University of New York Press, 1989.

Suzuki, Daisetz Teitaro, trans. *The Laṅkāvatāra Sūtra: A Mahāyāna Text*. Delhi: Motilal Banarsidass Publishers, 2003.

Thurman, Robert A. F., trans. *The Holy Teaching of Vimalakīrti: A Mahāyāna Text*. University Park, PA: Pennsylvania State University Press, 1976.

Tsomo, Karma Lekshe, ed. *Buddhist Women and Social Justice: Ideals, Challenges, and Achievements*. Albany: State University of New York Press, 2004.

Tuck, Andrew P. *Comparative Philosophy and the Philosophy of Scholarship: On the Western Interpretation of Nāgārjuna*. New York: Oxford University Press, 1990.

Umehara, Takeshi. "Heidegger and Buddhism." *Philosophy East and West* 20 (1970): 271–281.

Victoria, Brian. *Zen at War*. Lanham, MD: Rowman & Littlefield, Inc, 2006.

———. *Zen War Stories*. London and New York: RoutledgeCurzon, 2003.

Wang, Youru, ed. *Deconstruction and the Ethical in Asian Thought*. New York and London: Routledge, 2007.

Watson, Burton. trans. *The Zen Teachings of Master Lin-chi*. Boston: Shambhala Publications, Inc., 1993.

———, trans. *The Vimalakirti Sutra*. New York: Columbia University Press, 1997.

Welbon, Guy Richard. *The Buddhist Nirvāna and Its Western Interpreters*. Chicago, IL: University of Chicago Press, 1968.

Whitehill, James. "Is There a Zen Ethic?" *The Eastern Buddhist* 20 (1987), 9–33.

———. "Buddhism and the Virtues." In *Contemporary Buddhist Ethics*, edited by Damien Keown, 17-36. Richmond, Great Britain: Curzon Press, 2000.

Williams, Rowan. "Hegel and the Gods of Postmodernity." In *Shadow of Spirit: Postmodernism and Religion*, edited by Philippa Berry and Andrew Wernick, 72-80. New York: Routledge, 1992.

Wŏnch'ŭk 圓測. *Panya simgyŏngch'an* 般若心經贊 (Commentaries on the *Heart Sūtra*). Trans. Pak Insŏng 박인성. Korea: Chumin ch'ulp'ansa, 2005.

Wŏnyung 원융. *Kanhwa Sŏn: Sŏnjong tonbŏp sasang ŭi parŭn yihae* 看話禪: 禪宗 頓法思想의 바른 理解 (Kanhua Zen: The Correct Understanding of the Sudden Teaching of Zen Buddhism). Hapch'ŏn, Korea: Janggyŏnggak, 1993.

Wood, David. *The Step Back: Ethics and Politics after Deconstruction*. Albany: State University of New York Press, 2005.

Wright, Dale S. "Rethinking Transcendence: The Role of Language in Zen Experience." *Philosophy East and West* 42, no. 1 (January 1992):113–138.

———. "Kōan History: Transformative Language in Chinese Buddhist Thought." In *The Kōan: Texts and Contexts in Zen Buddhism*, edited by Steven Heine and Dale S. Wright, 200–212. New York, London: Oxford University Press, 2000.

Yampolsky, Philip B., trans. *The Platform Sūtra of the Sixth Patriarch: The Text of the Tun-Huang Manuscript*. New York: Columbia University Press, 1967.

Yi Chigwan 李智冠. "Hwaŏm sasang" 華嚴思想 (Huayan Thought). In *Han'guk Pulgyo sasangsa kaegwan* 韓國佛教思想史概觀 (An Introduction to the Intellectual History of Korean Buddhism), edited by Pulgyo munhwa yŏn'guwŏn, 65–106. Seoul: Tongguk taehak ch'ulp'anbu, 1993.

Yi Chungp'yo 이중표. *Aham ŭi chungdo ch'egye* 阿含의 中道體系 (The System of the Middle Path in the *Āgama*s). Seoul: Pulgwang ch'ulp'ansa, 1991.

———. *Kŭnbon Pulgyo* 근본불교 (Early Buddhism). Seoul: Minjoksa, 2002.

Yi Dong-hee 이동희. "Hegel ŭi Pulgyo ihae" 헤겔의 불교이해 (Hegel's Understanding of Buddhism). *Hegel yŏn'gu* (1997): 108–141.

Yi Tŏkchin 이덕진. "Chinul ŭi sŏnggi sŏl e taehan ilgoch'al-Chungguk Hwaŏm kyohak kwa kwallyŏn hayŏ" 知訥의 性起說에 대한 一考察: 中國 華嚴教學과 關 聯하여 (A Study of Chinul's Doctrine of Nature-Origination: in relation to Chinese Huayan Teachings). *Pojo sasang* 13 (2002): 391–422.

———, ed. *Chinul* 지눌. Seoul: Yemun sŏwŏn, 2002.

Yŏ Ikku 呂益九. *Minjung Pulgyo ch'ŏrhak* 民衆佛教哲學 (Philosophy of Minjung Buddhism). Seoul: Minjoksa, 1988.

Yü, Chün-fang. "Ta-hui Tsung-kao and Kung-an Zen." *Journal of Chinese Philosophy* 6 (1979): 211–235.

Yun Wŏnch'ŏl and Kang Inhae 윤원철, 강인해. "Chonggyo ŏnŏ rosse ŭi kongan" 종교언어로써의 공안 (The *Gong'an* as Religious Language). *Chonggyo wa munhwa* 7 (2001): 59–79.

Zimmerman, Michael E. "Heidegger, Buddhism, and Deep Ecology." In *The Cambridge Companion to Heidegger*, edited by Charles B. Guignon, 240–269. Cambridge: Cambridge University Press, 1993.

Index

About the Author

Jin Y. Park is Assistant Professor of philosophy and religion at American University. Her research areas include Buddhist-Continental comparative philosophy, Zen and Huayan Buddhist philosophy, ethics in Buddhism and postmodernism, and Buddhist encounter with modernity in Korea. Park is the editor of *Buddhisms and Deconstructions* (Rowman & Littlefield, 2006) and *Makers of Modern Korean Buddhism* (SUNY, forthcoming) and is currently working on the edited volume *Merleau-Ponty and Buddhism* (with Gereon Kopf) and *Comparative Political Theory and Cross-Cultural Philosophy: Essays in Honor of Hwa Yol Jung.* Park is also working on a monograph *Gendered Response to Modernity: Kim Iryŏp, the New Woman, and Korean Buddhism,* in which she explores modern Korean Buddhist philosophy in relation to the gender identity of the New Woman and new intellectual paradigms in modern Korea.